Reshaping Regional Relations

Reshaping Regional Relations

Asia-Pacific and the Former Soviet Union

EDITED BY

Ramesh Thakur
and Carlyle A. Thayer

Westview Press

BOULDER • SAN FRANCISCO • OXFORD

Published in 1993 in the United States of America by Westview Press, Inc., 5500 Central Avenue, Boulder, Colorado 80301-2877, and in the United Kingdom by Westview Press, 36 Lonsdale Road, Summertown, Oxford OX2 7EW

Library of Congress Cataloging-in-Publication Data
Reshaping regional relations : Asia-Pacific and the former Soviet
    Union / Ramesh Thakur and Carlyle A. Thayer, eds.
      p.   cm.
    Includes index.
    ISBN 0-8133-8506-7
    1. Former Soviet republics—Foreign relations—Asia.   2. Asia—
Foreign relations—Former Soviet republics.   I. Thakur, Ramesh
Chandra, 1948–   .   II. Thayer, Carlyle A.
JX1555.Z5   1993
327.4705—dc20   93-3617
                                                                               CIP

Printed and bound in the United States of America

The paper used in this publication meets the requirements
of the American National Standard for Permanence of Paper
for Printed Library Materials Z39.48-1984.

10   9   8   7   6   5   4   3   2   1

Contents

Tables and Figures

Glossary

ADB	Asian Development Bank
AFTA	Asean Free Trade Area
APEC	Asia-Pacific Economic Cooperation
ASEAN	Association of South-East Asian Nations
CGDK	Coalition Government of Democratic Kampuchea
CIS	Commonwealth of Independent States
CMEA	Council for Mutual Economic Assistance
CPSU	Communist Party of the Soviet Union
CSCE	Conference on Security and Cooperation in Europe
EAEC	East Asian Economic Caucus
EC	European Community
ECO	Economic Cooperation Organisation
FEER	*Far Eastern Economic Review*
FPDA	Five Power Defence Arrangements
FSU	Former Soviet Union
G-7	Group of Seven industrial states
GATT	General Agreement on Tariffs and Trade
GDP	Gross Domestic Product
GNP	Gross National Product
IAF	Indian Air Force
ICBM	Intercontinental ballistic missile
ICO	Islamic Conference Organisation
IMF	International Monetary Fund
KPNLF	Khmer People's National Liberation Front
KPRP	Kampuchean People's Revolutionary Party
LPRP	Lao People's Revolutionary Party
LTTE	Liberation Tigers of Tamil Eelam
MOFA	Ministry of Foreign Affairs (Japan)
MTCR	Missile Technology Control Regime
NAFTA	North American Free Trade Agreement
NAM	Nonaligned Movement
NATO	North Atlantic Treaty Organisation

NIC	Newly industrialising country
NLF	National Liberation Front
NPT	Non-Proliferation Treaty
NWFZ	Nuclear-Weapon-Free Zone
OECD	Organisation for Economic Cooperation and Development
PDPA	People's Democratic Party of Afghanistan
PECC	Pacific Economic Cooperation Conference
PLA	People's Liberation Army
PRK	People's Republic of Kampuchea
SAARC	South Asian Association of Regional Cooperation
SCMP	*South China Morning Post*
SEATO	South-East Asia Treaty Organisation
SLBM	Submarine-launched ballistic missile
START	Strategic Arms Reduction Treaty
SWB	*Summary of World Broadcasts*
TRADP	Tumen River Area Development Program
UN	United Nations
UNDP	United Nations Development Program
UNESCO	United Nations Educational, Scientific and Cultural Organisation
UNTAC	United Nations Transitional Authority in Cambodia
U.S.	United States
USSR	Union of Soviet Socialist Republics (the former Soviet Union)
ZOPFAN	Zone of Peace, Freedom and Neutrality

About the Contributors

Graeme Gill is Professor of Government and Public Administration at the University of Sydney. He has written widely on Soviet affairs. His most recent book is *The Origins of the Stalinist Political System* (Cambridge: Cambridge University Press, 1990).

Tsuyoshi Hasegawa is Professor in Russian and Soviet History at the University of California at Santa Barbara. His most recent work is a book edited jointly with Alex Pravda, *Perestroika: Soviet Domestic and Foreign Policies* (London: Sage, 1990). He is now completing a book jointly with Tsuneo Akaha, entitled *Soviet/Russo-Japanese Relations in the Perestroika and Post-Perestroika Period.*

R.A. Herr is Senior Lecturer in Political Science at the University of Tasmania. He is the editor of *The Forum Fisheries Agency: Achievements, Challenges and Prospects* (Suva: University of the South Pacific, 1990). His recent research centres on the role and legitimacy of non-state actors in South Pacific and Antarctic affairs.

Gary Klintworth is a Senior Research Fellow in the Northeast Asia Program, Research School of Pacific Studies, Australian National University. He has worked as a strategic analyst on the Asian-Pacific region for the Department of Defence of the Australian government, in the Australian Consulate-General in Hong Kong, and in the Strategic and Defence Studies Centre of the Australian National University. He is currently writing a book entitled *Taiwan's Changing Role in Asia-Pacific.*

D.J. McDougall is a Senior Lecturer in the Department of Political Science at the University of Melbourne. His most recent book is *Studies in International Relations: The Asia-Pacific, the Superpowers, Australia* (Melbourne: Edward Arnold, 1991). He is currently working on a study of political developments in the French overseas departments during the Mitterrand era.

William Maley is Associate Lecturer in Politics, University College, University of New South Wales. He was a Visiting Professor at the Russian Diplomatic Academy in 1992. Among other works, he has co-authored *The Transition from Socialism: State and Civil Society in the USSR* (London: Longman, 1991) and *Regime Change in Afghanistan: Foreign Intervention and the Politics of Legitimacy* (Boulder: Westview, 1991), and co-edited *The Soviet Withdrawal from Afghanistan* (Cambridge: Cambridge University Press, 1989).

Gerald Segal is a Senior Fellow (Asian Security) at the International Institute for Strategic Studies and editor of *The Pacific Review*. His publications include *The Soviet Union and the Pacific* (Boston: Unwin/Hyman for the Royal Institute of International Affairs, 1990) and *Openness and Foreign Policy Reform in Communist States* (London: Routledge for the Royal Institute of International Affairs, 1992).

Peter Shearman is Senior Lecturer in International Relations at the University of Melbourne. Author of *The Soviet Union and Cuba* (London: Routledge & Kegan Paul for the Royal Institute of International Affairs, 1987), he is currently writing a book entitled *International Relations Theory*.

Ramesh Thakur is Professor of International Relations and Director of Asian Studies at the University of Otago in New Zealand. His last book, written jointly with Carlyle A. Thayer, was *Soviet Relations with India and Vietnam* (London and New York: Macmillan and St Martin's Press, 1992). He is presently completing a book entitled *After Nonalignment: The Politics and Economics of India's Foreign Policy* (London: C. Hurst, forthcoming).

Pushpa Thambipillai teaches Politics and International Relations at the University of Brunei Darussalam. She has published extensively on Southeast Asian international relations.

Carlyle A. Thayer is Associate Professor of Politics at the Australian Defence Force Academy in Canberra. He is currently a Visiting Fellow in the Research School of Pacific Studies at the Australian National University and in 1993 will be a Research Associate at the International Institute for Strategic Studies in London. Among other works, Professor Thayer is the author of *War by Other Means: National Liberation and Revolution in Viet-Nam* (Sydney: Allen & Unwin, 1989).

William T. Tow is Senior Lecturer in International Relations at the University of Queensland. His most recent work is *Encountering the*

Dominant Player: U.S. Extended Deterrence Strategy in the Asia-Pacific (New York: Columbia University Press, 1991). He is now writing a book on contending post-Cold War regional security orders in Asia-Pacific.

Charles E. Ziegler is Associate Professor of Political Science at the University of Louisville, Kentucky, and Director of the Louisville Committee on Foreign Relations. Among other works, he is the author of *Environmental Policy in the USSR* (Amherst, MA: University of Massachusetts Press, 1987). His next book, *Foreign Policy Learning in the Gorbachev Era: Relations with East Asia,* will be published by Cambridge University Press in 1993.

1

Asia-Pacific After the Cold War

Ramesh Thakur

By history and geopolitics, Russia is a bridge between West and East. In a major foreign policy speech at Vladivostok on 28 July 1986, Mikhail Gorbachev located the Soviet Union firmly as an Asian-Pacific power, tried to define a new Soviet role in the region and launched a fresh approach to the problems of regional security and the Soviet Union's bilateral relations with Asian neighbours.[1] The theme was repeated in the much-publicised interview with *Merdeka,* the Indonesian newspaper, in July 1987, and again in another notable speech at Krasnoyarsk in September 1988. Gorbachev is no longer in power, having resigned on Christmas day 1991; the Soviet Union is no longer in existence, having broken up formally one day later. The momentous developments in world affairs pose important questions for the "mode of articulation" between Asia and the former Soviet Union (FSU). Will a four-power rectangle (China, Japan, Russia and the United States) provide a stable structure of Asian-Pacific order? Or will the events of the last few years focus Russian attention westwards?

At a roundtable discussion in Moscow on 26 November 1991, speakers noted that Moscow's international role was continuously shrinking and its positions won on global and regional issues were being progressively abandoned. Boris Zanegin of the Soviet Academy of Sciences said that the only direction of Russian foreign policy seemed to be "the search for donors and sponsors." Roald Lebedinskii of the foreign ministry proposed the convening of a conference of Russia and the Central Asian republics to

---

1. See Ramesh Thakur and Carlyle A. Thayer, eds., *The Soviet Union as an Asian Pacific Power: Implications of Gorbachev's 1986 Vladivostok Initiative* (Boulder and Melbourne: Westview and Macmillan, 1987).

work out a coordinated policy towards the Asian-Pacific region.[2] Speaking in Manila in July 1992, Foreign Minister Andrei Kozyrev said that "Russia remains a Pacific power."[3] During a visit to Kamchatka too he noted that Russia's Eastern policy should be no less active than that directed towards the West.[4] The purpose of this book is to explore the reality or verisimilitude and ramifications of this claim.

The Lead Players

A new world order for Asia-Pacific—the biggest and most diverse region in the world—is going to be a time-consuming enterprise. This is especially so because the ill-defined and inchoate concept of a new world order includes at least three distinct components. In the security sector, it is rooted in realism which views world order as the product of a stable distribution of power among the major actors. In this conception, aggressive behaviour is to be deterred and defeated by the great powers acting in concert on behalf of the world community. Its ideological component however draws inspiration from the liberalism of Woodrow Wilson and lays greater stress on the normative world order, expressed in particular in the promotion of democracy and human rights.[5] The third component is economic, whereby stable democratic governments will underpin an open trade and investment regime.

The framework for the world order resting on superpower rivalry was adopted at Yalta in 1945. Reflecting the two theatres of the Second World War, that order had two geographical components: Europe and Asia-Pacific. Since about 1989, the Yalta-based order for Europe has crumbled, but not for Asia-Pacific. The structure of power relations in the region is more fluid and complex than in Europe, resting on at least four powers: the United States, China, Japan and Russia. India is a fifth possible contender. For the moment, however, India is wracked by political turmoil, social ferment and economic drift. In external relations, on the one hand the situation in the subcontinent is quite sobering. During the 1980s India developed a formidable military capability. Both India and Pakistan are threshold or basement nuclear powers. On the other hand the government of India under the prime ministership of P. V. Narasimha Rao concluded that the most

---

2. BBC, *Summary of World Broadcasts (SWB)*, SU/1241 A3/1, 28 November 1991.

3. *Economist* (London), 25 July 1992, p. 25.

4. BBC, *SWB*, SU/1437 A1/4, 20 July 1992.

5. For a discussion of the conceptual tension between the realist and liberal antecedents of the new world order, see Joseph S. Nye, "What New World Order?" *Foreign Affairs* 71 (Spring 1992), pp. 83–96.

pressing priorities were economic liberalisation at home and friendship with the United States.[6] Consequently India is not covered any further in this introductory survey of Asia-Pacific; the implications for India of the breakup of the Soviet Union are analysed in chapter 8.

The Former Soviet Union (FSU)

Communism in the Soviet Union was blown away in the storm of protests that swirled up after the abortive coup of August 1991. The Baltic republics gained swift recognition of their independence from Moscow and the outside world. The eventual shape of the rest of the erstwhile Soviet Union remains blurred. There are at least four different routes down which the ex-union could travel. It could survive on the European Community (EC) model as a common market, linked by a common, almost certainly fully convertible, currency. It is worth remembering that if we exclude Russia, then in the remaining 11 republics, more than 40 percent of the output is traded with the rest of the FSU. (For Russia the figure is only 15 percent, so it is well-placed to survive a breakup of the ex-Soviet market.)

TABLE 1.1: Indicators of the Republics of the Former Soviet Union, 1990

| | Percentage share of former union's | | | | Wealth per capita (% of former union's average indicator) |
| | | | Products | | |
	Population	GNP	Industry	Agriculture	
Armenia	1.1	1.3	0.8	0.6	82
Azerbaijan	2.5	1.4	1.7	1.8	64
Belarus	3.6	3.8	4.1	5.9	103
Estonia	0.5	0.7	0.7	0.9	140
Georgia	1.9	1.7	1.2	1.4	84
Kazakhstan	5.8	5.3	3.5	6.9	91
Kirgizstan	1.5	0.9	0.5	1.3	53
Latvia	0.9	1.2	0.8	1.4	122
Lithuania	1.3	1.6	1.2	2.2	108
Moldova	1.5	1.2	0.8	2.2	80
Russia	51.3	58.7	66.4	46.2	117
Tajikistan	1.8	0.9	0.4	1.0	40
Turkmenistan	1.2	0.9	0.4	1.1	67
Ukraine	18.0	16.5	16.0	22.5	93
Uzbekistan	7.0	4.0	1.7	4.6	50

SOURCE: *Foreign Trade* 11–12/1991, p. 50.

---

6. See Ramesh Thakur, "India After Nonalignment," *Foreign Affairs* 71 (Spring 1992), pp. 165–82.

Alternatively (or in addition), the remaining republics could follow the military model of the North Atlantic Treaty Organisation (NATO) and stay together in an alliance with a unified command structure in charge of contingents contributed and controlled by each of the republics. Foreign policy would then be coordinated but not determined by the centre. As things have developed since the establishment of the Commonwealth of Independent States (CIS), this seems unlikely.

Instead the republics could be reduced to an association of sovereign states linked by bonds no stronger than the Commonwealth of Nations that brings together former British colonies in a loose organisational umbrella: a talking shop, an excuse for a periodic junket of government leaders and an occasional get-together of athletes, and an organisation for disbursing a few scholarships.

Finally, the constituent republics of the CIS could also fall apart completely into almost 40 countries. The FSU had comprised 15 Republics, 20 Autonomous Republics, 8 Autonomous regions and 10 Autonomous Areas.

Russia

The collapse of communism and the disintegration of the Soviet-East European empire marked tectonic shifts in the world political landscape. The Soviet Union is dead; long live democratic Russia? Fateful questions are not usually met with simple and direct answers. Early euphoria soon gave way to gloom as tensions threatened relations between Russia and Ukraine over nuclear weapons and the Black Sea fleet, conflict erupted between Armenia and Azerbaijan, a power struggle developed inside Georgia and Islam asserted itself in Central Asia.

In regard to communist ideology, analysts of later generations might debate whether the greater surprise was that it collapsed in the 1990s or that it lasted for more than 70 years in the Soviet Union. In power-political terms, the Soviet Union inherited the burden of an expansionist legacy from the Russian empire. In the words of the Russian historian Vassilii Kluchevskii, imperial Russia was "a bloated state of emaciated people."[7] The Soviet empire stretched ever outwards in a ceaseless effort at warding off outside threats to its historical centre. Imperial overstretch however itself produced an implosion of the Soviet empire.

But will Russia be able to provide enlightened, civilised, democratic and stable leadership despite a gaping void in its own history? Boris Yeltsin is

---

7. Quoted in Andrei Kozyrev, "Russia: A Chance for Survival," *Foreign Affairs* 71 (Spring 1992), p. 2.

Russia's first-ever elected president. Democratic and market forces moved centre-stage in Moscow in 1991, but goodwill is not enough for building a civil society. The world moved to help as best it could for fear of the explosive consequences should a still-nuclear armed Russia lapse into closed totalitarianism. Yet by the anniversary of Boris Yeltsin's triumph in August 1991, his reform government seemed to be on the verge of collapse. The reverses in economic policy, the threat of dismissal hanging over the reform-minded Prime Minister Egor Gaidar, the failure to evolve democratic political institutions and the appointment of army hardliners to the top echelons of the military leadership were reminiscent of the desperate tilt to conservatism by Gorbachev in the autumn of 1990. What Boris Yeltsin has in his favour is popularity with his public at home.

Mikhail S. Gorbachev had goodwill abroad. The *Guardian Weekly* described him as "the most important man in the world."[8] No living leader has so profoundly changed our lives as has Gorbachev. He transformed the Soviet Union, freed Eastern Europe, reunified Germany, ended forty years of the Cold War and nuclear confrontation between East and West, and he made sanity respectable again in relations between nations. Hence the description of his fall (or so it seemed on the morning after the coup) as not just a disaster for the USSR but "a tragedy of planetary proportions."[9]

The Soviet past burdened the new Russia also in the legacy of economic disaster. The Yeltsin government moved speedily to introduce a free-market economy, privatisation and liberalisation and, in foreign economic policy, to seek membership of or links with the International Monetary Fund (IMF), the World Bank, the General Agreement on Tariffs and Trade (GATT), the EC, the Group of Seven (G-7) industrial states and the Organisation for Economic Cooperation and Development (OECD). But clearly Russia has a long and difficult road to follow before goods, services, capital, people and ideas begin to move freely across political frontiers. By September 1992 there was some fear that the pace of reforms was slowing to a halt.

Efforts to promote civil society in Russia should be helped by the fact that the external environment is not hostile. To enmesh Russia still further in cooperative international exchanges, its leaders looked to deepen their involvement in such structures as the Conference on Security and Cooperation in Europe (CSCE) and the United Nations (UN). As the Gulf War showed, Gorbachev had already been moving to establish the old Soviet Union as a reliable partner in the community of civilised states. Under Yeltsin and Kozyrev, Russia has recommitted itself to establishing the UN as the centre for harmonising national, regional and global interests.

---

8. *Guardian Weekly*, 25 August 1991, p. 1.
9. *Ibid.*

They hope too that the experience gained in international forums can be applied to solve the problems surfacing between the CIS republics.

Not surprisingly, Russia's chief foreign policy priority has been relations with former fellow-republics in the CIS. Agreements signed at meetings in Minsk and Alma-Ata sought to establish the foundations of the new Commonwealth. Unsurprisingly again, the CIS encountered many teething problems, in particular outbreaks of disputes and conflicts of varying intensity and magnitude between as well as within the new republics. The nightmare scenario is of the former Soviet Union degenerating into the chaos and butchery of the former Yugoslavia.

The prospect is even more frightening in the case of the FSU because of the nuclear factor and the fate of the 27,000 nuclear warheads possessed by the FSU. During the attempted coup and its rapid collapse, most of the world's attention was centred on the efforts to resist and defeat the usurpers. Later it was learnt that the coup leaders had taken over the nuclear codes. Since then the world has agonised over the prospects of a number of new nuclear-weapon powers emerging as the FSU disintegrates into a mosaic of independent republics. Would each unilateral declaration of independence create a new nuclear power?

Reassuringly, there was no suggestion of a rogue nuclear launch during the coup attempt. There was of course no reason for the coup plotters to launch nuclear strikes: deterrence does not lose its logic in the middle of a coup. In fact the Commander of the Strategic Rocket Forces, General Iurii Maksimov, sent unmistakable signals to the outside world by withdrawing SS-25 mobile missiles into their garrisons. Western experts remained convinced of the reliability of the fail-safe systems in place in the Soviet Union based on a complex network of codes and identifications.

In a post-coup interview in *Izvestiia* on 30 August, General Maksimov said that there are good political, legal, technical and military reasons against scattering the Soviet strategic forces along ethnic lines.[10] Politically, strategic weapons have their sole utility as deterrents. To serve this purpose, they must be reliable, combat-effective and capable of launching credible retaliatory action. These attributes would be difficult to maintain in 15–40 countries.

Legally, the proliferation of nuclear-weapon states is prohibited by a number of international agreements to which the Soviet Union was a signatory. The most important of these is the Non-Proliferation Treaty, which the Soviet Union (along with the U.S. and Britain) helped to bring into being. The sudden emergence of a host of new nuclear powers would mark the end of the NPT: an odd outcome for a progenitor of the regime.

---

10. BBC, *SWB*, SU/1166 B/27, 2 September 1991.

Technically, the Strategic Rocket Forces is an integrated complex of scientific and production personnel and facilities from virtually all the republics. According to General Maksimov, it would be impossible to relocate and re-establish all the personnel and facilities on one territory. Even Russia's capacity to handle the economic and scientific requirements of a strategic force (research institutes, scientists, test sites, missile flight paths, attack warning systems) is questionable.

Militarily, the strategic forces need unified, centralised combat control. The fail-safe system which guards against unauthorised use of nuclear weapons was developed in the Soviet Union over decades and would be difficult to break into separate components. The production facilities are spread across several republics to ensure their survivability against surprise attack and so to enhance deterrence.

The bulk of the Soviet strategic nuclear arsenal is located in just four republics: Belarus, Kazakhstan, Russia and Ukraine. Belarus and Ukraine declared themselves to be nuclear-free zones. The horrors of years of nuclear testing at Semipalatinsk in Kazakhstan were revealed only after the breakup of the Soviet Union. Kazakhstan's President Nursultan Nazarbaev has now closed the testing site. Russia alone holds about four-fifths of the intercontinental nuclear weapons and half the heavy bombers. Tactical warheads designed for battlefield use are distributed more freely in the republics at large army bases, airfields and on warships. But even these are stored separately from their launch systems in fortified bunkers and heavily guarded by elite KGB troops.

The Strategic Arms Reduction Treaty (START) deals of 1991–92 are but footnotes to the history of the Cold War. For the next decade or generation, nuclear weapons will have a lesser effect on shaping the nature of relations between Moscow and Washington than at any time since World War II. The Cold War-related tensions of the nuclear balance will relax as Russia becomes more introspective and concentrates on rebuilding an economy in tatters. In the meantime, the verification and inspection procedures built into the START package will increase transparency and so enhance mutual trust.

Russia has maintained the momentum for arms control and disarmament partly from security considerations and partly too from the calculation that they will free resources and improve the conditions for the implementation of economic reforms. For the same reasons, Moscow shifted emphasis from arms buildups to confidence-building measures as the better guarantor of a more broadly conceived security. As a result of the Russo-American agreement of 16 June 1992, the number of strategic warheads will be reduced from about 20,000 in 1992 to 6,500 in 2003 (Figure 1.1).

FIGURE 1.1: U.S. and Russian Strategic Nuclear Warheads, 1992 and 2003

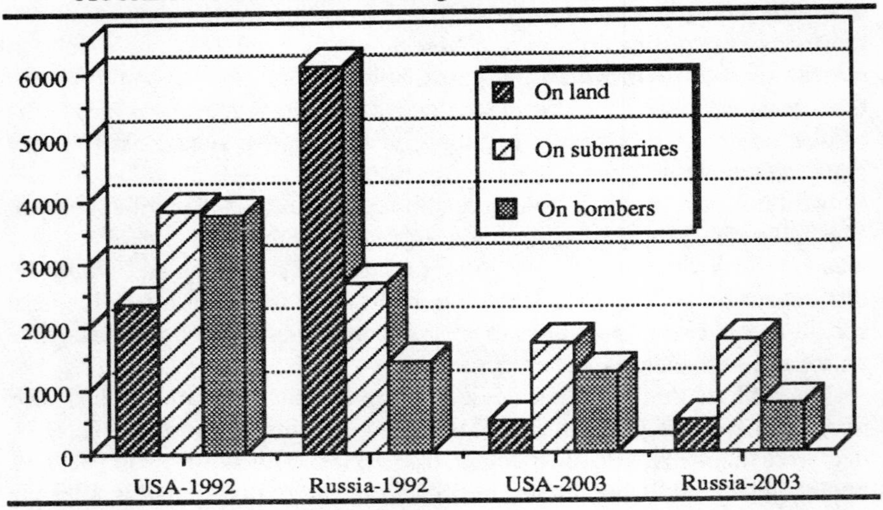

SOURCE: *Economist*, 5 September 1992.

Central Asia

Independent republics of the FSU have been rediscovering pre-Soviet geopolitical identities. The Baltic republics have been freed of any Asian pretensions while the Central Asian republics have been detached from Europe. There are tantalising hints of the re-emergence of the traditional map of Central Asia which used to comprise Afghanistan, Iran and the Central Asian states as a geopolitical whole. For example, plans have been laid for rail links connecting Alma-Ata with the province of Xinjiang and Turkmenistan with Iran in an effort to resurrect the old Silk Road. At the very least, the waning of Russian influence leaves room for other outside powers to establish cultural, economic and political links. For their part, the Central Asian states could be expected to recast their economies as autonomous units.

Central Asia is characterised by relative poverty and a volatile ethnic mix (Table 1.2). For example in 1990 about 200 people were killed in Kirgiz-Uzbek riots in the town of Osh in southwestern Kirgizstan. The potential for serious strife resulting from assertive ethnic nationalism is one reason why most of the Central Asian leaders had supported Gorbachev's goals of a strong centre to keep the military, the nuclear arsenal and one currency. Russians are the only ethnic group common to all five republics. Given Russia's dominance in the post-USSR CIS, the presence of Russian minorities in such large numbers adds to uncertainties about future relations between Russia and the other republics. On the economic front, the five republics had declared at Tashkent in August 1990 that they would move towards a new economic union. But prospects of a Central Asian common market are impeded by fears that the Uzbeks would dominate all others as well as by economic conflicts of interests. The May 1992 Central Asian summit in Ashkhabad ended with only two of the expected seven agreements on regional cooperation being signed. The modesty of the achievement was explained by the refusal of Turkmenistan to agree to a favourable price for its gas sales to the Asian countries of the CIS.[11]

As with most colonial empires, the creation of the five Central Asian republics in 1924 was based on artificial political boundaries which suited the interests and perceptions of the metropolitan capital. In keeping again with colonies in other parts of the world, the process of state-building was slow and superficial. Long-dormant cultural-national sentiments and economic grievances began to be expressed more openly from 1989 onwards and exploded in the aftermath of the failed Moscow coup of August 1991. An interesting political feature of Central Asia's transition to the post-USSR era was the transformation and survival of erstwhile communist leaders wearing nationalist mantles.

TABLE 1.2: Central Asian Indicators

	Kazakhstan	Kirgizstan	Tajikistan	Turkmenistan	Uzbekistan
Capital	Alma-Ata	Bishek	Dushanbe	Ashkhabad	Tashkent
Population (m)	16.7	4.4	5.1	3.6	20.3
Wealth per capita (% of USSR average)	91	53	40	67	50
Ethnic composition (%)					
Germans	5.8	–	–	–	–
Kazakhs	40.0	–	–	2.9	4.0
Karakalpaks	–	–	–	–	6.0
Kirgiz	–	52.4	–	–	–
Russians	38.0	21.5	10.4	12.4	10.8
Tajiks	–	–	58.8	–	3.8
Tatars	2.0	–	2.1	–	4.2
Turkmen	–	–	–	68.4	–
Ukrainians	5.4	–	–	–	–
Uzbeks	2.0	12.9	–	8.5	68.7

SOURCES: *Foreign Trade* 11–12/1991, p. 50; *Strategic Survey 1991–1992* (London: IISS, 1992), p. 151.

---

11. BBC, *SWB*, SU/1378 C3/2, 12 May 1992.

This was not always achieved without difficulty. In Tajikistan, for example, the Islamic Renaissance Party and other opposition groupings demanded the resignation of President Rakhmon Nabiev, saying that the old communist power structure had remained intact. By July 1992 unrest in the capital had spread to the rest of the country as communist, democratic and religious divisions were mixed up with regional rivalries. In the poorest of the former Soviet republics, President Nabiev was from the relatively prosperous north and he drew support also from the Kulyab region in the south adjoining Afghanistan. Opposition strength was concentrated in the Pamir mountains and in the southwestern region of Kurgan-Tyube. In addition, if civil war was to break out, there was always the prospect of Russian intervention to protect the half million Russians of Tajikistan.

In September 1992 Nabiev finally bowed out in the face of unrelenting pressure. Russian troops became more actively involved in protective duties in Tajikistan. President Islam Karimov of Uzbekistan blamed the continuing difficulties on external interference, especially Afghan rebels and Iran, and appealed to the UN for help in preventing Central Asia from becoming a new seat of tension or object of geopolitical games.[12] A Russian foreign ministry statement issued on 15 October referred to "acts of provocation" against Russians in Tajikistan and warned that "Russia will not leave in distress the Russian people who have found themselves outside their historical homeland through confluence of circumstances and will do everything necessary to protect their legitimate rights and interests." The Tajik foreign ministry responded on 19 October saying that it understood Russian concerns, but that the government was doing everything possible to protect all civilians who found themselves in the middle of armed clashes in the conflict zone.[13]

In economic policies, the Central Asian republics were less enamoured of unbridled market forces than Russia or East European countries. Partly because of their Asian identity and partly because of their lower levels of economic attainment, they looked instead to the newly industrialising countries (NICs) of Asia as more appropriate models of state-guided development. This had the added appeal to some Central Asian leaders of an authoritarian mode of governance. Kazakhstan's President Nursultan Nazarbaev visited South Korea in November 1990.

In external relations, the Central Asian republics moved to forge links between themselves and with moderate Islamic states in the neighbourhood. Turkey was attractive because of its strong secular nationalism, NATO membership, strong pro-Western capitalist outlook and links to the EC.

12. BBC, *SWB*, SU/1481 C1/3, 9 September 1992 and SU/1490 A1/2, 19 September 1992.
13. BBC, *SWB*, SU/1514 i, 17 October 1992 and SU/1516 i, 20 October 1992.

Uzbekistan in particular has been much impressed by the Turkish model. With the exception of Kazakhstan, the other four Central Asian republics have joined the Economic Cooperation Organisation (ECO) comprising Iran, Pakistan and Turkey. All three attended the two-day summit of Central Asian leaders in Ashkhabad on 9–10 May 1992. Tehran was the first to open embassies in the region, to make oil deals with some of the Central Asian states and to found the Caspian Council with Azerbaijan, Kazakhstan and Turkmenistan as well as Russia. Turkey has the advantage of being richer, connected to Western Europe and the United States through NATO and offering a model of a secular and market-economy state. Prime Minister Suleyman Demirel paid a week-long visit to the Muslim republics of the FSU in April 1992 and pledged more than $1.2 bn in credits, export guarantees and soft loans.[14]

The Central Asian republics remain concerned about the dangers of the rise of Islamic fundamentalism throughout the region. Central Asia and Azerbaijan have been experiencing an Islamic revival with new mosques being built and increased religious practices.[15] Insofar as this marked a renaissance of Islam, it was welcomed. Indeed Russian radio began a new program called the Voice of Islam in November 1991. Similarly, on 9 December 1991 the Russian foreign ministry greeted the intention of the six republics to join the Islamic Conference Organisation (ICO). Yet a commentary on Central Television on 11 December 1991, on the eve of a meeting in Ashkhabad by the Central Asian leaders, warned of a Muslim-Slavic divide.[16] The problem was that the Central Asians were angry that Yeltsin had signed a new Commonwealth treaty at Minsk on 8 December with fellow-Slavs Belarus and Ukraine. At the Ashkhabad meeting, the Central Asian leaders demanded the right to join the Commonwealth on equal terms and as co-founders. The Slavic republics agreed and a new treaty was signed at Alma-Ata on 21 December 1991.

East of Central Asia, China welcomed the prospects of new allies and markets in Central Asia and moved aggressively to exploit fresh opportunities. For example, delegations from Kazakhstan and Xinjiang held talks in Alma-Ata in May 1992 on expanding bilateral trade and economic relations.[17] Yet China too was concerned that its own nationalities problem could be exacerbated with the rising tide of ethnic sentiments, especially in

---

14. *Economist*, 16 May 1992, p. 32.
15. The number of mosques just in Tajikistan jumped from 17 to 2,870 within two years; Ahmed Rashid, "Clout of Clergy," *Far Eastern Economic Review*, 9 January 1992, p. 18.
16. BBC, *SWB*, SU/1254 B/5, 13 December 1991.
17. BBC, *SWB*, SU/1383 A3/1, 18 May 1992.

Xinjiang.[18] Iran's pleasant prospect of deepening relations with fellow-Islamic states to the north was tempered with the consciousness that the Central Asian Muslims are mainly Sunni and with the wish to improve relations with the West, dampen destabilising tendencies in Afghanistan and avoid importing ethnic tensions into Iran and Iraq. Egypt and Saudi Arabia in the meantime moved to protect Sunni interests in Central Asia.

United States

The collapse of the Soviet Union in the aftermath of the failed coup of 1991 underlined the status of the United States as the one unchallenged and unchallengeable world power. The events completed the American military domination of world affairs and the triumph of its political, economic and diplomatic systems. The United States is in no position to impose Pax Americana. But equally, no major world problem can be settled by working against the United States. Washington will remain reliant on coalitions whose membership may shift from issue to issue and region to region, but whose core will consist of NATO allies, Japan and other "like-minded" democracies. The pace and sweep of changes in Europe might keep the United States preoccupied with events across the Atlantic for the next few years. Some suggest that American interests in Asia-Pacific are peripheral or less urgent. Its strategic interests have been attenuated by the end of the Cold War and the disintegration of the Soviet Union. Its economic interests are on the rise but extend to only a few countries like Japan and the four dragons (Hong Kong, Singapore, South Korea and Taiwan). Given the reality of a political and economic multipolar pattern of relations in Asia-Pacific, the U.S. role in the region could be limited to playing the balancer.

The balancing wheel metaphor suits U.S. perceptions and preferences. Washington is the hub with spokes running to Japan, Taiwan and South Korea in Northeast Asia; the Philippines, Singapore and Thailand in Southeast Asia; and Australia in the Southwest Pacific. South Korea's economic success has helped to transform a narrow military protector-client relationship into a more genuinely equal and multidimensional partnership. The United States has treaty-based security relations with the Philippines and Thailand. While it is having to withdraw from bases in the Philippines, the U.S. concluded a base-access agreement with Singapore in 1991.

In addition to Singapore's decision on base facilities, Malaysia agreed to expand its military cooperation with the United States and to permit U.S. military personnel to be stationed in the country as administrative and

---

18. See Lincoln Kaye, "China Feels the Chill," *Far Eastern Economic Review*, 9 January 1992, p. 14.

technical personnel of the U.S. embassy. Brunei has given support to a continuing U.S. military presence in the region. It intends to sign a memorandum of understanding to facilitate increased U.S. navy visits. A state-owned Indonesian dockyard in Surabaya signed a maintenance agreement to service U.S. warships: the first time that Indonesia, host of the 1992 nonaligned summit, has permitted U.S. naval vessels to undergo repairs in its territory.[19] If allies are prepared to accept responsibility for the defence of home territories to the best of their abilities against the backdrop of a strategic "over-the-horizon" U.S. military presence, then a continued U.S. commitment to the peace and security of Asia-Pacific will meet the interests and the disposition of the United States. Australia is the southernmost spoke in the U.S. balancing wheel around the Pacific Rim.

Most regional governments acknowledge that the Pacific security framework established by the United States has been an important shield behind which they have pursued their search for peace and prosperity. In an address to the Asia Society in New York on 1 October 1992, Singapore's Foreign Minister Wong Kan Seng said emphatically: "no alternative balance in the Asia-Pacific can be as comfortable as the present one with the U.S. as the major player."[20] However, the bilateralism implied in the hub-and-spokes imagery suits the United States as the hegemon but is less satisfactory from the point of view of the spokes. The political infrastructure to sustain peace and prosperity in Asia-Pacific includes the network of dialogue and consultations already in existence. The most substantial forum is the Association of South-East Asian Nations (ASEAN), including the post-ministerial conferences between the ASEAN countries and a broader range of dialogue partners.

The Five Power Defence Arrangements (FPDA) were concluded in 1971. All partners are agreed that the FPDA, which at first blush might appear to be a postcolonial Commonwealth anachronism, provides a valuable basis for the three Western allies to contribute to regional security. The purpose of the FPDA is purely defensive. Its fixtures are equally limited. The FPDA has become increasingly useful as a training organisation. It contributes to the maintenance of interoperability by regular combined exercises. The FPDA is also useful as a medium for dialogue between the partners.

Malaysia and Singapore value the FPDA partly for the sense of security it provides, especially with the air of uncertainty hanging over the U.S. role in the region after the pullout from the Philippines, and partly for the opportunities to exercise with the more sophisticated Western defence

---

19. *Asian Defence Journal*, August 1992, p. 104.
20. "Post-Cold War Asia-Pacific Cooperation," para. 27. Text of speech supplied to author by the Singapore High Commission in New Zealand.

forces. Brunei, the only other ASEAN country that is a member of the Commonwealth club, is also considering whether to join the FPDA. For Britain, the arrangements will be the last remaining formal mechanism for demonstrating continued engagement in the Pacific after the handing over of Hong Kong to China in 1997. In addition to the FPDA, Australia has a web of bilateral security relationships with Brunei, Indonesia, Papua New Guinea and Thailand; New Zealand has bilateral military cooperation with Indonesia and Thailand.

In the view of most regional governments, the continued strategic engagement of the United States will remain the cornerstone of Asian-Pacific security. It is not that the regional governments trust or love the United States the most. Rather, they fear it the least. Different countries are variously uneasy or relaxed at the prospect of China, India, Indonesia or Japan becoming relatively more powerful as superpower political interest in Asia-Pacific wanes and their military presence contracts.

A basic goal of Asian-Pacific defence and foreign policies, therefore, will be to encourage and assist the United States to maintain its commitment to the region. To be reassuring, U.S. engagement with Asia-Pacific must be enduring; to be durable, the U.S. commitment needs to be clearly explained and understood. The likelihood of Russian power being used aggressively against Asian-Pacific countries is now negligible. But the economic dynamism and importance of Asia-Pacific is such that Washington cannot risk the possibility of a regional slide into chaos as has happened in Europe more than once in this century. At an annual turnover of more than US $300 bn, U.S. commerce across the Pacific is more than one-third bigger than that across the Atlantic. America's economic engagement with Asia-Pacific also includes U.S. investment of $61 bn in the region and $95 bn worth of Asian-Pacific investment in the United States. In an address to the Foreign Correspondents' Club of Japan in Tokyo on 22 November 1991, Secretary of Defense Richard Cheney summed up U.S. security policy in Asia in terms of six principles which mark a conceptual shift from deterrence of the enemy during the Cold War to reassurance of friends after, manifested operationally in a drawdown and not a pullback.

Japan

Existing defence links throughout Asia-Pacific already provide the necessary political and strategic infrastructure to support the U.S. security commitment to the region. The most important of these is the U.S.-Japan Mutual Security Treaty. Japan and the United States are vital to Asia-Pacific and indeed to the world, for between them the two biggest economies account for almost 40 percent of the world's GNP. In a sense the problem in U.S.-Japan relations reflects the ongoing process of adjusting to a change in the basis of the relationship. Bilateral dealings are conducted on a more equal footing, but the form and substance of the dealings do not fully reflect this change.

Japan was one of the chief beneficiaries of the Cold War. With the end of the Cold War and the collapse of the Soviet threat to the United States, Washington no longer has any reason to put strategic interests ahead of commercial calculations in its dealings with Japan. During the Cold War the United States allowed Japanese exporters generous entry into its markets in return for a strategic partnership in an Asia dominated by two communist giants. With the basis of the strategic alliance having dissipated, will the United States and Japan come into conflict?

This is unlikely because the disparate and sometimes conflicting U.S.-Japan interests have been held together (unlike EC-Japan relations) by a complex, multidimensional and growing web of relationships. Even short of an improbable conflict, the American people could withdraw support for a continuing mercenary role in Asia, for keeping order in a region that is dominated by a Japan which is perceived increasingly as a trade enemy rather than a trusted ally and friend. For their part, the Japanese may grow weary of financing a military presence designed chiefly to constrain their actions in Asia. (Japan is expected to bear about half the costs of stationing U.S. forces in Japan by 1995.)

The United States believes that Asian-Pacific countries should encourage Japan to play a still larger role in the region. Japanese contributions to regional security arrangements are likely to be viewed with equanimity in Canberra, Wellington and Washington, though not in all the other Asian-Pacific capitals. Racially homogeneous and not generally welcoming of foreigners, Japan has no tradition of cultural linkages and intercourse in Asia-Pacific. A militarily resurgent Japan would send ripples of anxiety around the Asian-Pacific countries even in the absence of any indications of hostile intentions. Japan's leaders have expressed sincere contrition for their wartime role in the region, but are yet to issue a formal apology.

A process of mutual reinforcement is at work. An independent Japanese security role is difficult to visualise unless there is a breakdown in the bilateral security relationship between Tokyo and Washington. An independent Japanese security role in Asia-Pacific would set off so many alarm bells around the Pacific Rim and provoke such a dangerous backlash from China, Korea and others that it is difficult to visualise policy-makers allowing the U.S.-Japan security relationship to lapse.

The other basis for the continuance of the U.S.-Japan security relationship is the continuing dispute between Japan and Russia over the "northern territories": the last significant territorial issue from the Second World War yet to be resolved. Taken over by Soviet forces in the closing days of the war, the islands are strategically important to Moscow for the defence of ballistic missile submarine bastions in the seas of Okhotsk and Japan. It remains to be seen whether Japan will turn around to viewing post-Soviet-collapse Russian forces as essentially defensive, whether lack of bargaining leverage will force Moscow to repatriate the northern territories to Japan in return for capital, credits and technology and whether this will erode the basis of Japan's alliance with the United States.

If Japan launches a policy of constructive engagement in Asia-Pacific by more generous programs of aid and technology transfers and conflict-resolution initiatives, then its presence will be welcomed. Aware of the sentiments that it arouses or could arouse in many parts of Asia, Japan is unlikely to seek to convert economic power and political influence into military muscle. Its security relationship with the United States will therefore remain a cornerstone of its foreign policy, despite increasing independence within that framework.

The Peacekeeping Operations Bill was finally passed by the Japanese parliament in June 1992, permitting up to 2,000 Japanese troops to serve with UN peacekeeping missions on condition that they are not involved in combat operations. It may be that the experience of limited Japanese military participation in peacekeeping operations will gradually assuage regional anxieties. One of the most frequently quoted remarks is that of Singapore's Lee Kuan Yew, that allowing Japanese troops to serve overseas would be like giving liqueur chocolates to an alcoholic.

In the meantime Japan remains attentive to regional demands and sensitive to regional concerns. Foreign aid is the most effective policy instrument available to Japan to demonstrate a tangible commitment to the prosperity, security and resilience of Asia-Pacific. Japan is now co-equal with the United States as an aid donor globally (US $9 bn and $10 bn respectively.)[21] Since about two-thirds of Japanese aid is disbursed within Asia-Pacific, Japan is the leading aid donor for many countries of Asia-Pacific. Many Japanese hope that bitter memories of wartime occupation will be erased by images of a kinder, gentler Japan. For today Japan seeks partnership, not conquest. It fosters such soft causes as disarmament and environmentalism: at the Earth Summit in Rio de Janeiro in 1992, Tokyo was prepared to provide hard cash and advanced technology to the cause of protecting the environment. In sum, building on its own history and on its

---

21. United Nations Development Programme, *Human Development Report 1992* (New York: Oxford University Press, 1992), Table 39, p. 198.

U.S.-crafted constitution, modern Japan aspires to a humane and civilian internationalism.

China

The relationship between Japan with its economic might and technological edge and China with its massive population and area will shape the new order in Asia-Pacific. The Chinese argue that a political role for China is welcomed by Asian-Pacific countries as a counter to Japan's growing economic might and makes the latter more palatable.

Regional governments would be happy to see Beijing and Moscow play a constructive role in ameliorating regional rivalries and tensions, for example in Cambodia and the Korean peninsula. A policy of constructive engagement has exposed the people of China to international influences and facilitated the development of a large market-oriented sector in parts of China's economy. Asian-Pacific governments remain keen to integrate China more fully into open regional and global trading arrangements.

Western perceptions of China tend to oscillate between the extremes of confrontation and fascination. For the first time in two centuries, leaders in Beijing can feel free of external threats from Japan, Russia, the U.S. or any other global or regional power. There are even expanding links with Taiwan through trade, tourism and investment. Today, the loss of ideological legitimacy with their own people is the greatest threat to the Chinese leaders. Yet the leadership feels vindicated in its chosen sequence of economic and political reforms by the chaotic collapse of communism in the Soviet bloc.

A Different Security Architecture

The relatively benign geostrategic environment notwithstanding, the system of security and stability already achieved in Europe seems to be as distant as ever in Asia-Pacific. There is a greater variety of political systems in Asia-Pacific, ranging from robust and explosive democracy in India and fragile democracies in Bangladesh, Nepal and the Philippines and something less than full democracies in many other countries, to communism in three countries.

Internal developments in the former Soviet Union had immediate and far-reaching consequences for Eastern Europe, but have lacked a similar resonance in the Asian communist countries. This because Soviet relations with the latter have been rather different from relations with Eastern European dependencies. Hence the domino effect of the collapse of communism in the Soviet Union on the satellite regimes in Eastern Europe in contrast to the capacity for independent survival of the Asian communists.

European achievements in arms control and disarmament have not been matched by comparable movement on Asian-Pacific fronts. Indeed Asia-Pacific is one of the few regions in the world, perhaps even the only one, where military spending is still rising. In September 1992, for example, Taiwan concluded deals for the purchase of 150 F-16 aircraft from the U.S. for $6 bn and another 100 Mirage 2000-5 from France for $7 bn. China for its part bought 24 Russian SU-27 fighters, one of the most modern aircraft in the ex-Soviet armoury.

Part of the difficulty in exporting success across regions arises from the fact that while Europe is a continent, Asia-Pacific is principally oceanic. Unchecked arms buildups reflect the existence of more multiple sources of threat to the peace and stability of Asia-Pacific than of Europe. The kaleidoscope of cultures, cleavages and conflicts in Asia-Pacific does not permit a simple intercontinental transposition of the European security architecture. In the South China Sea, for example, six nations assert conflicting claims over different parts of the Spratly and Paracel Islands and China flexed its muscles in 1992.[22]

Some of the European countries are only now beginning to experience the kind of destructive domestic violence and civil strife that has blighted India and Sri Lanka, for example, for what seems like an interminable period. Nor is there a readily apparent solution in sight to the problems of Tibet and East Timor. In addition to enduring low-intensity insurgencies, many countries are characterised by socioeconomic fragility and regime brittleness.

In sum, as the shroud of the Cold War lifts from Asia-Pacific, the region's own national and ethnic fault-lines stand out with greater clarity. The disparities in social and economic indicators are greater in Asia-Pacific. The compact symmetry of the Cold War has given way to more complex regional confrontations, and the threat and fear of a nuclear holocaust is being replaced by doubts and anxieties of neighbour's capabilities and intentions.

This is not to gainsay the important changes that are occurring in Asia-Pacific. Domestically, the military junta in Burma and the communist regimes in China, North Korea and Vietnam have set themselves obdurately against the international trend towards democratisation and human rights. Even so, democratic government remains entrenched in India and has been re-established in Bangladesh, Nepal and, perhaps less clearly, Mongolia. Political reforms continue apace in Hong Kong, South Korea and Taiwan. Internationally, Russia and the CIS are engaged in efforts to normalise

---

22. See Barry Wain, "China Puts the Squeeze on Vietnam," *Asian Wall Street Journal*, 30 September 1992.

relations with Japan and South Korea, having successfully done so with China; the two Koreas have joined the United Nations and are exploring closer contacts with each other; the withdrawal of nuclear weapons from South Korea facilitated the signing of international nuclear safeguards and inspection agreements by the North; China has mended fences with Vietnam, Indonesia and South Korea.

New Economic Order

The defining characteristic of Asian-Pacific salience in world affairs has been its economic dynamism. The four established dragons (Hong Kong, Singapore, South Korea and Taiwan) and the four emerging dragons (China, Indonesia, Malaysia and Thailand) grew thrice as fast as the OECD economies in the 1980s. They have proven the capacity to grow at a sustained rate of 7 percent a year, which doubles the size of an economy in one decade. Long-term forecasts issued by the OECD in August 1992 predict that Asia-Pacific's share of world economic product will rise from about one-quarter in 1990 to one-third in 2010 and one-half in 2040.[23]

The economic success of Asia-Pacific is attributed to several factors: sound economic management by relatively stable political regimes which ushered in rapid structural change, an industrious and increasingly well-educated workforce, high rates of savings and investment by instinctively thrifty peoples and the adoption of a managed-market strategy of economic development which struck a balance between the interventionist and the free-market state. The state was prepared to assist industries so long as industrial performance was responsive to international market signals as measured, for example, by a closing of the gap between domestic and international prices of the products in question.

Regional integration is yet another respect in which Asia-Pacific is unlikely to emulate developments in Europe. There is unquestionably an impetus towards strengthening regional cooperation. This will intensify as Asian-Pacific economies develop, expand and become more vibrant and diversified. External factors will impinge on them as well, for example the international trend towards free-trade areas. But because of the diversity of Asia-Pacific and the persisting problems, integration will occur only at subregional levels (for example ASEAN) and coexist peacefully alongside looser forms of pan-regional association (for example APEC and PECC).

The Pacific Economic Cooperation Conference (PECC) was formed in 1980 as a nongovernmental organisation in which officials, businessmen

---

23. *Otago Daily Times* (Dunedin, New Zealand), 10 August 1992.

and academics discuss regional problems. The Asia-Pacific Economic Cooperation (APEC) grouping amalgamates Asia, North America and Oceania in one large entity and promotes economic and political cooperation among the three subregions. Its agenda is expansive and it has already established itself as an important mechanism for sustaining market-oriented growth, reinforcing regional and global trade liberalisation and responding to the emerging challenges of interdependence.

In December 1990, Malaysia proposed the establishment of an East Asian Economic Group which would exclude the United States, Canada and probably Australia and New Zealand. In the face of U.S. hostility and Japanese reservations, other ASEAN countries transformed the Malaysian proposal into the East Asian Economic Caucus. It was given no institutional form or timetable, and the renaming emphasised its consultative role. Indonesian, Philippine and Thai officials privately concede that the Malaysian proposal was stillborn. Instead, meeting in Kuala Lumpur in October 1991, the ASEAN economic ministers adopted a framework proposal for an eventual common market linking their people in an ASEAN Free Trade Area (AFTA). The accord was signed at ASEAN's fourth summit meeting in Singapore (27–28 January 1992). The interesting thing about AFTA is firstly that it represents a reaction to market integration moves in the EC and North America, and secondly that it represents a recognition that economic cooperation in trade and investment is the chief vehicle for building a web of interlocking ties in Southeast Asia.

AFTA will start on 1 January 1993 for 15 product areas. The regional free-trade area is to be achieved under a 15-year scheme for reducing tariffs to between zero and five percent. The hope is that a graduated but timetabled tariff reduction will expand and diversify the manufacturing sector and attract foreign investment into a market of 320m people with a combined annual output of US $330 bn.

AFTA is designed to provide a framework for achieving regional economic integration that will interface with an open global trading system in order to sustain Asian-Pacific economic dynamism and avoid regional economic fragmentation. Yet the project is vitiated by several shortcomings and likely to be beset by many problems. The original Thai timetable of a ten-year phasing out of trade barriers was extended to 15 years. (But accelerated tariff cuts for some product categories was agreed to by ASEAN economic ministers meeting in Manila in October 1992.) Members may opt out of tariff-reduction arrangements in the case of sensitive or vulnerable manufactured goods (for example cement, textiles, electronics), while agriculture and services are omitted altogether. There is also the political problem of Vietnam's membership.

Developing countries cannot survive on trade among themselves, for they depend heavily on industrial-country markets and access to these will need to be maintained for many years. Most developing countries will be economic competitors for some time yet. Their economic relations with the industrialised countries are closer than with one another: only 17–18 percent of ASEAN trade is intra-area, compared to about the same proportion with the EC and another fifth with North America. Asian-Pacific countries face significant constraints on domestic market size; a smaller market means that the state continues to play a disproportionately larger role in their national economies; and as a result economic competition between them tends to be highly politicised.

The move to AFTA is motivated to an extent by a recognition of the fact that, through the twin combination of expanding populations and rising disposable incomes, Asia-Pacific is the world's fastest growing consumer market. The demographic balance sheet is being changed with growing populations, ascending life expectancy and declining infant mortality rates. Furthermore, the proportion of young adults in the whole population is rising in Asia-Pacific, and this in turn increases the number of households. For example, the number of South Korea's households is expected almost to double from 8m in 1985 to about 15m in 2005. And the new households will be located mainly in the cities: the last two columns in Table 1.3 show the rapid urbanisation of Asian-Pacific populations.

TABLE 1.3: East Asian Demographic and Economic Indicators

	Population growth rate (%)	Life expectancy (years)		Under 5 mortality rate (per 1000 live births)		GNP per capita (US $)		Urban population (%)	
	1960–90	1960	1990	1960	1990	1976	1989	1960	1990
China	1.8	47	70	203	42	410	350	19	23
Indonesia	2.2	41	61	225	97	240	500	15	31
Hong Kong	2.2	66	77	64	7	2110	10350	89	94
Malaysia	2.7	54	70	105	29	860	2160	25	43
Singapore	1.7	64	74	49	9	2700	10450	100	100
South Korea	1.8	54	70	120	30	670	4400	69	72
Thailand	2.5	52	66	149	34	380	1220	13	23
Industrial countries average	0.8	69	74	46	18	4850	17017	62	74

SOURCES: United Nations, *Human Development Report 1992* (New York: Oxford University Press, 1992); World Bank, *World Development Report 1992* (New York: Oxford University Press, 1992).

The structure of consumer demand will be transformed fundamentally with the trend towards more urban households centred on double-income nuclear families. Demand for housing will rise, as will demand for labour-saving and leisure activity consumer durables like household appliances and electronic entertainment machines. As in the West, an expanding middle class will demand better services in health and education and patronise the tourism and travel sectors more frequently.

Success for AFTA will transform the scale economies of operating in ASEAN markets, especially if it is linked to wider market-opening schemes throughout Asia-Pacific. Falling and disappearing market barriers would give further impetus to intra-regional trade in Asia-Pacific.

The greatest spur to Asian economic regionalism would be a collapse of the Uruguay Round of multilateral trade negotiations and the resulting rise of bilateral or regional trading arrangements around the world. The Uruguay Round began in 1986 and has already overrun its original deadline of 1990 by two years. Failure would impose long-term economic costs and short-term political costs.

Asian-Pacific countries have several reasons to fear failure of the Uruguay Round. First, it would signal the end of efforts to restore rule-based discipline to the older sectors of international trade that have been covered by GATT so far. Second, it would abort moves to extend disciplines to the newer sectors of agriculture and services (with the latter accounting for more than half the economic activities of industrialised countries). Third, a failure of GATT would represent a significant weakening of common institutions to underpin an increasingly interdependent global economy. Fourth, it could lead to a contraction in the rates of growth of world trade and national income, thereby depressing the economic prospects of the world's trading nations. Fifth, it would give fresh impetus to national and regional protectionism.[24]

The rise of regional trading blocs and discriminatory bilateral trading arrangements would in turn reinforce the reluctance of the industrialised countries to open their markets to developing countries and to the Eastern European countries and so produce an escalation of trade tensions worldwide. The failure of GATT would also provoke income-support and export-subsidy wars. The demand for protection would rise from firms and unions. With GATT having broken down, the supply of protection would increase by governments. A more frequent resort to unilateralism by a petulant American Congress and Administration determined to extract

---

24. See Jagdish Bhagwati, "Jumpstarting GATT," *Foreign Policy* 83 (Summer 1991), pp. 105–18.

concessions by flouting economic might could provoke panic reactions from other countries.

By contrast, a successful conclusion to the Uruguay Round including real agricultural reform would mean that market signals would play a greater role in guiding production decisions and consumption choices. Consequential global adjustments in agricultural demand and supply would reduce trade tensions, ease the burden on consumers and taxpayers, strengthen governments' capacity to withstand protectionist demands and maximise the growth prospects for the major agricultural traders of the world.

Asian economic integration could be accelerated also by the successful establishment of the North American Free Trade Area (NAFTA) agreed to by Canada, Mexico and the U.S. in August 1992. This for four reasons. Firstly because of the obvious demonstration effect. Second, if the Uruguay Round of GATT negotiations should fail, then the existence of two powerful regional blocs in the EC and NAFTA will generate pressures in other regions to integrate into equally powerful blocs for self-protection. Singapore Prime Minister Goh Chok Tong has noted that the Single European Market and NAFTA are defining the operating environment for ASEAN.

Third, given the competition between Mexico and Asian economies for the export of similar goods to the United States, the rationalisation of the North American market and the availability of cheap Mexican labour to U.S. businesses would have trade-diversionary effects at the expense of exports to the United States from the dynamic Asian economies.[25]

Fourth, North American industries that shed high-wage labour in Canada and the United States to relocate to Mexico, and have the added advantage of significantly enhanced economies of scale, will greatly improve their global competitiveness as well. NAFTA proponents respond that growth in North America will bring expanding markets for Asian traders and investors and thereby strengthen trans-Pacific economic links. This outward-looking interpretation is supported by Mexico's membership of PECC and its interest in participating in APEC.[26]

Equally, however, NAFTA is a powerful signal to everyone that the United States has alternatives to GATT which would bring its trade policy

---

25. Trade-creation occurs when the less efficient products are substituted by more efficient competitors within a free-trade area, and is a net welfare gain. Trade-diversion occurs when the more efficiently produced imports from out-of-area sources are abandoned in favour of intra-area inputs because of the price-distorting effects of frontier controls, and is a net welfare loss.

26. James A. Baker, "America in Asia: Emerging Architecture for a Pacific Community," *Foreign Affairs* 71 (Winter 1991/92), p. 7.

under more direct national control. For the view has gained ground in the U.S. political establishment that the United States has not been getting a fair deal from the multilateral trading system. It is time to use U.S. economic strength to pursue U.S. economic interests, not to police everyone else's interests. Unfortunately, the demand for fair trade can undermine the system of free trade. In addition, a diluted strategic interest in Asia-Pacific in the post-Cold War era could produce a hardening of bargaining stance on trade and other disputes that Washington has with Asian-Pacific countries: the latter have lost their strategic leverage.

The major industrial producers have been positioning themselves inside all three regional blocs (EC, North American and East Asian). Japanese executives reportedly concluded in 1991 that the attempt to incorporate Mexico inside a tripartite NAFTA, along with talk of extending it further south into Latin America, implied a threat of protectionist policies in the future.[27] Japanese commentators began to assert that their country had made enough concessions on structural adjustments; it was time for the United States to put its own house in order by achieving deficit reductions, savings and productivity increases.

Australia and New Zealand: The Odd Couple in Asia

It is clear then that the ending of the Cold War has brought some favourable portents to Asia-Pacific but that the contours of the region's security landscape are not yet fully set. Instead, the region is in transition. One of the uncertainties is the identity of Russia as an Asian-Pacific power. Another is the place of Australia and New Zealand in Asia-Pacific. Both have been engaged in a campaign to convince Asians that they too belong to Asia-Pacific. Where for two centuries Australia and New Zealand fought against their geographic reality in seeking security from Asia in the defence, trade and immigration spheres, they now seek security in Asia through cooperative security and economic arrangements. The "Coral Sea" concept of ANZUS, whereby the alliance was the main shield against an Asian threat, is now obsolete.[28] Instead, the security alliance with Australia and the U.S. is now conceptually enmeshed with a broader network of regional security arrangements (for example the FPDA discussed above).

---

27. William Pfaff, "Setting the Scene for Protectionist Trading Blocs," *International Herald Tribune,* 21 May 1991.

28. The phrase was used by Prime Minister Bob Hawke in an address to the Asia-Australia Institute in Sydney on 24 May 1991; Australia, Department of Foreign Affairs and Trade, *The Monthly Record* 62 (May 1991), p. 206.

In addition, the very fact of Australia and New Zealand being anglophile outposts in Asia-Pacific makes it possible for them to search for strategies of niche diplomacy. China and Japan, for example, value contacts with Australia and New Zealand precisely because the latter two countries can act as interlocutors between Asia-Pacific and the West. Therefore Australasia's wider international relationships will continue to be important for political, economic, security and identity interests. Moreover, to the extent that there is great cultural-cum-demographic diversity in Asia-Pacific and Australians and New Zealanders are not Asians, they can be equidistant from the regional fault-lines and help in the safer management of some of these fault-lines.

In the meantime, both Australia and New Zealand are being locked in the Asian-Pacific economic grid. In 1960, Asia took only 26 percent of Australia's merchandise exports, while Western Europe took 46 percent. A generation later, in 1990, Asia's share had climbed to 55 percent while Western Europe's share had fallen precipitously to 16 percent. New Zealand has undergone a similar transformation in its trading relationships. In 1972, 15.6 percent of New Zealand exports went to Asia; by 1992 they had climbed to 35.7 percent.

Whether or not Russia, Australia and New Zealand can be regarded as Asians, they are Pacific. Australia and New Zealand are already involved in a number of pan-Pacific associations and organisations like APEC and PECC and post-ministerial consultations with ASEAN. The search for Asian-Pacific identity by Russia will therefore take it as far afield as Australia and New Zealand.

Conclusion

In the meantime, the search continues apace for prosperity and security in Asia-Pacific. International relations in the Pacific have lacked the institutional structures that have absorbed periodic stresses across the Atlantic and helped to stabilise relations. The multilateral structure across the Atlantic has also firmly anchored an American presence in Europe if on a continually readjusting basis. The strategic rationale for U.S. presence in the Pacific has never been as stark and simple as in Europe, and the cultural and political divides across Asia-Pacific are deeper and more variegated.

Items for continuing discussion on the regional agenda include:

- the future of Hong Kong and Taiwan;
- the nature of the U.S. role as a balancing wheel;
- the future of the two Koreas;

- nuclear proliferation in the Indian subcontinent and the Korean peninsula;
- conventional arms transfers;
- regional peacekeeping;
- the reintegration of Vietnam and Cambodia into the Southeast Asian mainstream;
- the nature of links between a more integrated ASEAN and wider Asian-Pacific, North American and European economies;
- the place of Australia and New Zealand in Asia-Pacific and
- the future roles of India, China, Japan, the United States, Russia and the Central Asian states.

History is not yet at an end in Asia-Pacific. The chapters that follow attempt to trace a historical rearticulation of the former Soviet Union and its successor-states with the countries of Asia and the Pacific.

2

The Agenda for Reform in Russia
Linkages Between Domestic and Foreign Policies

Graeme Gill

One of the most important characteristics of the Gorbachev period of Soviet politics was the close linkage between foreign policy and domestic considerations. While in no political system is there a complete rupture between the domestic and international spheres, in the last half of the 1980s the connection was even closer in the USSR than it had been elsewhere.

There were two chief elements of this linkage: legitimation and policy interlocking. At the level of legitimation, the foreign policy-domestic situation nexus was most clearly evident in the part played by foreign policy in the authority-building program Gorbachev sought to design. In an endeavour to build up the authority necessary to implement change, Gorbachev sought to build a policy program embracing both domestic and international components.[1] Within this enterprise, foreign policy assumed an increasingly prominent place as the period wore on. This was chiefly because of the way in which, throughout this period, a series of achievements was registered in the foreign arena, mainly in the form of greatly improved relations with the West (particularly in the arms control area), while in the domestic arena successes were more ambiguous.

The personalised nature of foreign policy, with key parts being played by Mikhail Gorbachev and his Foreign Minister Eduard Shevardnadze, meant that achievements in this arena buttressed their personal stature and added lustre to their domestic authority. Furthermore, because foreign policy was directly and openly tied in with *perestroika*, the successes achieved in the

---

1. For an early discussion of this, see Graeme Gill, "Power, Authority and Gorbachev's Policy Agenda," in Ramesh Thakur and Carlyle A. Thayer, eds., *The Soviet Union as an Asian Pacific Power* (Boulder, Westview Press, 1987), pp. 19–38.

foreign arena gave added authority to the reform program generally, a development which was particularly important given continuing domestic problems.

But there was also a more direct policy linkage apart from the legitimation implications. The central aim of the Gorbachev foreign policy was to seek rapprochement with the West and in particular a greatly improved relationship with the U.S. While the intrinsic value of improved relations was clearly important, there were also economic considerations behind this policy line. With the Soviet economy facing increasingly straitened circumstances, a major aim of improving relations was to decrease Soviet defence expenditure, thereby releasing resources into domestic restructuring.

But defence expenditure could be reduced only if stability was achieved in relations with the West, thereby reducing the need for increasing investment on arms development, production and deployment. Furthermore, a reduction in tension with the West was also seen as a prerequisite for gaining access to increased trade and investment. Both of these were considered to be important sources of stimulus for the Soviet economy, as alternative means of gaining the financial and material inputs essential for economic restructuring. In this sense foreign policy was directly linked with the success of the domestic program of restructuring: the improved relationship with the West was a vital means of generating extra resources for economic reform. Foreign policy was thereby seen as a means of underwriting *perestroika*.

In the immediate post-*perestroika,* post-Soviet age it is not clear that foreign policy can perform the same functions. The situation is complicated by the breakup of the Soviet Union into fifteen independent states, eleven of which combined together to form the Commonwealth of Independent States (CIS).[2] In place of one foreign policy, there were in principle now fifteen, although there was some coordination provided through the Commonwealth structure.

This chapter will focus upon Russia. This is the biggest and most powerful of the post-Soviet successor-states and the acknowledged legal successor in terms of occupancy of the UN Security Council seat. Furthermore in any discussion of policy in Asia-Pacific, Russia is the post-Soviet state with the largest stake in this area. It retains a presence in the region that is qualitatively different from that of the only other states with such a connection, those of Central Asia.

---

2. The Soviet republics which did not join the CIS were Estonia, Latvia, Lithuania and Georgia.

The Russian Federation, or Russia, retains basically the same geopolitical location as its Soviet forebear and therefore many of the same strategic interests. Its territory still stretches from the Pacific coast to the Polish border (although the Russian territory around Kaliningrad that shares a border with Poland has now been turned into an enclave, separated from the unbroken expanse of Russia by Lithuania and Belarus), and from the Arctic Ocean to the Chinese border and deep into the Caucasus region.

Although the separation of the other states has broken large areas off from the Russian periphery, the Russian core remains extensive and far-flung. This has ensured that its interests remain defined as vital in all the geographical theatres in which the USSR was active; Russia remains recognised as, and sees itself as, a great power with essential interests in the Asian-Pacific, Central Asian, Caucasus and European regions. The balance of where those interests lie remains uncertain and has been the subject of debate within the Russian policy elite between those who see the first priority as seeking greater integration with the West, and those who wish to see Russia exploit her position to play the role of bridge between Europe and Asia. (This is discussed more fully in the next chapter by Peter Shearman.) However both sides acknowledge that Russia has interests in both regions.

Although Russia shares many of the geopolitically determined vital interests of the Soviet Union, its capacity to act effectively to realise those interests has been reduced. One important respect in which this has been the case is geopolitical. With the emergence of new independent states on its borders where formerly there were Soviet republics, new potential centres of instability and uncertainty have opened up which are not amenable to direct and immediate Russian action.

As the successor-states asserted their new-found independence, direct Russian intervention in their domestic affairs was rebuffed whenever it seemed likely. The sharp response evoked by the Yeltsin government's threat to consider redrawing borders in the case of discontented Russian ethnic minorities in other republics warned that government of the sensitivities of its neighbours and was instrumental in its adoption of a much less aggressive policy on this issue. In this sense Russia's room for action is restricted: it is faced with many new states which, reflecting their Soviet experience, are very sensitive to the slightest hint of Russia exercising a hegemonial role over them. Russian pursuit of its foreign policy must, therefore, be managed with these sensitivities in mind.

Russia's capacity to exercise an outward-looking naval policy has been severely circumscribed by its new geopolitical circumstances. While its access to the Pacific and Arctic Oceans has remained unchanged, that to the

Baltic Sea has been narrowed by the loss of ports in Estonia, Latvia and
Lithuania, and access to the Black Sea through its main Crimean ports has
been lost to Ukraine; access exists directly only through ports at the eastern
end of the sea, which (with the exception of Novorossiisk) are much less
developed for either large-scale commercial or military use. The squabble
with Ukraine over ownership of the Black Sea fleet simply underlines the
reduced capacity enjoyed by Russia in this region. Furthermore this is the
only point of access and egress which is ice-free all year round so its loss,
in the context of the more restricted usage of the Baltic Sea outlet, is
particularly severe.

Russia's physical capacity to exercise a vigorous foreign policy is also
diminished compared with that of the USSR. The loss of the resources that
went with the independence of the other republics has clearly been a blow to
the Russian economy, although this may have been offset by the
disappearance of the financial subsidy that Russia effectively paid to at least
some of the republics throughout much of the Soviet period.

But the chief constraint upon an activist foreign policy has been the
dramatic decline of the economy. The failure of *perestroika* to arrest the
gradual decline of the Soviet economy and the speed with which this decline
accelerated at the end of the 1980s, reflected most clearly in the dramatic fall
in industrial production in 1991 and 1992, meant that there was an economy
falling into major recession. This meant that there were few resources
available to expend on foreign policy matters. The activity of the armed
forces was severely curtailed, thereby limiting its "show the flag" role and
reducing its capacity for effective action, and there was some reduction of
diplomatic representation. The poor performance of the economy clearly
restricted Russian capacity to pursue its foreign policy aims with vigour.

The Domestic Policy-Making Arena

In all states, including post-Soviet Russia, foreign policy is partly shaped
by domestic considerations. In Russia, the central factor to consider is the
extraordinarily fluid nature of the political situation which has prevailed
since the dismemberment of the Soviet Union. The way in which political
power has been structured is especially important here.

A year after the failure of the coup, no stable form of the structuring of
power had been achieved. The clearest evidence of this has been the
prolonged nature of the attempt to draft a new constitution for Russia. A
new draft constitution was presented to the Congress of People's Deputies
in April 1992, but this body adopted the draft "in principle" after much

argument[3] and established an editorial commission to examine possible changes.[4] This has meant that Russia has been operating on the basis of the RSFSR Constitution that was put in place during the Soviet period, albeit significantly amended.

Even following the end of the USSR in December 1991, this basic legal instrument remained in force in the absence of anything to replace it. With the public rejection of virtually all things Soviet, this left a constitutional vacuum within which Russian politics had to be played out. Within these constitutional ambiguities, there were four areas of the structuring of power which were of concern: the nature of executive power, the role and functioning of the legislature, channels for popular involvement and the bureaucratic command structure.

The focus of executive power is the office of president, initially filled by Boris Yeltsin. The office of Russian president was created (following popular approval in a referendum in March 1991 accompanying the union-wide referendum on the future of the USSR) in late May 1991. The legislation gave the president the power to appoint ministers and issue decrees but not to veto laws or dissolve parliament, and it established a Constitutional Court as a watchdog to balance the powers of the chief executive.

When the election was held on 12 June, Yeltsin was victorious with nearly 57.4 percent of the vote. This was important because it gave Yeltsin a popular mandate that no other Russian leader had possessed. The personal authority that this endowed was substantially reinforced by the part Yeltsin played in defeating the coup. Regardless of the precise nature of the role he played in the dynamics of the coup, it is clear that at the public level he was the personality who emerged with reputation and stature most enhanced by these events. In the immediate aftermath of the coup, Yeltsin's personal authority was at its height. In the months following, and particularly under the impact of the price rises in early January 1992, that popular authority began to wane, and although twelve months after the coup Yeltsin's

---

3. Debate was based principally upon a dispute over whether Russia should adopt a presidential or parliamentary system. There was significant support for the latter among congress deputies while the draft assumed a presidential system.

4. For the draft, see *Argumenty i fakty*, 12 March 1992, and for the decision on the editorial commission, *Shestoi s'ezd narodnvkh deputatov rossiiskoi federatsii. Dokumenty, doklady, soobshcheniia* (Moscow, 1992), pp. 21–23. For one discussion of the official draft, see *Nezavisimaia Gazeta*, 28 March 1992. A Federation Treaty was signed between the constituent elements (excluding Tatarstan and Chechnia) of the Russian Federation on 31 March, but this was designed purely to regularise relations between these units, not to structure power at the all-Russian level. The treaty was confirmed by the Congress of People's Deputies on 10 April. *Rossiiskaia Gazeta*, 13 April 1992.

popularity remained high,[5] it had declined from the levels it had earlier achieved.

In late 1991 Yeltsin consolidated his position at the peak of the Russian government. At the end of October the Russian legislature adopted two measures, the first postponing elections for a year and giving Yeltsin the power to make all senior appointments and impose a vertical line of authority (see below), and the second giving him the right to issue decrees assisting economic reform even if these formally conflicted with existing law. This latter power was to last until 1 December 1992.

On 6 November 1991 Yeltsin took up the post of Prime Minister, a position he held simultaneously with the presidency until his chief economic adviser and First Deputy Prime Minister Egor Gaidar was made acting Prime Minister in June 1992. In August 1992, despite vigorous criticism in the Congress of People's Deputies during its April meeting, Yeltsin foreshadowed extending his executive power to rule by decree until the end of his five-year term in 1996.[6] Despite this apparent strengthening of his power, Yeltsin's position remained somewhat uncertain. This reflects the continuing ambiguity of the presidency within Russian leading circles.

One reason for the continuing uncertainty surrounding Yeltsin and his position is that he did not take action to consolidate any form of institutional power base apart from the office of the presidency itself. Despite urgings from some supporters, Yeltsin did not seek to establish a "presidential party" which could both organise support for him inside the legislature and seek to give him a firm, organised standing within the populace as a whole.

Furthermore the organisation which had supported him during the presidential election in mid-1991, Democratic Russia, ceased to act as a firm organisational base following the coup as the essential cement of its unity, opposition to the communists, dissolved and Democratic Russia itself began to splinter. With this, Yeltsin and his policies came under increasing criticism from this quarter.

Yeltsin's failure to develop his own partisan support structure has been defended by the claim that, once such a structure had been established, there would be a scramble by all to join it with the result that it would constitute less a solid support base than merely another arena within which the differences dividing Russian political circles could degenerate into conflict.

---

5. By this time his popularity had dropped below that of his vice-president Aleksandr Rutskoi. According to one survey, if the presidential election had been held in June 1992, Yeltsin would have gained only 33 percent of the vote. Elizabeth Teague & Vera Tolz, "The Civic Union: The Birth of a New Opposition in Russia?," *RFE/RL Research Report* 1:30 (24 July 1992), p. 3.

6. *Moscow Times*, 28 August 1992.

But Yeltsin's failure to generate a solid organisational base left him vulnerable: he has relied on the powers vested in his office,[7] which are subject to erosion when that office rubs against other bodies in the power structure, and his personal popularity, which by its nature is fickle. He has therefore lacked the sort of personal power base which could give certainty and stability to his position.

The nature of executive power is also complicated by the uncertainty surrounding the institutional relationship between the government and the Security Council and the nature of the membership of these bodies. The government seems formally to have been given responsibility for the management of day-to-day affairs and for formulating and implementing policy, while the Security Council was designed to oversee questions of domestic and foreign policy relating to the security of the federation. There was no clear demarcation of responsibilities between these two bodies and the resulting ambiguity was bound to cause conflict, particularly given that Yeltsin seemed to envisage the Security Council as becoming the key strategic decision-making body in the country.[8]

The uncertainties created by this institutional ambiguity were exacerbated by the political differences among the personnel of the executive branch. Yeltsin's commitment to radical economic reform is reflected in his appointment of Egor Gaidar as First Deputy Prime Minister in November 1991,[9] and his promotion as acting Prime Minister seven months later. Gaidar brought with him into the administration a team of younger economists committed to radical and swift economic reform and it was under his guidance that during the first half of 1992 government expenditures were slashed, many prices freed and foreign economic activity substantially liberalised.

---

7. And of course on the range of advisers and support staff attached to that office. In mid-1992 these consisted of some nine presidential counsellors, five advisers to the president, a presidential consultative council, a series of commissions, committees and agencies, and an administrative bureaucracy . For details, see "Key Officials in the Russian Federation: Executive Branch," *RFE/RL Research Report* 1:29 (17 July 1992), pp. 68–72. For a slightly different configuration, see A. Papp, ed., *The Supreme Government Bodies of Russia* (Moscow: Panorama, 1992), pp. 10–11.

8. *Izvestiia*, 11 June 1992. On 7 July a presidential decree strengthened the Security Council by calling for all of its decisions to be accompanied by a presidential decree, gave its secretary special powers to implement its decisions and called on all heads of ministries and local administrations to fulfil its instructions. *RFE/RL Research Report* 1:30 (24 July 1992), p. 77.

9. Although Yeltsin apparently had to be pushed to appoint Gaidar by some of the leaders of Democratic Russia. Peter Pringle, "Gaidar & Co: The Best and the Brightest," *Moscow Magazine*, June/July 1992, p. 31.

There was significant opposition from within leading levels of the power structure to the speed and some aspects of the reform program introduced by Gaidar. One of the leading figures with reservations was Vice President Aleksandr Rutskoi. Former air force colonel and Afghan veteran, Rutskoi has had close links with the conservative military-industrial sector of the economy. Reservations about the reform program within the leadership seemed to be strengthened by the entry into the government in June 1992 of three representatives of the industrialists' lobby, Vladimir Shumeiko, Georgii Khizha and Viktor Chernomyrdin. These people represent the managers of major state industrial enterprises. Although there is no evidence that they are opposed to economic reform, they clearly have a concern to protect the interests of the state industries, and yet if Gaidar's reforms were to succeed, this would require the substantial dismantling of many state-owned enterprises.

The strengthening of the voice of the industrialists' lobby in the government added an extra note of dissonance to the policy-making arena and strengthened the reservations about the government's program within the government itself.[10] The close links between the extra-parliamentary leader of the industrial lobby (see below) Arkadii Volskii, the military-industrial complex and Rutskoi substantially strengthened reservations about the Gaidar reforms among influential sections of the policy elite.

This is linked to the government-Security Council relationship. The Security Council was established in the spring of 1992.[11] The complexion of this body is mixed, but it has had a solid core of people with connections to the security-military-industrial sector—Rutskoi and Iuri Skokov plus the non-voting ministers of defence, internal affairs and security.[12]

Apart from Yeltsin, Gaidar was the only member linked closely with the young reform economists he carried into government; it is striking in this regard that the more sympathetic Foreign Minister Andrei Kozyrev, who one would have thought would have been on the Security Council, appears not to have been a member. If this body is less favourably disposed towards reform than the Gaidar leadership, this plus the institutional uncertainty

---

10. Following the appointment of these representatives of the industrialists' lobby, one newspaper speculated that the ranks of the reformers in the government had been reduced to Gaidar and Deputy Prime Minister Aleksandr Shokhin. *Nezavisimaia Gazeta*, 2 June 1992.

11. Its first meeting was on 3 May. Its membership consisted of Yeltsin, Rutskoi, Sergei Filatov (First Deputy Chairman of the Supreme Soviet), Gaidar (Acting Prime Minister), Iuri Skokov (presidential counsellor for regional affairs as secretary) as well as some non-voting members including the ministers of defence, internal affairs and security. Personal communication, Moscow, August 1992.

12. This has added importance in the light of the tension between Rutskoi and Kozyrev and the former's attempts to have the latter sacked.

between it and the government created significant potential for policy disagreement and the blocking of further policy development.

The second area of concern in the structuring of power is that of the legislature. Russia inherited from the Soviet period a two-tier legislative arrangement, a Congress of People's Deputies which was to meet approximately twice each year and a standing Supreme Soviet. Both were elected in 1990 and were unsympathetic to the program of reform fostered by Gaidar. Certainly at the Sixth Congress of People's Deputies in April 1992, the government and its policies came under stinging attack, a development that was blunted only by its threat to resign and the behind the scenes compromises worked out between the government and less conservative deputies led by First Deputy Chairman of the Supreme Soviet Sergei Filatov.[13] A similar assault was launched at the following session in September.

But it is not just the attitude to government policy which is important here. Also significant is the fact that there is no clear relationship between the legislative and executive branches. Both president and legislature (at least the Congress of People's Deputies) possess a direct popular mandate, but lack a clearly formulated or institutionalised mechanism for regulating relations between these two branches of government. This is exacerbated by the basic disagreement between Yeltsin and the legislature, led aggressively by Supreme Soviet Chairman Ruslan Khasbulatov, over whether the system should be parliamentary or presidential in type. This was clearly demonstrated at the Congress when the legislature attempted to curb the president's power of appointment of ministers and to make economic policy by decree.[14]

Clearly the legislature has sought to expand its role and authority in the policy sphere, an aim which Yeltsin, with his commitment to a presidential rather than parliamentary style of government, was bound to reject. Yeltsin consistently drew away from seeking to send this body to the electorate, probably because he was not certain that a newly-constituted legislature would be more amenable to his plans. Indeed, with a renewed public mandate, and one gained within the context of popular disillusionment with the effects of the reform program, he might only get a more hostile legislature reinforced by popular support.

---

13. For one discussion, see Alexander Rahr, "Winners and Losers of the Russian Congress," *RFE/RL Research Report* 1:18 (1 May 1992), pp. 1–7. The proceedings have been published in *Rossiiskaia Gazeta*, 7 April–5 May 1992.

14. Ultimately Yeltsin was empowered to make such appointments until 1 July, after which appointments had to be approved by the legislature, and to retain the power to rule by decree in economic matters until 1 December.

Nor has Yeltsin sought to counteract this by attempting to construct a disciplined parliamentary core of supporters within the legislature, or even assiduously to court that 40 percent or so of deputies who seem most amenable to the sorts of reforms for which he has stood. The legislative-executive relationship has thus remained uncertain, with Yeltsin doing little to stabilise this.

The third area of concern in the structuring of power is that of channels for popular involvement. The avowed aim of the Yeltsin administration, and indeed the public aim of most of the political forces in action in Russia, is the achievement of a democratic Russia. Such an aim is seen as involving the generation of viable, mass-based political parties, but the emergence of such parties has been retarded.

Parties began to emerge on the Soviet scene in 1989–90 and although the collapse of communism stimulated the development of independent political organisation, mass-based parties have not come to dominate the public scene. Those parties which have emerged have for the most part essentially been elite-centred groupings with few organisational roots among the populace. The difficulties they have had in the regular production of party newspapers has greatly hindered any attempt to develop a broad mass-based organisational structure. So too has the concentration on nuances of policy difference, an emphasis which has been an important factor in encouraging the splintering of the emergent party structures. Indeed, the parties seem to have developed little from the stage they had reached under *perestroika:* they remain principally notable-centred political groupings, gaining support from within a narrow band of the populace and with few roots in the mass population.

This nature of the parties has a number of significant consequences. One is that parties have not played a major part in structuring proceedings in the legislative arena, thereby compounding the failure of such proceedings always to contribute fruitfully to policy debate. Of course given that the Congress and Supreme Soviet were elected in the Soviet period when competitive party elections were impossible and when the Communist Party could still dominate parts of this process, it was impossible for new parties to dominate the legislative chamber. Nevertheless deputies have tended to band together into more or less discernible groupings in the chamber.[15] However these have not crystallised into political parties extending outside the chamber.

As yet the mode of party formation common in much of the West, the generation of a mass-based structure to provide the support for a

-----

15. For a review of these, see *Nezavisimaia Gazeta,* 24 April 1992. A survey of the parties by Sergei Stankevich will be found in *Izvestiia,* 20 April 1992.

parliamentary grouping, has not happened. In this sense, the way in which the debate is structured in the chamber is not connected in any direct organisational way with shifts of opinion among the populace.

Another consequence, directly linked with this, is that the parties do not act as vehicles for the aggregation of popular interests. Their lack of deep roots among the populace means that they are not particularly sensitive to the needs, interests and views of the mass of the people in whose name they often talk. More importantly, this means that the mass of the populace may not see the parties as potential means of realising their interests or of placing pressure upon the government to meet their demands. In this sense, the parties do not act as the necessary bridge between governors and governed, thereby not helping to decrease the sense of distance between these two groups.

Another aspect of this is that the parties do not act as means of mobilising the populace into politics. The extensive popular apathy that appears to have set in has not been counteracted by vigorous party activity to involve the people in continuing political life. As a result, there has developed a gulf between the populace as a whole and its immediate concerns and the official political process. The latter takes place in substantial isolation from popular activity, despite the fact that politics fills the pages of the press and the Russians remain avid readers. But reading about political issues tends by and large not to be translated into political activity. The politics of the elite is therefore not closely anchored in the continuing activity or sphere of immediate concern to the Russian people.

The lack of close connection between the politics of the elite and the active concerns of the populace means that the former is much more fluid and less stable than it would have been had its roots been firmly planted among the populace. It is a politics of the elite in which those who are well organised can have a disproportionate effect.

In the year since the coup groups have not been slow to organise in order to press their particular interests; most of these groups have been conservative or establishment-oriented. The most important of these have been the so-called "national-patriotic forces," a constellation consisting of an amalgam of communists, Russian nationalists and those with military-industry experience and connections. This shadowy force has representatives within leading political circles (including Vice-President Rutskoi).

Important too has been the emergence in the middle of 1992 of an organisation of production managers, principally managers of state enterprises during the Soviet period; these formed a professional organisation (the Russian Industrialists and Entrepreneurs Union) which then spawned a political pressure group (the All-Russian Renewal Union) which, in turn, combined with a couple of political parties to form a centrist bloc entitled Civic Union designed to place pressure on the government.[16] In alliance with the remnants of the old official communist trade union structure, this body has exerted pressure on the government to modify its economic reform plans in such a way as to prevent enterprises from going bankrupt.[17]

The failure of elite politics to be firmly rooted in mass politics makes the political process susceptible to being unduly shaped by powerful organised pressure groups like the Civic Union. The only thing standing between them and the public interest is the will-power of elite politicians, and this is a frail defence against concerted self-interest.

The final area of concern in the structuring of power is that of the bureaucratic command structure. The post-Soviet authorities needed an administrative structure which worked efficiently and effectively if they were not only to govern Russia, but also to bring about the major reforms which they had on their agenda. Much of the central state apparatus remained formally intact from the Soviet period, although sections of it had been severely affected by problems of worker demoralisation and its capacity to operate effectively was therefore hindered. This was particularly the case in the economic command structures, but it also affected other sectors as well.

In taking over the existing hierarchies, the new authorities also wished to reduce them in size: the reduction in size of the geographical area to be added and the planned withdrawal of the state from much of the type of activity it had been involved in during the Soviet period both dictated a slimming down of the state apparatus. It is not clear that the planned reductions in staff have taken place nor that the reorganisations that have accompanied the takeover of the ministries has resulted in short-term improvements in operating efficiency.

A more clearly discernible problem with the emerging bureaucratic command structure was the fraying of relations between the centre and the localities. While the coup led to some shifting of elites at the centre, with the partial displacement of the communist Gorbachev-focused elite by that centred around Yeltsin, in many areas it has had little effect on the local

---

16. The other parties in the bloc were the People's Party of Free Russia (led by Rutskoi), the Democratic Party of Russia (led by Nikolai Travkin), and a parliamentary faction of deputies called Smena. See the discussion in Teague & Tolz, "Civic Union," and in *Nezavisimaia Gazeta*, 26 May 1992.

17. See the discussion in Elizabeth Teague, "Russia's Industrial Lobby Takes the Offensive," *RFE/RL Research Report* 1:32 (14 August 1992), pp. 1–6.

power structure. This is most widely recognised in Central Asia, in parts of which the republican communist parties were able to sustain their rule under another name. This situation also applied in many parts of Russia.

It is not that the communist party as an organisation was able to maintain itself intact, but that the power structures that operated within the formal party hierarchy and the informal norms governing personal and power relations at the local level were able to sustain themselves. Even if exactly the same people did not hold onto office (although in many cases they did), the patterns of power and the principles upon which they rested continued to structure the local political situation. The immediate effect of this has been that, as in the Soviet period, many local power centres have sought to play an independent role from the centre.

Local political leaders, claiming that they had the best interests of their own region and its inhabitants at heart and with a wary eye to their own survival, have placed the needs of their own region above those of the centre; embargoes on food shipments out of the region is a case in point. This has meant a fraying of the command structure, with the Moscow authorities unable to make their writ run easily throughout Russia as authorities at all levels (from autonomous republics like Tatarstan and Bashkortostan to regions like Sakhalin) have pursued policies independent from and often at odds with those of the centre.

The Yeltsin administration was aware of these problems from the outset. In November 1991 when Yeltsin gained the right effectively to rule by decree for twelve months, he was also granted a 12-month postponement of the local elections due in December and the right to appoint into the regions plenipotentiaries answerable only to himself.[18] These presidential representatives were seen as the means whereby Yeltsin could exert central control over the local authorities.

However the results of these appointments have not always been what the centre had hoped. While there were cases in which the presidential envoy was able to move into an area and assert presidential authority effectively, many cases seem to have taken on one of two other forms. The first is that Yeltsin's appointee was frozen out by the local authorities. He may have been confronted with a united front by the local soviet and its chairman, or he may have entered into the sort of continuing conflict between soviet and chairman that has been all too typical of power at these levels, but in either event he was unable to clearly establish his authority in the region.

---

18. These regional administrators were to be able in their turn to appoint heads of lower-level executive bodies. *Rossiiskaia Gazeta*, 5 November 1991.

Second, the presidential appointee found that the only way he could hope to exercise any influence over the local situation was by throwing in his lot with the local power holders. In this sense, instead of being able to exert central control over the situation, he became captured by local power holders and therefore ineffective as a representative of the centre. In either event, the use of presidential plenipotentiaries has not been sufficient to establish an integrated administrative system through which the government could ensure obedience to its will.

Policy Implications

The picture of the emergent political process sketched above is one which emphasises the fluidity and ambiguity of that process. The president's and the government's lack of a firm organisational basis, the ambiguous nature of institutional relationships, the nature of legislative politics, the isolation of the politics of the elite from that of the masses and the absence of an integrated and effective administrative structure mean that the conduct of political life is very weakly structured by accepted rules, regulations and norms.

Rules regulating political conflict and mechanisms for resolving that conflict are undeveloped. It is this which so magnifies the importance of organisation in the playing out of political life. Where rules are few and only lightly worn, the impact of effective organisation is increased; organised pressure is more difficult to withstand in the absence of support from clearly accepted norms and rules. Furthermore, in this sort of situation, individual policy issues are likely to erupt into major political disputes. Where there are few rules governing the structuring of the political agenda and its working out, policy issues can take on a life and an importance of their own. These two characteristics of the Russian scene, the potential power of organisation in the midst of uncertainty and the role of policy as a source of potential instability and conflict, have been evident in the post-Soviet period.

The major policy issue in the post-Soviet period has been economic reform, and more specifically the attempt rapidly to move to a market economy. It is on the commitment to this aim that the rationale of the Gaidar government rested. The way in which the government sought to realise this policy aim generated significant opposition from within the politically active section of the Russian population. Such opposition was based on the immediate social effects of the price increases introduced in January 1992 and upon the wish to defend established positions and privileges: both management and workers were opposed to the sorts of changes which might lead to bankruptcies, enterprise closures and unemployment.

This policy of a rapid move to the market also had foreign policy implications which fed into this question. Just as one of the basic assumptions upon which *perestroika* rested was an improved and economically fruitful relationship with the West, so the Gaidar policy also assumed Western involvement. The broad policy outline was designed to be acceptable to the IMF, the World Bank and the G-7,[19] while the conduct of the policy of transition to the market assumed substantial Western aid.

Moreover it was assumed that full marketisation would mean integration into the broader global market. These sorts of assumptions were familiar to all who took an interest in national affairs, but they were not very palatable to everyone, particularly those who had reservations about the course of marketisation and its consequences.

The attitude to the IMF, the World Bank, the G-7 and the West more generally was bound to cause resentment in some circles. For some, this seemed like throwing over everything for which they and their parents had struggled; it was a surrender to the traditional enemy, an abandonment of past positions and the wholesale adoption of those which a short time ago had been vigorously criticised. But even for those for whom ideology was not a moving force, the wholesale importation of things Western—from experts, to goods, culture and capital—was a blow to Russian nationalism. It was like selling one's most treasured possessions at reduced prices. More importantly, it was perceived as sacrificing the essential Russianness on the altar of the material values of the West.

These sorts of attitudes merged into a moderately coherent anti-Western, Russian nationalist, almost Slavophile ethos which pervaded sections of the population generally as well as segments of the politically active elite.[20] This was the intellectual core which sustained the so-called national patriotic forces and it has been the means for bringing together elements of those forces with the managerial-worker opposition noted above. In the fluid situation that characterised national politics, this group has been emerging as an organised and vigorous force. The strength of this conservative force cannot be measured accurately, but it is clear that it has had an influence upon policy-making in both the domestic and international spheres.

The strength of national-patriotic sentiment has imposed clear restrictions upon the freedom of manoeuvre of the Russian government in ordering its relations with its neighbours. Perhaps the clearest instance of this is in its

---

19. Although this does not mean that all IMF demands were met. The early reluctance to raise fuel prices to world levels is one instance of primacy being accorded to domestic political considerations rather than the demands of international capital.

20. For extreme expressions of this, see *Russkii Vestnik*, the conservative, patriotic weekly newspaper.

relations with the other members of the CIS. With the breakup of the USSR, there was inevitably going to be disagreement over how Soviet resources were to be divided between the former constituent parts of the union. The prolonged debate over the Black Sea fleet was only the most public of such disagreements.

In this situation, the force of national-patriotic sentiment restricted the flexibility enjoyed by the Russian government; it could not be seen to be giving up any of the Russian birthright. The same was true in regard to the vexed question of the place of the substantial Russian minorities in the other former republics of the Soviet Union. Where these came under pressure or discrimination, as for example in Moldova and Estonia, there was pressure from national-patriotic sources, including Rutskoi,[21] for Russia to become directly involved. The government could not be seen to be leaving fellow-countrymen to their fate. Reflective of this was the rumour in autumn 1992 that responsibility for relations with the CIS would be taken away from the Ministry of Foreign Affairs and placed in a special ministry for relations with the CIS headed by Sergei Stankevich, who had taken a firm stand on the protection of Russian minorities outside Russian borders.[22]

The concern not to be seen to be forsaking the Russian patrimony was also reflected in a particularly acute fashion in the issue of the northern islands which is discussed fully in chapter 6 by Tsuyoshi Hasegawa. Other parts of the Asian-Pacific region have been seen in some quarters as having a potential role to play in Russian economic restructuring. The successful economies of the region, particularly South Korea, Taiwan and Singapore, were seen as potential sources of trade and investment, particularly in the Russian Far East. Furthermore, in some quarters the economic success of some of these countries has been seen as providing a model which Russia might do well to try to emulate; South Korea in particular has been commonly referred to in this regard.[23] The applicability of the experiences of these countries as models for Russia is highly dubious, and certainly they are not relevant if Russia seeks a democratic path to marketisation.[24] Yet

---

21. See Alexander Rahr, "Winners and Losers of the Russian Congress," *RFE/RL Research Report* 1:18 (1 May 1992), p. 6.

22. See his comments in *Izvestiia*, 8 July 1992 and *Rossiiskaia Gazeta*, 28 July 1992.

23. Kazakhstan has also looked in this direction, with President Nazarbaev apparently seeing Singapore and Korea as models relevant to Kazakh needs. See the discussion in Bess Brown, "Central Asia and the East Asian Model," *RFE/RL Report on the USSR* 3:6 (8 February 1991), pp. 18–19.

24. From the Soviet period the calls for an "iron hand" as a means of introducing the market and democracy have sometimes been associated with positive references to the Korean experience. See, for example, A. Migranian, "Dolgii put' k evropeiskomu domu," *Novyi mir* 7 (1989), pp. 166–184.

their experiences and wealth ensure that they will remain within the vision of Russian elites searching for solutions to their economic difficulties.

The Asian-Pacific region is also relevant in terms of development of the Russian Far East. The greater integration of the Far East into the dynamic economies of the Asian-Pacific region has been on the agenda since Gorbachev's Vladivostok speech in July 1986. Little progress was made during *perestroika,* in part because the Far East did not get the levels of investment from Moscow that were deemed necessary to develop the local economy in such a way as to be able to enter the broader regional economy.

With the collapse of the Soviet Union, the liberalisation of conditions under which foreign capital could enter and operate and the increasing propensity on the part of local authorities to act independently of Moscow, interest in this area has grown. One manifestation of this has been the proposal to develop a major trading and processing centre on the Tumen River, a project which would involve Russia, China, North and South Korea, Japan and Mongolia. Another has been the major increase in cross-border trade with China, a development that promises to generate its own set of stable market relationships independent of outside considerations. Another has been the international tendering for oil drilling rights off Sakhalin.

What is most significant about these developments is that they have relied overwhelmingly on local initiative, not that from Moscow. In this sense, they reflect the absence of an integrated administrative framework noted above. Indeed, significant problems have been encountered in advancing with the Sakhalin oil drilling project because of conflict between the authorities in Moscow and the local leader over how the project is to proceed. It is likely that this conflict is the harbinger of the future: as the region finds itself dragged more into the Asian-Pacific market, its relations and links with Moscow are likely to become increasingly strained.

But in the immediate short-term future, the Asian-Pacific region is likely to be a low priority on the Russian foreign policy agenda. As the Russian government struggles to extricate itself from the remnants of the Soviet experience and to maintain its international standing as a great power, its focus will remain concentrated principally upon its CIS partners and the West. However until a stable and agreed structure of national politics emerges, issues will continue to be worked out in an unpredictable fashion. This applies as much to foreign policy issues as to those of a domestic nature, and it does mean that issues relating to Asia-Pacific may leap to a prominent place in the political debate at any time despite the government's own priorities.

3

Russia's Three Circles of Interests

Peter Shearman

Since the "Peoples' Democracies" began transforming themselves into peoples' revolutions in 1989, and the subsequent ending of the East-West bipolar Cold War confrontation, academic journals have been full of articles assessing the significance of these radical changes for international stability. Much of the focus of this literature has been on European security issues (especially that relating to the "question" of a unified Germany) and on the position of the United States in the emergent "new world order." Although there has been an increase in collaboration recently between Western specialists on international relations and their counterparts in the East, what has been lacking in the pages of scholarly journals is a detailed analysis of where post-Soviet Russia fits in any future scenario of global order.[1] This is a remarkable omission given the crucial role that Russia is likely to play in any of the potential futures on offer, due to its geostrategic position, its military status, its resource endowments and potential economic power as well as its current economic crisis, its mixed ethnic and cultural population, and the very large concentrations of Russians living in neighbouring newly-independent post-Soviet states. This chapter provides a critical analysis of Russian foreign policy in the post-Cold War era seeking to identify any basic trends in overall strategy.

Utilising the basic assumptions and concepts of Western theories of international relations it is possible to identify two orientations in the Russian academic and foreign policy communities: an idealist orientation with a stress on international organisation, common human values, the

---

1. There are exceptions, the most interesting produced by Russian officials and scholars. These will be referred to later in this chapter.

primacy of the individual, international law and collective security; and a realist orientation with a stress on nation-states, power and national security.[2] During the early period of Mikhail Gorbachev's reformism the idealists seemed to dominate, both in the realm of ideas and in setting the foreign policy agenda. However, by 1990 realist ideas were paramount in academic debates and in the Soviet Ministry of Foreign Affairs.

Following the disintegration of the Soviet Union in December 1991 President Boris Yeltsin and his foreign policy officials have dropped the rhetoric of new political thinking completely as Russia has been groping for a new conception of its national security. What Dean Acheson once remarked of Britain is now true of Russia: it has lost an empire but has yet to find a role. Realists under Yeltsin came to dominate in all important positions in the foreign policy apparatus, as the idealists among the original "new thinkers" (Eduard Shevardnadze, Aleksander Iakovlev, Vladimir Petrovskii) have departed the scene or taken up other, less important posts. Thus Russia's new self-perceived role in international relations will be based on a worldview that gives less attention to international institutions like the United Nations than it does to the balance of power between states. The fact that there is a general consensus on what constitute the main dynamics in international relations does not, however, provide a necessary logic or blueprint for what is in the Russian national interest or for a grand strategy to obtain them. Realists can and do disagree on foreign policy objectives, strategies and tactics.

Russia as a Great Power

There is a consensus on one basic principle: to ensure the maintenance of Russia as a "great power" in international politics. For Shevardnadze and the "old" new thinkers, the language of the "great powers" was reflective of a past era from which it was necessary to escape. For the incumbent Russian Foreign Minister Andrei Kozyrev and the "new" new thinkers, "For natural reasons alone, Russia is doomed to the status of a great power."[3] Kozyrev, following Shevardnadze's resignation as Soviet Foreign Minister in December 1990, said in an interview that he favoured "a course taking us away from the policy of new thinking to a policy of common sense."[4] Others criticised Shevardnadze's conception of new thinking as "utopianism" which threatened to undermine the real "national interests" of

---

2. See Peter Shearman, "New Thinking Reassessed," *Review of International Studies* 19 (1993; forthcoming).

3. A. Kozyrev, "Russia Looks West," *Moscow News* 39 (29 September–8 October 1991).

4. In *International Affairs* (Moscow) 3/1991, p. 131.

the state.[5] Crucial to these national interests is "the retention of Russia's special role in world politics" and its "high international status."[6]

While Russians recognise that their international position has been weakened they also widely believe that in an emerging multipolar world Russia can play a pivotal balancing role between Europe and Asia. This is the public presentation of where Moscow's elites perceive Russia's future great-power role to be. Postwar France under Charles de Gaulle is often referred to as a model for post-Cold War Russia. Although its international position had been weakened, de Gaulle's "realism" sought to give France an important balancing position between the European Community, North America and the Pacific states.[7] Ultimately, de Gaulle's successors tied France firmly to Europe as a leading advocate of regional integration. Britain also, weakened by the Second World War, sought to maintain its influence in three circles: the Commonwealth, North America and Europe. Ultimately Britain had to make a choice and, not without a great deal of continuing division and Mrs. Margaret Thatcher's departure from office, Britain chose the European circle. No longer based upon a hegemonic position in the communist East in conflict with the capitalist West, Russia's great-power status is now said to be based upon its geopolitical position situated between East and West. This is an argument that is constantly made by influential Russian commentators, scholars and politicians.[8]

Political scientist Andrei Kortunov, criticising the foreign policy of Gorbachev, Shevardnadze and Iakovlev for its lack of any "grand strategy" also refers to Gaullism of the 1960s, seeing the potential for Russia to utilise its relatively weakened international position as a balancer between a united Germany and the EC, the United States and the Pacific states.[9] The concept of the "balance of power" and the correlation between polarity and stability were topics introduced into Soviet academic debates, pre-*glasnost,* by Vladimir Lukin.[10] Lukin is an "Americanist" and an international relations specialist, formerly of the Institute for the Study of the USA and Canada,

5. For example see Andrei Kortunov, "New Dogma of the New Think," *Moscow News* 40 (14–21 October 1990), p. 3.

6. A. Bogaturov, M. Kozhokin and K. Pleshakov, "Mezhdu vostokam i zapadom: kontseptsiia vneshnei politiki RSFSR v perekhodnyi period," *Nezavisimaia gazeta,* 25 September 1991.

7. See Alfred Grosser, *French Foreign Policy Under de Gaulle* (Boston: Little Brown, 1965).

8. Those specifically using the de Gaulle analogy include Andrei Kokoshin, the Russian Deputy Defence Minister, in *New Times* 8 (February 1992), pp. 26–27, and Stephen Sestanovich, "Inventing the Soviet National Interest," *National Interest* 20 (Summer 1990), pp. 3–16.

9. Andrei Kortunov, "Rossiia i de Goll," *Moskovskie novosti,* 9 September 1990.

10. Following the publication of his book, *"Tsentry sily": kontseptsii i real'nosti* (Moscow: Mezhdunarodnye otnosheniia, 1983).

later appointed head of the Russian State Committee for Foreign Affairs and Foreign Economic Relations, before Yeltsin appointed him as the Russian ambassador to the United States in April 1992. Lukin and Andrei Kokoshin, his former colleague at the USA Institute (appointed Deputy Minister of Defence by Yeltsin) have been influential in developing, from their shared realist perspective concerning the dynamics of international relations, a new strategy for Russian foreign policy. One important objective is to ensure that Russia remains a great power, a key actor in the emerging multipolar balance of power.

What determines Russia's place in the post-Cold War international multipolar system is said to be its weight in relation to other states in the distribution of power capabilities. Weakened by its loss of empire and economic malaise with the end of the Cold War, Russia nevertheless is still one of the major powers in the international system due to its geopolitical position, its conventional and nuclear military power, the size and rich resource endowment of its territory and the size, literacy and skill of its population.[11] For Foreign Minister Kozyrev "The diversity and collision of interests will persist and states will continue... to rely on military force as the only real guarantee of their security." He calls explicitly for "realism" in foreign policy and in assessing Russian state interests, and this requires maintaining a nuclear deterrent and, in order to ensure its effectiveness, the continuation of nuclear testing.[12]

A desire to be and be seen to be a great power does not imply that the Russian leadership continues to hold to former Soviet Foreign Minister Andrei Gromyko's view that no problem of international relations can be resolved without considering Moscow's interests. On the contrary, in defining Russia's national interests and its new great-power role there is a consensus among foreign policy elites that the Soviet Union had over-extended itself on the global plane which undermined Moscow's interests.[13] This was particularly the case in supporting distant Third World regimes at considerable economic cost for questionable strategic or political benefit. The logic of Soviet Third World policy was the bipolar competition for influence with the United States rationalised in ideological terms as part of the global class conflict, with Moscow as the centre of proletarian interests and Washington representing the interests of monopoly capitalism. The

---

11. This is a theme constantly pursued by many Russian officials and academics. Lukin argues that due to these factors "Russia is doomed to be a great power"; *Moscow News* 19 (10–17 May 1992), p. 4.

12. Interview in *Izvestiia*, 2 October 1991. See also Andrei Kozyrev, "Confidence and Balance of Interests," *International Affairs* (Moscow), 11/1988, pp. 3–12.

13. Among many others making this point of over-extension was Eugene (Evgennii) Bazhanov, now Head of the Russian Diplomatic Academy. See his "V chem zhe nashi gosudarstvennyie interesy," *Izvestiia*, 12 April 1991.

actual forces and dynamics determining Soviet international behaviour were less ideological and more the shifting balance of power and strategic security threats and perceptions. Yet Soviet ideology did to a degree shape the agenda of foreign policy and oblige the Soviet leadership to make some "fraternal commitment" to states of "socialist orientation."

With the demise of communism the Russian Foreign Ministry has no need to qualify, rationalise or justify its policies on the basis of Marxist-Leninist ideology. Now that there is no longer a communist second world struggling for influence with the capitalist first world in the turbulent Third World, Russian policy is free to be far more discriminatory in choosing friends, allies and commitments on the basis of a realistic appraisal of what is in Russia's national interests. As a true status quo power Russia's foreign policy discourse and diplomatic language no longer suffer from the contradictions that so frustrated Henry Kissinger during the détente of the early 1970s.[14] Like France and Great Britain, weakened after World War II and hence forced to retreat from empire, Russia, emerging weakened after the Cold War has lost its empire and has been withdrawing from overseas commitments from Cuba to Angola. But like postwar Britain and France, post-Cold War Russia has been searching for a role which still accords it great-power status. As will be demonstrated below, however, there has been no consensus on how to achieve this objective and foreign policy has been an area of conflict and confusion in domestic Russian politics.

Issue Salience and the Foreign Policy Agenda

The saliency of issues on the foreign policy agenda of states is determined in large part by perceptions of threat. The logic of Soviet participation in the arms race, Soviet Third World interventions and the Brezhnev doctrine during the Cold War were all dependent variables in the competition with the West, with the United States in particular perceived as a threat to Soviet state, or "national," interests. Traditionally anything that undermines a state's territorial integrity and survival as a sovereign entity is considered to be its main threat. In an increasingly interdependent world, with the perceived decreasing utility of the military as an instrument for gaining foreign policy objectives and with global problems (pollutants, terrorists, viruses, currency exchange rate fluctuations) national interests are

---

14. For instance the Soviet Union's insistence on using the term "peaceful coexistence" in bilateral agreements, which to the Americans implied a Soviet commitment to support national liberation movements in the Third World. For how this affected negotiations, for example, on the Basic Principles Agreement during the détente era see chapter 5 of Alexander L George, *Managing U.S.-Soviet Rivalry: Problems of Crisis Prevention* (Boulder: Westview, 1983), pp. 107–18.

being redefined as sovereignty is being undermined. Given the crisis in the Soviet economy and polity in the 1980s the priority for Gorbachev and Shevardnadze was to save the Union, and to do so it was necessary to cut back on defence expenditure, on overseas economic and military commitments and hence to formulate a foreign policy strategy to ensure the realisation of these basic goals. Soviet foreign policy was driven by an overriding domestic economic imperative. This led to a strategy designed to open up to the outside world for economic aid and investment.

As with Gorbachev and Shevardnadze, so with Yeltsin and Kozyrev, the most salient foreign policy issue has been linked to domestic economic imperatives. The major "threat" to the integrity of the state continued to be the prospect of total economic collapse and domestic political instability. With the Cold War over it is not the fear of an external threat of war so much as the fear of civil disorder that has determined Yeltsin's foreign policy orientation. Kozyrev has referred to the fact on a number of occasions that for the first time in its history Russia is not faced with a clearly defined potential external enemy. However, Russia's foreign policy agenda following its independence and the establishment of the Commonwealth of Independent States (CIS) has been determined in large part not so much by Yeltsin and Kozyrev, but by events themselves. Russia's foreign policy as a result has been reactive rather than proactive.

It has also often been difficult to discern who and what institutions actually have the competency to make policy. The fact that most domestic actors agree on the basic overall objectives of Russian foreign policy, and what essentially is in the Russian national interest (maintaining Russia's great-power status, ensuring domestic stability and developing the economy), has not led to a common definition of what this means in practice. Nor has it led to a consensus on the most appropriate strategy and tactics to achieve foreign policy objectives.

One way of looking at Russian foreign policy during 1992 is to think in terms of three concentric circles: the first circle incorporating the former Soviet republics around the periphery of Russia, the second circle consisting of the "West" (incorporating North America, Europe and Japan) and the third circle consisting of the "rest" (mainly what used to be termed the "Third World"). For the most part during the first year of post-imperial Russian statehood the planned focus of active foreign policy has been targeted on the second circle in order to gain economic assistance from the leading capitalist states to assist domestic economic development. However, the Russian leadership has found itself reacting to events in the first circle, forcing it to spend an inordinate amount of time and energy dealing with problems previously associated with Soviet domestic politics. The third circle initially played a relatively minor role but has been increasing steadily in saliency. It has been the relative weight attached to each of the three circles that has provided the battleground for domestic individual and institutional competition over the course of foreign policy.

Policy Controversy and the Second Circle

In a speech to the European parliament in April 1991 Yeltsin placed his Western credentials on the table: "I am convinced that Russia must return to Europe... as a renewed democratic state."[15] Although he was talking about Russia's future position as a bridge between East and West as the major Eurasian power in terms of its geopolitical position, Yeltsin clearly perceives Russia's basic political orientation as part of the "West." In the context of the old (and some say ongoing) great debate between the Westernisers and the Slavophiles, Yeltsin and Kozyrev would fit into the first category. Kozyrev has argued that Russia's destiny is as an integral part of the West, as "a reliable partner in the community of civilised nations." He regards the "supertask" of foreign policy to be to ensure the "improvement of the everyday lives of Russian citizens."[16] This has entailed the wooing of the West.

Three main factors have undermined the extent to which Yeltsin and Kozyrev have been able to implement their foreign policy focus on the second circle: domestic political opposition, the reluctance of the West to deliver and the need to react constantly to events in the first circle.

In any evaluation of the opposition to Yeltsin's "Western" policy, one has to consider the psychological milieu. Britain found it difficult to adjust to the end of empire, and Suez, 1956 was a major psychological blow.[17] France's retreat from empire was even more traumatic and, in granting independence to Algeria, President de Gaulle brought the Fifth Republic to the brink of civil war. The Soviet Union's sudden demise in 1991 marked the end of the last of the great European empires. Despite its ideological protestations about proletarian internationalism the Communist Party of the Soviet Union inherited and continued to rule the former Tsarist Russian empire as a traditional hegemonic power. From its birth in 1917 until the advent of "new political thinking" in the late 1980s the Russian Soviet empire's foreign policy was based upon competition with the "West."

15. Quoted in John Morrison, *Boris Yeltsin: Bolshevik to Democrat* (London: Penguin, 1991), p. 29.

16. Andrei Kozyrev, "A Chance for Survival," *Foreign Affairs* 71 (Spring 1992), pp. 9–10.

17. For a discussion on how this impacted on Britain's perceptions in reference to the three circles see David Saunders, *British Foreign Policy* (London: Macmillan, 1990).

During the Cold War period (1946–89), it was the "American threat" which determined Soviet foreign and security policies.

In 1989 Moscow lost its external East European empire. In 1991 it lost its internal empire and the communist ideology that helped to hold it together. Ronald Reagan's "evil empire" was no more and the Cold War was over. Like all wars, there were winners and losers. Despite what Shevardnadze and Gorbachev, and Bush and Baker, said about both sides winning the peace, there was a growing perception among sections of Russian society that indeed the Cold War had been won and lost. And as losers Russia found itself in the humiliating position of having its leaders shuttling around Western capitals, cap in hand, begging for economic assistance from the victors. Neither Britain nor France, notwithstanding Marshall Aid, found themselves in quite such a humiliating situation with the end of empire. This sense of humiliation is almost palpable when one visits Moscow and soon becomes evident when conversing with elites, even with the most liberal of the reformers.[18]

In his power struggle against Gorbachev Yeltsin had taken advantage of the prevailing manifestation of Russian nationalism, arguing that Russian history, culture and traditions had suffered more under the Soviet system relative to other nations. Lenin had referred to the old Tsarist empire as a "prison of nations" and many Russians argued that under the communist party Russians had suffered the most severe form of imprisonment. Other Soviet nationalities had their own separate cultures and languages which were allowed to "flourish," whereas even the Russian language became meshed with "Sovietisation." Russian identity was actually therefore undermined by the Soviet state, with this second-class status institutionalised in the federal administrative structure where Russia was the only one of the fifteen republics not to have its own separate party, governmental and public organisations.

This then was the backdrop to Yeltsin's diplomatic focus on the West, on the second circle. In the initial euphoria following the failure of the coup attempt and the subsequent demise of the Soviet Union in 1991, Yeltsin's position seemed unassailable. He enjoyed democratic legitimacy, enormous domestic and international popularity for his brave role in opposing the coup and he was apparently unhindered even by a loyal opposition in formulating policy. But the military-industrial complex was still intact, the old bureaucrats still in place in the command economy and the Russian parliament (whose composition was determined under only a partially

---

18. This has certainly been my own experience. Lukin suggests that there is a danger that this sense of humiliation could give rise to a foreign policy based upon Russian chauvinism; Vladimir Lukin, "Our Security Predicament," *Foreign Policy* 88 (Fall 1992), pp. 57–75.

democratic system) was becoming increasingly conservative. Yeltsin was forced to give up his position as head of government and to develop a Russian Ministry of Defence. The Defence Ministry was necessary, it was argued by Colonel Dmitrii Volkogonov (who headed a commission to establish it), to counter similar intentions by Ukraine, Belarus and other former Soviet republics to create their own defence ministries.[19]

The Western-oriented foreign policy was promoted most enthusiastically by Yeltsin himself, Kozyrev and acting Prime Minister Egor Gaidar. Gaidar came under constant criticism from conservatives in the Russian parliament and the military for what they argued was his kowtowing to the IMF and other Western financial institutions. Kozyrev has been criticised for following the Western line on issues from Afghanistan to Yugoslavia. And Yeltsin has borne the brunt of attacks from the military both for his apparent overactive unilateral arms control initiatives and for his lack of initiative in ensuring the well-being of Russian citizens resident in other former Soviet republics. It is not only the communists and extreme nationalists who have been levelling these criticisms at the conduct of Russian foreign policy. For example Georgii Arbatov, Director of the Institute for the Study of the USA and Canada in Moscow has criticised Gaidar for moving too rapidly towards American-style capitalism and attacked the IMF for treating Russia like a Third World country.[20]

When the Russian Defence Ministry was being created there was debate in Moscow as to whether the first minister should be a military official or a civilian. In the event Colonel Pavel Grachev (formerly commanding officer of Soviet paratroop units) got the job. (Kokoshin, Arbatov's deputy at the USA Institute, was appointed Grachev's First Deputy Minister.) That a military official should be appointed to this senior governmental post was a disappointment to the liberal reformers in Moscow.

The military had always been opposed to participation in an anti-ballistic missile defence program with the United States and when Yeltsin announced on a visit to Washington that Russia should join the U.S. in developing such a system it came as a surprise not only to the White House in Washington, but also to Yeltsin's "White House staff" in Moscow. Vladimir Moskvin has written that Yeltsin's announcement also "stunned specialists in the Russian foreign ministry and the General Staff of the armed forces."[21] Aleksei Arbatov, the Director of the Centre for Arms Control and Strategic Stability in Moscow, has constantly argued that Russia should not become involved in a strategic defence initiative for it would complicate the

---

19. See *Krasnaia zvezda*, 14 April 1992.
20. *Radio Liberty Daily Report* 145 (31 July 1992).
21. *New Times* 15 (April 1992), p. 9.

balance of power, push back the prospects for disarmament, be far too costly and could compromise Russian sovereignty.[22]

Yeltsin had also announced that Russian nuclear weapons would no longer target the United States and he told the Russian parliament on his return from Washington that Russia and the U.S. no longer consider themselves potential adversaries.[23] But it would appear that Yeltsin had not informed parliament of this important change in Russian nuclear strategy in advance. Yeltsin had also announced a general intention for further radical cuts in nuclear arsenals, a moratorium on nuclear testing and a continuation of a no-first-use policy of nuclear weapons. Speaking at the London Royal United Services Institute, Defence Minister Grachev said that although more cuts are possible, they would now need to include Chinese, French and British nuclear weapons.[24] In an address to students at the Moscow State Institute for Foreign Relations, Marshall Evgenii Shaposhnikov, Chief of Staff of the CIS armed forces, acknowledged that some eight months after Yeltsin's announcement Russian strategic nuclear missiles were still aimed at U.S. targets. He also stated that Russia would resume nuclear tests if "Western countries do not stop."[25]

General Aleksandr Lebed, since his appointment by Yeltsin to command the Russian 14th army in Moldova, has made repeated attacks on the government, stating that Russia would do well "to stop begging around the world, like goats begging for carrots."[26] The Russian parliament debated a motion of no confidence in the government in September in which one member, Viacheslav Liubimov argued that "This government has a pro-Japanese, pro-American and pro-German policy."[27] Another indication of military conservatives gaining influence in policy was Yeltsin's appointment of General Boris Gromov as Deputy Defence Minister in July 1992. Gromov, an Afghan war hero, was a stern critic of Gorbachev's reformism and the role he played in the August events is not totally clear, although he did refuse to attack the Russian White House. Colonel Aleksander Rutskoi, Yeltsin's Vice President (another hero of the Afghan war) has also strongly criticised the emphasis of Russian diplomacy on the West, being particularly critical of Kozyrev himself, calling for his resignation and the replacement of "theoreticians" in government with "people of practical knowledge."[28] Rutskoi's resignation plea came after Kozyrev, in an interview with

22. *Nezavisimaia gazeta*, 4 March 1992.
23. *Izvestiia*, 13 February 1992.
24. *Radio Liberty Daily Report* 14 (27 July 1992).
25. Quoted in the *Australian*, 28 September 1992.
26. *Moscow News* 28 (12–19 July 1992).
27. Quoted in the *Australian*, 30 September 1992.
28. *Radio Liberty Daily Report* 135 (17 July 1992).

Izvestiia, warned of a possible military coup.[29] The influential chairman of the Russian parliament Ruslan Khasbulatov and a close Yeltsin adviser Sergei Stankevich have also been critical of Kozyrev's handling of foreign policy. Stankevich was often cited as a potential successor to Kozyrev as foreign minister or as head of a newly created Ministry of Commonwealth Affairs. Despite his earlier "democratic" credentials as deputy mayor of Moscow and a flirtation with the U.S. constitution as a model for Russia, Stankevich has since argued that Western liberal democracy is not necessarily the appropriate vehicle for Russia's development, but rather represents a "naive idealism."[30]

Yeltsin has been unable to keep full control over foreign policy due to domestic conservative opposition to its Western direction. There has been no coherence in foreign policy making, and it has been unclear at times who and which institutions have the competence to make policy. The president and vice president often articulate diametrically opposed views on important foreign policy issues. Yeltsin says one thing when overseas, often, as with his nuclear targeting strategy, without apparently consulting the relevant authorities in Moscow, only then later to say another on returning home. Yeltsin appears to have diminishing control over national security policy, as conservative military commanders and defence officials are increasingly monopolising decision making. He has been faced with criticism and opposition from members of parliament from both the "right" and "left," and the Russian Security Council, dominated by conservatives, was becoming increasingly powerful during the second half of 1992.

Another good example of the problems that Yeltsin and Kozyrev have faced from domestic political opposition in trying to construct a coherent foreign policy relates to Japan. When in opposition to Gorbachev Yeltsin had given some indications that Russia would be prepared to compromise on the issue of the Kuril Islands. Kozyrev and some Asian specialists in the Russian Foreign Ministry had hinted that international law could provide the basis for a settlement of the issue (some seeing this as a way for Russia to save face since the Japanese case would be stronger). Those in the ministry who opposed returning the islands to Japan were placed in diplomatic posts which excluded them from having any influence on the issue. Many observers assumed that Yeltsin's visit to Japan, scheduled for September 1992, would result in the "sale of the century" with Russia receiving vast

---

29. *Izvestiia,* 30 June 1992.

30. For his earlier views on the U.S. constitution see Richard Sakwa, *Gorbachev and his Reforms, 1985–1990* (Hemel Hempstead: Philip Allan, 1990), p. 148. Dmitri Simes in "Russia Reborn," *Foreign Policy* 85 (Winter 1991–92), pp. 41–62, refers to Stankevich's "naive idealism" critique. For Stankevich's criticism of Kozyrev see *Izvestiia,* 7 July 1992.

sums of much-needed hard currency in exchange for islands of little value or utility.[31] In the event Yeltsin snubbed the Japanese and at the last hour postponed his visit (see the chapter by Hasegawa in this volume).

Opposition to any deal over the islands came from those bureaucratic and institutional quarters that one would perhaps most expect: the military-industrial complex. A document was submitted by the Russian General Staff to a special closed session of the parliament called to debate the issue. Russia's defence chiefs opposed the return of the islands on a number of grounds. It would, it was argued, compromise Russia's defences in the Pacific, weaken the Pacific Fleet, stimulate further territorial demands by Japan, act as a model for other nations with territorial claims on Russia and compensating for the weakened security would ultimately be very costly. The military argued that the Kuriles were vital for Russian national security interests. Again, there was also the perceptual, psychological question of appearing weak in the face of another great "Western" power. Arkadii Volskii, head of an industrial lobby in Moscow stated that "It is a mistake to think that Russia is so weak that all sorts of demands can be made" and Lukin, Russia's Ambassador to the United States, has argued that Japanese monopoly should not be permitted in the development of Russian oil and gas deposits in the Far East.[32] It was particularly galling for the Russian leadership when Japan succeeded in 1992 in putting the issue of the disputed islands on the agenda of the G-7 summit in Munich. In the end Russian pride and military logic won out over the need to gain financial assistance. One year after the failed coup, Russia's Western-orientated foreign policy had not received the hoped for dividends in the form of large economic commitments from the G-7 and it was being held hostage by domestic politics. Energies put into the second circle were also being undermined by having to react constantly to events in the first circle.

Policy Controversy and the First Circle

Compared to the disintegration of the Soviet empire, the French and British retreats from empire were relatively uncomplicated. The Soviet empire's collapse was clumsily arranged and, given its suddenness, there were no carefully worked out institutions and constitutional mechanisms to manage it. Under these circumstances it is perhaps remarkable how relatively little conflict and bloodshed have resulted.

---

31. On the history behind the dispute over the islands see the appendix to Wolf Mendl's chapter, "The Soviet Union and Japan," in Gerald Segal, ed., *The Soviet Union in East Asia: Predicaments of Power* (London: Heinemann, 1983), pp. 65–67.

32. Quoted in the *Guardian Weekly,* 20 September 1992.

With the demise of the USSR in 1991 fifteen new states came into existence, most of which have significant Russian minorities. A mechanism to share out debts, property and other assets and liabilities had not been worked out. Overnight the world faced the prospect of three new nuclear powers, one of which, and the least likely to give them up, becoming Europe's largest state (covering almost twice as much territory as a united Germany and with a population almost as large as France's) with the largest standing army (a commitment to maintain 400,000 troops). Moreover this country, Ukraine, is in dispute with Moscow, which claims large parts of its territory. (Nuclear weapons were also deployed in Belarus and Kazakhstan). Russia and Ukraine are also in conflict over the Black Sea Fleet and the distribution of gold and diamond reserves and property abroad. Ukraine is estimated to have nearly 1,500 strategic nuclear missiles, which it is increasingly less inclined to see withdrawn to its former coloniser and potential foe.[33] It has been suggested that "Ukraine, Russia's key partner in the new commonwealth, daily defines its new sovereignty largely in terms of ways it does not want to be part of Russia."[34]

The Crimea, ceded to Ukraine by Nikita Khrushchev, is, in the minds of most Russians, an integral part of "Mother Russia" and it is inconceivable that it should not be under the jurisdiction of Russian authorities. An opinion poll conducted in thirteen Russian cities asked: "Do you think the Crimea must be part of Ukraine or Russia, or an independent state?" Sixty-six percent said Russia, 11 percent an independent state, 12 percent did not know, and only 7 percent thought it should belong to Ukraine.[35] The domestic political agendas in both countries have been set in large part by issues pertaining to national sovereignty and, given the history of their relations, Russians and Ukrainians are clearly in for some testing times. Neither President Yeltsin in Russia nor his counterpart, President Leonid Kravchuk in Ukraine would wish to see their relations deteriorate or resort to conflict, but they are not able to control their respective political agendas. Rukh, the movement that mobilised for Ukrainian independence under Gorbachev, passed a resolution at its Congress in March 1992 for Kravchuk to pull Ukraine out of the CIS and to announce presidential rule over the Crimea, and has been successful in forcing the replacement of the Prime Minister.[36] And Yeltsin has been confronted with domestic pressures from

---

33. On the number of nuclear weapons see *Komsomolskaia pravda*, 26 March 1992.

34. Francis X. Clines in the *New York Times*, 29 December 1991, cited by Teresa Rakowska-Harmstone, "Chickens Coming Home to Roost: A Perspective on Soviet Ethnic Relations," *Journal of International Affairs* 45 (Winter 1992), p. 547.

35. *Moscow News* 20 (17 May 1992).

36. *Radio Liberty Daily Report* 43 (3 March 1992).

communists, nationalists and the military not to cede any claims to the Black Sea Fleet or to the Crimea. Vice President Rutskoi has referred to Crimea as sacred Russian territory and his advice to the leaders of other republics of the former Soviet Union is to "make no mistake: no one will surrender an inch of the sacred land to you."[37]

The Deputy Director of the Russian Institute for Europe, Sergei Karaganov, has suggested that with the disintegration of the USSR some "national borders may require correction due to the mixture of nationalities within present republican areas," predicting conflicts over resources and local arms races.[38] Of the population of Ukraine, 21 percent is Russian, and there are large numbers of Russians living in the Baltic Republics, Moldova, and Kazakhstan. Yeltsin himself hinted during the turbulent months leading to the collapse of the USSR that Russia's borders with Ukraine and Kazakhstan were not immutable. The issue of Russians living in the other members of the CIS has become an important issue in Russian domestic politics. Officials have been forced to take a stand on this issue due to a rising wave of nationalism across Russia and to the particular problems confronting Russians in Moldova, the Baltic States, the Crimea, the Caucuses and Central Asia. Although Yeltsin won a clear majority in the first round of voting for the Russian Presidency in June 1991 (57 percent of the vote), the ultra-nationalist Russian V. V. Zhirinovskii, with a clearly anti-semitic, anti-Muslim and revanchist manifesto, garnered over six million votes. In the year since the election nationalist sentiments have clearly increased as Russians search for a new identity, for scapegoats and for solace during severe economic times. Politicians have been capitalising on these sentiments and hence exacerbating and feeding them for their own personal, instrumental ends. Zhirinovskii may not be a direct personal threat to Yeltsin's position, but the ideas he propagates could well be.

The Estonian presidential elections in September 1992 effectively disenfranchised one third of the population, overwhelmingly ethnic Russians, due to new laws on citizenship. Fully 90 percent of the population of Narva, Estonia (almost entirely Russian), are not eligible for Estonian citizenship.[39] Some 10,000 Russians demonstrated in Tallin, the Estonian capital, in March 1992 against the new laws pertaining to citizenship.[40] Clearly the Russian government has to react to these issues and events.[41] Likewise, and more immediately problematic, has been the conflict between the Moldovan authorities and the self-proclaimed (by ethnic

---

37. *Kommersant*, 3 February 1992.
38. "Vneshnaia politika posle putcha," *Nezavisimaia gazeta*, 21 September 1991.
39. RIA Novosti, 10/9 1992.
40. *Radio Liberty Daily Report* 57 (23 March 1992).
41. In October 1992 the treatment of Russians in the Baltic states was the pretext used by Yeltsin to announce a suspension in the withdrawal of Russian troops; editors.

Russians) Dniester Republic, and that between Georgians and Abkhazians in the Caucuses. Lebed, the commander of the 14th Russian army in Moldova issued public threats against the Moldovan government warning it against intervention, Vice President Rutskoi has issued similar warnings, and even CIS Commander Shaposhnikov has taken an increasingly hard line stance in relation to the treatment of ethnic Russians by former Soviet republics. All three have been blunt in their criticism of the Russian foreign ministry's failure, as they see it, to defend adequately the interests of Russians in the other republics.

Yeltsin and Kozyrev have been forced, both by the events themselves, and by domestic political pressures, to respond to incidents in Moldova, the Baltic Republics, and other areas of the former Soviet Union with similar ethnic problems (e.g., South Ossetia, Nagorno Karabakh, Abkhazia). Kozyrev has come to stress as his "top priority" the "protection of Russians in other CIS states... using powerful methods if necessary."[42] This harder line followed an article in *Nezavisimaia gazeta* by Stankevich, who in 1992 had become the main defender of these Russians, and who here was arguing that concern for their fate in other states does not mark interference in their internal affairs, but was rather the duty of the Russian government.[43] Stankevich has praised Rutskoi's foreign policy proposals to defend Russian minority rights in South Ossetia and has joined the Vice President (and other powerful voices) for increased authoritarian rule in order to extricate Russia from its present crisis.

That the CIS has dominated Russian foreign policy was evident in Kozyrev's statement to the 6th congress of the Russian parliament for it was "wholly devoted to Russia's position in the CIS" and it also "contained a meaningful admission that the highest percentage of president-hours spent on foreign policy, concerns work with the CIS countries."[44] In January 1992 Yeltsin disappeared from Moscow without any explanation when he was due to meet the visiting Japanese foreign minister. He later emerged in Ukraine having emergency talks concerning the Black Sea Fleet. Summits with Shevardnadze over Abkhazia, with Kravchuk over the Black Sea Fleet, or Mircea Snegur over the Dniester Republic, have come to dominate Russia's foreign policy agenda rather than summits with Presidents George Bush and François Mitterrand or Chancellor Helmut Kohl. Whatever Yeltsin's own preferred priorities, developments in places like South

---

42. Interview in *Nezavisimaia gazeta*, 4 April 1992.

43. *Nezavisimaia gazeta*, 28 March 1992. Later Stankevich praised Rutskoi for showing determination in pursuing Russia's interests in Moldova and Georgia; see *Rossiiskaia gazeta*, 28 July 1992.

44. See *Moscow News* 18 (3–10 May 1992).

Ossetia, the Crimea and the Dniester region have been setting the agenda for him, as well as serving as political fodder in domestic power struggles.

Russia Turns to the Third Circle

Although not ignored completely, the "third circle" was far less salient in the initial Yeltsin foreign policy strategy. But during 1992 Yeltsin's foreign policy focus on the West for economic aid was faced with increasingly effective opposition from an unholy domestic alliance of right and left, and his energies have been pushed off track by the constant need to respond to developments in the CIS states in defence of Russian nationals' interests. The third circle too became more important, as Russia, in its search for a new post-imperial role, perceived certain developing countries as offering not only regional influence but also alternative sources to the West for modern technologies and trade opportunities.

There is an emerging consensus, which perhaps Yeltsin himself the great survivor may yet join, that Russia's policy has been too heavily focused upon the West, the second circle, at the expense of the first and third circles. As Viktor Kuvaldin put it, mistakes in Russian foreign policy have been due to a "thoughtless pro-Western course with a strong American emphasis."[45] Ambassador Lukin in Washington is an expert on the Pacific, and he has argued that Russia should not become too dependent upon Japan as the latter emerges as a global power. Rather, he suggests, countries like South Korea should be given the opportunity to assist in the exploration of the Russian Far East.[46] Kozyrev visited South Korea in March 1992 where he sought to acquire commitments for investments in Russia while making promises that his government would do all it could to prevent North Korea developing nuclear weapons.[47] Shortly after postponing his trip to Tokyo Yeltsin rescheduled and reconfirmed his trip to South Korea for November. In November 1991 the two Koreas, Russia, Mongolia and China signed an agreement for the development of a three-billion dollar project to construct a port in the border region of the Tumen (Tumyntsian) River. The objective is the creation of a free-trade zone. South Korea has signed a contract to develop a gas field in Yakutia. Russia's foreign trade statistics for 1992 show the greatest increase in trade to be with China and South Korea and, as Gary Klintworth notes in his chapter, economic interdependency between these states will increase further. Russian CIS General Staff Chief Viktor Samsonov visited China (and North Korea) in March 1992.

---

45. Viktor Kuvaldin, "Is There a Third Way?," *Moscow News* 30 (26 July–2 August 1992).
46. *Guardian Weekly,* 20 September 1992.
47. *Radio Liberty Daily Report* 54 (18 March 1992).

Russia has basically abandoned Cuba, the outpost of Marxism-Leninism in the Western hemisphere, but it has been more circumspect in relations with former communist allies closer to home in the Asian-Pacific region. For example, while cutting back on military supplies to North Korea, and despite Kozyrev's promise to prevent the transfer of nuclear technology, Russia renewed the old Soviet-North Korean Treaty of Friendship and Cooperation in July 1991 (originally concluded in 1961). Russia's Deputy Foreign Minister, Georgii Kunadze stated on the treaty's renewal that "We and the Korean People's Democratic Republic share common concerns of a strategic nature."[48] Although cutting back on arms transfers to countries that cannot afford to pay for them and cutting off arms supplies to Iraq in accordance with UN resolutions, during 1992 the military-industrial complex has fought a successful lobbying campaign to increase arms sales. One of Yeltsin's advisers suggested that Russia transform its domestic military-industrial complex into an arms-exporting industry in order to gain scarce hard currency.[49] A new military committee was established in June 1992 to supervise arms sales with Vice President Rutskoi being given overall responsibility for overseeing the export of arms.

Culturally Russia may not be a true Asian power but its present leadership does have a good understanding of the workings of the communist system still operative in five Asian countries. It is, therefore, perhaps better able to deal with these regimes than are Western nations. The non-communist dynamic Asian economies may also provide a more suitable model of political and economic development for Russia than the more established democratic Western states.

Furthermore, despite Yeltsin's goal of integrating Russia into West European civilisation, Moscow, shorn of its control over Ukraine, Belarus, Moldova and the Baltic states, is actually now geographically more distant from Western Europe than when it was the capital of the USSR. This has led Russians from both ends of the political spectrum to reevaluate Russia's foreign policy focus on the West. Lukin, for example, sees Russia not so much as between Europe and Asia but, in terms of levels of economic development, as "occupying some strange middle space between two 'Europes'." He argues that "Russia can become an important balancer" between China, Japan and other states in Asia-Pacific, "preventing any one of them from dominating others without itself posing a threat to the region."[50] Twice in this same article Lukin states that the most likely threat to regional security would derive from conflict or crisis in the Koreas (a

---

48. *Ibid.*, 143 (29 July 1992).
49. Mikhail Maley, interview in *Rossiiskaia gazeta*, 28 February 1992.
50. Lukin, "Our Security Predicament," pp. 60, 70.

perception shared by former U.S. Secretary of State James Baker). Russia's balancing policy should be designed to prevent this.

On the conservative side, Stankevich argues that there have been two basic orientations in Russia's foreign policy: Atlanticism (the U.S. and the West: our second circle) and Eurasianism (CIS and Asia-Pacific: our first and third circles), with, in his view, too strong an emphasis on the former at the expense of the latter. However, he talks not only in terms of the "national interest" as a guide to foreign policy, but also in terms of a "mission" for Russia in its international relations.[51] For Stankevich the central mission should be the protection of Russian nationals living in former Soviet republics. But it is much more than that, for it is argued that "Russia's mission in the world... is to initiate and support a multilateral dialogue of cultures, civilizations, and states." Stankevich sees Russia as "the conciliator, Russia connecting, Russia combining." Bruce Porter points out that over the centuries the only connecting Russia has done is in the form of "military conquest and annexation."[52] Although Stankevich is not calling explicitly for military conquest or the annexation of neighbouring states, his missionary zeal will ring alarm bells in those states that have historical justification for worrying about Russia's intentions.

Stankevich has also argued that the Russian foreign ministry has almost totally ignored other, non regional, "second-echelon" (our third circle) states, and that this has been a serious omission. He prescribes a policy targeted on countries such as Mexico, Brazil, Chile, Argentina, South Africa, Turkey and India: "Like us they want to integrate into the world economy without losing identity and while defending their national interests."[53] In Asia-Pacific he calls for close collaboration with other regional "middle rank powers." However, in defining Russia's national interests in terms of a "mission" Stankevich's conception of Russia's role in the world is not as a normal state acting as balancer (cf. Lukin), but as a unique state acting as protector of Russians based on the idea of Russian exceptionalism and manifest destiny.

In the autumn of 1992 conservative forces appeared to be gaining the upper hand in foreign and security policy. Foreign policy was no longer being influenced by new political thinking academics in ivory towers, but by practitioners reacting to real world events on the ground. The original new

---

51. See Sergei Stankevich, "Russia in Search of Itself," *National Interest* 28 (Summer 1992), pp. 47–51. This is an adaptation of his piece in *Nezavisimaia gazeta*, 28 March 1992.

52. Bruce D. Porter, "Comment" (on Stankevich's article), *National Interest* 28 (Summer 1992), p. 54.

53. Sergei Stankevich, speech to a conference on Russian foreign policy, *International Affairs* (Moscow) 4–5/1992, pp. 81–104.

thinking idealists are now voicing their concern at recent developments, suggesting that they could harbour a dangerous turn in foreign policy. The spectre now haunting Eurasia we are told is a form of Russian fascism. For example Aleksander Iakovlev, Gorbachev's former foreign policy adviser, suggests that placing the old CPSU on trial in Moscow is to misunderstand the nature of the threat, for the threat is no longer communism but neo-fascism "boosted by our traditional intolerance... chauvinism, radical nationalism, economic dislocation, social instability, and impoverishment of the society."[54] Kozyrev has also written about the "dangerous prospect of fascist ideology staging a comeback in some form."[55]

The dangers of such an occurrence are real, but nationalism in some less dangerous form will likely shape the short-term future of Russian foreign policy as Russia reborn seeks a new role for itself in a changing world. Whereas the end of the Cold War, as James Schlesinger puts it, "represents a moment of triumph for the United States,"[56] it represents a difficult period of humiliation and readjustment for Russia. The victor in the Cold War has not only failed to finance Russian reforms, it has also not reciprocated Russian disarmament and moratorium policies. To add insult to injured Russian pride the United States has put pressure on Russia not to supply India with space rocket technology and Iran with submarines. Russia's policy in the third circle had hitherto been fairly pragmatic and circumspect, involving a withdrawal from expensive Third World commitments. The focus has been on the more dynamic newly-developed Asian economies, such as South Korea. This is likely to continue, and although Cuba, Vietnam, and North Korea are unlikely to enjoy a reversal of the cuts in Russian aid over the past two years, Moscow will possibly turn more to the third circle both to gain access to economic assistance and modern technologies and to enhance its own international status.

In a recent article Ken Booth refers to the erosion of sovereignty and, influenced by James Rosenau,[57] trends in "post-international relations." Like other post-realists Booth exaggerates the extent to which others ignore new "turbulent" and transformative dynamics in world politics, and his mocking idea that sovereignty has now become "the colour of the flag people wear on their post-fordist boxer shorts" underestimates (unfortunately, perhaps) the continuing vitality of nationalism and the idea

---

54. Aleksander Iakovlev, "Reliving the Past Experience," *Moscow News* 28 (12–19 July 1992), p. 3.

55. Kozyrev, "Chance for Survival," p. 5.

56. James Schlesinger, "New Instabilities, New Priorities," *Foreign Policy* 85 (Winter 1991), pp. 3–24.

57. James Rosenau, *Turbulence in World Politics* (New York: Harvester-Wheatsheaf, 1990).

of sovereignty.[58] This is certainly true of the geographical space that we used to know as the Soviet Union. As John Chapman more accurately points out: "The paradox remains that although national interests are now more difficult to conceive and promote, given the decline in the power of sovereign states to control their affairs, nationalism still shapes world politics."[59] Russia's national interests are certainly being defined in terms of nationalism, sovereignty, territorial integrity and power. The question ultimately is the mix in which these aspects blend.

Still absorbed by problems in the economy, Russia's foreign policy outside of its own immediate geographical region will be increasingly low-key (about fifty consulates and embassies are planned for closure to save money: even the Ukrainian ambassador has no staff, lives in a hotel and only has use of a car due to the generosity of a relatively wealthy local friend).[60] Russia is likely to play a decreasing role in international institutions like the United Nations and to become far less accommodating to the West in arms control issues. Its foreign policy will focus increasingly on the former Soviet republics in the first circle and the more prosperous states in the third circle. As the short-lived embassy in Papua New Guinea is vacated, along with many others in least-developed nations, the foreign ministry will enhance its representation in the larger CIS states and the more economically dynamic Third World states.

The most dangerous scenario for global stability will be, and it is not a remote possibility, if Russia's tensions with any of the other former Soviet republics (especially Ukraine) erupts into military conflict. If this happens then Stankevich's missionary conception will not only win out in the battle for defining the Russian national interest, but it will take on a new form of crusaderism. Thus far though, all things considered, Russia has managed its decline from empire without risking war. So long as Russian national interests are defined in traditional terms and its government seeks to balance rather than to challenge the emerging order, international stability will be enhanced. With the end of the Cold War, in each of the three circles, maintaining stability has become more complex and unpredictable. But as a central component in each one, Russia's role will be critical.

58. Ken Booth, "Security and Emancipation," *Review of International Studies* 17 (October 1991), p. 315.

59. John Chapman, "The Future of Strategic Studies: Beyond Even Grand Strategy," *Survival* 34 (Spring 1992), p. 114.

60. Interview in *Moscow News* 20 (17–24 May 1992), p. 8.

4

Russia as an Asian-Pacific Power

Gerald Segal

Visitors to Siberian Russia are often told of the great Siberian dilemma: If a fisherman falls through the ice, does he clamber out and freeze to death instantly or stay in the water and die in three minutes from hypothermia? Russian morbidness is legendary, but such an attitude can be said to reflect Russia's state of mind about its position in the Asian-Pacific region. Yes, there are many fish to be caught in the prospering Pacific, but no matter what policy Russia adopts, there are serious problems and risks. A Russia that seeks integration with the region will find itself a minor player with vulnerable outposts on the Pacific. A Russia that waits for investment from Moscow will wait for ages before anything gets done.

The debate between the first, more maritime school, and the second, more continental school, well pre-dates the existence of the Soviet Union and will outlast it for some time.[1] The death of the Soviet Union has merely accentuated the starkness of the choice. The new Russia lacks the resources to invest heavily in its Pacific territory and as its defence budget shrinks and its armed forces rust, Russia will lose its main claim to great-power status in the Pacific—its military clout. With its small population and expensive labour costs, the Russian Far East is primarily attractive to other states in Asia-Pacific as a raw material exporter and possibly as a source of inexpensive arms. And yet, even the prospect of getting access to these raw materials depends to an important extent on Russia's ability to invest in infrastructure in the region. In sum, the key to the future of Russian policy in Asia-Pacific is the fate of its domestic reforms.[2] Given the deep

---

1. Milan Hauner, *What is Asia to Us?* (London: Unwin/Hyman, 1989)
2. Gerald Segal, *The Soviet Union and the Pacific* (Boston: Unwin/Hyman, 1990).

uncertainties about the reforms and the current leadership, there can be little optimism about Russia in the Pacific.

The Domestic Base

The uncertainty in Russia about its policy in the region derives from multiple sources. As we have already suggested, there are deep-rooted debates about how much of a commitment Russia should make to its Pacific territories. The investment costs and the harshness of the living conditions have always made them think more than twice about a major commitment. The lure of the vast Siberian resources and more recently the wealth of the states of East Asia have ensured the survival of romantic Russian dreams of tapping their Pacific potential. These desires and dilemmas predated the creation of the Soviet Union and Russians were among some of the earliest dreamers of the Pacific Century. And yet Russia has consistently failed to realise its perceived potential and it has remained primarily a power walking on an unstable and solitary military leg. Unlike the other white-settler states which reached Pacific waters, including Canada and Australia, the Russian population on the Pacific has remained much more of an "outpost culture" unsure of its staying power.

The Russian debate about how much to invest in the Pacific is in fact part of a much larger debate about Russia's fundamental interests. Because of its vast Eurasian landmass, even pre-1917 Russia regularly debated whether it was primarily European or Asiatic. As the majority of its wealth depended on relations with Europe, it was always clear that Russia was primarily a European power, but an ambiguous one and never fully accepted by other Europeans. As the Russian empire absorbed Ukraine and the Baltic states, its European weight was more pronounced. Russians settled in large numbers in Central Asia, but never really established large communities in the Far East. The Russian bear faced Europe, and it usually showed its backside to the Pacific.[3]

The revolutionary events of the late twentieth century have reopened these discussions because for the first time in nearly a century Russia has begun to concentrate on what constitutes its national interest. The disintegration of the Soviet Union was also the disintegration of important parts of the Russian empire. The loss of the other republics in Europe pulled Russia further back from Europe. But the loss of the Central Asian republics has also tightened the belly of the bear as the Asian population has fallen away. What is left of the Russian empire is some of its earliest holdings, the

---

3. The image is that of a former Japanese ambassador to Britain; Kazuo Chiba, "Japan and the New World Order," *Pacific Review* 4:1 (1991), p. 1.

territory stretching to the Pacific. But this is also some of the least populated and most forbidding parts of the Russian empire. While parts of Siberia might also be vulnerable to fissiparous tendencies, it is not inevitable just because Central Asia, the Caucasus, Ukraine and the Baltic states have escaped from Muscovy's control.

What remains is a more ethnically coherent Russia but one that still thinks of itself as primarily European. Culturally this is certainly so, and at a time when basic features of national interest are being discussed, culture looms large. To be sure, there is a major debate in Russia about this national interest and the meaning of Russia as a Eurasian state.[4] Those more geopolitically inclined will look at a map and see a Russia that has most of its land in northern Asia. But a demographic map shows most of its population is in Europe. Those arguing for a more Asian-focused Russian national interest suggest that Russia will need support from Central Asia in its struggle with Ukraine, as a counter to the United States and as a balance against excessive dependence on Western Europe. They point to the natural wealth of Siberia and the potential for investment from East Asia. But they ignore the fact that millions of ethnic Russians are to be found in Central Asia and disputes in this region are likely to be at least as intense as in Europe. East Asians have little reason to do business with a Russia that is not a threat and offers only costly opportunities. Thus while the Russian debate over its interests and orientations simmers on, it is unlikely that the outcome will be a decision to ditch Europe and focus on Asia. At best, there may be a decision to fudge the choice and dream of serving as a land bridge across Eurasia. But the image of being a land bridge is the most discredited of Mackinder-like geopolitics and bears no resemblance to how the global market economy really functions. It is true that the Conference on Security and Cooperation in Europe (CSCE) has extended itself to include the Central Asian states, and the CSCE extended from Vancouver to Vladivostok, but that was always a geographic quirk that was never intended to suggest European responsibility for Asian security. In reality, there is little that joins the interests of Europe and Central Asia, apart from Russian interests.

Of course, Russians, even of the Eurasian school, have yet to think through properly which parts of Asia concern them most. When they wish to stress the potential gains for Russia, it makes far more sense to refer to

---

4. The material on these debates is growing rapidly. See for example "Does Russia Have a Foreign Policy," Russian TV, 3 June 1992; in BBC, *Summary of World Broadcasts (SWB)*, SU/1402 A2/1–4; Vladimir Erneianenko, "Russia between Europe and Asia," *Moscow News Weekly Edition*, no. 16, 1992. See also analysis in Alexander Rahr, "Atlanticists versus Eurasians in Russian Foreign Policy," *RFE/RL Research Report*, 29 May 1992; Natalie Gross, "Russian Strategy—East or West," *Jane's Intelligence Review*, June 1992; and "Russia Looks East," *Economist*, 4 July 1992.

the booming economies of East Asia and the potential for aid from these states. Reference to Central Asia is usually made in more negative terms, dwelling on the major risks that involve key Russian interests. The presence of nuclear weapons in Kazakhstan, the presence of large Russian populations in many of the Central Asian states, the strength of Islamic feelings, and the illogicality of frontiers are all causes for concern to Russian planners. In 1992 as various teams in Moscow were busy trying to define a Russian national interest, various participants found that a vast amount of time was being spent discussing Central Asia, but more in terms of threat than opportunity. It was hard to make a persuasive case that Russia stood to gain much from closer relations with the Central Asians, although it was acknowledged that neither could Russia ignore the problems of the region. Whether it was through the CSCE or some residual mechanism of the CIS (Commonwealth of Independent States), Russians hoped that they would not have to face these problems on their own. But despite the extension of the CSCE to this region, it was increasingly clear that the richer countries of Europe were unlikely to support Russia in sorting out its relations in Central Asia. Indeed, should Russia use force to settle territorial or ethnic disputes, it ran serious risks of losing much needed aid. Clearly there was a great deal more thought that needed to be given to the idea of Russia as a Eurasian power.

A more modernised geopolitician might argue that the logic of the disintegration of the Soviet Union will go a bit further and suggest that a much looser Russian federation or even a further shrunken Russia might well be emerging. The distance of 6,500 km from Moscow to Vladivostok is only marginally more than that from Moscow to Montreal.[5] If one defines the Russian Far East as that 60 percent of the Russian republic (including the administrative regions of East Siberia and the Far East), this region of 10.3m km^2 would be the largest country in the world. With a population of some 17m and an average density of 1.6 per km^2, this Russian Far East is in the league of Mongolia as one of the most lightly populated states in the Pacific. More than three-quarters of these people are of Russian origin, more than 80 percent are urban and most are spread out along rail lines and the southern frontier with Mongolia and China. The people live on the edge of a climate not really fit for human habitation. More than half the land is subject to permafrost, and ice fog hangs over the cities and towns. Building factories and bridges under these conditions, let alone living an outdoor life, is difficult. Metals become brittle, lubricants freeze and skin sears in the cold. The psychological stresses of such life are a serious problem. In

---

5. Details in Segal, *Soviet Union and the Pacific* and Michael Bradshaw, *Siberia at a Time of Change* (London: Economist Intelligence Unit, March 1992).

summer, heavy rains cause the rivers to flood, marshes to spread and mosquitos with legendary appetites for human blood to flourish.

Of course, the climate is not all bad. Visitors to Vladivostok are pleasantly surprised to find a "Black Sea resort" feel to the town—the climate is milder than Moscow and people bathe in the Amur basin well into September. The growing of rice and grapevines suggests there is plenty of scope for a pleasant life in the area. The citizens enjoy the rough-and-ready romantic image of their region. Vladivostok enjoyed a boom time in the 1920s when it was a small but very cosmopolitan town. In the immediate aftermath of the Russian revolution the Soviet Union established a Far Eastern Republic in the hope of playing on anti-Japanese sentiment and playing down the communist component of the new regime. The FER was disbanded after Japan retreated from Russian territory in 1922, but between 1922 and 1938 the territory was given special status and remained less affected by the communist revolution than European Russia.

During the Second World War, Russia focused on the threat in Europe and only joined the war against Japan in the final months. It was kept out of the administration of vanquished Japan, but was allowed to seize islands in the southern Kuriles. The Soviet Union put greatest stress on its relations with China, especially as it became clear that a communist government was coming to power. As the Cold War deepened, the Soviet Union paid more attention to its territory in the Far East because a number of major conflicts were waged in the region. We now know that Russian pilots flew in combat against American troops in the Korean War.[6]

In short, there is an obvious tradition of greater independence for the Russian Far East, even in living memory. The geopolitics of the Russian Far East also suggest that there is good reason for the Russian people on the Pacific to seek their own way if politics in Moscow continues to be confused or to result in decisions that are contrary to the interests of Russians in the Pacific. Whether this further fragmentation of Russia is formal or not, the result is likely to be the emergence of a region that looks remarkably like Australia—at least in the sense of being thinly populated with vast resources to sell to resource-poor states in the Pacific. Such a Russia-on-the-Pacific would be unable to sustain much of an armed forces and might eventually also look even less threatening than a far wealthier Australia. Being so close to the far more powerful states of Japan, China, and perhaps even a united Korea, it might be the Russians who would feel threatened. As a result, the Russians on the Pacific are unlikely to seek full independence from Moscow, although they may well take far more control

---

6. Jon Halliday, "Secret War of the Top Guns," *Observer,* 5 July 1992.

of their own resources, economic policy and even aspects of foreign relations. Such a more independent and maritime type of Russia-on-the-Pacific might well be the most sensible outcome, but its prospects depend primarily on the fate of the political changes back in Moscow. In the meantime, Russians on the Pacific have to see their region in large part through the eyes of their masters in Moscow.

Military Power

When thinking about the Russian military interest in Asia-Pacific, many of the old dilemmas return. Russians speak with pride about the fact that their settlers had reached the Pacific when the British were just reaching the North American Great Lakes. Russian naval power spread across the north Pacific to Astoria in northern California before imperial overstretch took its toll. Russian military power then concentrated on land war and vast swathes of territory were taken from a fading Chinese empire. Russia manoeuvred among the great powers of the Pacific as China was sliced up.

The Russian empire was wrenched back to reality by the rise of Japanese power and the defeat in 1904–05. Japan's seizure of Korea and large sections of China was contested by Russia, but in the end the Soviet Union was ineffective, especially at a time of domestic turmoil and uncertainty in Moscow. As the Soviet Union grew militarily strong, Japan lost territory to the new superpower and the United States saw the Soviet Union as the main rival in Asia-Pacific. Wars in Korea and Vietnam could not have been waged with such devastating effect if not for Soviet military power. The fate of East Asian politics in the 1945–91 period was deeply affected by the overlay of Cold War politics. The Soviet Union may not have been a natural East Asian power, but it certainly was a power in East Asia.

Of course, much of this power was illusory in the Pacific, as it was to some extent in Europe, although it was not known to be the case at the time. In the Pacific, the Soviet Union was far more a one-legged power, relying on the military instrument without a fully supportive economy. The situation was somewhat akin to the 19th century British empire that operated in the Pacific. Once the decision was taken to give independence to its colonies such as Australia, it was seen that Australia in and of itself had little intrinsic military power. The Russians in the Pacific are in somewhat of an analogous position in that they are now finding out just how little real military power they have in the region.

It is obvious that Russian military power in Asia-Pacific will shrink (see Table 4.1 and Figure 4.1).[7] The Pacific fleet now spends most of its time in port in the northwestern Pacific. Ships are rusting. Sailors are hard to find and many of those in service are not being paid. Many ships are being taken off the order of battle and others have no fuel. There is certainly little rationale for anything like the kind of massive navy the Soviet Union once deployed. At this stage it is hard to judge how far the reductions will go. Nuclear-powered submarines (SSNs) are less affected by fuel shortage, but the utility of nuclear-propelled ballistic missile submarines (SSBNs) or attack submarines must be in great doubt. Of course, as the Strategic Arms Reduction Treaty (START) accords reduce the number of land-based intercontinental ballistic missiles (ICBMs), the Russian SSBN fleet with its submarine-launched ballistic missiles (SLBMs) become of increasing importance. With serious doubts about the Black Sea and Baltic Fleets, the Russian Pacific Fleet assumes greater importance in strategic terms.

TABLE 4.1: Soviet/Russian Forces in East Asia

	1989–90	1990–91	1991–92	1992–93
Far Eastern TVD[a]				
Tank divisions (TD)	7	6	7	7
Motor rifle divisions(MRD)	42	39	35	35
Submarines	120	110	98	86
Ballistic missile submarines (SSBs)	24	24	24	21
Principal surface combatants	77	69	63	55
Carriers	2	2	2	1
Cruisers	11	15	14	14
Destroyers	8	7	7	7
Forces in Mongolia	60000	37000	3000	3000
Forces in Vietnam	2800	2800	2800	500

a. TVD: *Teatr Voennykh Deistvii.* Soviet/Russian strategic planning divides the world into a number of continental and maritime TVD.

SOURCE: International Institute for Strategic Studies, *Military Balance,* 1989–1993.

---

7. On some problems see ITAR-TASS, 5 July 1992, in BBC, *SWB,* SU/1427 C3/6; Radio Moscow on 27 July 1992, in BBC, *SWB,* SU/1445 C3/1. For other details see Gerald Segal, "Russia and East Asia Have a Security Deal to Make," *International Herald Tribune,* 11 June 1992.

FIGURE 4.1: Soviet/Russian Forces in East Asia

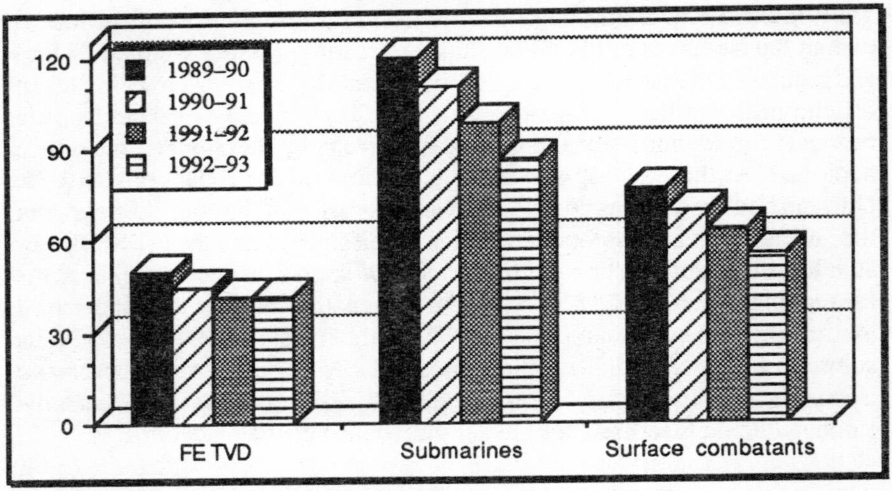

SOURCE: IISS, *Military Balance,* 1989–1993

Assuming that the SSBN fleet will remain a major part of Russian nuclear policy, there is an obvious need for major naval facilities in the northwest Pacific. But this is not the same as arguing that Russia will have major conventional naval forces in the region. Certainly surface ships are not needed as much to support an SSBN fleet. The lack of bases elsewhere in East Asia since the loss of those in Vietnam, means less range for conventional ships, even if they could get the fuel and sailors they need. Vietnam is no longer seen as an ally in need of defence and the South Pacific is no longer seen as a zone of future contention. China is no longer seen as a major military problem, at least not at sea, although it is possible that Russia might become involved in some future international effort to keep the peace in the South China Sea and deter further Chinese aggression. In short, the Russian Navy needs far fewer ships because it will spend more time closer to home ports. At a minimum, the Russian Navy looks like being cut in half and perhaps even as much as 70 percent. Assuming relatively fewer cuts in the submarine force, perhaps more than 70 percent cuts can be expected in the surface fleet. One aircraft carrier is already out of commission and the other one will not be able to operate all-year round. Thus the Russian capability to project naval power on the surface and in the air is severely circumscribed.

Only two countries, the United States and Japan, may upset this scenario of a navy in retreat. The United States, the previous main adversary, is reducing its own forces in the Pacific, albeit not at anything like the same rate. Should the United States retain major forces in the region, there may well be voices in the Russian Navy arguing for limits on Russian cuts. Some Russians have already argued that the United States is not reciprocating Russian reductions, although part of this line of argument is an anachronistic residual of the time when there were two superpowers and the Soviet Union had illusions that it could compete with the United States.[8]

A far more significant trend is the growing collaboration between the U.S. and Russian navies as both countries grow concerned about the future of the northern Pacific if China and Japan should increase military spending. The Russians can also see that the United States is likely to make swinging cuts in its order of battle. The withdrawal of all tactical nuclear weapons by the Americans has allowed Russia to do the same and feel more secure about reducing its forces. Russia watched with relative equanimity as the United States built up major naval forces to deal with the 1990–91 Gulf War and it might well take a relaxed view of American forces dealing with risks in the South China Sea or threats to Taiwan. American naval action closer to Russia's home bases, for example in a Korean crisis, might well provoke a much more vigorous Russian response. But Russia would prefer to operate in cooperation with the United States and other states, and the Russian Foreign Minister's remarks in July 1992 suggest that such a scenario might be possible in support of an operation in the South China Sea mandated possibly by the United Nations or the Association of South-East Asian Nations (ASEAN). Vietnam has not yet agreed to provide basing facilities for such a Russian policy and may be unwilling to antagonise China by doing so.[9] In order to avoid falling out with China, Russia would need a multilateral effort to cloak its continuing engagement in the region as a naval power, which, under certain circumstances, might even include a continuing presence in Vietnamese bases. Andrei Kozyrev was clear that Russia "does not intend to disappear from the map of Asia" and wants to remain "a major and strong Asian power."[10] Its only hope of doing so is in the context of multilateral collective security.

But Russian naval interests are likely to focus on northwestern Pacific waters and on the intentions of Japan. In the short term, the retreat of Russian naval power is perceived by some in Japan as an increased military threat. But it is a fact of geography that by retreating to its home ports,

---

8. For example, Radio Moscow on 2 July 1992, in BBC, *SWB*, SU/1423 A1/1.

9. *Far Eastern Economic Review (FEER)*, 6 August 1992, p. 11. The fact that Radio Moscow has rented part of its transmission facilities to Vietnamese anti-communist forces will not help Russia's cause. See *FEER*, 13 August 1992, p. 7. See also Voice of Vietnam, 30 July 1992 in BBC, *SWB*, FE/1456 A1/2; and Thayer's chapter below, pp. 206–09.

10. ITAR-TASS, 22 July 1992, in BBC, *SWB*, FE/1441 A1/3 and interview on Radio Moscow on 26 July1992, in BBC, *SWB*, SU/1444 A1/3–4.

Russia increases the number of ships closer to Japan. Until the navy rusts or is scrapped, Japan will have to learn to be more subtle in its assessment of capabilities and intentions. Should Japan persist in viewing Russian capabilities as far more impressive than they are, then a resulting Japanese naval buildup might well stimulate Russia to restrict the scrapping of its fleet.

Should Russia perceive Japanese naval power to be on the increase, even while that of the United States is declining, Russia might well see this as an increased cause of concern. Should this condition persist while the Russo-Japanese territorial dispute is unresolved, tension will be significant. Russian fears about its vulnerability and the memories of the 1905 defeat will loom large and Russians increasingly link what they see as Japanese revanchism about the northern territories to Japan's power before 1945. As a result, it is far from certain that there will be a territorial settlement between Russia and Japan. As Russians grow increasingly fed up with their weakened state and the constant surrender of territory, there is far less willingness to give up land to Japan. Russian military officials also argue that to give up the disputed territories would be a military risk because forces would be divided, radar fields would be lost, sea bastions for the SLBMs would be compromised and relocation costs would be considerable.[11] Arms control and confidence-building measures with Japan might help reduce some of these worries, but it seems evident that basic trust of Japan is lacking. Of course, aid from Japan is desired, but increasingly seen as something that will come as part of discussions on a G-7 level. Russians also fear the rise of Japan in Asia and it can be argued that with major reductions in Russia's land-based strategic arsenal, it becomes all the more important to protect the sea bastions in the Far East. Russo-Japanese relations are discussed at greater length later in this volume, but suffice it to say that the fate of the Russian military power in the Pacific depends to a large extent on choices made in Japan. To an important extent, the dispute over the Kuriles is merely a reflection of the wider struggle for power as Japan rises and Russia declines. For that reason alone, it is not surprising that some Russian officials are keen to internationalise the dispute

---

11. This is a complex subject, but for a flavour of recent Russian nationalism see a statement by Marshal Evgenii Shaposhnikov on 21 June 1992 reported by NHK in BBC, *SWB*, FE/1495 A1/4–5 and G. Kudnadze on 24 July on Moscow TV in BBC, *SWB*, SU/1444 A1/1–2. Andrei Kozyrev also noted that Lenin was prepared to sell Kamchatka, but to a Russian nationalist this revelation only confirms hatred of communists and makes a deal on the Kuriles less likely. See ITAR-TASS, 18 July 1992 in BBC, *SWB*, SU/1437 A1/4. For views in the Russian Supreme Soviet debate on the subject and comments by government officials at the time, see various reports in BBC, *SWB*, SU/1446 C2.

with Japan and bring in the United States.[12] Whether Washington is involved as a guarantor of any agreement, or just in the sense of a more multilateral confidence-building regime in the region, it can only strengthen the Russian case to try to broaden the discussion to wider security issues. What is at stake are more important questions of how the post-Cold War order should be shaped, and obsessive discussion about the islands obscures the larger picture.

To an important extent this concern with Japan is unusual, at least in the sweep of history. Traditionally, Russia has been concerned primarily with China and threats on land, and Russian officials still see China as the major power in the region.[13] Since 1945, Russian soldiers have died in combat in the Korean War when flying out of Chinese bases and along the disputed Sino-Soviet frontier. In the 1960s and 1970s the Soviet Union invested heavily in building up their forces facing China. In the 1980s, the most significant reductions in the Soviet forces were in those deployed along the Sino-Soviet frontier. The main peace dividend was earned before the ending of the East-West Cold War and as a result of the ending of the East-East Cold War. Agreements on border disputes were reached in the dying days of the Soviet Union and reconfirmed in 1992. Chinese workers began contract labour in the Russian Far East in the late 1980s and their numbers are increasing in the early 1990s.[14] China and the Soviet Union/Russia have engaged in de facto arms control along the frontier and China continues to make major reductions in its northern forces.

Because so many of these changes predated the ending of the East-West Cold War, it is harder to be certain about the size of the reduction of Russian land forces. Like China, Russia is now more concerned with threats in Central Asia than along the Sino-Russian frontier. With large Russian minorities across frontiers in Central Asia that have little basis in historical or ethnic facts, it is easy to see why Russian defence planners can expect to have major worries about insecurity in Central Asia. European history is littered with unhappy experiences of conflict resulting from similar conditions, and the inherently unstable process of state-building in Central Asia will surely make it more difficult for Russia to manage the problem. Russia has the most powerful armed forces in the region, but unlike China, Russia faces the problem of whether to intervene to protect Russians whereas China fears that those of Turkish descent in Central Asia will seek to unite with brethren in China. Thus there is little coincidence of interests,

---

12. M. Poltoranin reported in *Izvestiia*, 5 August 1992 in BBC, *SWB*, SU/1454 A1/4–5.

13. Andrei Kozyrev interviewed in *International Herald Tribune*, 27 July 1992.

14. On peasants from Heilongjiang as market gardeners in Siberia see *Komsomolskaia Pravda*, 21 July 1992, in BBC, *SWB*, SU/1442 A1/2.

and plenty of tinder for conflict. Russia faces no easy choices, but in any case it is clear that concern with Central Asia will assume far more prominence than concern with China.

The reductions of 120,000 along the Russian side of the border with China may well turn out to be much larger. Troop levels may well fall to those of the 1950s, and certainly much lower if economic problems persist in Russia and the Russian Far East is given more control over its domestic and foreign relations. To some extent, troop reductions are limited more by the absence of anywhere to house redeployed forces. The lack of a coherent military doctrine, and shortage of fuel and spare parts have made a mess of Russian planning procedures and encouraged a sense of ad hocery in Russian defence policy. Tanks are being sold off in Siberia to the timber industry and helicopters are being sold to anyone who wants to buy them. One general said in June 1992 that one third of personnel had been cut, but largely because soldiers from former republics such as Ukraine were bringing their people home.[15] Russia was watching its forces melt away, and thus a Russian Far East that does not have good relations with China will be highly vulnerable.

In sum, Russia looks set for a long period of military retrenchment. Apart from the SSBN and remaining ICBM deployments, one can expect reductions far more than the 50 percent figure which is usually mentioned. Should Russia dissolve into a much looser federation, even 75 percent cuts would appear to be a conservative guess. Russia is headed back to a force posture akin to that in the late 19th century. The increased lethality and range of weapons, along with its nuclear arsenal, will give it more power relative to its neighbours than it had in the late 19th century, but it will be nothing like the menace it was in the Cold War days.

The only and major exception to this scenario is the question of Northeast Asian security. Russia's primary interests in the Pacific are in this sub-region where it meets Korea, Japan, China and a highly engaged United States. Until the question of Korean reunification is managed, and the extent of the retreat of U.S. power is known, Russia will remain wary and engaged in regional diplomacy. Should Japan and China fill the vacuum left by the superpowers and should the two local powers come into more direct conflict, Russia will remain a key force in the balance of power.

As a result, Russian military power will probably concentrate on retaining significant forces in the Northeast Asian theatre. But it will rely primarily on diplomacy and alliance politics, much as Russia did in the age of rival empires a century before. Now, as then, a premium will be placed

---

15. *Jane's Defence Weekly*, 20 June 1992 p. 1052.

on good relations with China and keeping China in play as an anti-Japanese force. In this light, Russia's improving military relationship with China makes good sense. Sales of SU-27 aircraft or even the possible sale of an aircraft carrier are important ways to keep China friendly and make Russia more able to deal with Japanese or even American power.[16] One can expect Russia and China to develop closer relations at the level of defence industries, including possible co-production of new weapons. China may buy the services of Russian scientists and seek Russian military technology. Russia will have to watch how far these contacts go for fear of losing control of China and possibly even seeing the weapons used against Russia in the future.

In the short term, Russia has the potential to export not only bargain-basement weapons, but also begin co-production arrangements with a wide range of states which no longer see Russia as a threat and which want to take advantage of Russia's military expertise. Malaysia, Taiwan and even South Korea are countries with money to spend, expertise of their own and perceived security needs.[17] One of the most striking trends is the rapidly warming relations between Taiwan and Russia, leading to the same kind of de facto relations that Taiwan has with Western states. Russia seems a bit surprised just how easy it has been to establish such ties with Taiwan and is anxious to explore what this means in terms of economic aid and possibly even military relations. Taiwanese interest in this kind of cooperation is tempered by concern with China's reaction, but at a time of Sino-Russian military deals, Taiwan and Russia may well have an opportunity to do business.[18]

Needless to say, such a wide-ranging sales programme will upset regional balances and be a major cause of concern for those such as the United States anxious to manage the post-Cold War world and retain market share in the weapons business. But a Russia that otherwise finds it hard to sell manufactured goods in the region and desperate for hard currency, will take much persuading not to explore such possibilities. For this reason alone, Russia will remain actively involved in regional security in Asia-Pacific and especially in Northeast Asia.

---

16. The Varyag aircraft carrier being completed in Ukraine is not necessarily Russia's to sell. See one report on its joining the Ukrainian fleet on Radio Moscow 6 August 1992 in BBC, *SWB*, SU/1454 C1/4. For a sensible survey of these issues see Tai Ming Cheung, "Ties of Convenience," a paper for the Conference on PLA Affairs sponsored by the Chinese Council of Advanced Policy Studies, Taipei, June 1992.

17. On the Malaysian case, see *FEER*, 23 July 1992, p. 11.

18. On recent contacts, see *Free China Journal*, 26 June and 10 July 1992 and *China News*, 30 June 1992.

An obvious route for Russia to stay involved at low cost is support for arms control in the region. In part because Soviet foreign policy was seen to have been mischievous in suggesting such ideas in earlier years as a way of undermining American alliances, Russian initiatives are still treated with much caution. Yet Russia, and increasingly even the United States, are finding that in a time of retreating power, arms control or multilateral collective security offers a way of keeping involved at lower cost. Proposals increasingly focus on Northeast Asia and that is also the area of Russia's most acute concern. Possible action in the South China Sea also cannot be ruled out. One can expect Russia not to lead efforts for regional arms control, but certainly to be an active and keen participant.[19]

Economic Interests

When Russians think of the international economy these days they cannot help but begin with a domestic bias. Their need for reform at home is so dire that they are anxious to do business with nearly anyone who can help. In Asian terms, this makes Russia see Central Asia as at worst a burden and at best a backwater. It is to East Asia that Russians look for aid and trade prospects. What is more, East Asia has also been seen as a source of ideas about reform and alternative models of development.[20] During the Gorbachev era, Russians saw that East Asian economic success was often built on the basis of a limited political pluralism and often an economy with many features of a command economy. The so-called Capitalist Development State holds many attractions for Russian reformers who wish to transform their large state industries into effective multinationals. For some with neo-authoritarian tendencies, the limited pluralism in East Asia is also attractive, especially at a time of revolutionary transition. At least one Japanese report to the CIS contradicts the IMF (International Monetary Fund) line on the best strategy for reform by arguing that the former Soviet Union can learn a great deal from the way Japan used its Capitalist Development State to recover from defeat in 1945.[21]

Of course, there are vast differences between the Russian political and economic culture and that in East Asia, but at least in these terms there is something more to the concept of Eurasianness. Russian culture is more

---

19. On recent changes in U.S. policy, see James Winnefeld et al., *A New Strategy and Fewer Forces* (Santa Monica: RAND, 1992). On arms control in the region see Patrick Cronin "Pacific Rim Security," *Pacific Review* 5:3 (1992) and Gerald Segal, "Northeast Asia: Common Security or A La Carte," *International Affairs* 67 (October 1991).

20. This is the theme of Gerald Segal et al., *Openness and Foreign Policy Reform in Communist States* (London: Routledge for the RIIA, 1992).

21. *FEER*, 13 August 1992, pp. 59–60.

authoritarian than that in Western Europe, although whether it has many of the beneficial features of a Confucian culture is far less obvious. The Russian economy is also very different from most in East Asia in that its strength in international trade is as an exporter of raw materials. It has few of the advantages such as cheap labour and a work ethic that made it possible for Japan and the NICs (newly industrialising countries) to prosper in their initial stages. In short, there is much that the Russians still have to learn about how business is done in East Asia.

There are also major structural problems in Russian economic relations with East Asia. Before the Soviet Union collapsed, it accounted for less than four percent of all trade within the Pacific, a level akin to that of Thailand or Canada. On a per capita basis, using the population of the Russian Far East rather than that of all the Soviet Union, this was not a bad performance. But China's and even Hong Kong's share of Pacific trade was three times higher and France was a more important trading partner for Pacific states. Total Soviet trade with the Pacific was similar to that between the Soviet Union and Czechoslovakia.

This not insignificant but nevertheless disappointing trade performance was not very different from the general problems that the Soviet Union faced in trade with the Western market economies. The key to any change in this performance depends on the structure of the Russian economy and the reforms that are undertaken. In the period before 1991, there were remarkable consistencies in the pattern of Soviet trade in the Pacific. For some two decades both imports and exports hovered between five and ten percent of total Soviet imports and exports. Figures were up to about 25 percent in the 1950s, but that was a unique period. In the more representative twenty years before the 1991 revolution, only a quarter of the already much reduced exports were generated within the Russian Far East. The Soviet Union traded with a remarkably consistent group of states and exported mainly raw materials.[22]

This consistent pattern of trade has changed little since the disintegration of the Soviet Union, largely because the Russian economy has yet to carry out real reforms, at least for any length of time. Without major reforms, there can be no hope of changing the structure of trade and economic relations. Yet it would be illusory to expect that even massive reforms will bring about swift and major changes in the Russian economic position in Asia-Pacific. Raw materials are likely to persist as the basis of exports and Russia has little hope of becoming a major exporter of manufactured goods

---

22. See more complete data in Segal, *Soviet Union and the Pacific*, ch. 6.

to the booming economies of East Asia. In that sense, domestic reform will change the pattern of imports more than the pattern of exports.

Exporting of raw materials is not necessarily a bad market niche to have. Canada and Australia have done very well and their market position must be the best that Russia can aspire to reach. Of course, the export of raw materials depends in part on world market prices, which in turn depends on growth in the global economy. The ability of Russia to put these raw materials on the market depends on the amount of investment in infrastructure, as well as the inherent difficulty in getting at the resources. With the well-known difficult climatic conditions in Russia, the amount of investment would necessarily have to be higher than in many competing countries.

The sources of investment in Russian raw materials are restricted. Major American and European multinationals are obvious candidates, many of whom have already been in business in the Russian Far East. From within the Pacific, expertise exists in Canada and Australia, but major capital can probably only come from Japan and some of the NICs such as South Korea and Taiwan. These East Asian states need raw materials, but have signed long-term deals with others, such as Australia and Canada. But Japan and the NICs will need resources well into the long term and new deals have to be set up. Investing in Russia becomes more likely if there is a sense that a reforming Russian economy is stable and profits can be earned. Continuing unrest in Russia will put off foreign investors.

International politics also weaves its way into many of these economic calculations. Japanese investment is restricted by a government anxious to obtain the return of the disputed northern territories. South Korean investment is made more likely by the desire to improve relations with Russia in order to pressure North Korea. Taiwan might invest in order to diversify supplies and keep Russia from growing too close to China. General worry about oil and gas supplies from the Persian Gulf may make a calculation of risk in Russia seem less dangerous.

Given the difficulties of getting at Russian raw materials, the strength of the local environmental lobby and the long-term nature of planning for such investment, there will be no swift change in Russia's economic relations with its major trade partners in Japan and South Korea. The small, and likely to remain small, population of the Russian Far East, will limit the ability to afford imports, especially at a time of major economic hardship in Russia.

Economic cooperation with Japan remains restricted by the territorial dispute and a more general fear that Russia might still be a problem for a rising Japan. South Korea, on the other hand, and in part for the same reasons that made Japan wary, sees greater reason for pressing ahead with closer relations. Seoul sees Russia, especially in its weakened form, as a useful counterweight to both China and Japan. It is therefore more keen to explore the joint development of production zones either in the Tumen region or in Russia. It is keen to discuss cooperation in generating nuclear power.[23] Thus Russia may well find South Korea as a more promising source of finance and a partner in developing raw materials for export and even primary processing. Yet, for all the reasons already identified, such developments are likely to be slow and fraught with difficulties.

Only trade with China holds out any prospects for more steady and more swift improvements. Russia can export some manufactured goods as well as timber to China, and China can export light industrial goods and food. Greater independence for China's regional economies and more freedom for the Russian Far East to strike its own deals was the basis of trade growth before 1991. This decentralisation and the dislocations of economic reform also led to problems with payments and deliveries. But the essential conditions for trade looked encouraging. The reduction in military tension along the frontier also helped natural cross-border trade flourish. Chinese workers are now being used to build the new Russian border checkpoints.[24]

But apart from the major trade partners in Northeast Asia, it is hard to see Russia becoming a major economic player in the Asian-Pacific region. Southeast Asia has never figured as a major trade partner and this is unlikely to change. Russia would very much like to find a firmer footing for trade, but so far it has only been able to suggest that arms sales might be a lever for a wider trading relationship. In the short term, Russia's political role and its stake in such processes as the ASEAN post-ministerial conference depends mostly on Russia's residual military role in the region.[25] The NICs of Southeast Asia might need Russian raw materials but they are farther from the source and may find it easier to deal with Latin America, the Arab world or even eventually with Central Asia. Russia certainly sees little reason to focus on developing new trade relations in Central Asia, although it is true that the region may well be useful as one willing to import Russian manufactured goods that otherwise would be hard to market in the West. The Central Asians will find it hard to pay in real money and their economies are in such poor shape that Russia will not want to invest much in developing markets in this region. But it will be quite some time before

23. ITAR-TASS, 21 April 1992, in BBC, *SWB*, SU/1362 A3/2, Yonhap on 9 April in BBC, *SWB*, FE/1356 A2/2 and *International Herald Tribune*, 23 April 1992.

24. Interfax on 1 July 1992, in BBC, *SWB*, SU/1424 A1/1.

25. Andrei Kozyrev making the more optimistic case in his interview on Radio Moscow on 26 July 1992, in BBC, *SWB*, SU/1444 A1/3–4.

the old economic ties from the Soviet period are broken and more natural ones established. As with so much else in this field, the key is the nature and pace of reform in Russia and the other parts of the former Soviet Union.

Once again, the image of Russia in the post-Cold War Pacific is of a form of Australia, but in the vital and sensitive Northeast Asian region. The extent to which Russia makes the best of its opportunities depends on its ability to carry out real domestic reforms. Manipulating political issues, for example in Korea or in relations with Japan, will also help ensure a better future. But in the end, Russia will remain a marginal economic player in the Pacific. All the more reason for Russia to see its major priority in Europe and the Atlantic world.

Russia and the Pacific Century

Now that the Soviet Union has been dismantled, it is only natural that Russia should be asking fundamental questions about its national interest. So long as this necessary process of self-examination takes its course, there can be few certainties about Russia's role in the Asian-Pacific region. It does seem clear that Russians will conclude that they are unique, for they alone span Eurasia. But it is not at all clear what being Eurasian means in practice. Geopoliticians once regarded such control of the "heartland" as vital to great-power status, but in the late twentieth century, the heartland might be better regarded as a no-man's land of little interest.

Russia seems to be culturally of Europe but not necessarily part of it. As the Slav heartland, it comes from a distinct European tradition, but one equally distinct from the more prosperous Western Christian tradition. As far as Asians are concerned, there is no question that Russia is a white-settler state, somewhat more in their midst than Australia, but still on the fringes. In the world of new and complex interdependence, being a white-settler state in Asia is not a major handicap, for East Asia prospers because it is increasingly integrated into a global market economy. But Russia has been far less integrated in this way than the East Asians and therefore offers little except its services as a mine, quarry or aquarium. Russians need to be careful not to confuse their own fascination with East Asia, with how East Asians will tend to regard Russia as a yet another European has-been power.

Russia faces tough choices about its role in the world and in Asia. Its obvious worry about Central Asia is shared with no one except China, and Central Asia will remain a burden far more than an asset. Russia needs to choose whether it wants to be primarily Asian or European, to engage in reform or not and to centralise or decentralise. The first choice is really a false one—Russia is and will remain European-of-a-sort. But should the Russians choose to explore the meaning of Eurasia, they will wander down geopolitical byways for ages and to no advantage. Should Russia fudge or fail in the challenge of reform, it will fulfill its "promise" as a wasteland rather than a heartland. Should Russia fail to decentralise, it may find reform far harder and it will certainly find it more difficult to sustain a presence in East Asia, Central Asia as well as Europe. Ultimately, the choice is for Russia to make, although outsiders can and will have an effect on the margins.

5

Russia and the Emerging Asian-Pacific Economic Order

Charles E. Ziegler

One striking development in international relations in recent years is the expansion of regional economic cooperation, reflected in the European, North American and Asian-Pacific groupings. The wide cultural and economic diversity of Asian-Pacific nations, together with their relative geographical isolation, has inhibited the development of formal institutional arrangements. Nonetheless, a number of economic organisations—the Pacific Economic Cooperation Conference (PECC), the Asia-Pacific Economic Cooperation (APEC) initiative, and the Association of Southeast Asian Nations (ASEAN)—have been created. Asia-Pacific is home to some of the world's most dynamic producers and demonstrates tremendous potential for future growth. The countries of this region, broadly defined, account for over half of the world's Gross National Product and nearly forty percent of its trade. Increasingly, the Asian-Pacific nations are trading as a bloc. Intra-regional trade among Asian-Pacific nations is close to 65 percent, only marginally lower than that for the European Community member nations.[1] Although institutional development has proceeded slowly, with member-nations favouring informal linkages, Asian-Pacific nations have taken the first steps towards developing more effective regional economic regimes.[2]

---

1. See Peter Drysdale, "Soviet Prospects and the Pacific Economy," in Peter Drysdale in association with Martin O'Hare, ed., *The Soviets and the Pacific Challenge* (Armonk, NY: M. E. Sharpe, 1991), p. 5; also, Andrew Elek, "Trade Policy Options for the Asia-Pacific Region in the 1990's: The Potential of Open Regionalism," *American Economic Review* 82 (May 1992), p. 7.

2. On Asian-Pacific regional integration, see Norman D. Palmer, *The New Regionalism in Asia and the Pacific* (Lexington, Mass: Lexington Books, 1991); Andrew Elek, "The Challenge

To date, Russia and the former Soviet Union (FSU) have played only a marginal role in the Asian-Pacific economic order. In the 1960s and 1970s, Soviet trade and economic cooperation with the region was heavily influenced by political and strategic considerations. In the 1980s, as Mikhail Gorbachev and his reformers outlined their plans to restructure the moribund Soviet economy, several rather optimistic scenarios for developing Siberia and the Soviet Far East and integrating the Soviet economy into the Asian-Pacific region were developed. By the time that the Soviet Union collapsed in December 1991, few of Gorbachev's ambitious goals had been realised.

This chapter surveys efforts made by the new Russian Federation towards establishing closer ties with the Asian-Pacific economic order. Despite claims by Foreign Minister Andrei Kozyrev that Russia seeks a balanced position between Europe and Asia,[3] the evidence suggests that the Russian Federation's foreign economic policies were, at least during the first year, oriented largely towards Europe and the United States. Very little has been accomplished in terms of Russian participation in Asian-Pacific multilateral organisations. A few bright spots exist in Russia's bilateral economic ties, most notably with China, Taiwan and South Korea, but Russia's chaotic domestic situation will seriously constrain efforts to integrate the country's economy into the Asian-Pacific economic order.

Background

Perhaps "unrealised potential" is the most accurate description of Soviet Far East development plans and trade and economic cooperation with the Asian-Pacific region. The territory east of the Urals contains more natural wealth than is found anywhere else on the planet. Substantial deposits of oil, natural gas, coal, timber, gold, diamonds and various minerals are located throughout Siberia and the Far East. The eastern coastal areas are rich fishing grounds. However, the vast distances and harsh environmental conditions in the region, combined with a poorly developed infrastructure, make extraction and transportation of these resources difficult and costly. Moreover, development plans for the region have continually been

---

of Asian-Pacific Economic Cooperation," *Pacific Review* 4:4 (1991), pp. 322–32; and Donald Crone, "The Politics of Emerging Pacific Cooperation," *Pacific Affairs* 65 (Spring 1992), pp. 50–83.

    3. Andrei Kozyrev, "Russia: A Chance for Survival," *Foreign Affairs* 71 (Spring 1992), p. 15.

hampered by labour shortages and underpopulation.[4] These problems became more acute in the latter part of the 1980s, as migration into the Far East diminished and, together with the exodus of significant numbers of young people, contributed to the aging of the region's population.[5]

In reference to Soviet developmental policies, it is useful to distinguish between Western Siberia, Eastern Siberia and the Far East. By far the richest oil and natural gas fields are concentrated in Western Siberia, primarily Tyumen oblast, which in 1989 accounted for 64.4 percent of all Soviet oil production.[6] The Brezhnev regime's foreign trade strategy concentrated on exploiting Tyumen's energy resources for hard-currency earnings through sales to Western Europe. While this may have fuelled overall economic growth during the 1970s, declining energy prices in the 1980s combined with Gorbachev's ill-considered economic policies made Western Siberia, in the words of a noted scholar, a "massive geographic sinkhole" that contributed to the Soviet economy's downward spiral.[7]

By contrast, Eastern Siberia and the Soviet Far East are less richly endowed and have remained largely peripheral to the FSU and Russian economies. Security issues dominated Moscow's approach towards the region throughout Soviet history. In the 1930s and during the Second World War, the Kremlin's preeminent consideration was containing an expansionist, imperial Japan. Far more disturbing to Moscow was the later emergence of a hostile People's Republic of China, armed with nuclear weapons, populated by a billion people and sharing a 7,500 km disputed border with the Soviet Union. Finally, the Western Pacific was ringed with American facilities—in Japan, South Korea, the Philippines, South Vietnam and Australia—which together with American naval forces were dedicated to containing communist (that is, Soviet) expansion in Asia.

In sum, any propensity towards trade and economic cooperation with Asian-Pacific nations was overshadowed by Moscow's preoccupation with ensuring its security militarily. Apprehensive about possible ideological contamination, Moscow's leadership had effectively isolated the Soviet economy from the capitalist international economy, and as a result the centrally planned economy produced few goods that were competitive on world markets. Only about eight percent of total Soviet trade was conducted

---

4. See Allan Rodgers, ed., *The Soviet Far East: Geographical Perspectives on Development* (London and New York: Routledge, 1990).

5. E. Motrich, "Demografiia i ekonomika DVER," *Problemy dal'nego vostoka* 6 (June 1991), pp. 28–29.

6. Michael J. Bradshaw in "Panel on Siberia: Economic and Territorial Issues," *Soviet Geography* 32 (June 1991), p. 397.

7. Leslie Dienes, "Siberia: *Perestroyka* and Economic Development," *Soviet Geography* 32 (September 1991), pp. 445–46.

with Asian-Pacific nations at the start of the Gorbachev period. A limited number of projects had been carried out with socialist and capitalist countries during the postwar period, but few could be considered successful for any of the parties involved. In short, the Soviet Far Eastern economy was both peripheral to Asia's economic calculations and heavily dependent on rather than a major contributor to the larger Soviet economy.

Trade with socialist countries of Asia-Pacific—the People's Republic of China, Vietnam, Cambodia, Laos, North Korea and Mongolia—accounted for the bulk of Soviet economic activity in the region. Trade and economic cooperation with these countries was clearly influenced by political factors. Sino-Soviet trade, for example, fluctuated dramatically depending on the state of relations between the two communist giants. In 1959, before relations deteriorated significantly, turnover exceeded $2 bn, constituting nearly half of China's total for that year. Sino-Soviet trade dropped to a low of $47m in 1970, following the outbreak of armed clashes along the Ussuri river, and rebounded to nearly $4 bn when relations were normalised in 1989. However, by the late 1980s China had established itself as a significant trading nation in the world economy: $4 bn constituted only 3.6 percent of China's total trade.[8] The USSR had also cooperated with China on some 178 construction projects during the 1950s, but Nikita Khrushchev withdrew Soviet technicians as relations worsened. Many of these projects were revived following the conclusion of a major trade agreement between the two countries in July 1985.

Vietnam constitutes another example of Soviet political goals dominating economic considerations. Soviet policy towards Vietnam during the war attempted to take advantage of U.S. involvement and to challenge the Chinese for influence. Estimates are that from 1965 to 1974 the USSR supplied Vietnam with around $3.25 bn in military assistance. After the Tet offensive, Soviet military assistance declined relative to economic largesse.[9] Soviet trade with Vietnam grew rapidly after the Vietnamese and Chinese clashed in 1979, increasing to $4.9 bn in 1980–85.[10] Moscow and its East European allies granted the Vietnamese free credits, preferential pricing arrangements, subsidies and generous barter arrangements through the Council for Mutual Economic Assistance (CMEA), to which Vietnam was

8. Pu Shan, "Sino-Soviet Economic and Political Relations," in Drysdale, ed., *The Soviets and the Pacific Challenge*, p. 104.

9. See Ramesh Thakur and Carlyle A. Thayer, *Soviet Relations with India and Vietnam* (London: Macmillan, 1992), pp. 115–21, 173–76.

10. Abraham S. Becker, "The Soviet Union and the Third World: The Economic Dimension," in Andrzej Korbonski and Francis Fukuyama, eds., *The Soviet Union and the Third World* (Ithaca and London: Cornell University Press, 1987), p. 73.

admitted in 1978. As of late 1992, Vietnam's total debt to the FSU states was approximately 10 billion roubles.

For the Brezhnev regime, the economic expense of supporting Vietnam was well worth the strategic access to Southeast Asia. Following the signing of a Soviet-Vietnamese friendship treaty in 1978, Soviet forces were granted access to port facilities at Cam Ranh Bay. By 1984 the Soviet Union was providing Vietnam with about $1 bn annually in economic aid and the East European states contributed another $0.5 bn each year. The USSR supplied all Vietnam's oil imports, most of its food and textile imports, and was involved in hundreds of aid projects. Several thousand Vietnamese workers were employed in the Soviet and East European economies.[11] However, as Sino-Soviet and Soviet-American relations improved during the Gorbachev era, Vietnam became less critical to Moscow's Asia policy.

Soviet economic ties with North Korea were influenced by two factors: the state of Sino-Soviet relations and Kim Il-sung's nationalistic policy of self-reliance (*juche*). Soviet-North Korean trade and economic cooperation dropped off in the late 1950s as Pyongyang emulated China's Great Leap Forward, and then expanded in the second half of the 1960s as China turned inwards during the Cultural Revolution. Trade stagnated during most of the 1970s, although cooperation agreements signed during this decade resulted in Soviet assistance for the North Korean energy, oil refining, cast iron and steel, metallurgy, ore extraction and chemical fertiliser industries.[12]

Economic cooperation between the USSR and the Democratic People's Republic of Korea expanded in the late 1970s and early 1980s, as Sino-Soviet relations deteriorated over Vietnam, Afghanistan and Sino-Japanese normalisation. Soviet trade in the early 1980s constituted nearly one-third of North Korea's total foreign trade. Approximately 3,000 Soviet economic advisers were assigned to North Korea, Moscow granted Pyongyang credit on highly favourable terms and frequently wrote off large debts. Following Kim Il-sung's 1984 trip to Moscow, his first in 17 years, the Soviet Union agreed to supply North Korea with modern weaponry, including MIG-23 fighter aircraft. And in 1984 Soviet-North Korean trade reached a new high of 712m roubles.[13] However, relations remained testy. Moscow was

11. See Daniel S. Papp, *Soviet Policy Toward the Developing World in the 1980s* (Maxwell, Alabama: Air University Press, 1986), pp. 349–55.

12. V. I. Andreev and V. I Osipov, "SSSR-KNDR: kursom vzaimovygodnogo sotrudnichestva," *Problemy dal'nego vostoka* 3 (March 1983), pp. 8–22; Harry Gelman and Norman D. Levin, *The Future of Soviet-North Korean Relations* (Santa Monica, CA: RAND, October 1984), pp. 19–21.

13. A. Muratov, "The Friendship Will Grow Stronger," *International Affairs* (Moscow) 9 (September 1985), p. 26.

disturbed by North Korea's terrorist adventures and annoyed at its refusal to openly acknowledge Soviet assistance.

Throughout the postwar period economic ties with most non-communist nations in Asia-Pacific were minimal to nonexistent. Japan was by far the most significant economic partner for the Soviet Union—total trade turnover between the two countries expanded from a mere $21m in 1957, the year after diplomatic relations were established, to $5.2 bn in 1981.[14] A series of development projects in the fields of timber, oil and natural gas, and coal were initiated in the mid-1960s, with Japan supplying machinery, credits, steel pipe and extraction equipment in exchange for payment in raw materials. Coastal trade developed between the northern Japanese island of Hokkaido and Primorskii krai, and Japan helped expand port facilities at Nakhodka and Vostochnyi.

Despite natural complementarities existing between the two economies, Soviet-Japanese economic cooperation could not avoid the influence of politics. Although the Kuril islands dispute was the major obstacle to large-scale cooperation, U.S. pressures, particularly in the early Reagan years, also constrained Japan's economic links to the USSR. More importantly, following the oil shocks of the 1970s Japan diversified its energy sources, adopted stringent conservation measures and shifted away from energy-intensive industries, significantly reducing the country's demand for imported energy. By the time that Gorbachev began to implement *perestroika* and open up the Soviet economy, Japanese businesses were less than eager to participate in energy-related joint projects.

Japan accounted for 1.91 percent of all Soviet exports and 3.99 percent of imports in 1980. By comparison, the ASEAN countries together comprised only 0.13 percent of exports and 1.33 percent of imports. Australia and New Zealand combined accounted for only 0.02 percent of total Soviet exports and 2.11 percent of imports.[15] In contrast, over 40 percent of Soviet trade was conducted with the centrally planned economies of Eastern Europe and about 25 percent with Western Europe. Moscow had virtually no contact with some of the more dynamic Asian economies until well into the Gorbachev period. For example, political considerations precluded formal trade relationships with either South Korea or Taiwan, although some indirect trade with Seoul was reportedly conducted through Japan in the early 1980s.

Until Gorbachev, Soviet leaders had paid scant attention to Asia's increasingly dominant position in the world economy. In international

---

14. John J. Stephan, "Japanese-Soviet Relations: Patterns and Prospects," in Herbert J. Ellison, ed., *Japan and the Soviet Quadrille* (Boulder: Westview Press, 1987), p. 142.

15. Drysdale, "Soviet Prospects and the Pacific Economy," p. 4.

relations, Moscow was concerned with power, and power was conceptualised almost exclusively in terms of military capabilities. Soviet foreign policy accorded prime importance to the United States and Europe, not East Asia. China and the United States dominated Soviet policy towards Asia-Pacific because from Moscow's perspective these nations threatened Soviet security. Japan was viewed as largely a vassal of the United States, not a regional power in its own right. In short, Moscow's approach to Asia-Pacific was dominated by political and security considerations rather than trade and economic issues.

Gorbachev's Reforms

Perestroika reversed the longstanding Soviet policy of maintaining a closed economy protected from the impact of international capitalism. The absence of external competition, Moscow's reformers realised, had allowed Soviet industry to stagnate as the rest of the industrialised world experienced rapid scientific and technological development.[16] Initial goals in reforming Soviet foreign trade included abolishing the Ministry of Foreign Trade's monopoly status; devolving responsibility for foreign trade to ministries and enterprises; encouraging the diversification of exports to eliminate Soviet dependence on exporting energy and unprocessed raw materials; and achieving a more efficient allocation of imports.

Ideological strictures had precluded the acceptability of learning from the example of successful capitalist economies, or from reforming socialist states such as China. Under Gorbachev, a new openness encouraged critical evaluation of Soviet economic institutions and for the first time allowed serious consideration of alternative models. Scholars could now objectively assess past Soviet development policies in the Far East, evaluate such experiments as China's special economic zones and argue for the importance of foreign direct investment to stimulate the Soviet economy.[17]

If *perestroika* was a failure, then Gorbachev's foreign trade reforms and Moscow's grandiose plans for revitalising the eastern sector of the USSR and integrating it into the Asian-Pacific economic order were even less successful. In July 1987 the Communist Party Politburo adopted a wildly optimistic program, never implemented, for investing 232 bn roubles in Russia east of Lake Baikal through the year 2000. Few specifics were ever

---

16. See Abel Aganbegyan, *Inside Perestroika: The Future of the Soviet Economy* (New York: Harper & Row, 1989), pp. 173–226.

17. See for example, V. Ivanov and P. Minakir, "O roli vneshneekonomicheskikh sviazei v razvitii tikhookeanskikh raionov SSSR," *Mirovaia ekonomika i mezhdunarodnye otnosheniia* 5 (May 1988), pp. 59–70.

published regarding this program, which seems to have been inspired by Gorbachev's remarks in Vladivostok a year earlier. The basics included improving the region's transportation infrastructure, providing more housing and consumer amenities to encourage migration into the Far East, making the region self-sufficient in agriculture and energy and developing an export base for high value-added products.[18]

Gorbachev's efforts to reduce tensions on the Soviet Union's eastern flank, as part of his "new thinking" in foreign policy, led to significant improvements in trade relations with some Asian countries—most notably, China and South Korea. New thinking reconceptualised the Soviet position in Asia-Pacific, de-emphasising the significance of military power in the region while stressing the importance of developing economic links to energise domestic reform plans.

Normalising Sino-Soviet relations was the centrepiece of Gorbachev's Asian-Pacific policy. Negotiations initiated in 1982 were accelerated after Konstantin Chernenko's death and, after Moscow had satisfied each of Beijing's "three conditions," full governmental and party ties were restored at the May 1989 summit. Throughout the process of political negotiations, however, economic cooperation had expanded rapidly. A major five-year trade agreement was signed in July 1985, border trade expanded and Soviet technicians returned to assist the development projects abandoned in 1958. Sino-Soviet trade increased rapidly during the 1980s, from a low of $110m in 1981 to $3.6 bn 1989 (see Table 5.1).

Agreements on economic, scientific and technical cooperation were concluded between the Soviet Union and China during the Gorbachev-Deng summit and during Premier Li Peng's April 1990 visit to Moscow. In March 1991, concerned over growing Soviet instability, Beijing offered Moscow a commodity loan worth $730m to purchase foodstuffs and textiles, repayable over a five-year period.[19] Moscow also agreed to sell China two nuclear power stations, two thermal power stations and pulp and flax mills. As economic conditions deteriorated further, the Soviet Union found itself in the position of offering to sell its former enemy sophisticated military aircraft.[20]

The new approach towards Soviet interests in the region led, somewhat belatedly, to a reassessment of relations with the two Koreas. Under Gorbachev, the Soviet Union continued and even expanded economic

---

18. See Charles E. Ziegler, "Soviet Strategies for Development: East Asia and the Pacific Basin," *Pacific Affairs* 63 (Winter 1990–91), pp. 451–68.

19. *Pravda*, 5 March 1991; *Izvestiia*, 20 March 1991.

20. Sophie Quinn-Judge, "Cannon for Fodder," *Far Eastern Economic Review (FEER)*, 28 March 1991, p. 11.

assistance to Pyongyang and followed through on agreements to supply advanced weaponry concluded under Chernenko. By 1988, however, Moscow was openly soliciting economic ties with South Korean businesses and trade organisations. South Korea's technological capabilities and surplus investment capital made it a potentially valuable partner in Moscow's development plans. Conservatives in the Soviet leadership resisted abandoning Pyongyang and full diplomatic relations were not established until September 1990, after Gorbachev's meeting with Roh Tae Woo in San Francisco.

Economic ties between the Soviet Union and South Korea expanded after the 1988 Seoul Olympics. A Korean trade show was held in Moscow in July 1989, commemorating the opening of a Korean Trade Promotion Corporation office there. Permanent trade missions were established in Seoul and Moscow during 1989, with trade more than doubling from the previous year. In August 1990 Moscow proposed cooperation on 22 industrial and 40 consumer projects, involving petrochemicals, defence plant conversion, natural gas and coal development and the production of household appliances (refrigerators, washing machines, microwave ovens and so forth).[21] Hyundai established cooperative ventures with Soviet firms in shipbuilding, forestry products, computers, automobiles and petrochemicals. Samsung, Lucky Goldstar and other major Korean companies opened negotiations on joint ventures. Following the normalisation of relations in September 1990, South Korea agreed to provide the Soviet Union $3 bn in loans over three years.

Soviet and Russian economic relations with Asia-Pacific have been almost exclusively bilateral. During the Soviet period Moscow was as a rule hostile to all regional organisations, preferring to deal with atomised countries. Under Gorbachev, this suspicion and hostility was replaced with a readiness to recognise and cooperate with ASEAN, PECC, APEC and the Asian Development Bank (ADB). However, by the time that the Asian-Pacific organisations were convinced that Moscow really had fundamentally changed its policies, the Soviet Union was beginning to disintegrate and Asian affairs were a secondary consideration.

After the Coup

The August 1991 coup and subsequent disintegration of the Soviet Union heightened the sense of uncertainty among some Asian-Pacific nations regarding trade and economic cooperation with the successor-states. In the

---

21. *SUPAR Report* 10 (January 1991), pp. 114–15.

year following the coup, Russia's foreign policy was largely adrift. Under President Boris Yeltsin, relations with CIS members, Europe and the United States overshadowed ties with Asia. Russia moved to strengthen its economic ties with the western world through participation in the International Monetary Fund, the World Bank and the European Bank for Reconstruction and Development. In addition, the Russian government hired Western economists such as Harvard's Jeffrey Sachs and Swedish economist Anders Aslund to advise on making the transition to a market economy. By late 1992, although Russian officials were declaring Asia to be equally important with Europe, Moscow's actions suggested a continued Eurocentric bias.

For example, Russia's Far East was neglected throughout much of 1992. Although the region suffered from the general chaos affecting most of the FSU, the region's relative ethnic homogeneity lowered the potential for violent confrontations. President Yeltsin signed a decree in April granting the Russian Far East preferential treatment and greater autonomy in foreign economic activities, including special privileges in retaining foreign exchange earnings.[22] Privatisation of industry and agriculture accelerated and Vladivostok, long closed to foreigners, was finally opened at the beginning of 1992. Plans were made to develop the city into a special economic zone with UN and Japanese assistance.[23] And yet Moscow seemed only distantly concerned with events east of Baikal.

Many Western observers consider Japanese assistance critical to successful Russian participation in the Asian-Pacific economic order. In the wake of Russian parliament speaker Ruslan Khasbulatov's remarks to Japanese Prime Minister Toshiki Kaifu in September 1991 there was speculation that Russian reformers would move quickly to strike a deal on the Kuril islands in exchange for massive Japanese investment in the ailing economy. However, such conjecture underestimated the strength of Russian nationalism and the conviction among a large segment of the Russian public, across the ideological spectrum, that the Kuriles were rightfully Russian territory. This sentiment is especially strong in the Kuriles themselves, on Sakhalin and in the Far East more generally. Sakhalin's chief executive, Valentin Fedorov, has lobbied intensively to preserve Russian sovereignty over the islands, as has Oleg Rumiantsev, head of the Russian parliament's Constitutional Committee. Cossack groups in the Far East have declared their intention to fight for "Russian" territory.

---

22. Interfax, in *Foreign Broadcast Information Service—Soviet Union*, 28 May 1992.
23. *Izvestiia*, 2 January 1992.

TABLE 5.1: Soviet Trade with Asian-Pacific Nations, 1980–91 (US $m)

	1980	1985	1986	1987	1988	1989	1990	1991
Japan	4778	4356	5303	4997	5964	6094	5883	5345
China	491	2065	2691	2545	3261	3637	3838	3964
N. Korea	925	1349	1829	2074	2809	2532	2715	NA
S. Korea	–	–	–	185	278	600	890	1202
Singapore	281	278	176	243	227	259	301	531
Australia	1269	661	776	548	646	931	341	383
Thailand	191	85	98	74	122	365	270	308
Hong Kong	49	121	97	133	182	151	215	268
Taiwan	–	–	–	–	7	73	101	225
Malaysia	344	217	153	187	180	345	223	157
New Zealand	258	113	127	119	195	212	195	142
Indonesia	98	89	62	105	83	152	139	88
Sri Lanka	43	41	37	30	16	32	48	52
Philippines	229	48	31	46	48	47	52	49

Sources: *Direction of Trade Statistics* (Washington, DC: IMF, June 1992), p. 132; *Direction of Trade Statistics Yearbook* (Washington, DC: IMF, 1991), p. 395; *Direction of Trade Statistics Yearbook* (Washington, DC: IMF, 1986), p. 394; *Korean Newsreview*, 10 June 1989, p. 22; *Economist*, 31 March 1990, p. 32; Joseph S. Chung, "Foreign Trade of North Korea: Performance, Policy and Prospects," in Robert A. Scalapino and Hongkoo Lee, eds., *North Korea in a Regional and Global Context* (Berkeley: University of California, Institute of East Asian Studies, 1986), p. 86; "Prospects of North Korea Economic and Trade" (Japan External Trade Organisation, December 1991); *Free China Journal*, 25 August 1992, p. 2; *Far Eastern Economic Review*, 30 May 1991, p. 50; Korea Trade Center. IMF statistics are derived from reports by FSU trade partners.

As Moscow's hold over the periphery weakened and conservatives' influence in Russian foreign policy increased, it became increasingly difficult for Russia's central authorities to reach agreement with Japan over the protests of newly-empowered locals, leading Yeltsin to postpone his visit to Tokyo until a more auspicious time. Although a solution of the dispute might have resulted in guaranteed credits for investment, not many Japanese businesses seem eager to take advantage of the "opportunities" available in the Russian Far East. In Russia, there is still a significant contingent of the population that views foreign investment as "exploitation" of the motherland and any attempt to return the Kuriles as a betrayal of Russia's heritage.

Following the coup, a number of Japanese companies doing business in the Soviet republics suspended operations pending a stabilisation of the political situation. Others, however, were optimistic that weaker central control would make it easier to arrange credit and conclude deals directly with local enterprises, bypassing the monopolistic (and nearly insolvent)

Vneshekonombank and bureaucratic central ministries.[24] By mid-1992 about a dozen Japanese companies had established operations in Vladivostok and the total number of Japanese-Russian joint-ventures had increased to 43. However, the total capitalisation of these joint ventures was only 138m roubles. Many Japanese businesses continued to be wary of investing in Russia given Tokyo's refusal to offer credit assurance.[25]

Russia's relations with China survived the coup, and commerce, especially border trade, continued to grow. The two nations signed a trade pact in early March, the first official agreement since the Soviet collapse. Trade between China's Heilongjiang province and the Russian Far East, which share a 3,000 km frontier, approached one billion Swiss francs (approximately $730m) in 1991. As border controls were relaxed, shopping and tourism became commonplace in cities on both sides. Chinese consumer goods are in high demand among Russians, although they have few finished products to offer in exchange.

China has been concerned about political instability in the FSU and the possible effect of such turmoil on ethnic minorities in the border areas. The revival of Islam in the newly-independent Central Asian states and the possible impact on China's minorities worries Beijing. The Russian Far East is more ethnically homogeneous than Central Asia and does not present the separatist appeal of the newly-independent republics on China's western border. However, separatist movements have emerged calling for the formation of a Far Eastern Republic. Some of these movements—for example, Vozrozhdenie ("Resurrection") are seeking autonomy through parliamentary means, while others (for example the Far East Republican Party) are prepared to use illegal or violent methods to achieve their goals. These separatist movements and the highly chaotic situation in the Russian Far East are a source of concern to conservative Chinese leaders preoccupied with maintaining political stability in their country.[26]

Beijing was also disturbed by Moscow's rapidly expanding economic ties with Taiwan. Soviet-Taiwanese trade had expanded significantly in the months preceding the coup—trade turnover during the first seven months of 1991 was larger than in all of 1990, and the total for 1991 was three times the 1989 level (see Table 1). Taiwan is primarily interested in obtaining energy and raw materials—crude oil, aluminium, copper, chemical raw

---

24. See, for example, reports in Kyodo, 27 August 1991; and *Nikkei Weekly*, 31 August 1991; in *SUPAR Report* 12 (January 1992), pp. 43–44.

25. *SUPAR Report* 13 (July 1992), p. 32; *Japan Times*, 30 June 1992.

26. For a more extensive discussion of security and instability in the Russian Far East, see Charles E. Ziegler, "Russia, the United States, and Post-Cold War Security in the Asia-Pacific Region," paper presented to the Fourth Bedford Colloquium on Soviet Military-Political Affairs, Bedford, Nova Scotia, 10–13 August 1992.

materials, coal and iron ore—in exchange for computers, electronic goods and similar high-technology products. In June 1992 former Pacific Fleet commander Vladimir Sidorov led a delegation of senior military officers to Taipei amid rumours that Taiwan might consider purchasing Russian arms.[27] However, Russian weapons would pose serious interoperability problems for the Taiwanese military. And even trade in civilian items has been constrained by Moscow's refusal to grant Taiwanese goods preferential tariff rates.

Taipei was encouraged by developments in Russia following the 1991 coup. The director-general of Taiwan's Board of Foreign Trade, Sheu Keh-sheng, said that his country would encourage direct trade with enterprises in the FSU. In late August China's External Trade Development Council (CETRA) announced plans to open a trade office in Moscow and expressed interest in opening offices in other republics. The first Russian-Taiwanese joint venture—the Elecs East Taiwan Corp. Ltd. was established in late August 1991 in Taiwan, to export computers and other electronic equipment to the FSU in exchange for raw materials.[28] Taipei and Moscow reached agreement in May 1992 to establish coordination councils, similar to those that Taiwan has with Tokyo and Washington in the absence of full diplomatic relations.[29]

Despite rapid improvements in Russian-Taiwanese economic relations since the dissolution of the USSR, the People's Republic of China remains far more important for Moscow, both as an economic partner and as a potential security concern. Yeltsin's scheduled visit to Beijing in November 1992 underscores the centrality of the PRC in Russia's Asian policy. The Yeltsin government has tried to reassure the Chinese leadership that Russia does not plan to extend diplomatic recognition to Taipei. In mid-September, the Russian President signed a decree on relations with Taiwan, expressly reaffirming the "one-China" concept and acknowledging Taiwan to be an indivisible part of China.[30] For its part, Taiwan has rejected any intention to seek formal political ties with Moscow.

Economic relations with the Republic of Korea during Gorbachev's last two years looked very promising, doubling from $600m in 1989 to just over $1.2 bn in 1991. As the Soviet Union disintegrated, however, Seoul's initial enthusiasm waned. South Korea had used the lure of trade and

---

27. *FEER*, 9 July 1992, pp. 8–9. Admiral Sidorov's visit may have played a role, albeit a secondary one to electoral politics, in President Bush's September announcement that the United States would sell 150 F-16 fighters to Taiwan.

28. *SUPAR Report* 12 (January 1992), pp. 75–76.

29. *Free China Journal*, 19 May 1992, p. 1.

30. *RFE-RL Daily Report*, 18 September 1992.

investment to encourage Moscow to pressure North Korea into dialogue with the South on reunification. As Moscow's limited influence over Pyongyang diminished and its foreign debts mounted, the economic costs of doing business quickly surpassed the political benefits. In early December 1991 Seoul reversed its liberal trade policies towards the Soviet Union and China, announcing a tougher stance calculated exclusively on economic criteria. The South Korean government put a temporary hold on $1.2 bn in tied loans and, as the Soviet Union disintegrated, moved to seek individual payment guarantees from the newly-independent republics.

Virtually all of Russia's involvement in the Asian-Pacific economy has been through bilateral arrangements. Under Yeltsin, participation in regional economic organisations has not proved to be a top priority in Russian foreign policy. Prior to the breakup of the Soviet Union, Moscow was seeking to join PECC, was observing Asian Development Bank operations and had applied for membership in APEC.[31] However, the new Russian Federation has so far expressed little interest in these organisations.[32] Russia did confirm its membership in the UN Economic and Social Commission for Asia and the Pacific (ESCAP) as the successor-state to the USSR in April 1992, and participated in the ASEAN's 1992 post-ministerial conference. But for the most part Russia's serious internal problems precluded an activist policy towards Asia-Pacific.

In the foreign policy realm, Moscow was preoccupied with the impending Russian-Japanese summit and the increasingly prickly issue of the Kuriles throughout much of 1992. Russia's Japan policy, of course, was constrained by domestic considerations. The cancellation of Yeltsin's September visit to Tokyo illustrated the strength of public opinion against any concessions on the islands. Given Japan's dominant position in Asia, continuing tensions between the two nations will constrain Russia's effective participation in the Asian-Pacific economic order. Moreover, Russia's vociferous conservatives display a strong isolationist streak, have been wary of cooperation in international forums and generally view foreign investment as "exploitative." These factors work against significant Russian integration into the Asian-Pacific economy.

Perhaps the major economic development potential for the Russian Far East lies in the Tumen River Area Development Program (TRADP). The idea for developing the border area shared by Russia, China and North

---

31. "SSSR i aziatsko-tikhookeanskii region: sozdan Sovetskii natsional'nyi komitet," *Mirovaia ekonomika i mezhdunarodnye otnosheniia* 5 (1988), pp. 57–58; *Wall Street Journal,* 9 May 1988, p. 17; *FEER,* 14 November 1991, p. 27.

32. The Central Asian republics of the FSU recently approached the ADB about membership. See Jonathan Friedland, "Freshmen at the Feast," *FEER,* 14 May 1992, p.55.

Korea into a modern, major trade and transport facility was first advanced by the Chinese at a conference in Chanchung in July 1990.[33] This proposal was discussed at the UN Development Plan's Northeast Asia Regional Program meeting a year later, and a management committee of representatives from Russia, China, North and South Korea, Mongolia and Japan was established in October 1991. The UNDP appropriated $3m for an 18-month feasibility study, with a detailed report to be submitted to the six participating nations by the end of 1993.[34]

This project envisions investment of some $30 bn over 20 years to build up to 11 specialised harbours, air, rail and road terminals, power plants and telecommunications facilities, and the modern infrastructure to support an urban community of 500,000. The idea is to take advantage of existing regional complementarities—Russian and Mongolian natural resources, Chinese and North Korean surplus labour, and South Korean and Japanese capital and technology. Ideally, TRADP will have a spillover effect on the backward surrounding area, promoting growth in neighbouring economic zones. Russian plans to develop free economic zones around Khabarovsk and Sakhalin have been public for several years; more recent plans have envisioned a zone around Vladivostok. In December 1991 Pyongyang established an economic zone along the Tumen river, and the PRC in late April 1992 announced the creation of a Hunchun City economic zone. Japan's northwestern coastal areas, which have lagged behind the rest of the country, are expected to benefit from the project. Seoul is encouraged by the potential contributions of the zone towards meeting some of the massive costs of anticipated North-South reunification.

Conclusion

Soviet postwar regimes shared a myopic view of the Asian-Pacific region derived from a Stalinist obsession with ideological and military affairs. This perspective inhibited Moscow's ability to adapt to rapidly changing events in the region, which were dominated by economic processes. Although Soviet leaders' obsession with military production distorted the entire country's industrial base, the impact was particularly severe in Russia's Far East. Gorbachev and the reformers shifted Moscow's focus towards the importance of economic strength in international affairs and recognised

33. Mark J. Valencia, "Economic Cooperation in Northeast Asia: The Proposed Tumen River Scheme," *Pacific Review* 4:3 (1991), pp. 263–71.

34. Lincoln Kaye, "Hinterland of Hope," *FEER*, 16 January 1992, pp. 16–17; Li Haibo, "Tumen River Delta: Far East's Future Rotterdam," *Beijing Review*, 20–26 April 1992, pp. 5–6.

Asia's growing prominence in world affairs. Gorbachev eliminated the Soviet military threat to Asia, but Yeltsin has yet to make Russia economically relevant to most of its Asian neighbours.

The factors inhibiting greater Russian participation in the Asian-Pacific economy appear overwhelming in the short run. They include unpredictable and excessive taxing policies that discourage foreign investment; nationalist resentment at letting foreign companies exploit natural wealth and pollute the environment; continued conflicts between Moscow and local governments over jurisdictional authority; the threat of hyperinflation; major difficulties in privatisation and defence conversion; and a massive foreign debt. In the Far East, these problems are magnified by a shaky population base, the heavy concentration of defence industries, adverse climatic conditions and the presence of large numbers of demobilised and disaffected soldiers.

In the year since the abortive coup, Russia's leaders have understandably concentrated their energies on resolving the monumental political, economic and social problems confronting their country. Their priorities are to protect the Russian population in former Soviet republics, solve tense and sometimes violent ethnic disputes, work out viable arrangements among the highly specialised and economically interdependent republics of the former Soviet Union, and enlist European and American aid in stabilising and rebuilding the devastated economy. Asia and the emerging Asian-Pacific economic order appear to be only marginally important to Russia's immediate future.

6

Japan

Tsuyoshi Hasegawa

There is a general consensus that relations between Japan and the former Soviet Union (FSU) are in a state of stalemate. The validity of this consensus can be illustrated by the fact that Japan and the Soviet Union failed to sign a peace treaty for almost half a century after the end of World War II. This is truly an abnormal situation, when one considers the rapid transformations that have been taking place in the rest of the world. We are now living in a new world, a post-*perestroika*, post-Gorbachev, post-Soviet, post-communist world. New players are on the stage, and new values and new policies are emerging in the FSU. But in Russo-Japanese relations, the same old theme is being played out to the same old tune.

Although Russo-Japanese relations can be characterised as a stalemate, it is wrong to assume that they have been at a standstill. If measured by the same yardstick that was used to measure the relationship between the two countries during the Brezhnev period, significant changes have taken place. In order to be able to suggest specific ways in which both countries can break the stalemate, it is important to understand why these changes have taken place and why they have not produced a breakthrough.

This chapter attempts firstly to identify the nature of changes that have taken place in Japan's relations with the FSU in recent years, and secondly to examine closely how various aspects of the restructuring process after the August coup are affecting these relations.

Changes in Soviet-Japanese Relations

The great stumbling block for normalisation of relations between Japan and the FSU is the northern territorial dispute. There are two causes for the intractability of this issue. The first cause is on the Soviet side and has to do with the sequence of events, Soviet priorities and the dynamics of Soviet politics. Mikhail Gorbachev's foreign policy priorities had focused on the United States and Western Europe. Mending fences with Japan was low on his priority list; even in Asia, it ranked below Sino-Soviet rapprochement. Second, Gorbachev's foreign policy had domestic repercussions. By the time Gorbachev turned his attention to Japan, nationalism within the Soviet Union asserted itself as the most powerful disintegrating force of the Soviet political system. Obviously, he could not accept the Japanese argument that the northern territories had been seized illegally by Stalin while rejecting the Baltic states' insistence on independence. Also the democratic movement that he himself fostered led to a situation in which he could no longer ignore public opinion. Polls indicated that an overwhelming majority of Soviet citizens, especially those who lived on the disputed islands, were opposed to giving up any territory to Japan.

Furthermore, by 1990 conservative critics within Russia began voicing opposition to perceived unilateral concessions to the West. Related to this was the third element, the sequence of events. After the German reunification it became impossible for him to make another major concession to Russia's former enemy. To make matters worse, the radical reformers led by Boris Yeltsin capitalised on the territorial question to discredit Gorbachev. By the time Gorbachev finally visited Japan in April 1991, attacked both from the right and the left, he had no leverage on the matter. The chance to resolve the northern territorial issue fell victim to the domestic political dynamics in the Soviet Union.[1]

The second cause for the intractability of the northern territorial dispute is what I call the northern territorial syndrome that paralysed Japan's policy towards the Soviet Union. If we examine Gorbachev's dazzling successes in achieving reconciliations with his previous adversaries, we can safely conclude that Gorbachev's initiatives were met with reciprocal concessions from the other side. Gorbachev's new political thinking succeeded in turning previous zero-sum games into positive-sum games. Japan was an exception. The overriding assumption held by the Japanese government until now has been that since Moscow needs Tokyo more than the other way round, Japan can conduct negotiations from a position of strength. When Gorbachev initiated the new course of foreign policy based on his new political thinking, Japan made the northern territorial issue a litmus test for the changing attitude of the other side, taking the "entrance approach" (*iriguchiron*), which meant that Japan would not consider rapprochement

---

1. See Tsuyoshi Hasegawa, "Gorbachev's Visit to Japan and Soviet-Japanese Relations," *Acta Slavica Iaponica*, 10 (1992), pp. 65–92.

with the Soviet Union without first getting back the northern territories, as opposed to the "exit approach" (*deguchiron*), which took the position that the solution to the territorial question should come along with the culmination of the improvement of bilateral relations in other spheres.

This does not mean that the attitude of the Japanese government remained inflexible all the time. In fact, it has changed significantly over time. At first, the Japanese government was sceptical about the possibility of *perestroika* changing the Soviet system fundamentally. When drastic changes began to take place after 1987 and Gorbachev's new political thinking began to yield tangible results in East-West relations, the Japanese government grudgingly admitted that Gorbachev's policy was changing the international political landscape but took the position that although the Cold War might be over in Europe, it still persisted in Asia. In its view, the new political thinking did not extend to Asia. It was only after the collapse of East European communism in 1989 and under the danger of international isolation that the Japanese government finally came around to accepting, albeit reluctantly, that it was in the interest of the Western alliance, including Japan, to help the Soviet Union make a transition to democracy and a market economy.

Japan's Ministry of Foreign Affairs (MOFA), which had previously taken a strict "entrance approach," modified its position in 1989 to adopt a policy of "expanded equilibrium" (*kakudai kinkô*), by which it took the position that both countries should expand the realm of cooperation even though the territorial dispute remained unresolved. Since the level of cooperation was to be determined by the degree to which the Soviet Union responded constructively to the territorial dispute, this was different from the "exit approach." The policy of "expanded equilibrium" was thus a partial abandonment of the intransigent "entrance approach."

Once a crack was opened in the foundations of the "entrance approach," various sacrosanct principles began tumbling down as well. The principle of "inseparability of politics and economics" (*seikei fukabun*) had been another cornerstone of Japanese attitude towards the FSU. It meant that Japan would refuse to grant large-scale economic aid to the FSU and improve economic relations by removing the ban on credit from the Export-Import Bank of Japan to promote trade. The Japanese government also gave up the demand of immediate return of all the northern islands as a precondition for improvement of relations. The Japanese strategy during the Gorbachev-Kaifu summit in April 1991 was to have Gorbachev reaffirm the validity of the 1956 Joint Declaration, by which the Soviet government had pledged the return of the two islands, Shikotan and the Habomai group, after the conclusion of a peace treaty.[2]

All these changes, however, came too late to alter the nature of Moscow-Tokyo relations. The Japanese consistently erred on the side of caution and conservatism. The Japanese government misjudged the seriousness of *perestroika,* when it began. When it finally recognised the importance of *perestroika,* it ignored all clear signs of changing Soviet foreign policy not merely in Europe and the U.S. but also in Asia. The new direction in Soviet foreign policy in Asia that was to culminate in rapprochement with China and South Korea was already visible in Gorbachev's Vladivostok speech in July 1986.[3] Rather than seizing this opportunity, the Japanese government dismissed the Vladivostok speech and all visible signs of the new political thinking as mere propaganda that did not amount to anything, since the Soviets showed no indication of changing their position on the northern territorial question. Had the Japanese government adopted much earlier the policy that it was to pursue during the Kaifu-Gorbachev summit, the resolution of the northern territorial question might have been possible before German reunification.

This tendency of the Japanese government to fall constantly behind rapidly developing events in the Soviet Union and Soviet foreign policy initiatives can ultimately be traced to the northern territorial syndrome, which can be defined as an affliction akin to a mental block that paralyses one's ability to see and comprehend rationally one's own interests that go beyond the fixation of the northern territories. In an ordinary state a specific policy on specific issues towards the Soviet Union stems from a general and comprehensive Soviet policy, which in turn is determined by the general framework of the international system it wants to promote. In Japan, the northern territorial issue has constituted almost the entirety of Japan's Soviet policy. In other words, a comprehensive Soviet policy has been held hostage to the northern territorial problem in Japan.

Japan managed to reach a position of global power without dealing with the Soviet Union. Trade with the Soviet Union always represented less than two percent of the total volume of Japan's trade. As long as the U.S.-Japan Mutual Security Treaty was in good shape, Japan could be protected under the U.S. nuclear umbrella, delegating the major tasks of solving security conflicts with the Soviet Union to the United States. Unlike West European countries, which have lived under the constant threat of superior Soviet forces just across the border, the possibility of Japan being attacked directly

---

2. See *ibid.*

3. See Ramesh Thakur and Carlyle A. Thayer, eds., *The Soviet Union as an Asian Pacific Power: Implications of Gorbachev's 1986 Vladivostok Initiative* (Boulder: Westview, 1987).

by the the Soviet Union had been remote. Thus, while the Soviet Union, for better or worse, occupied a central place in the foreign policies of West European countries, Japan had the luxury of being able, in large measure, to ignore this troublesome neighbour. The northern territorial problem provided a convenient excuse for Japan to ignore the Soviet Union precisely because of its intractability.

The beauty of the problem was that the northern territories are not vitally necessary for Japan. No Japanese live there and they are not essential for Japan's economic needs. Japan can therefore afford the luxury of keeping the territorial dispute unresolved. In fact, as long as the Cold War continued, the territorial problem served as a convenient means to keep Japan's relations with the Soviet Union adversarial. One might add that the existence of the dispute between Japan and the Soviet Union was also convenient for the United States, since it could exploit this question as a guarantee that prevented Japan from straying from the U.S.-Japan alliance.

The situation changed drastically when Gorbachev came to power. The utility of the northern territorial question ended with the termination of the Cold War, and the changing policy of the U.S. towards the Soviet Union. As the United States and Western Europe began to seek rapprochement with the Soviet Union, the northern territorial issue became an important impediment to Japan pursuing a course that was synchronised with the rest of the Western alliance. The shifts in the Japanese government's policy represented its adjustment to the changing circumstances.

Nevertheless, the paradigmatic shift in the international system did not force the Japanese to reexamine the foundations of their policy towards the FSU. Rather, the changes that took place in Japan's policy towards the FSU were but superficial adjustments to the changing circumstances without being accompanied by a fundamental reappraisal of the entire policy towards the FSU. The past policy that justified the territorial claim as Japan's foreign policy *goals*, although it was nothing but a *means* to prevent rapprochement with the Soviet Union, began to haunt Japanese foreign policy. The Japanese became prisoners of the northern territorial syndrome, which left them unable to address the obvious question of what Japan's policy towards the Soviet Union should be and what position the territorial question should occupy in this overall framework of Japanese-Soviet relations.

Hopes and Pitfalls: August–December 1991

One may surmise that the end of communism in the Soviet Union and the disintegration of the Soviet empire must have tremendous impact on improving Russo-Japanese relations, since the very source of Soviet expansionism that has constituted a major threat to Japan has disappeared. As an important member of the Western alliance, Japan is expected to follow the concerted effort by the Western alliance to assist Russia's transition to democracy and a market economy. Moreover, those who took over the stewardship of Russian foreign policy under Yeltsin are free from past prejudices and display sensitivity to Japan's position on the territorial issue. One might reasonably expect that under the combined impact of all these factors, after the August 1991 coup Russo-Japanese relations would have quickly gained the momentum for rapprochement that had proven elusive under Gorbachev. This would be a false assumption. Russo-Japanese relations have remained in a state of stalemate. In fact, the sudden cancellation of Yeltsin's trip only four days before the scheduled date of visit of 13 September 1992 may have set the clock back to a situation that is far worse than the one that existed towards the end of the Gorbachev era.

Immediately after the failure of the coup, prompted by the increasing role played by the Russian Federation in bilateral relations, both sides were optimistic. Reflecting the shift of power relations from Gorbachev's Soviet government to Yeltsin's Russian government, it was clear that suddenly the Russian Foreign Ministry was in the driver's seat. And the driving force behind the new Russian policy towards Japan was Georgii Kunadze, who had been one of the most outspoken critics of the intransigent Soviet policy towards Japan in the past, and most sympathetic to the Japanese position.[4] Before he became Deputy Minister of the Russian Foreign Ministry, Kunadze had already advocated that the only realistic solution to the territorial dispute was for both sides to reaffirm the validity of the 1956 Joint Declaration, which stipulated that the Soviet Union would return Shikotan and Habomais to Japan after the conclusion of a peace treaty.[5] It was in this belief that he began an energetic campaign to reach a compromise solution with Japan along this line, which might be called the Kunadze option. Foreign Minister Andrei Kozyrev basically supported the position of his deputy who, unlike his self-effacing boss, asserted himself with a strong personality and an energetic leadership.

Riding on the crest of his popularity after the collapse of the coup, Yeltsin was eager to seize the Japan issue in order to undercut Gorbachev's authority further by intruding in bilateral negotiations with Japan. It was for this purpose that in early September he sent his trusted aide Ruslan Khasbulatov, then acting chairman of the Russian Supreme Soviet, to Japan, and conveyed the message that he believed that new relations

---

4. *SUPAR Report* 12 (January 1992), pp. 49–50.

5. Georgii Kunadze and Konstantin Sarkisov, "Razmyshliaia o sovetsko-iaponskikh otnosheniiakh," *Mirovaia ekonomika i mezhdunarodnye otnosheniia*, No. 5, 1989.

between Russia and Japan should be operated without any distinction between "the victor" and "the vanquished" in the previous war, that the disputed territorial issue would be solved on the basis of "law and justice," and further that the length of time within which the territorial dispute should be solved in his original five-stage proposal should be able to be shortened.[6]

Yeltsin had already proposed a five-stage solution to the northern territorial dispute in January 1990 when he visited Japan as the leader of the reformist opposition to Gorbachev. This proposal included: (1) recognising the existence of the territorial dispute; (2) declaring the islands a free economic zone; (3) demilitarising the islands; (4) concluding a peace treaty and (5) leaving the solution of the territorial dispute to the next generation, and solving it within 15 to 20 years. In the meantime Yeltsin was elected chairman of the Russian Supreme Soviet, and later President of the Russian Federation. As the head of state his role was reversed: he was now in the position of having to uphold the integrity of the Russian territory.

As Yeltsin's political role changed, so did the meaning of Yeltsin's five-stage solution. When Yeltsin initially made this proposal, it represented a radical departure from the intransigent official Soviet position. When Gorbachev was preparing his visit to Japan, however, this formula was turned into a conservative criticism to the realistic alternative that Gorbachev might have chosen. By 1991 the Soviet government already recognised the existence of the territorial dispute and the initial step of demilitarisation was promised by Gorbachev at the summit. After the Gorbachev-Kaifu summit the crucial question of the territorial dispute had shifted to two questions: whether the Joint Declaration of 1956 would be honoured, and whether the Soviets were prepared to acknowledge Japan's sovereignty over Etorofu and Kunashiri. Yeltsin's five-stage proposal that gave negative answers to both questions, therefore, was a step backward from the Gorbachev-Kaifu Joint Statement, and therefore could serve as no basis for a realistic solution to the territorial dispute.[7]

It was obvious that there were fundamental discrepancies between the Kunadze option and Yeltsin's five-stage proposal. But it was difficult for the Japanese to see these discrepancies at the time, partly because Yeltsin's suggestion to solve the territorial question on the basis of "law and justice" was interpreted by the Japanese to coincide with the Kunadze option. Thus,

6. *SUPAR Report* 12 (January 1992), pp. 49–50. Khasbulatov became the chairman of the Supreme Soviet of the Russian Federation. In this capacity, he began distancing himself from Yeltsin later, when Egor Gaidar's economic policy was implemented in January 1992.

7. See Wada Haruki, "Hoppô ryôdo mondai o saikô suru: sorenpô no shûen o mukaete [Reexamining the Northern Territorial Problem: In the Face of the End of the Soviet Union]," *Sekai*, No. 2, 1992, p. 221.

despite these fundamental discrepancies that were to play a decisive role on the eve of Yeltsin's scheduled trip to Japan, the Khasbulatov mission was taken by the Japanese as a positive development.

The Japanese side also reciprocated the willingness to step up the pace of improvement with the FSU. At the end of September, while in New York, Foreign Minister Tarô Nakayama enunciated five new principles that were designed to serve as a new framework to guide Japan's relationship with the Soviet Union and Russia after the coup. These five principles called for (1) setting up aid for Soviet reform; (2) strengthening cooperation with the Russian Federation; (3) assisting the Soviet Union in its efforts to be accepted as a constructive partner in Asia-Pacific; (4) supporting the Soviet Union's campaign to integrate itself with the global economic system via special status in the IMF and World Bank; and (5) seeking an early resolution to its territorial dispute in order to conclude a peace treaty.[8] Following these new principles, the Japanese government announced in October that it would grant aid to the Soviet Union amounting to $2.5 bn.[9] The government spokesman took pains to explain that this aid was to be granted to the Soviet Union without a resolution of the territorial issue.

Despite the overall optimism, however, there were basically three negative factors that were eventually to surface as major impediments for rapprochement. The discrepancies between Yeltsin's position and the Kunadze option was the first such negative factor. Second, there was an immediate backlash to Kunadze's initiatives. There were diverse political groups that registered opposition to the Kunadze line for different political motives. The first group were residents of the islands themselves, who in resolutions of local soviets, rallies and petitions to Yeltsin and Gorbachev, registered their protest at any negotiations with regard to the return of the islands.[10] The second voice of opposition to the Kunadze option came from Valentin Fedorov, governor of Sakhalin, who adopted the most militant position against the transfer of islands to Japan presumably for his personal political reasons of trying to prop up his sagging popularity. The third group were national-patriotic politicians in the Russian Supreme Soviet, who formed a parliamentary group called Russian Unity (*Rossiiskoe edinstvo*). The fourth group was the military, which began to reassert itself after the initial setback that it suffered from the coup attempt.

At the end of September, Kunadze visited the disputed islands to explain his position on the territorial issue. It turned out that he had charged straight

---

8. *SUPAR Report* 12 (January 1992), p. 51.

9. *Asahi Shimbun*, 9 October 1991; *SUPAR Report* 12 (January 1992), pp. 39–40.

10. *Asahi Shimbun*, 16 September 1991; *Svobodnyi Sakhalin*, 18 September 1991, quoted in *SUPAR Report* 12 (January 1992), p. 50.

into a hornet's nest. At one meeting at a fisherman's house on Shikotan, "he was almost clobbered by the people."[11] Fedorov assailed Kunadze's visit as "an ideological preparation for the surrender of some of the islands to Japan" and urged the local residents to register protest "through meetings, declarations, short-term strikes."[12] Fedorov then toured around the islands, accompanied by Nikolai Pavlov and Sergei Baburin, two of the most prominent conservative people's deputies to the Russian parliament. On every island he visited, Fedorov fulminated about Kunadze's betrayal and fanned xenophobic appeal to defend the Russian land.[13] The Kuril issue— the national-patriotic group refused to call it the northern territorial problem—gave this group, which represented a curious mixture of the former communists and right-wing nationalists, a rallying point. On 17 October, *Sovetskaya Rossiia*, published an interview with Baburin and Pavlov. Baburin rejected the 1956 Joint Declaration as "extremely anti-constitutional, and anti-state from the political and spiritual point of view."[14] The military also joined the chorus of opposition to Kunadze. In the beginning of November newly-installed Soviet Defence Minister Evgenii I. Shaposhnikov submitted a report to the Russian Supreme Soviet. This statement warned that had Russia returned Kunashiri and Etorofu to Japan, the Ekaterina Strait between the islands would fall completely into Japan's control, and that in that case Japanese and U.S. submarines would be able to penetrate into the Sea of Okhotsk without any difficulty.[15]

The third negative factor in Russo-Japanese relations after the August coup was in Japanese domestic politics. In November a new government under Prime Minister Kiichi Miyazawa was formed. Miyazawa appointed to the post of foreign minister his powerful rival Michio Watanabe. On the one hand, the initial expectation was that the Miyazawa cabinet, unlike its predecessor, would be a strong cabinet. Miyazawa, as the head of the Miyazasa faction, had been a powerful contender for premiership since the fall of Yasuhiro Nakasone in 1987. Assisted by Watanabe, head of the Watanabe faction (former Nakasone faction), who also needed diplomatic success to boost his political influence for his bid for future premiership, the Miyazawa government might have been able to assert a strong leadership for concluding a peace treaty with Russia, had it chosen to do so.

On the other hand, however, the Miyazawa government was a creation of political compromises and manoeuvres, in which the Takeshita faction

---

11. *Pravda*, 8 October 1991, quoted in *SUPAR Report* 12 (January 1992), p. 53.

12. *Asahi Shimbun*, 4 October 1991; *SUPAR Report* 12 (January 1992), pp. 51–52.

13. *SUPAR Report* 12 (January 1992), pp. 53–54.

14. *Sovetskaia Rossiia*, 17 October 1991, quoted in Wada, "Hoppô ryôdo mondai o saikô suru," p. 222.

15. *Asahi Shimbun*, 13 November 1991.

played a decisive part. Thus, the Takeshita faction's Shin Kanemaru had to be installed as vice-premier to oversee the general operation of the Miyazawa government much like the arrangement under the Kaifu government. This meant that the powerful young maverick, Ichirô Ozawa of the Takeshita faction, who was known to have a visceral dislike for Miyazawa, was free to criticise the government's policy.

If Japan were to strike a deal with Russia, the narrow passage through which Russia and Japan could find an acceptable ground would have been somewhere along the Kunadze option. This would have meant a major departure from the official position that Japanese governments had upheld consistently since 1956: the return of the four islands. For such a policy to be implemented, strong leadership was required in order to twist the arms of MOFA and to silence the opposition within the ruling Liberal Democratic Party. Miyazawa was not prepared to risk his political life to achieve rapprochement with Russia, which was low in his priority. Thus, he let MOFA dictate the agenda of his cabinet's policy towards Russia.

On the surface Russo-Japanese relations immediately after the August coup moved in a positive direction. General optimism seems to have captured the policy-makers on both sides. Nevertheless, under this optimism, there were a number of pitfalls that eventually proved to be deadly obstacles capable of dealing a heavy blow to the momentum for rapprochement.

Russo-Japanese Relations after the End of the Soviet Union

The end of the Soviet Union in December 1991 eliminated the ambiguities that existed in Japan's two-track diplomacy. Initially, the transfer of negotiations to the Russian Foreign Ministry exerted a positive impact on Russo-Japanese relations, since the Russian policy towards Japan was now led by the Russian Foreign Ministry. Indeed, for the first couple of months after the end of the Soviet Union, it seemed that the momentum for rapprochement that had begun after the failed coup in August continued to accelerate.

The Japanese government granted Russia immediate diplomatic recognition as the Soviet Union's successor-state. On 28 December, Kozyrev told Japanese Ambassador Sumio Edamura that Russia would honour all treaties and agreements signed by the FSU. More specifically, Kozyrev said that "the Russian government recognises the legality of the 1956 Japan-Soviet Joint Declaration, including an item concerning the return to Japan of the Habomai islands and Shikotan on the conclusion of a peace treaty," although he hastened to add that the recognition of the Joint

Declaration "will not immediately lead to the automatic, immediate handover of the islands to Japan."[16] Watanabe and Kozyrev held their first meeting on 27 January in Moscow. Watanabe pledged that he would do everything in his power to move forward bilateral relations without letting them slide backward, but pointed out that for drastic improvement of relations the territorial question could not be evaded. He then proposed that once Russia agreed to return the four islands, Japan was prepared to be flexible with regard to the timing and the means of their return.[17]

The first foreign ministerial conference between Watanabe and Kozyrev augured ill for the future, although it was hardly recognised so at the time. Certainly, Watanabe's endorsement of Russia's transitional process to democracy and a market economy was a positive move. Nevertheless, the position that Japan would be flexible about the timing and method of transfer of islands only after Russia pledged the return of all four islands was a step backward from Kaifu's position during his summit with Gorbachev. Moreover, Watanabe's first official trip to Moscow was marred by another incident. His scheduled meeting with Yeltsin was cancelled suddenly when Yeltsin disappeared mysteriously from Moscow. This would not be the last time that Yeltsin cancelled a scheduled meeting with the Japanese.

Nevertheless, the momentum for rapprochement seemed to have been maintained. After a brief meeting with Miyazawa in New York, Yeltsin announced that his visit to Japan was to take place in mid-September.[18] The first working group meeting between Russia and Japan was held in Moscow on 10–11 February. The Russian side was headed by Kunadze and the Japanese side by the new Deputy Foreign Minister Kunihiko Saitô. Certainly, there was some progress on the territorial dispute. The Russians not only affirmed the validity of the 1956 Joint Declaration, but also agreed that the Shimoda Treaty of 1855 that had drawn the border between Uruppu and Etorofu had been concluded peacefully. Thus, the Russians repudiated for the first time the previous Soviet claim that the Shimoda treaty was forced on Russia by Japan under duress during the Crimean War. During the negotiations Kunadze said that Moscow "must overcome a 1960 government memorandum that negated the Japan-Soviet joint declaration." To this Saitô replied that "if Moscow can accept in principle the return of the islands to Japan, the details can be worked out later." The differences were narrowed, but they were still a long way from agreement, since Kunadze was talking about the return of two islands while Saitô stood firm on four.[19]

16. *Nihon Keizai Shimbun*, 28 December 1991; *SUPAR Report* 12 (January 1992), p. 60.

17. *Yomiuri Shimbun*, 28 January 1992.

18. *Ibid.*,1 February 1992.

19. *Nihon Keizai Shimbun*, 11 and 16 February 1992; *SUPAR Report* 13 (July 1992), p. 54.

Kozyrev's second meeting with Watanabe on 20–21 March, which was officially the first Russo-Japanese foreign ministerial conference since Russia became an independent state, did not produce a breakthrough on the territorial issue, either, although it was accompanied by a number of atmospheric improvements. With regard to the territorial issue, Kozyrev said that Russia would "take over" the 1956 Joint Declaration, but stopped short of committing himself to the return of the two islands after the conclusion of a peace treaty. It appears that Kozyrev's position was a step backward from his own previous pledge, and presumably, this retreat reflected the growing domestic opposition to territorial concessions. Faced with this retreat, Watanabe in turn rejected Kozyrev's demand that Japan cease linking large-scale economic assistance and full-fledged bilateral economic ties to the territorial question.[20]

Despite the willingness of the Russian Foreign Ministry to achieve a breakthrough by adopting the Kunadze option, it could not ignore the political reality at home. The collapse of the Soviet Union, the formation of the Commonwealth of Independent States (CIS), Yeltsin's handling of diaspora in the Baltic states and new frictions with Ukraine over the fate of the Black Sea Fleet and the Crimea inflicted on the Russians a deep sense of humiliation. The awakened Russian nationalism was easily exploited by the former communists and the reactionary national-patriotic group to discredit Yeltsin and his government. Furthermore, Yeltsin's government launched the ill-conceived radical economic reform led by Prime Minister Egor Gaidar in January 1992. Gaidar's "shock therapy" led to immediate hyper-inflation. Yeltsin's popularity that had reached its zenith after the August coup dwindled sharply.

As popular discontents with Yeltsin's government mounted, its inner circles began to splinter. Vice-President Aleksander Rutskoi began distancing himself from the president, sharply criticising Gaidar's shock therapy. Khasbulatov, who had securely installed himself as chairman of the Russian Soviet, used parliament as a bastion from which to attack Gaidar's economic reform. The Constitutional Commission of the Supreme Soviet, headed by Oleg Rumiantsev, and the Committee for International Affairs and External Economic Relations, headed by Evgenii Ambartsumov, asserted their constitutional power to challenge the executive branch. The nationalist-patriotic group, led by Baburin and Pavlov, turned up the volume of their protest against the Kunadze option. Constitutional struggle, ideological motivation and personal political ambitions were mingled into the parliamentary opposition to the Kunadze option, and the "Kuril issue"

---

20. *Asahi Shimbun*, 22 March 1922; *Nihon Keizai Shimbun*, 21 March 1992 (evening ed.); *SUPAR Report* 13 (July 1922), pp. 54–55.

became a focal point for these diverse groups to rally around against the Yeltsin government.

Kozyrev's retreat on the territorial issue reflected the Foreign Ministry's recognition that a flexible response to Japan's demands would have to be reexamined under domestic pressure. Aleksander Panov, newly-installed chief of the Russian Foreign Ministry's Asia-Pacific division, warned that unless Japan changed its intransigent position, it would be unlikely to solve the territorial dispute when Yeltsin visited Japan in September.[21] Suddenly a red light began to blink in front of Russo-Japanese relations that had appeared to be moving along smoothly.

Yeltsin's relations with the military also cast a dark shadow on Russo-Japanese relations. As Gorbachev found it imperative to rely on the military to prop up the quickly collapsing regime during his final days, so Yeltsin too needed the support of the military for the survival of his government. In May Yeltsin decided to form the Russian military, which quickly took over the bulk of functions of the former Soviet military. Already gone was his strident criticism of the military and the military-industrial complex. Radical military reform programs were pushed aside. Suddenly, the military's role in domestic politics had increased. Yeltsin appointed Pavel Grachev, a veteran officer in the war in Afghanistan, not a civilian, as a temporary Defence Minister.[22] The military's increasing muscle in domestic policy was reflected in its outspoken criticism of the Foreign Ministry's position on the territorial issue. Contradicting Kozyrev's statement on the reduction of the troops on the northern islands, the General Staff of the CIS armed forces recommended that no reduction of troops should be made.[23] For the military as well, the "Kuril issue" became a focal point of their influence in domestic politics.

The Japanese government displayed an amazing lack of sensitivity to these domestic pressures. In April, Watanabe announced in Ôtawara, Tochigi Prefecture, the Japanese government's latest official position. He stated that Japan would be prepared to accept Russia's right of administration over the northern territories as long as the Russian government accepted Japan's "residual sovereignty" over the islands.[24] Cabinet Minister Kôichi Katô reconfirmed the Watanabe statement by saying that the Japanese government had consistently held the view that as long as

---

21. *Mainichi Shimbun*, 2 April 1992. Panov became Ambassador to South Korea in June 1992.

22. Aleksei Zagorskii, "Russian Security Policy in Asia-Pacific: From USSR to CIS," Paper Presented to the conference on Pacific Security Relations after the Cold War, Hong Kong, 15–18 June 1992, p. 12.

23. *Nihon Keizai Shimbun*, 3 April 1992.

24. *Asahi Shimbun*, 18 April 1992; *SUPAR Report* 13 (July 1992), p. 56.

the Russian government recognised that the four islands were an inalienable part of Japanese territory, Japan would respond flexibly as to the timing, method and conditions of their return to Japan. Katô, however, added a major clarification: the Japanese government's policy to recognise Russia's right of administration would not be extended to Habomais and Shikotan.[25]

This policy was a step backward from the Kaifu government's position during the summit with Gorbachev. At the summit, the purpose of the Japanese government was to have Gorbachev reaffirm the 1956 Joint Declaration. But one year later, the objective of the Japanese government was no longer to have Yeltsin reaffirm the 1956 Joint Declaration; it upped the ante by adding another condition: Russia's recognition of "residual sovereignty" over Etorofu and Kunashiri. At a time when the Russian Foreign Ministry was fighting a lone battle under mounting pressures from all sides, and when Western allies were increasingly becoming critical of Japan's reluctance to aid the Soviet Union, the reason for this changing position was difficult to understand. Perhaps the Japanese government had concluded that Russia's weakness provided Japan with a golden opportunity to strike a better bargain.

Whatever the reason behind the newly-acquired intransigence, Japan's position proved to be a fatal impediment to a solution of the territorial issue. It was tantamount to waving a red flag in front of a raging bull that was gathering all its force against the Kunadze option. Immediately after Katô's clarification, the Russian Foreign Ministry flatly rejected the proposal as unacceptable.[26] From this time on, the differences between the two sides became increasingly noticeable. Watanabe's negotiations with Kozyrev and Yeltsin in Moscow in May only accentuated the differences on both sides.

Confronted with the difficult prospect in the forthcoming summit with Yeltsin, the Miyazawa government and MOFA displayed a bizarre sense of diplomatic strategy by appealing to the Western allies at the G-7 summit in Munich in July to put pressure on Russia to change its position. The most important goal of the Japanese government for the G-7 summit in Munich was to have the northern territorial issue included in the political statement. For this purpose, the government dispatched Ambassador Nobuo Matsunaga, who was to attend the summit in place of the hospitalised Watanabe, to Germany and France to obtain prior approval. Initially, Chancellor Helmut Kohl and President François Mitterrand were opposed to including the territorial issue in the Political Statement. But a deal was struck between Japan and these two hard-nosed European powers. Japan would raise no objections to Western aid to Russia in return for the inclusion of the

25. *Yomiuri Shimbun*, 20 April 1992.
26. *Asahi Shimbun*, 23 April 1992.

territorial issue in the Political Statement. In the end, the G-7 agreed to include in the Political Declaration the expression: "We welcome Russia's commitment to a foreign policy based on law and justice. We believe that this represents a basis for full normalization of the Russian-Japanese relationship through resolving the territorial issue."[27]

Although the Japanese government congratulated itself for scoring a diplomatic victory for having the territorial issue included in the G-7 Political Statement, the Japanese conduct in Munich actually revealed how far the Japanese sense of reality was at variance with the rest of the Western world. A simple comparison between Japanese and Western newspapers that reported the summit will make this point crystal clear. While Japanese papers made the territorial issue the focal point of the summit, this question was hardly mentioned in Western newspapers. Moreover, the inclusion of the G-7's wish to solve the territorial question on the basis of "law and justice" could well be turned against Japan, if Japan were to insist on the intransigent position. Already, Germany and France expressed strong dissatisfaction with Japan's unreasonable intransigence. Even the American pledge to support Japan obviously was mere lip service.[28]

If Japan behaved badly at the summit, Yeltsin also displayed his typical *muzhik* (peasant) horse-trading mentality in Munich. Incensed by Japan's effort to internationalise the territorial issue, Yeltsin accused Japan of not spending a penny for aiding Russia. Not only did this statement outrageously ignore the whole range of Japan's assistance to Russia and the CIS; it was also an affront to the outpouring of goodwill from ordinary Japanese citizens, displayed in donations for emergency food and medical aid as well as for medical treatment of patients with severe burns who were brought to hospitals in Hokkaidô.[29] Moreover, Yeltsin's insolent assumption that took other nations' moral obligations to assist Russia for granted was regarded as shameful blackmail and lacking in dignity commensurate with the status of a great power.

Thus, by July it became apparent that Russia and Japan were no longer speaking a common language. The prospect of failure at the forthcoming

---

27. *Asahi Shimbun*, 6 and 9 July 1992; *Nihon Keizai Shimbun*, 4, 8, 9 and 9 (evening ed.) July 1992; *Mainichi Shimbun*, 8 and 9 July 1992; *Yomiuri Shimbun*, 8 and 9 (evening ed.) July 1992; *New York Times*, 2 July 1992; *Wall Street Journal*, 7 and 9 July 1992; *Los Angeles Times*, 6 July 1992; Kimura Hiroshi, "Ronten: samitto, 'Hô to seigi' no imi" ("The Issue: Significance of 'Law and Justice' in the Summit"), *Yomiuri Shimbun*, 10 July 1992.

28. Tsuyoshi Hasegawa, "Hoppôryôdo shôkôgun ni ochiitta nihon" ("Japan that Is Afflicted with the Northern Territories Syndrome"), *Chûôkôron*, No. 9, 1992, p. 88.

29. One of the most celebrated cases was that of Kostia, a small boy who was brought to Sapporo and operated on in the Sapporo Medical University Hospital. All the hospital costs were paid by the fund created by citizens' donations, and others volunteered as interpreters.

summit between Miyazawa and Yeltsin was a foregone conclusion. What both sides should have done at this point was to seek ways to avoid a disaster, but they continued to behave as if they could bridge the irreconcilable differences before the summit.

Plunging into Disaster: July–September 1992

The domestic situation after July went from bad to worse in Russia. The "Kuril problem" was no longer one of many controversial issues, but became the most hotly debated issue during the summer. Conservative opposition became more active and vociferous. But the opposition was no longer confined to the national-patriotic group. As the opposition of the radical reformers led by Yeltsin to any territorial concessions was decisive in the failure of Gorbachev's trip to Japan in April 1991, so the opposition that came from the left succeeded in dealing a coup de grâce to the Kunadze option. Moreover, the "Kuril issue" became an issue in the fierce infighting among Yeltsin's inner circle.

As Yeltsin's visit to Japan approached, the nationalist-patriotic group intensified its opposition to territorial concessions. On 10 July, 52 people's deputies, including Baburin and Pavlov, sent an open letter to Yeltsin registering opposition to any territorial concessions to Japan. The letter threatened that the transfer of any islands to Japan "will bring about destructive results to the state" with the warning that territorial concessions to Japan would inevitably provoke territorial claims against Russia from other countries.[30]

The second meeting of the working group for a peace treaty was held on 15–16 July in Tokyo. As expected, discussions on the territorial issue were at complete cross purposes. The Japanese side insisted on Russia's recognition of Japanese sovereignty over the islands. The Russian side refused to grant any concessions, citing domestic difficulties.[31] In fact, the domestic situation in Russia was deteriorating precipitously. At the end of July reactionary opponents of the Kunadze option were joined by radical reformers interested in challenging Yeltsin's power. This force was led by Rumiantsev and Ambartsumov, who supported the conservatives' demand calling for hearings on the Kuril issue at the Committee for International Affairs and External Economic Relations. The lone protest by the Foreign Ministry was drowned out by the outcry of the coalition between the right and the left in parliament.[32]

---

30. *Mainichi Shimbun*, 11 July 1992 (evening ed.).

31. *Yomiuri Shimbun*, 17 July 1992; *Nihon Keizai Shimbun*, 19 July 1992.

32. Aleksei Zuichenko, "Vizit v Iaponii pod voprosom?" *Nezavisimaia gazeta*, 24 July 1992.

"Closed" hearings on the Kuril issue were held on 28 July. Essentially, four groups of opinions were expressed. The first group expressed the view that insofar as Russia was a law-abiding state and the Russian Federation had pledged to observe all treaties and agreements concluded by the Soviet Union, the only foundation on which Russia should conclude a peace treaty would be on the basis of the 1956 Joint Declaration. Kunadze presented the Foreign Ministry's view, and this position was supported by S. A. Filatov, First Deputy Chairman of the Supreme Soviet, who chaired the hearings, as well as most of the experts. The opposite pole was represented by nationalist-patriotic deputies, who heaped invectives upon Kunadze and opposed any transfer of the islands. Also two military representatives warned that any transfer of the Kuril islands would put the Russian defensive capability in the Pacific in jeopardy. The third group, represented by Ambartsumov and S. A. Mikhailov, chairman of the sub-committee on the Asia-Pacific Region of the Committee for International Affairs and External Economic Relations, raised objections to the immediate transfer of the two islands, which would not serve Russian national interests, although they were prepared to accept the 1956 Joint Declaration as a binding commitment. Ambartsumov was highly critical of Japan's attitude that amounted to blackmailing Russia on territory while refusing economic assistance. This group recommended the postponement of Yeltsin's trip, citing the lack of national consensus on the territorial issue. The fourth opinion was offered by representatives of the Kuril islanders themselves, who pleaded that whatever the outcome of the negotiations, the Russian government should take the islanders' interests into consideration.[33]

In the end, however, what was said at the hearings did not matter. The hearings were a political demonstration engineered by the opposition to the impending compromise the Foreign Ministry was working hard to reach with the Japanese government.[34] And it was Rumiantsev and Ambartsumov who were most responsible for staging this political demonstration in an attempt to flex the muscle of parliament vis-à-vis the executive branch.

During the hearings Rumiantsev published his own report on the Kuril issue. Developing detailed rebuttals against the Foreign Ministry's position in nine specific aspects, Rumiantsev assailed the ministry's position as capitulation to Japan's illegal and historically unfounded claims and betrayal of Russia's economic, political and geopolitical interests. As the solution to the territorial question, he explained that of all possible formula for territorial solution, his preferred solution would be what he called the 2+2+0 option:

---

33. "Rossiia-Iaponiia, a mezhdu nimi Kurily," *Rossiskaia gazeta*, 4 September 1992.

34. See Vladimir Vozhskii, "V etoi bor'be pobeditelei ne budet," *Nezavisimaia gazeta*, 25 July 1992.

Kunashiri and Etorofu to remain within the Russian jurisdiction, and Habomais and Shikotan to come under the joint sovereignty of Russia and Japan, while Japan should obtain no islands exclusively. Since there was no national consensus on the territorial question, however, Rumiantsev recommended the postponement of Yeltsin's trip.[35] After the hearings, Ambartsumov sent a recommendation to Yeltsin on behalf of the Committee for International Affairs and External Economic Relations that Yeltsin should postpone his trip to Japan.[36]

It is also important to understand that the Kuril issue was not merely a debate between the Yeltsin government and its opponents, but was also closely connected with the internal power struggle among Yeltsin's closest advisers. When Yeltsin's visit to Japan was announced, those who favoured the Kunadze option occupied the most influential position closest to Yeltsin. The ad hoc committee to prepare Yeltsin's visit was formed in May. The committee was headed by First Deputy Prime Minister Gennadii Burbulis, who was at the time the most powerful adviser to Yeltsin.[37] The Burbulis committee had submitted its recommendation that advocated the Kunadze option and it was rumoured to have been tentatively approved by Yeltsin by mid-July.[38] This explained in part the move on the part of Rumiantsev and Ambartsumov to hasten the parliamentary hearings. Confronted with a parliamentary revolt, Burbulis decided to send Information Vice-Minister Mikhail Poltoranin to Japan in the beginning of August to buttress its recommendation.[39]

Nevertheless, the power relations among Yeltsin's advisers had already changed by then. In May, Presidential adviser Iuri Petrov's influence suddenly grew stronger, overshadowing that of Burbulis. It was Petrov who played a major part in working out the details of the newly-formed Russian military. Around the same time, the Security Council was established. Coined as a new Politburo, the Security Council became the highest decision-making body in the Yeltsin government. Although Burbulis was a member of the Security Council, he was outnumbered by newly-

---

35. See O. G. Rumiantsev, *Rosshiisko-iaponskie otnosheniia i problema territorial'noi tselostnosti Rossiiskoi Federatsii: Deviat aspektov, Doklad*, Special Supplement, No. 2, Biulleten "Konstitutsionnyi Vestnik," (Moscow: Constitutional Commission of the Russian Federation, July 1992); also its shortened version, "Vopros o Kurilakh mozhet 'vzorvat' vsiu vneshniuiu politiku Rossii," *Nezavisimaia gazeta*, 25 July 1992; "Vopros o Kulilakh: argumentatsiia Olega Rumiantseva," *Nezavisimaia gazeta*, 26 July 1992.

36. *Nihon Keizai Shimbun*, 29 July 1992.

37. *Yomiuri Shimbun*, 23 May 1992. One of the most interesting aspects of this committee was that it excluded Valentin Fedorov, and included his rival Anatolii Aksenov as a representative from the Kuril islands.

38. Based on interview with a Japan specialist in Moscow, 5 September 1992.

39. *Asahi Shimbun*, 5, 6 August 1992.

emerging conservatives such as Council secretary Iuri Skokov, Vice-President Rutskoi, Defence Minister Grachev and Minister of Internal Affairs Viktor Barannikov.[40] It was in this context that the "Kuril issue" became the focal point of a power struggle between Petrov and Burbulis. Poltoranin's mission to Japan could be interpreted as Burbulis's attempt to regain influence by bypassing Petrov. Burbulis then submitted his final recommendation as the head of the Burbulis committee.

Yeltsin's acceptance of the Burbulis report would have meant Petrov's defeat. Thus, Petrov launched a counterattack. He had a secret session of the Security Council convened on 19 August, which was attended just by Gaidar, Grachev, Barannikov, Filatov and Skokov. Neither Burbulis nor Kozyrev was present. At this session it was pointed out that Japan's aid was smaller than that of other advanced countries and that the return of any islands would worsen the domestic political situation. On this basis the Security Council decided to overturn Burbulis' recommendations, and not to accept the return of any of the islands.[41]

On 22 August, Petrov flew to Tokyo. Presumably his trip had two aims. First, it was necessary to talk to Japanese officials to find out Japan's intentions for the purpose of examining the veracity of Burbulis' recommendations. There was another motive. It was rumoured that Yeltsin had already made up his mind to name Petrov as Kozyrev's successor as Minister of Foreign Affairs.[42] His Tokyo trip was therefore the first test of his diplomatic skill. In his meetings with Hisashi Owada of MOFA and Miyazawa, Petrov repeated the difficulty of making any territorial concession, and yet demanded greater economic aid from Japan. Both Owada and Miyazawa responded that Japan would stand firm on its demand for the return of all the islands, and that as long as Russia was not prepared to return the islands, Japanese economic aid to Russia would have its own limitation.[43] It is unlikely, however, that at this point Petrov was deliberating on the possibility of cancelling Yeltsin's visit to Japan. In fact, he stated that he hoped to make Yeltsin's visit a historically significant event. There is no reason to suspect that this was not his true intention, since the success of Yeltsin's trip to Japan on his terms, not its cancellation, would be essential to achieving his political ambition.

In the meantime, Yeltsin held a press conference at the Kremlin on 21 August. Asked about his trip to Japan, he complained bitterly that Japan's

40. *Asahi Shimbun*, 19 May 1992.

41. *Ibid.*, 26 August 1992.

42. Sergei Boguslavskii, "Daitôryô sokkin pâji no imbô [A Conspiracy to Purge the Presidential Advisers]," *AERA* 39 (29 September 1992), p. 17.

43. *Nihon Keizai Shimbun*, 25 and 26 August 1992.

aid was the smallest of all advanced nations, and in strong terms accused
Japan of adopting the principle of inseparability of politics and economics
by making Russia's territorial concessions the prerequisite of economic aid.
Asked about his approach to the territorial question, he stated: "I have at my
disposal twelve different proposals for the solution to this question. I will
reveal my option only on the second day of the summit in Tokyo."[44] Two
things were clear from his statement. First, at this point he did not entertain
the thought of cancelling his trip. Second, he intended to adopt one of these
twelve proposals depending on what Japan would offer at the negotiating
table, thus abandoning the Burbulis committee's recommendation. The
Kunadze option was in deep trouble.

Totally oblivious to these domestic developments, the Japanese
government formulated its final position. To various suggestions coming
from Russia along the Kunadze option, MOFA reacted with suspicion,
believing that they represented a concerted effort to force an agreement on
Japan without resolving the territorial question. MOFA wrongly concluded
that Yeltsin was already committed to the Kunadze option. But the Kunadze
option would leave the question of the sovereignty of Etorofu and Kunashiri
unresolved, and in their judgement, this was precisely the major point of
this proposal.[45] On the basis of this judgement, at the end of August the
government decided (1) to reject Russia's demand to conclude agreements
on investment protection and on economic cooperation, (2) to conclude 5–
10 agreements covering the prevention of maritime accidents, peaceful use
of the space, new opening of consular offices and expansion of cultural
exchanges, and (3) to issue a joint statement summarising the results of the
summit including progress on the territorial question. This decision was the
reaffirmation of the official position that Japan would tie its economic
cooperation to Russia's acceptance of Japanese sovereignty over the
northern territories, precisely the point that Yeltsin was trying to persuade
Japan to repudiate.[46] With this decision in hand Watanabe visited Moscow
from 29 August to 4 September to make last-minute arrangements for the
summit.

Watanabe and MOFA seemed to believe until the last moment that the bait
of Japan's economic cooperation would be enough to induce Yeltsin to
recognise sovereignty over the entire northern territories. It was obvious that
such a policy was not merely unacceptable to any Russian government; in
addition, such a crude formulation of economic cooperation and the
territorial issue would have made it impossible for even those who were

44. *Nihon Keizai Shimbun*, 22 August 1992.
45. *Nihon Keizai Shimbun*, 10 August 1992; *Asahi Shimbun*, 4 September 1992.
46. *Nihon Keizai Shimbun*, 26 August 1992.

most favourably disposed to Japan's position to accept it. Little wonder then that Watanabe's meetings with Kozyrev and Yeltsin were not merely unproductive, but also brief.

The first sign that Yeltsin's closest advisers were contemplating the possibility of cancelling his trip to Japan was protest raised by the secret service on 3 September that the Japanese authorities prohibited Yeltsin's bodyguards from bearing arms. The spokesman of the secret service stated that if their demands were not satisfied by the Japanese side, he would recommend the cancellation of the trip.[47] Since there was absolutely nothing in security procedures that was different from those that had been consistently followed for all visits of foreign heads of state to Japan including Presidents Bush and Gorbachev, it was clear that the issue of Yeltsin's security was merely a red herring that was raised to be exploited as a convenient excuse for the possible cancellation of the trip. On the night of 6 September Yeltsin appeared on a satellite program between Moscow and Japan (Nemuro and Niigata). His reference to the territorial question to the Japanese audience was unusually blunt. He stated that he had at his disposal fourteen proposals for the territorial question, thus adding two more than he had revealed at the news conference a week before, but he severely warned that whatever proposal he chose at the summit, the Japanese should not expect any part of the islands to be handed over to Japan during his visit.[48] But there was not a hint in his television appearance that a cancellation of the trip was a serious option. By this time the Russian advance party had already arrived in Tokyo. Both sides had made the final arrangements for Yeltsin's schedule. On 8 September a spokesman for the Russian government met a group of Japanese correspondents in Moscow and expressed the hope that Yeltsin's trip would serve as a starting point for further improvement.[49]

At 3 p.m. on 9 September Yeltsin was scheduled to hold a news conference on his forthcoming visit to Japan. When the scheduled time arrived, his press secretary Viacheslav Kostikov announced that the press conference was postponed until further notice. Obviously, something went wrong. As it turned out, the Security Council was called suddenly and it was there that the final decision to cancel Yeltsin's trip was made. Yeltsin immediately placed a call to Miyazawa. In what was described as a rancorous 35-minute conversation, Yeltsin not only cited the Russian domestic situation as the reason for the cancellation, but also blamed Japan

---

47. *Asahi Shimbun*, 4 September 1992.
48. *Ibid.*, 7 September 1992.
49. *Ibid.*, 9 September 1992 (evening ed.).

for connecting economic assistance with the territorial issue.[50] Finally, at 7 p.m. the press secretary announced that Yeltsin had decided to cancel his trip to Japan and South Korea, only four days before his scheduled departure.

Watanabe's last visit to Moscow must have provided a major impetus for the cancellation of Yeltsin's visit. The realisation that the Japanese side had not budged an inch to the last moment must finally have convinced Yeltsin of the futility of the trip. Nevertheless, the last minute drama leading to the cancellation may have been connected to the power struggle among Yeltsin's closest advisers. One version takes the view that the cancellation was a political move on the part of Skokov, Grachev, Barannikov and Evgenii Primakov (head of the KGB) against not only Burbulis but also Petrov. According to this version, with the decision to cancel the trip to Japan, Yeltsin shifted the power balance within his government decisively in favour of the military-industrial complex. The Kuril issue was thus used as a prelude to a major government shakeup to the right.[51]

Whatever the motive, the cancellation of Yeltsin's trip to Japan was a major setback in Russo-Japanese relations. It definitely shifted the relationship to a condition that is worse than the one that existed at Gorbachev's disastrous visit to Japan. It also made the resolution of the territorial dispute extremely unlikely. Rapprochement between Russia and Japan that had seemed within reach had again eluded both countries.

Prospects

In July 1992 in a short essay I wrote that the cancellation of Yeltsin's trip would be a reasonable option.[52] Cancellation could have served the interests of both countries, if both sides decided that the summit without agreement on the territorial issue would be counterproductive. Nevertheless, the timing of the decision and the manner in which Yeltsin presented this decision could not have been worse for the future prospect of Russo-Japanese relations. At first, Yeltsin cited Japan's inability to take sufficient measures to insure his security as the main reason for the cancellation. Later, he explained that the real reason was Japan's trying to buy the Russian territory with big yen. To this travesty, reminiscent of Soviet diplomacy in the days

---

50. *Asahi Shimbun*, 10 and 11 September 1992; Vera Kuznetsova and Sergei Parkhomenko, "Piatnadtsatyi variant resheniia Kuril'skoi problemy," *Nezavisimaia gazeta*, 10 September 1992.

51. Boguslavskii, "Daitôryô sokkin pâji," p. 17. Vera Kuznetsova also thinks that Skokov played a major role in the decision. See Vera Kuznetsova, "Iaponskie strasti prodolzhaiut sotriasat' Rossiiu," *Nezavisimaia gazeta*, 11 September 1992.

52. Hasegawa, "Hoppô ryôdo shôkôgun," p. 96.

of Andrei Gromyko, the Japanese government responded calmly, at least at the official level, maintaining that it did not intend to change its course despite the cancellation.[53] On the one hand, it is promising that Japan decided not to retaliate against this unprecedented diplomatic humiliation, although at the psychological level the sense of wounded pride is bound to manifest itself in various ways. Particularly significant is the damage this cancellation has inflicted on the popular perception of Russia as a whole and Yeltsin in particular. On the other hand, however, the Japanese government's refusal to change its course also has negative implications.

It is clear that the Russian domestic situation and the Japanese intransigent stand were the two major factors that caused the disaster in September. Obviously, the cancellation of the summit was Yeltsin's admission of the failure of his own foreign policy. But it was also a major setback for Japanese foreign policy. The Japanese government made a major error in strategy when it upped the ante in April 1992 by insisting on Russia's acceptance of "residual sovereignty" over the northern territory. It constantly underestimated the importance of domestic opposition to the Kunadze option, and did not lend an iota of support to the isolated political force that was most favourably disposed to Japan's position. Behind all these errors, there existed the northern territorial syndrome.

As long as Japan is unable to rid itself of the northern territorial syndrome, as long as Japan does not realise that rapprochement with Russia is in itself in Japan's interest, not a favour to give Russia, and as long as Japan takes the position that it is Russia's loss, not Japan's, to keep relations in a state of stalemate, it is unlikely that the territorial issue will see a final settlement, regardless of the domestic situation in Russia. It is clear, however, that the outside world is increasingly watching Japan's intransigence with irritation, and that it is beginning to treat Japan's northern territorial syndrome as a manifestation of the general malaise of Japanese foreign policy. In this sense the solution of the northern territorial issue is a litmus test for Japanese foreign policy itself.

---

53. *Asahi Shimbun*, 10 and 12 September 1992.

7

China and East Asia

Gary Klintworth

Sino-Russian relations were officially normalised on 16 May 1989 when Soviet party Secretary General Mikhail Gorbachev met Deng Xiaoping in Beijing. Their summit meeting came after almost three decades of tension and border clashes that had on several occasions threatened to erupt into war. According to Gerald Segal, what Gorbachev achieved was the most important shift in the strategic balance in Asia-Pacific since Sino-U.S. détente in 1972.[1] The great-power rivalry between China and Russia that had helped shape U.S. strategic policy in the 1970s was over: the Beijing summit had "ended the past and opened up the future," said Deng Xiaoping; Gorbachev's visit represented a "new starting point" in Sino-Soviet relations after "a tortuous course in the past" said President Yang Shangkun.[2]

The path to normalisation started in the late 1970s but was interrupted by the Soviet invasion of Afghanistan in 1979 and the Soviet-backed Vietnamese intervention in Cambodia in 1978–79. Both wars became key— but with hindsight transient—obstacles to normalised Sino-Russian relations. The way ahead was eased by the election of Ronald Reagan as U.S. president in 1980. Reagan's views on Taiwan prompted a reassessment by China of its place in the strategic triangle with the Soviet Union and the United States. Soviet President Leonid Brezhnev meanwhile carefully reassured Beijing in a speech at Tashkent in August 1982 that the Soviet Union recognised Beijing as the sole legal government of China and that Taiwan was an integral part of one China.

---

1. Gerald Segal, *The Soviet Union and the Pacific* (London: Unwin Hyman, 1990), p. 193.
2. Xinhua, Beijing, 18 and 16 May 1989 respectively.

As well as reassurances from Moscow on the Taiwan issue, China reassessed the nature and likely outcome of the wars in Afghanistan and Cambodia. Afghanistan was seen to be a problem more for the West than for China and, in any case, Chinese military analysts had concluded that it would do to the Soviet economy what Vietnam had done to the U.S. From Beijing's perspective, the Soviet withdrawal from Afghanistan was a foregone conclusion. So too in Cambodia where the Vietnamese had commenced withdrawing military forces in 1982–83 and promised to be out of the country altogether by 1990.

Ideological differences between Moscow and Beijing had begun to dissipate with the death of Mao Zedong in 1976. When Mikhail Gorbachev became general secretary of the Communist Party of the Soviet Union (CPSU) in March 1985, he took the Soviet Union down the reformist route that Deng Xiaoping had taken China a decade before. There had moreover been no clashes or incidents on the Sino-Soviet border for several years.[3] The last border alert was in 1979 when China attacked Vietnam, the Soviet Union's Asian ally. In other words, by the mid-1980s, China and the Soviet Union were more than ready for the summit meeting that took place between Mikhail Gorbachev and Deng Xiaoping in Beijing in May 1989.[4]

The joint communiqué issued after the summit (see Appendix 7.1) declared that the meetings on 15–18 May 1989 between Mikhail Gorbachev and Chinese leaders, including Deng Xiaoping, "symbolised the normalisation of relations between the two countries." The two sides stated that their relationship in future would be based on the five principles of peaceful coexistence which were "the universal principles guiding state-to-state relations." Both supported the peaceful resolution of disputes. In a reference to China's deep-seated concern about containment and encirclement by the Soviet Union—or any other great power—the two sides undertook not to "use or threaten to use arms against the other by any means, including the use of territorial land, water, or air space of a third country bordering on the other side."

China's sensitivity on this issue was manifested in the attention given to the Cambodian issue in the joint communiqué. Soviet agreement that Vietnam should withdraw "completely" from Cambodia and that Cambodia should be "independent, peaceful, neutral and non-aligned" indicates Soviet

---

3. In fact, despite confrontations, such as occurred in 1969, Russia is the only great power not to have fought a war with China; Vladimir Miasnikov, "Soviet-Chinese Relations: Historical Experience," seminar paper, Canberra, July 1989.

4. For background and details of the normalisation process, see Gary Klintworth, "Gorbachev's China Diplomacy," in Ramesh Thakur and Carlyle A. Thayer, eds., *The Soviet Union as an Asian Pacific Power* (Boulder: Westview, 1987), p. 39.

acceptance of China's claim to keep it and all other foreign powers out of Indochina. In this regard, the joint communiqué added that neither side would seek hegemony of any form in the Asian-Pacific region or other parts of the world.

The two sides agreed moreover to cut their military forces on the border "to a minimum level commensurate with normal, good neighbourly relations." The Soviet Union simultaneously announced the withdrawal of its forces from Mongolia. Both sides agreed to settle the boundary question in a "fair and reasonable manner in accordance with international law and a spirit of mutual understanding and accommodation."

Moscow reassured Beijing on the one-China issue while Beijing undertook not to join the United States in any form of anti-Soviet alliance. It was Soviet concern about the China-U.S. military relationship in the 1970s that led the Soviets into Vietnam in an attempt to break out of the hostile ring they saw encircling them, while it was President Reagan's ambiguity about Taiwan that helped China to decide not to side with the U.S. against the Soviet Union.

Moscow-Beijing Détente

The impact of Sino-Soviet détente on Russian and Chinese society was indirect but nonetheless profound. One can surmise, for example, that the decline in external threat perceptions in the 1980s removed one of the pillars underpinning authoritarianism in both Beijing and Moscow. In China's case, this contributed to the events that culminated in the Tiananmen Square massacre in Beijing in June 1989. Paradoxically, Gorbachev's physical presence in Beijing in May 1989, Chinese student admiration for his liberalism and demands that Zhao Ziyang—the Chinese Gorbachev—should follow the same course, fuelled the political crisis in Beijing that led to the killings at Tiananmen.

Today the relationship is as might be expected between two large neighbouring nuclear-armed states with complementary economies, faced with urgent reconstruction and reform priorities at home, a shortage of foreign exchange and an absence of major political or strategic differences.

China is familiar with Soviet-Russian technology and it is available at a lower political and financial cost than from Japan or the West.[5] China is also accustomed to dealing with Russians. Many of China's top leaders such as

---

5. The Chinese and Russian Academies of Science signed a second five-year agreement for cooperation over 1991–95 in ecology, microelectronics, magnetic fluid-electric generation, organic matter oxidation, laser technology, plasma, geotectology and plant physiology: Xinhua, Moscow, 9 May 1990.

Premier Li Peng, party Secretary General Jiang Zemin, Foreign Minister Qian Qichen and vice chairman of the Military Commission Liu Huaqing all served time in Moscow and speak Russian.

On 23–26 April 1990 Premier Li Peng took a comprehensive team of military and economic advisers to Moscow. They signed several agreements with the USSR, including long-term economic, scientific and technological cooperation in areas that included fuel and power, metallurgy, transport, communications, agriculture, electronics, forestry, health and environmental protection and peaceful uses of outer space. China and the USSR agreed on the mutual reduction of military forces on the Sino-Soviet border and "guiding principles for enhancing trust in the military fields"—confidence building measures—including regular military exchanges. There were to be regular consultations at foreign minister level; and continued negotiations for "a just and reasonable solution to the border issue left over by history."[6] Under the terms of a border agreement signed during Li Peng's visit, both sides undertook to "reduce their military forces to the lowest level suited to normal good neighbourly relations between the two countries on an equal basis for mutual security."[7]

In June 1990 Liu Huaqing, a vice chairman of the Chinese Central Military Commission, went to Moscow: the most senior Chinese military leader to do so since the 1950s. He was accompanied by Major General Shen Rongjun, Vice Minister of the Commission of Science, Technology and Industry for National Defence; Lin Zongtang, Minister of Aerospace Industry; and Li Lanqing, Vice Minister of Foreign Economic Relations and Trade.[8] Liu and Soviet chief of staff Mikhail Moiseev said they had agreed on the principles for establishing military economic relations.[9] Moiseev said that China and the Soviet Union had also agreed on one main point: "we must forget past injury and build our relations on a new basis."[10]

Another high-level military exchange occurred in May 1991 with the visit to Beijing of the Soviet Defence Minister Dmitrii Yazov. China and the USSR formally acknowledged that they no longer perceived a threat from each other.[11] In August 1992, Russian Defence Minister Pavel Grachev met Chinese Defence Minister Qin Qiwei in Moscow to reaffirm that military-to-military exchanges and undertakings given by the USSR would be honoured by Russia.[12] They also discussed military cooperation, arms sales

6. Xinhua, Moscow, 27 April 1990.
7. Xinhua, Moscow, 26 April 1990.
8. Xinhua, Beijing, 15 June 1990.
9. Xinhua, Moscow, 7 June 1990.
10. Reuter, Moscow, 4 June 1990.
11. *SCMP*, 12 May 1991.
12. Reuter, Moscow, 25 August 1992; TASS, Moscow, 25 August 1992.

(including SU-27 fighter aircraft) and further troop reductions along the border.[13]

Demilitarisation and demarcation of a long-disputed border and agreement on a posture of non-provocative defence have been integral to a new Sino-Russian relationship. While the precise details on border force reductions have not been revealed, Russia has been steadily cutting troop levels and closing weapons plants near China. Mikhail Gorbachev announced a unilateral cut of 120,000 in May 1989. Troop levels of about 270,000 have been reduced to around 150,000.[14] Six rounds of talks have been held so far with more to come, and with most withdrawals being made by Russia. Another 60,000 troops from the Commonwealth of Independent States (CIS) were to be withdrawn in 1992, along with "thousands of tanks and artillery pieces and 350 combat aircraft and helicopters" said CIS chief of staff General Viktor Samsanov.[15] All Soviet troops in Mongolia—first deployed in 1966—were withdrawn in 1989.

A treaty was signed in March 1992 demarcating the more difficult eastern sector (with the exception of Heixiazi, near Khabarovsk). Russia gave China Damanski island (Chenpao in Chinese), a small island of 1 km^2 that was the focal point of vicious fighting along the Ussuri (Wusuli) river in 1969. Most of the border has now been demarcated and representatives from Russia, Tajikistan, Kazakhstan and Turkmenistan are meeting with the Chinese to resolve the remaining relatively minor areas in dispute in the west. These are remarkable achievements given the history of Sino-Soviet relations.

Détente has enabled Beijing and Moscow to work together in the UN Security Council. They liaise on issues such as Iraq, the Gulf War and the UN, the future role of the U.S., Taiwan, Afghanistan, nuclear proliferation in the Korean peninsula, regional stability and a solution for Cambodia. Both have joined the ASEAN (Association of South-East Asian Nations) post-ministerial conference as dialogue partners. Chinese Foreign Minister Qian Qichen and his Soviet counterpart Eduard Shevardnadze met regularly to discuss Cambodia: both sides agreed to stop supplying weapons to the warring factions and the Phnom Penh government and to support a comprehensive solution in Cambodia.[16] They agreed to "hold regular

---

13. *Jane's Defence Weekly*, 5 September 1992, p. 24.

14. Aleksei Zagorskii, "Russian Security Policy in Asia-Pacific: From USSR to CIS," Paper presented to the conference on Pacific Security Relations After the Cold War, Hong Kong, June 1992.

15. Reuter, Moscow, 27 February 1992.

16. Xinhua, Harbin, 3 September 1990.

consultations about Asia-Pacific regional issues, especially about promoting the settlement of conflicts in Asia."[17]

On the Gulf issue, Beijing and Moscow expressed a preference for avoiding the use of force, reflecting their concern about unbridled American military supremacy and its dominance of the security agenda at the UN. Both states supported the UN process and the role of international law. Both came out in opposition to Iraq's invasion of Kuwait and called on Iraq to withdraw its troops from Kuwait without preconditions. But Qian Qichen said that both China and the USSR insisted that the dispute should be settled through political and peaceful means within the scope of the UN Security Council resolutions and the use of force should be avoided. They did not, he said, agree with the view of "some countries" that a settlement could be reached only through the use of military force.[18]

Party Secretary General Jiang Zemin visited Moscow from 15 to 19 May 1991, the most senior Chinese leader to do so since 1957. The joint communiqué issued on 19 May acknowledged the unique economic complementarity of the two economies and the "remarkable potential" for economic cooperation. It noted with "satisfaction that thanks to their joint efforts, friendly and cooperative relations between the two countries in the political, economic, trade, scientific and technological, cultural, military and other fields were developing steadily."[19] Looking to the future, the communiqué promised that new ways would be sought to deepen economic cooperation, including with third parties like South Korea and Japan.

Trade between China and the former Soviet Union (FSU) has shown a steady rise since 1980 (Table 7.1). Trade between Xinjiang and the Central Asian Republics has doubled every year since 1986. Since April 1989, enterprises and companies in China and the FSU have had the right to import and export directly. The Soviet Union became China's fifth-largest trading partner by 1991 (after Hong Kong, Japan, the U.S. and Germany). China on the other hand was the USSR's twelfth-largest trading partner in 1991. Total trade in 1992 is estimated to be worth US $5 bn. Moscow has also been able to open up trade relations and commercial contacts with Hong Kong and Taiwan, both previously off-limits to the Soviet Union.[20] Taiwan

---

17. Xinhua, Harbin, 3 September 1990.

18. Xinhua, Harbin, 3 September 1990 and *SCMP*, 2 September 1990.

19. *Beijing Review*, 27 May–2 June 1991, p. 13.

20. Moscow has been circumspect in its approaches to Taiwan, to the point of checking its dealings with Taipei with the Chinese embassy in Moscow. Soviet relations with China had a difficult and controversial history: "they are of such tremendous importance to us that we have to be very cautious and reasonable and we must abstain from any interference in their affairs;" Eugene Bazhanov, Diplomatic Academy, Russian Foreign Ministry, interview, Canberra, April 1992. But Boris Yeltsin's Russia seems much less inhibited, with reports that it would be

was ranked 48th amongst the USSR's trading partners in 1991, after being 56th in 1990. Trade with Hong Kong has shown a steady increase. The colony was ranked 36th amongst the USSR's trading partners in 1991, up from being 42nd in 1990.

China and Russia are natural trading partners. China has a comparative advantage and excess capacity in light industrial technologies while Russia has the heavy industrial and military technology that China needs. Russia wants Chinese cooperation in food production and light industries. China wants to tap Russia's skills in power generation, aircraft technology, biological engineering, and basic scientific research. It is looking to recruit Russian scientists and other specialist personnel.

China exports goods hard to get in Russia such as fresh fruit, meat products, edible oil, vegetables, soya beans and maize (8m tonnes in 1988), building materials, light industrial goods such as car batteries (400,000 in 1988), photocopiers, telephones, electronic parts, computers and software, textile plant and processing equipment, non-ferrous metal ores and various rather ordinary consumer goods in oversupply in China (such as clothing, shoes, furniture, stationery) and household electrical items (such as television sets and radios). Leading Chinese imports from Russia include transport aircraft, aircraft engines, chemical fertilisers, industrial chemicals,

TABLE 7.1: Soviet Trade with China, Taiwan and Hong Kong, 1980–91 (US $m)

Year	China's		Taiwan's		Hong Kong's	
	Exports	Imports	Exports	Imports	Exports	Imports
1980	228.30	264.10	0	0	14.9	36.2
1981	122.60	154.00	0	0	18.1	44.9
1982	142.50	243.10	0	0	23.4	38.8
1983	319.10	440.70	0	0	21.8	61.9
1984	585.10	670.10	0	0	40.7	39.5
1985	1937.30	1916.50	0	0	72.8	47.7
1986	1229.90	1472.10	0	0	42.0	55.3
1987	1247.10	1290.50	0	0	38.4	94.8
1988	1475.70	1801.80	0	7.86	54.3	128.1
1989	1849.30	2146.70	20.50	55.07	103.6	96.8
1990	2047.90	2212.80	59.17	59.35	124.6	90.0
1991	1860.40	2108.90	67.15	70.06	217.5	49.6

SOURCE: IMF international trade data.

willing to sell Russian military aircraft and other equipment to any country, including Taiwan. "As long as anyone can afford the prices, we have no reason not to sell," said Russian Admiral Vladimir Sidorov on a visit to Taipei; *Free China Journal*, 26 June 1992.

nuclear and thermal power generators, aluminium, copper, tungsten, machine building products, cement, timber, motor vehicles (22,000 motor cars and lorries in 1988), gasoline, rubber products, aquatic products, freight wagons (2000 in 1988), trains (12 electric locomotives in 1988), steel, pig iron (450,000 tonnes in 1988), coal (30,000 tonnes were shipped up the Amur River in 1989) and oil (300,000 tonnes in 1988).[21]

The problem in Sino-Russian relations is no longer political. It is, rather, infrastructural, with a primitive transport system incapable of handling the rapid expansion of border trade. The result has been a huge backlog of freight and a rush to build new river ports, highway border crossing points, ferry crossings, bridges, new direct road routes through the Mongolias, new bus routes and telecommunication links.

Chinese ships can now use the Heilong and Songhua Rivers to transit Russian territory to reach the Pacific Ocean. Harbin is to be developed as an inland port and joint container shipping centre. New air links have been established between major cities such as Irkutsk and Shenyang; Moscow and Beijing; Alma-Ata and Urumqi; and Khabarovsk and Harbin. In addition, agreements signed in 1990 have opened up air corridors across China and the FSU cutting flight time and giving greater freight capacity from Hong Kong to Europe.[22] New rail links between Alma-Ata and Urumqi open up the possibility of uninterrupted rail travel from Rotterdam across Europe, Central Asia, China's northwest and central plains to the Chinese eastern port city of Lianyungang in Jiangsu Province. Provided there is enough injection of Japanese and South Korean capital, Sino-Russian cooperation with North Korea on the Tumen River project could eventually see rail links between Europe and a multinational Asian terminus centred on Russia's Vladivostok, Chongjin in Korea and Hunchun in China.[23]

One of the most important areas of Sino-Russian cooperation has been in nuclear, thermal and hydroelectric power generation. High voltage power grids are being built to supply hydroelectricity generated on the Amur/Ussuri river to consumers in China's industrial northeast. There are plans for a chain of seven new hydroelectric power stations on the Amur River to meet China's huge demand and coincidentally contribute to the integration of China's Northeast with the Russian Far East. Russia is

---

21. TASS in BBC Monitoring Service, 9 June 1989.

22. *SCMP*, 6 May 1990.

23. See "A Rotterdam in the Orient in the Making," *Beijing Review*, 35(16) 20–26 April 1992, p. 5; and generally Peter Rimmer, "Ports, Inland Transport Linkages and Regional Development: A Western Pacific Rim Conspectus" in Korea Maritime Institute, *The Public Sector's Role in Logistics for the 21st Century* (Seoul: Korea Maritime Institute, The 2nd KMI International Symposium, 2–7 July 1990) pp. 259–312.

building a nuclear power plant in Shenyang, in Liaoning Province, a nuclear reactor in Anhui and coal-fired heat and power stations elsewhere in China's northeast in exchange for Chinese goods. Russia and China are cooperating in oil exploration in Central Asia and in building pipelines to transport liquefied coal from fields in Shanxi Province to nearby power stations.

The Russian Far East has rich resources but suffers from a shortage of labour. With a population of just 7.2m in an area of 6.22m km^2, it needs at least 200,000 labourers to develop a viable timber industry.[24] China meanwhile has abundant labour but lacks natural resources like timber. Détente has enabled the two sides to set in motion a grand scheme first envisaged in the 1950s to exploit the comparative advantages of two complementary, neighbouring economic regions.[25] There are now over 30,000 Chinese workers in the Russian Far East engaged in building houses, logging Russian forests, growing vegetables, assembling refrigerators and diesel engines, building roads and repairing railways.

China is helping convert Russian factories from weapons production to the manufacture of consumer goods. A tank repair plant near Chita on the border with China is being converted into a passenger car factory with the help of Chinese engineers.[26] China is building a VCR plant in Zelenogorsk near Moscow and modernising a Russian tractor factory near Krasnoyarsk. Russian technicians meanwhile are renovating Soviet-built industrial plants like the Baotou steel plant, the fifth biggest in China.

There is scope for cooperation in textile processing, a labour intensive industry. Russia is one of the world's largest producers of cotton, flax and chemical fibres. China has a rapidly expanding textile processing industry that supplies 7 percent of the world market.[27] It is eager to import Russian raw materials for re-export as clothes or textiles either back to Russia or to markets in Europe and North America. It plans to set up a flax processing factory, a silk processing factory and cooperative ventures in cotton spinning in Baotou in Inner Mongolia using Russian materials.[28]

There has clearly been a rapid growth in the size and diversity of Sino-Russian trade, scientific cooperation, contracts, service agreements, joint

---

24. *China Daily*, Beijing, 2 September 1989 and Xinhua, Beijing, 19 August 1990.

25. Allen Whiting, *Siberian Development and East Asia, Threat or Promise* (Stanford: Stanford University Press, 1981), p. 178.

26. BBC Monitoring Service, 8 May 1992.

27. Kym Anderson, *Textiles and Clothing in Global Economic Development: East Asia's Dynamic Role* (Canberra: Australian National University, Pacific Economic Papers, No 206, April 1992), p. 18.

28. Xinhua, Beijing, 6 July 1989.

ventures, shipping and shopping agreements,[29] barter arrangements and resource sharing. This has been matched by agreements on double taxation, investment protection and other legal and financial matters. New consulates have been opened in Shenyang and Khabarovsk.

Problems and Concerns

Not all was sweetness and light however. There were uncertainties subsequently with the fragmentation of the Soviet Union, the formation of independent Central Asian Republics and the collapse of the CPSU. China also expressed concern about the disposal of nuclear weapons in the former Soviet Union. Li Peng said on 11 December 1991 that China was worried by the "great chaos" in the Soviet Union and that the situation there was unpredictable.[30] China in fact offered US $730m in food credits to the USSR in 1991 to try and prop up the CPSU.

The collapse of the CPSU fuelled new concern in China about its northern neighbour. Independence for the Soviet Union's Central Asian Republics and Mongolia stimulated concern about separatist movements in China's inner Asian frontiers, long a troublesome region because of secessionist sentiment and anti-Han demonstrations (see Map). Ethnic minorities particularly in Xinjiang and Tibet have a long history of unrest and have been a cause of tension and suspicion between China and the FSU. The newly-independent Muslim republics in Central Asia are suspected of being even more inclined to seize the Muslim chunks of Xinjiang. China's Turkic speaking minorities include 8.4m Muslims in the northwest, mostly Uighurs (7.2m), Kazakhs (1.1m) and Kirgizs (140,000).[31] Adjacent to Mongolia's population of 2m are around 4.8m ethnic Mongolians in China's Inner Mongolia Autonomous Region and its neighbouring provinces.[32] There are also 4m Tibetans.

China's relations with the newly-independent Muslim states in Central Asia seem to have stabilised however. China has diplomatic relations with Kazakhstan, Uzbekistan, Kirgizstan, Turkmenistan and Tajikistan and has offered them financial credits and technical assistance. A second option has been to send military reinforcements to Xinjiang to crush any signs of separatism on the Chinese side of the border.

---

29. Shanghai's Hualian retail shopping group plans to open retail stores in St Petersburg, Vladivostok and Khabarovsk.

30. *South China Morning Post (SCMP)*, 13 December 1991.

31. *Research Paper on China's Minorities* (Taipei: National Chengchi University, 1991), pp. 4–6.

32. *Ibid.*

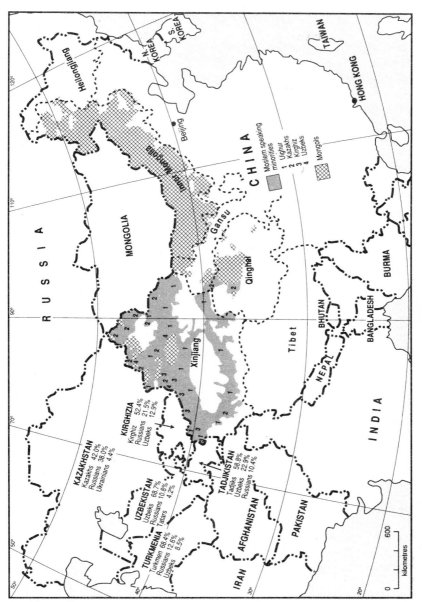

China's Inner Asian Frontiers and the Muslim Republics

Another worrying consequence of the collapse of communism in Eastern Europe was the conclusion—not least in China—that Chinese communism might be next.[33] The credibility and relevance of communism in Asia was under attack both internationally and domestically. While one Cold War may have ended, China emerged as the new target of the pro-democratic anti-communist forces in the Western world.[34]

The collapse of the Soviet Union almost immediately weakened China's strategic value to the U.S. Together with the impact of the Tiananmen massacre, it led the U.S. to cut off its military relationship with Beijing and reassess its relationship with Taiwan. The shift in U.S. strategic priorities in relation to the two Chinas was reflected starkly in the decision by President George Bush to sell the Taiwanese 150 General Dynamics F-16 fighter aircraft. The U.S. had previously refused to approve the sale of such a modern fighter aircraft and had, on the contrary, engaged in supplying China with fighter aircraft avionics and naval technology so as to bolster the defences of the People's Liberation Army (PLA) against a southward thrust by the Soviet Pacific Fleet. With no Soviet threat to worry about, the U.S. finds it has less need of China.

China's relative decline is reflected in criticism of China by the West, especially the U.S., over human rights, Tibet, prison labour, arms exports, and for being the last bastion of anti-democratic communism. The Soviet factor had shielded China from such criticism in the past. China believes that the collapse of the USSR has left the U.S. in too powerful a position. These perceptions have led to what U.S. Secretary of State Lawrence Eagleburger has described as the prospectively "rough patch ahead" in Sino-U.S. relations.[35]

---

33. There are however key differences between Soviet and Chinese communism. Soviet communism was in place for 70 years while in China it has only had a life of 40 years; China has the overseas Chinese as well as the visible example and influence of Taiwan and Hong Kong; China, with Deng Xiaoping in charge, started on the road to economic reform in 1979 (if not in the 1960s) and had phenomenal success once agriculture was privatised whereas Gorbachev started with political reform without a sound economic base; China is a more homogeneous society than the USSR with most Chinese believing in the notion of one China; Beijing was not confronted by the West as the Soviet Union was by NATO and Radio Free Europe—indeed, the West helped China against the Soviet Union; and China's history was one that accepted authoritarianism. For the rural hundreds of millions of Chinese, good government is synonymous with enough to eat—which they got from Deng Xiaoping—and not a free media or free elections. China's economic growth has been in the double digits whereas Soviet/Russian growth has been negative. For a discussion, see Peter Ferdinand, "Russian and Soviet Shadows over China's Future?" *International Affairs* 68 (April 1992), pp. 279–92.

34. According to a Chinese central government document cited in the *International Herald Tribune,* 22 April 1992.

35. USIS Wireless File, EPF502, 4 September 1992.

TABLE 7.2: China's Trade with the United States and Japan, 1980–91 (US $m)

Year	U.S.		Japan's	
	Exports to China	Imports from China	Exports to China	Imports from China
1980	3755.00	1164.40	5168.90	4032.20
1981	3602.70	2062.40	6183.00	4746.60
1982	2912.00	2502.40	3901.70	4806.40
1983	2173.20	2476.80	5495.20	4517.00
1984	3004.30	3381.40	8056.90	5155.00
1985	3955.70	4224.20	15178.40	6091.40
1986	3106.30	5240.60	12463.20	5078.60
1987	3497.30	6910.40	10087.20	6391.80
1988	5016.80	9261.30	11062.10	8046.40
1989	5807.40	12901.00	10533.90	8394.70
1990	4807.20	16295.80	7655.90	9210.40
1991	6287.10	20305.10	10078.50	10264.80

SOURCE: IMF international trade data.

Still, China has no Soviet card to play, while at the same time it needs the U.S. as a source of foreign exchange, an export market vital to the Chinese economy and a source of technology. China's state sector is virtually bankrupt so new employment opportunities and the current annual economic growth rate of 12 percent are heavily dependent on exports to the United States from labour-intensive light industries in southern China. More than a quarter of Chinese exports of around US $72 bn in 1991 went to the U.S. China has had a steadily widening trade surplus with the U.S. since 1983, with a record US $14 bn in 1991 (Table 7.2). The U.S. moreover still commands Chinese respect as the world's supreme military power, especially after the Gulf War. China may thus be forced to swallow its pride and accept that the West is going to be more critical and that reunification with Taiwan will not be on terms dictated by the mainland.

Benefits of Détente

Despite these negative consequences, Sino-Soviet détente has brought many positive consequences from Beijing's viewpoint. A list might include the following:

1. Rapprochement with the Soviet Union and later Russia occurred on Chinese terms: that is, an end to the Soviet encirclement strategy in Afghanistan, Vietnam, Mongolia and the Far East.

2. The Soviet Union accepted the Chinese position on Cambodia and withdrew its support for Vietnam. Like the U.S. and the French before

them, the Russians have thus departed from China's doorstep leaving small neighbours to deal with China as best they can. Countries like Vietnam and Mongolia can no longer afford to ignore China's claims to dominant regional influence. Hanoi has promised not to re-intervene in Cambodia and it replaced the outspoken Nguyen Co Thach with a foreign minister more amenable to Beijing. Mongolia used to depend on the USSR for fuel but now barters copper and wool for oil from China.

3. The withdrawal of the Soviet Union from Indochina consolidated China's historical ascendancy as a rejuvenated "Middle Kingdom" in Asia-Pacific. For the first time in nearly two centuries, China is no longer threatened by a European or Asian power. Russia, the U.S. and Japan know that China is prepared to go to war when the stakes are high enough. The U.S. fought China in Korea and indirectly in Vietnam while China was prepared for war with the USSR over Vietnam in 1979. China is thus relatively confident about its great-power status and relaxed about its security environment.

4. The absence of a threat from the north gave China more leeway to concentrate on domestic economic reform. China was able to keep defence expenditure under restraint for the decade 1980–90 (Table 7.3). No increases in real terms occurred until 1990 and these were insufficient to bring the level of expenditure back to what it had been in 1980.[36]

5. China was able to revise and rationalise its defence strategy—rather than fighting a destructive "people's war" defensively inside Chinese territory, the PLA moved to develop the capability to project military force beyond China's borders and protect the maritime approaches to the mainland, particularly in the South.

TABLE 7.3: China's Military Expenditure, 1981–92
(US $m at 1988 Prices and Exchange Rates)

1981	1982	1983	1984	1985	1986	1987	1988	1989	1990	1991	1992
7600	7800	7700	7600	7200	7100	6800	6900	5800	6400	6003	6700

SOURCES: *SIPRI Yearbook 1991* (New York: Oxford University Press, 1991), pp. 157,169–73; and Wang Bingqian's Report on the State Budget, *FBIS China*, 10 April 1992, p. 1.

---

36. Chinese defence spending declined from the late 1970s, to the late 1980s. According to a 1988 CIA report, China's military operating budget declined by about one-fifth from the previous eight years, while defence expenditure as a share of total government expenditures dropped from one-third to one-fifth in 1987; and defence as a percentage of GNP fell from 12 percent to 5 percent over the same period; Richard A. Bitzinger, *Chinese Arms Production and Sales to the Third World* (Santa Monica, CA: RAND Note N-3334-USDP, 1991), p. 25.

6. Access to sophisticated military technology, particularly fighter aircraft, is one of the most important benefits gained. China's military aircraft industries have been struggling to develop new generation fighters from designs developed in the Soviet Union in the 1950s and 1960s.[37] China is reported to have acquired 24 SU-27 aircraft, with another 14 to follow, at a price of US $25m each. With the SU-27, China is getting a long range combat aircraft with a multirole capability well beyond anything in its present air force inventory. Chinese defence experts have shown an interest in, and the Russians are more than keen to sell, other modern weapons platforms, including the T-72 tank, anti-missile missiles, TU-22M Backfire bombers and the SU-24 (a variable geometry, long range, large payload strike aircraft like the F/B-111), the MIG-29 (comparable, if not superior to, the F-16) and the MIG-31 fighter aircraft.[38] If acquired, each of these items would provide a quantum leap in China's military technology and, once deployed, an upgrading of China's defence capabilities.[39] Acquisition of just a few Backfire bombers (range 4,000 km or more) would boost China's ability to project military power in the Western Pacific.[40]

7. As well as military technology, China has found an alternative to the West for the supply of relatively modern heavy industrial technology, again without the need to spend foreign exchange. Over 95 percent of Sino-Russian trade is done by barter using Swiss francs as the medium of exchange. For example in 1992 China bartered 500 railway wagons full of

---

37. For a detailed discussion see Harlan W. Jencks, *Some Political and Military Implications of Soviet Warplane Sales to the PRC* (Kaohsiung: Sun Yat-Sen Centre for Policy Studies, SCPS Paper No 6, April 1991).

38. *Flight International,* 26 February 1992; and Tai Ming Cheung "Loaded Weapons," *Far Eastern Economic Review,* 3 September 1992, p. 21. One should note that China's practice has been to avoid becoming dependent on imported military technology. China preferred to obtain a few samples plus the technical blueprints so that it could manufacture the weapons in China. Reports of large-scale Chinese purchases of Russian aircraft and missiles and their subsequent operational deployment should therefore be treated with caution.

39. Some reports suggest Russia and China might cooperate in the assembly of MIG-29s or MIG-31s in China. TASS, Moscow, 25 August 1992, reported that in the first high-level Sino-Russian (as distinct from Sino-Soviet) military talks, China's Defence Minister Qin Qiwei and Russian Defence Minister Pavel Grachev agreed in Moscow on further arms cuts on their border, military scientific cooperation and the possibility of Russian aircraft technology sales to China.

40. One should however be wary about giving uncritical credence to every newspaper report about Russian arms sales to China. The Russians have no intention of creating a "military monster" on their back-door or in Asia, said Egor Rogachev, Russian ambassador to China; interview, Beijing, 21 October 1992. Besides, the PLA is being squeezed for funds and could not afford all the things it was reported to be looking at, said Senior Colonel Pan Zhenqiang, Deputy Director, Institute for Strategic Studies, National Defence University, Beijing; interview, 20 October 1992.

light industrial goods for four TU-154M passenger jets in a deal worth US $321m.[41]

8. Russia and the other members of the CIS provide a growing new market for exports of light manufactured goods in oversupply in China.

9. The possibilities for economic cooperation with Russia, particularly in the supply of energy, timber and industrial raw materials, in exchange for items in which China has a comparative advantage, look very promising indeed.

10. The collapse of the Soviet Union was a shock but it also had useful lessons for China. Chinese leaders were assured that even if Tiananmen was the wrong result, China's demographic, economic and political circumstances could not permit political pluralism. But while the collapse of the Soviet Union politically and economically reinforced confidence that tight political control was essential in China, it also underlined the need for continued reform, that is, the transformation of communism implicit in the open door policy and the development of "socialism with Chinese characteristics."

11. After the civil unrest and the bread queues that followed the collapse of the CPSU, the Chinese on the mainland and governments in Taiwan and Japan agreed that overthrowing communism in China was not a desirable outcome. Fear of Soviet-like chaos therefore has propped up the authority of the Chinese Communist Party both within China and in the Asian part of the Asian-Pacific region. This has led Taiwan, South Korea and Japan, among others, to choose economic-based policies that work with rather than against Beijing in order to bring about the gradual transformation of communism on the mainland.[42]

12. Currently the most advantageous position in the lesser triangle between China, Japan and Russia is held by Beijing. Yeltsin visited Beijing in December after the 14th Party Congress of the Chinese Communist Party, whereas he abruptly cancelled his visit to Japan that had been scheduled for September 1992.

Regional Effects of Sino-Russian Rapprochement

Sino-Russian relations have progressed full circle. In the past, the degree of tension in Sino-Soviet relations was an important factor in the strategic analysis of security planners throughout the Asian-Pacific region. Sino-

---

41. Reuter, 29 July 1992. Xinhua, Urumqi, 3 November 1989 reported an exchange of 160 Xinjiang camels for 400 goats, 38 oxen, 38 horses, and 20 foxes from the FSU.

42. This is one of the reasons why Mao Zedong launched the Cultural Revolution, that is to resist "sugar-coated bullets."

Soviet rivalry contributed to the suspicious state of Sino-Indian relations, China's alliance with Pakistan, the deadlocked Cold War in the Korean peninsula and the leverage of North Korea vis-à-vis its two communist neighbours. It ensured the tightness of the Japanese-U.S. security relationship and the forward posture of U.S. military units in the Western Pacific. It led to the Soviet naval presence in Cam Ranh Bay and China's hostility towards Vietnam. It was the basis for American military technology transfers to China and Western deference to China over Hong Kong and Taiwan. In particular, the Soviet factor gave focus to the threat perceptions that China found it shared with the U.S. and the non-communist states of Asia-Pacific: it provided a bridge for China to develop closer relations with the ASEAN states, the U.S., Australia and Japan.

Not surprisingly, therefore, there have been important region-wide security and economic benefits flowing from the end of the Sino-Soviet Cold War. It contributed directly to tension reduction and peace-building between China and neighbours such as India, Vietnam and South Korea.

Relations between China and India are the best they have been since 1962.[43] A negotiated solution in Cambodia was facilitated by regular talks between Chinese and Russian officials, including Vice Foreign Minister Egor Rogachev (presently ambassador in Beijing). China and the USSR-Russia have been able to contribute to the effective operation of the UN Security Council and the expectation that the UN will be able to break free from the shackles that made it moribund during the Cold War.

Tension in the Korean peninsula in particular has eased dramatically as a direct result of the Sino-Soviet rapprochement. China, feeling threatened by the USSR, bid against Moscow to retain influence in North Korea. Soviet rivalry with China strengthened North Korea's leverage and its willingness to contemplate the use of force against South Korea.[44] Moscow's perception of being encircled by hostile forces, including China, led to a close alliance with Pyongyang. Even up to the mid-1980s, the Soviet Union was prepared to supply North Korea with new tanks, anti-aircraft and long

---

43. Ramesh Thakur commented (Canberra, 1 October 1992) that India has a political problem with China. The security issue had dissipated and was now manageable, to the extent that India had withdrawn at least three mountain divisions from the Sino-Indian border and established a dialogue on security and confidence-building measures with Beijing. See Ramesh Thakur and Carlyle A. Thayer, "Postscript," *Soviet Relations with India and Vietnam, 1945–1992* (New Delhi: Oxford University Press, 1993); and Gary Klintworth, "Chinese Perspectives on India as a Great Power," in Ross Babbage and Sandy Gordon, eds., *India's Strategic Future* (London: Macmillan, 1991), p. 91.

44. The Soviet Union signed a Treaty of Friendship, Cooperation and Mutual Assistance with North Korea on 1 July 1961. Ten days later China signed a Treaty of Friendship Cooperation and Mutual Assistance with North Korea. Such was the pattern of Sino-Soviet relations in the Korean peninsula for the next decade or so.

range artillery, modern combat aircraft and various missile systems.[45] In return, the Soviet Union gained access to North Korean ports at Wonsan and Chongjin and overflight rights for intelligence collection by TU-95 BEAR D naval reconnaissance aircraft.

North Korea's strategic circumstances began to deteriorate after the deaths of Mao Zedong in 1976 and Leonid Brezhnev in 1982. North Korea's only allies reassessed their strategic and national economic priorities and concluded that they shared a common strategic interest in war avoidance as far as the Korean peninsula was concerned. North Korea was thus found to be an embarrassment and a burden to Moscow and Beijing. Both chose to drop Pyongyang in favour of economic and trade linkages with South Korea. Sino-Russian rapprochement enabled Moscow to normalise relations with Seoul on 30 September 1990 and Beijing followed suit on 24 August 1992.

The Russian foreign ministry, in a statement issued on 25 August 1992, said that the establishment of Sino-South Korean relations was "a major step in overcoming the vestiges of the Cold War in the Korean peninsula" and Moscow, with others like China, would now work to create "an effective peace and security structure in Korea."[46] In his visit to Beijing in September 1992, South Korea's President Roh Tae Woo elicited an undertaking from China's President Yang Shangkun that Beijing would nudge Pyongyang on the nuclear issue and make a contribution to achieving peace in the Korean peninsula. Thus, North Korea, no longer able to play China off against the Soviet Union or vice versa, has had to think twice about the nuclear option—if it ever was an option.[47] It has also been forced to come to terms with South Korea, Japan and the West.[48]

---

45. The Ministry of National Defence, *Defense White Paper 1989* (Seoul, 1989).

46. TASS, Moscow, 25 August 1992.

47. Ryukichi Imai suggests North Korea may have deliberately exposed the Yongbyon facility to the prying eyes of U.S. satellites in as part of its game strategy to negotiate the withdrawal of U.S. nuclear weapons from South Korea; in *Security and Development in the Asia-Pacific Region* (Tokyo: IIGP PP 61E, August 1991), p. 11. Dr. Hans Blix, Director General of the International Atomic Energy Agency, after an inspection of North Korea's Yongbyon Nuclear Research Centre in May 1992, said that it could not be considered to be a full-scale reprocessing plant although it could be upgraded; the IAEA had found no evidence that North Korea intended to use the "tiny amount" of plutonium it had produced for a weapons program; the amount was less than would be required to produce a nuclear weapon; and he had seen no evidence that the North Koreans had removed equipment from Yongbyon: *SCMP*, 17 May 1992. Blix said that the IAEA was not giving a clean bill of health but nor did it want to sound an alarm: USIS Wireless File, EPF403 23 July 1992.

48. Suk-Hong Chung, Assistant Minister for Research and Studies on the ROK National Unification Board, said that North Korea realised its strategy of revolution in the South had failed and it had therefore changed its policy towards the South from confrontation to coexistence; interview, Seoul, May 1991.

Sino-Russian détente, together with normalised Chinese and Russian relations with South Korea have opened up possibilities for wider regional economic cooperation in Northeast Asia.[49] While there are signs that states in Northeast Asia are still building up their armed forces qualitatively, and while Russia and Japan are still engaged in their dispute over the Kuriles, attention is switching to the potential for regional trade and economic cooperation in Northeast Asia.

Normalised relations between Japan and North Korea and, ultimately, between South Korea and North Korea seem likely to match Sino-Russian détente, the dramatic progress made in China's relations with Taiwan since 1987, normalised relations between Japan and China and, more recently, between Seoul, Beijing and Moscow.[50]

The Chinese are about to cement an even closer political relationship with Japan after the historically important visit to Beijing and Xian by the Japanese Emperor Akihito in October 1992. China needs Japanese political support to fend off U.S. pressure over matters such as human rights and democracy. With the exception of Hong Kong, Japan has become China's most important trading partner.

As old rivalries in Northeast Asia give way to moves that exploit Russian resources, Chinese manpower and Japanese and South Korean technology and capital, the accompanying geoeconomic linkages hold out the possibility of a new East Asian economic order.[51] For non-Russians and non-Chinese, it may well seem rather grandiose. But given the rapidly growing Japanese and South Korean demand for energy and the resources available, especially gas, in central and western Yakutia and Sakhalin island in the Russian Far East, it is possible to envisage sub-regional zones of economic cooperation and development around the Sea of Japan, the Tumen River area and the Yellow Sea, all within the wider regional zone of Northeast Asia.[52]

With the end of the Russian-Chinese Cold War, and possibly a settlement of the Japanese-Russian dispute over the Northern Territories, Northeast Asia could fulfil its pre-war promise of becoming the industrial "cockpit of

---

49. See Stuart Harris, "Varieties of Pacific Economic Cooperation," *Pacific Review* 4:3 (1991), pp. 1, 10; and Haruo Nakayama, "New Dynamism in the Asian Economy," Asia Club Papers No. 2, May 1991, Tokyo Club Foundation for Global Studies, pp. 313–27.

50. For details on the growing China-Taiwan nexus see Gary Klintworth, "Taiwan's New Role in the Asia-Pacific Region," *Current Affairs Bulletin* 69 (July 1992).

51. Foreshadowed in Mikhail Gorbachev's Krasnoyarsk speech in September 1988. See also the report by V. I. Ivanov and N. M. Baikov, eds., *Soviet Far East: Minerals and Resources* (Moscow: Institute of World Economics and International Relations, 1989).

52. See for example Segal, *Soviet Union and the Pacific*, pp. 188 ff; and Eugene M. Khartukov, "Energy Developments in the Russian Far East," paper presented to "Asian Energy Markets to 2000," Pacific Rim Forum, San Diego, 1992.

Asia," a regional zone of dynamic economic development that involves South Korea, Taiwan, the United States, China's Northeast and the Russian Far East.[53] Such a zone would match the dynamic economic region comprising Taiwan, Hong Kong, Guangdong and Fujian in the south of China. There, the economic and political impact of investment from Hong Kong and Taiwan is such that one can foresee a process of Taiwanisation of mainland China, starting from its southern provinces.[54]

Both economic zones—one in the north and one in the south—are being matched by a middle zone around Shanghai, thus combining in a three-pronged assault on China's economic backwardness, and ultimately perhaps, its political transformation.

Beijing has in mind a regional grouping that accomplishes something more than just economic cooperation.[55] The Chinese perceive a kind of Northeast Asian Co-prosperity Sphere that might eventually include Taiwan, Hong Kong, Mongolia, the Koreas, Japan and Russia, preferably no doubt with China as the kingdom in the middle. It would keep Japan in its place and function as an East Asian Economic Zone that would match the North American Free Trade Area (NAFTA) and the European Community (EC).

The Japanese have in mind a Sea of Japan economic zone that includes northern China, the Russian Far East, the Korean peninsula and Japan. Nomura, Japan's biggest securities house, notes that the Northeast Asian economic zone has the largest potential in Asia in terms of its endowment of natural resources and complementary economies.[56] The zone is rich in natural resources, including energy, timber, metals and sea foods. It has a population of almost 200m, plentiful labour, a large market, surplus capital and advanced technologies from two of the world's leading industrial economies.

This Japanese vision of Northeast Asia would appear to have suffered a serious setback with the cancellation of Boris Yeltsin's visit to Tokyo and the continuing dispute over the Kuriles. The Japanese and Russians may never satisfactorily settle the Kuril dispute, a deep-seated issue with

---

53. See Saburo Okita and others, "Japan's Response to the Changing Soviet Union," Japan Forum on International Relations, Tokyo, 1991.

54. See for example François Heisbourg, "The New Strategic Environment: Traditional Players and Emerging Regional Powers," *Contemporary Southeast Asia* 14 (June 1992), pp. 1, 9.

55. See for example "Tumen River Delta: Far East's Future Rotterdam," *Beijing Review*, 20–26 April 1992, p. 5; "New Spring in Sino-Japanese Ties Heralded," *Beijing Review*, 6–12 April 1992, p. 4; "New Blueprint for an Old Industrial Base in Liaoning," *Beijing Review*, 17–23 February 1992.

56. The Nomura report was issued in March 1991; cited in *SCMP*, 10 April 1991, and Harris "Varieties of Pacific Economic Cooperation."

profound strategic and political consequences for both Russia and Japan. Russia moreover still maintains significant military forces in the Far East and Japan still has the world's third-largest defence budget. Nonetheless, Boris Yeltsin said in Seoul on 19 November that Russia would be cutting its submarine production and would withdraw its sea-based nuclear weapons from the Pacific.[57] The Japanese Defence Agency references to Russia as a threat in its annual defence white paper[58] and its defence budget is also under downward pressure.

At the same time, the giant Mitsui group joined American oil interests to bid successfully for the potentially rich Sakhalin oil and gas project, the biggest resource development in the Pacific region to date. It will supply oil and liquefied natural gas to lucrative markets in Japan and South Korea.[59] Japan is currently Russia's fifth-largest trading partner, after Germany, Italy, Poland and Czechoslovakia. Although trade between Japan and Russia has expanded rather slowly from US \$4.7 bn in 1980 to US \$5.4 bn in 1991 (see Table 5.1 above), its composition reflects the complementarity of the two economies. Russia exports mainly energy, cotton, lumber, non-ferrous metals, and gold whilst importing Japanese steel, machines and chemicals.[60] Russian-Japanese-South Korean economic cooperation around the Sea of Japan creates the potential for what Robert Scalapino calls a NEZ, a natural economic zone.[61] It is on Japan's doorstep in East Asia and coincidentally a relatively safe distance from both Moscow and Washington. (Moscow is 8,500 km by train from Khabarovsk.) According to the Nomura report, the decay of central power in Russia was pushing eastern Siberia into the lap of its dynamic Pacific Rim neighbours because they were the only ones capable of developing its rich potential.[62]

In Seoul the same idea of regional cooperation involving the Northeast Asian economies and the Russian Far East is rapidly taking shape.[63] It was

57. Reported in the *International Herald Tribune*, 20 November 1992.

58. Defence Agency, *Defence of Japan* (Tokyo, 1990).

59. "BHP's \$10 billion Soviet Oil Strategy,"*Australian Financial Review*, 26 July 1991; "BHP Looking at Huge Siberian Deal," *Australian Financial Review*, 17 September 1992.

60. SOTOBO (Japan Association for Trade with the Soviet Union and Socialist Countries of Europe), *Monthly Bulletin on Trade with USSR and East Europe*, 2 (1988), pp. 28–29, cited in Yasushi Toda, "Trends in Soviet-Japanese Trade," paper presented to the AAASS 20th National Convention, Honolulu, 20 November 1988.

61. Robert Scalapino, "Northeast Asia—Prospects for Cooperation," *Pacific Review* 5:2 (1992), pp. 101, 102. See also Mark Valencia, "Economic Cooperation in Northeast Asia: The Proposed Tumen River Scheme," *Pacific Review* 4:3 (1991), p. 263.

62. Quoted in *SCMP*, 10 April 1991.

63. See Ahn Byong-joon "The Korean Peninsula and Peace and Stability in East Asia," paper presented to Korea 1991 Workshop, Northeast Asia Program, Australian National University, Canberra, 12 August 1991; and the remarks of Dr Suh Jan Won, Vice President of Korea's Institute for International Economic Policy, Korean Feature, *Australian*, 18 September 1992, p. 14.

highlighted by Yeltsin's visit to South Korea in November 1992 and his commitment to a further easing of military tension in the region. It is being actively planned by corporations like Hyundai, South Korea's largest industrial conglomerate. Soo-Sam Chae said Hyundai, in anticipation of the rapid growth in South Korean demand for resources in the 1990s, intended investing substantial amounts (in the tens of billions of dollars) in energy and resource projects in the Russian Far East.[64] It was already a partner in the Svetlaia Joint Venture to process and export timber and wood-pulp products from the Russian Far East using ethnic Russian-Korean labour. Other South Korean *chaebols* (conglomerates) such as Samsung and Daewoo are active in seeking energy joint ventures in the Russian Far East.[65] Trade between South Korea and the USSR is given above in Table 5.1. South Korea was the USSR's 26th-largest trading partner in 1991.

Meanwhile trade between China and South Korea, worth around US $5 bn in 1991, is expected to double to US $10 bn in 1992. China is already South Korea's fifth-largest trading partner and some of South Korea's biggest multinationals such as Kia, Hyundai, Samsung and Daewoo have set up joint ventures in China's Northeast. China's industrial heartland and South Korea's west coast are just one day apart by ship across the Yellow Sea. The new relationship between China and South Korea was symbolised by President Roh Tae Woo's visit to Beijing in September 1992, with agreements signed on trade, investment, scientific cooperation, and prospectively, sea and air links and double taxation. As Shandong's Governor Jiang Chunyun remarked, "the geography is obvious to everyone."[66]

North Korea will find it very difficult to resist this regional economic dynamic. Pyongyang is in fact equally interested in transforming the Sea of Japan into a "sea of prosperity" and it could benefit from participation in the Tumen River economic development project, or in allowing Sakhalin LNG to be piped overland to South Korea.

Prospects

There is some contempt in the Russian leadership over China's adherence to communism and concern about the political stability of China, with the Deng leadership succession around the corner. Equally, however, there is appreciation that China, with 1.2 bn people, has been able to feed its people

---

64. Soo-Sam Chae, Senior Executive Vice President of Hyundai Resources Development Corporation, interview, Seoul, May 1991.

65. *SCMP*, 1 October 1990.

66. *SCMP*, 21 July 1988.

and is making rapid progress economically, far more so than the CIS. Moscow knows moreover that China, whether communist or capitalist, is geographically Russia's largest neighbour and that Moscow will have to work with whatever leadership emerges in Beijing. The Chinese leadership meanwhile has been quietly critical of Russia's abandonment of communism.

Relations therefore will not return to what they were in the 1950s. Nonetheless, reform is underway in two large neighbouring economies sharing the longest land border in the world. They have never fought a war in the past. They have instead cooperated extensively and are doing so once again. Each has much to learn from the other and much to gain from barter trade and economic cooperation. China has an oversupply of light industrial goods. Russia has advanced military technology, plentiful raw materials and the surplus power capacity needed by China. The present trend towards growing economic interdependence is likely to continue. Sino-Russian economic growth will be boosted by cooperation with South Korea and, subject to resolution of the Kuril dispute, Japan.

Sino-Russian détente may have solved China's concern about a military threat from the north. It has however freed the PLA to look beyond the defence of northern China. It has boosted China's confidence and given the PLA access to advanced Russian weapons. Not surprisingly, this has generated speculation and concern in the region about an expansionist China.

Japan fears that the easing of tension on the Sino-Russian border will enable China to look south and east. Japan is especially concerned about the possibility of Chinese naval and air forces being developed with Russian technology to support China claims to off-shore territories, including the Japanese-claimed Senkaku islands (Diaoyutai) in the East China Sea. Earlier in Paris Japan had vetoed the sale of British air-to-air refuelling technology to China.[67] Japanese foreign ministry officials indicated that Japan might curtail economic assistance to China if Beijing went ahead and bought an aircraft carrier from Ukraine.[68]

Taiwan is also concerned that Beijing, undistracted in the north, will switch defence resources south to reinforce its claims to Taiwan, given its policy of not renouncing the use of force against the island.[69] Similar

---

67. Phil L. Midland, "China, Japan or Both–the Integration of the Pacific into U.S. National Security Strategy," (unpublished paper, Harvard University, 1988), p. 12.

68. Xu Dan, Deputy Director of China's Institute of Contemporary International Relations, quoted by UPI, Tokyo, 9 September 1992.

69. There is no evidence that the PLA has redeployed forces to areas adjacent to the Taiwan Straits but it is a possibility now that Taiwan has approval to buy F-16 fighter aircraft. Some reports suggest that China will deploy its new SU-27s to Wushu, 150 km south of Shanghai.

concerns about the PLA concentrating its attention on the south have been expressed in New Delhi and Hanoi. Indian strategists are interested in finding out where the missiles in China's strategic rocket force are located and in which direction they are pointed now that Russia is no longer perceived to be an imminent threat.[70] Fear of China has led Vietnam to try and link up with ASEAN as soon as possible.

In the absence of a common regional interest in confronting an expansionist Soviet Union, and perceptions of an isolationist U.S., instinctive fears have similarly re-emerged amongst the ASEAN states and Australia of a big China filling a perceived power "vacuum" in the South China Sea.[71] (There may be scope, paradoxically, for a continued Russian naval presence at Cam Ranh Bay.) China is again being portrayed as a threat to regional peace and security, a result for which China has itself partly to blame.[72]

Such assessments will need sensitive handling by all members of the Asian-Pacific region, including China, Russia and the United States. Beijing will have to go out of its way to reassure member-states in forums such as APEC and the ASEAN post-ministerial conference of its long-term commitment to regional economic cooperation, a security dialogue and the negotiated settlement to territorial disputes in the South and East China Seas.[73] China might also need to consider publication of a defence white paper setting out its security perspectives, its strategic objectives, its force structure planning and the detail of its defence equipment purchases. Russia will need to be circumspect in its arms sales policy to China and the region.

---

70. China's Second Artillery Corps has at least 200 mobile strategic missile systems; *Beijing Review*, 10–16 August 1992, p. 5.

71. For an early exposition of this theme see Des Ball, "Foreword," in Gary Klintworth, *China's Modernisation: The Strategic Implications for the Asia-Pacific Region* (Canberra: Australian Government Publishing Service, 1989), pp. iii–v.

72. See Harlan Jencks, "China's Defence Build-up: A Threat to the Region?" and Taeho Kim, "China's Military Build-up in a Changing Security Climate in Northeast Asia," papers presented to the 1992 Conference on PLA Affairs, Chinese Council of Advanced Policy Studies, Taipei, June 1992.

73. Xu Dan, Deputy Director of China's Institute of Contemporary International Relations, took a step in this direction by reassuring a Japanese audience that China had not purchased the *Varyag*, the Ukrainian-built aircraft carrier and that it would not fuel a regional arms race. Much more needs to be done.

APPENDIX 7.1: Sino-Soviet Joint Communiqué
(Beijing, 18 May 1989)

1. At the invitation of President Yang Shangkun of the People's Republic of China, M. S. Gorbachev, President of the Presidium of the Supreme Soviet of the USSR and General Secretary of the Soviet Communist Party, paid an official visit to the People's Republic of China (PRC) from 15 to 18 May 1989.

Chairman Deng Xiaoping met with President Gorbachev in Beijing on 16 May. The two leaders exchanged views on Sino-Soviet relations and international issues of mutual interest.

President Yang Shangkun, General Secretary Zhao Ziyang of the Chinese Communist Party and Premier Li Peng of the State Council of the PRC held meetings and talks respectively with President Gorbachev.

2. The leaders of China and the Soviet Union found it useful to exchange views on bilateral relations. The two sides agreed that the Sino-Soviet high-level meeting symbolised the normalisation of relations between the two countries. This is in conformity with the interests and aspirations of the Chinese and Soviet peoples and contributes to the maintenance of world peace and stability. The normalisation of Sino Soviet relations is not directed at any third country, nor does it harm its interests.

3. The two sides stated that the People's Republic of China and the Union of the Soviet Socialist Republics would develop their relations on the basis of the universal principles guiding state-to-state relations, namely, mutual respect for sovereignty and territorial integrity, mutual non-aggression, non-interference in each other's internal affairs, equality and mutual benefit and peaceful coexistence.

4. Both sides expressed readiness to resolve all the disputes between the two countries through peaceful negotiations and neither side would use or threaten to use arms against the other by any means, including the use of territorial land, water or air space of a third country bordering on the other side.

The two sides held the view that strict observance of the above points would help enhance mutual trust and establish good-neighbourly and friendly relations between the two countries.

5. The leaders of China and the Soviet Union confirmed the statement on the question of Kampuchea issued by the foreign ministers of the two countries on 6 February 1989 and, in view of later developments, had an overall and in-depth exchange of views on the settlement of the Kampuchean question.

The two sides took note of the decision of Vietnam to withdraw all its troops from Kampuchea by the end of September 1989 under effective international supervision.

They shared the concern and considered it essential that no civil war in Kampuchea should follow the complete Vietnamese troop withdrawal and that future Kampuchea should be an independent, peaceful, neutral and nonaligned state. To this end, they expressed support for national reconciliation with the participation of the four parties in Kampuchea. The Chinese side advocated the establishment in Kampuchea of a provisional quadripartite coalition government headed by Prince Sihanouk during the transitional period after the complete Vietnamese troop withdrawal and prior to the end of a general election. The Soviet side maintained that the internal problems of Kampuchea, including preparations for the general election under international supervision, should be solved by the Kampuchean people themselves. It expressed welcome to intensified efforts for dialogue among the Khmer parties and its readiness to support any agreement reached by the Kampuchean parties on different aspects of the Kampuchean question.

The two sides pledged to respect the results of the general election of the Kampuchean people under international supervision.

They held that with the withdrawal of Vietnamese troops from Kampuchea, the countries concerned should gradually reduce and eventually stop all their military aid to any of the parties in Kampuchea.

The two sides stood for the convocation of an international conference on Kampuchea as soon as possible.

They reaffirmed their continued efforts to promote an early political settlement of the Kampuchean question in a fair and reasonable way. They agreed to continue their discussions on the Kampuchean question, including the remaining differences in this regard.

6. The two sides agreed to take measures to cut down the military forces in the areas along the Sino-Soviet boundary to a minimum level commensurate with the normal, good-neighbourly relations between the two countries and work for increased trust and continuous tranquillity along the border areas.

The Chinese side welcomed the announcement of the Soviet Union to withdraw 75 percent of its forces from the People's Republic of Mongolia and hoped to see the complete pullout of its remaining forces from that country within a specified short period of time.

7. The two sides favoured a fair and reasonable settlement of the Sino-Soviet boundary question left over from the past, on the basis of the treaties concerning the present Sino-Soviet boundary and of the generally recognised principles of international law and in a spirit of consultations on an equal footing and mutual understanding and mutual accommodation.

The leaders of the two countries decided, in line with the above-stated principles, to speed up the discussions on those sectors along the Sino-Soviet boundary where agreement was yet to be reached, so as to work out a mutually acceptable way to resolve the eastern and western sectors simultaneously. They entrusted the two foreign ministers to conduct discussions devoted to the boundary question when necessary.

8. The two sides agreed to work for the development of the economic, trade, scientific, technological, cultural and other relations in a planned way on

the basis of the principles of equality and mutual benefit and to deepen mutual understanding and promote exchanges between the two peoples.

9. The two sides considered it beneficial for them to share information and experience regarding their socialist development and reforms and exchange views on bilateral relations and international issues of common concern. Their differences on certain matters should not stand in the way of progress of bilateral relations.

10. The two sides agreed that the Communist Party of China and the Communist Party of the Soviet Union would develop their contacts and exchanges in accordance with the principles or independence, complete equality, mutual respect and non-interference in each other's internal affairs.

11. The Chinese side reiterated that Taiwan is an inalienable part of the People's Republic of China. China is firmly opposed to any attempt designed to create "two Chinas," "one China, one Taiwan" or "the independence of Taiwan."

The Soviet side expressed support to this position of the Chinese government.

12. The Chinese side reiterated that the People's Republic of China pursues an independent foreign policy of peace and adheres to the principled position of not entering into alliance with any country.

The Soviet side stated that its foreign policy, based on the supreme value of peace, is to work steadfastly for real disarmament, including nuclear disarmament, its underlying principle being that the security of one country should not be ensured at the expense of another. It stood for giving priority to the value of the entire mankind and for peaceful competition between different social and economic systems under the conditions of free choice and balanced interests.

13. The two sides stated that neither side would seek hegemony of any form in the Asian Pacific region or other parts of the world. Both deemed it essential to denounce the attempt or action of any country to impose its will on others or seek hegemony of any form anywhere in the world.

14. The two sides took the view that peace and development are the two most important questions in the world of today. They expressed welcome to the easing of the long-standing world tensions and made positive appraisal of the efforts of various countries for arms reduction and relaxation of military confrontation and the progress achieved in settling regional conflicts. The two sides indicated readiness to continue their respective efforts in these aspects.

They stood for enhanced prestige of the United Nations and hoped to see its greater role in international affairs, disarmament and settlement of global problems and regional conflicts. All the countries, big or small, strong or weak are entitled to participate as equals in international activities.

15. The two sides expressed concern over the world economic situation and particularly the deteriorating economies in developing countries, the growing gap between North and South and the worsening debt issue. They considered

it urgent to establish the new international economic order while taking into consideration the interests of all peoples and on the basis of the principle of equality and mutual benefit.

16. The two sides held that solutions to the global economic, social, population, ecological and other problems would be of great significance to the maintenance and development of the world civilisation and improvement of the quality of life of mankind. They stated that it was necessary to get more attention to those problems from the international community, the United Nations and other international organisations and seek coordinated measures to alleviate and tackle them.

17. China and the Soviet Union deemed it necessary to promote a fundamentally healthy development of international relations. To this end, the Chinese side proposed to establish a new international political order on the basis of the Five Principles of Peaceful Coexistence and the Soviet side proposed to foster new political thinking in international relations. The understanding of the present international relations by each side is manifested in their respective propositions and concepts as stated above.

18. The two sides considered it important to have contacts and dialogues between leaders of the two countries and intended to continue to do so in the future. President Gorbachev, on behalf of the Soviet leadership, invited Comrades Deng Xiaoping, Yang Shangkun, Zhao Ziyang and Li Peng to pay official visits to the Soviet Union. The Chinese side expressed thanks for his invitation.

8

South Asia

Ramesh Thakur

South Asia is one of the world's more sharply defined regions in physical characteristics, shared histories and considerable economic and administrative coherence inherited from the British Raj. Yet until the 1980s South Asia was conspicuous for having failed to produce a regional organisation. Regionalism was progressively weakened after the departure of the British as the independent countries went their separate ways politically, economically and in foreign policies. To take one simple but telling measure, intra-area trade declined from an already-meagre 3.24 percent in 1980 to 2.66 percent in 1990.[1]

The region, defined by the membership of the South Asian Association of Regional Cooperation (SAARC), comprises Bangladesh, Bhutan, India, the Maldives, Nepal, Pakistan and Sri Lanka. Afghanistan and Myanmar (Burma) lie on the periphery of the region and could conceivably become members of SAARC in the future. While they are of interest to and their affairs concern some SAARC members, they are not for the present themselves SAARC members and therefore not included in this chapter.

The region's combined population of 1.13 bn represents 21.4 percent of the world's people. It is also a population characterised by poverty, illiteracy and low life expectancy (see Table 8.1). Moreover, South Asian countries do not fare well on these measures even by developing-country standards, let alone by world or industrial-country standards. In addition, most of them are wracked by problems of internal security and economic scarcities which threaten them with political destabilisation and territorial disintegration.

---

1. *Direction of Trade Statistics Yearbook 1986* and *1990* (Washington, DC: IMF, 1986 and 1990), pp. 222–23 in each case.

TABLE 8.1: South Asian Indicators

	Population (million, 1990)	GDP/capita (PPP[a] $, 1989)	Life expectancy (years, 1990)	Adult literacy (%, 1990)
Bangladesh	115.6	820	51.8	35.3
Bhutan	1.5	750	48.9	38.4
India	853.1	910	59.1	48.2
Maldives	0.2	1118	62.5	95.0
Nepal	19.1	896	52.2	25.6
Pakistan	122.6	1789	57.7	34.8
Sri Lanka	17.2	2253	70.9	88.4
Developing countries	4070[b]	2296[c]	62.8[c]	64[c]
World	5280[b]	4622[c]	64.7[c]	–

a. PPP = purchasing power parity; b. total; c. average.

SOURCE: UNDP, *Human Development Report 1992* (New York: Oxford University Press, 1992).

Yet, on the positive side, South Asia too has been infected by the worldwide movement towards greater democratisation and market freedoms. Pakistan's shaky democracy has survived to date through 1991 with Prime Minister Mohammad Nawaz Sharif still at the helm, Sri Lanka's regime has so far proven viable against the secessionist threat from the Liberation Tigers of Tamil Eelam (LTTE), Bangladesh and Nepal moved to elected governments in 1991 and the resilience of India's long-established democracy was demonstrated with the election of a Congress minority government despite the assassination of former and aspiring prime minister Rajiv Gandhi by suspected LTTE terrorists in June 1991.

South Asia remains important in world affairs, if not quite to the same extent as during the Cold War. To the west and east, it straddles and links two other areas of vital interest, namely the Middle East and Southeast Asia. To the northeast it borders the sole remaining communist giant which shares a long and troubled frontier with India. To the northwest while Afghanistan is no longer occupied by foreign invaders, its fate is still unsettled. The breakup of the Soviet empire has also produced fresh turmoil in the Central Asian republics of the former Soviet Union (FSU). To the south the region juts out athwart important sea lanes of communication and supply in the Indian Ocean. It continues to be a focus of international attention: for the continuing tragedy of Afghanistan; for the possibility of nuclear proliferation; for the transregional repercussions of another India-Pakistan war; for the presence of extensive debilitating poverty and efforts to alleviate it; for India's importance as the leading Third World and most populous worldwide democracy; for India's leadership role among developing countries; and for Pakistan's central role in the Muslim world and as a geographical conduit to Afghanistan and Central Asia.

India

India by itself accounts for 76 percent of South Asia's total population, 73 percent of its land area and 77 percent of its economic product. India's position in the region is distinctive also for the fact that all other states save the Maldives share a border with India but not with each other. Consequently, all other states can in the nature of things interact with one another only through India. With India being so dominant in South Asia, Soviet relations with the region were decidedly Indocentric. One key statistic is the trade figures. In 1990, Soviet trade with Bangladesh was worth 53.1m roubles, with Pakistan 182.4m roubles, with Sri Lanka 32.7m roubles and with other South Asian countries virtually nil. So, excluding India, total Soviet trade with the rest of South Asia was a paltry 268.2m roubles, compared to 3.2 bn roubles with India.[2]

Looking back at the period since the Second World War in its entirety, the most successful bilateral relationship for India and the Soviet Union was with each other. The year 1955 was crucial in the development of Indo-Soviet relations. In addition to the highly successful exchange of visits by Nikita Khrushchev and Jawaharlal Nehru, there was the agreement for the construction of the Bhilai steel plant in the public sector and the first visit of Soviet oil experts. The Moscow-New Delhi ties that developed thereafter were broad, deep and durable. A host of framework agreements, treaties of cooperation and joint committees gave organisational structure to bilateral relations independently of personal and party fortunes in either country.

The breakup of the Soviet Union disrupted India's most important channel of defence supplies, took away a major export market, left it more vulnerable to hostile resolutions at the United Nations, introduced fresh instabilities in its northern neighbourhood and brought new competitors for foreign aid. Yet efforts will continue to preserve friendly ties with the CIS republics. In January 1992 India agreed to grant Rs. 32 bn worth of technical credits to Russia to pay for Indian goods;[3] the credits would be repaid with Russian oil, petrochemicals and fertilisers. India also gave Rs.

---

2. *Foreign Trade* (USSR), 4/1991, pp. 34–36.

3. BBC, *Summary of World Broadcasts (SWB)*, SU/1291 A3/2, 30 January 1992. Technical credits effectively convert trade into barter deals. The old agreements used to approve trade in advance. The country which failed to export sufficient goods gave technical credits instead: deliveries of goods in exchange for other goods.

150m in humanitarian assistance, with Prime Minister P. V. Narasimha Rao saying that India would consider similar contributions to other republics of the FSU.[4] India also moved aggressively to establish political, military and economic relations directly with the newly-independent republics.

Political

Homage to the Soviet Union for having stood by India in its various hours of need was a familiar refrain by Indian politicians and scholars. In the 1980s, it was India that stood by the Soviet Union during its international difficulties in Afghanistan and Cambodia. Yet by 1990 there was a perceptible end-of-era sense about the Indo-Soviet relationship. There was "much anguish" in India as a result of the *glasnost*-induced critical attention in the Soviet media to Indian opposition to the Non-Proliferation Treaty (NPT), the lease of a Soviet nuclear-propelled submarine to India, soft-currency trade and debt repayment arrangements and the suspect stability of the National Front government in New Delhi.[5] After Prime Minister V. P. Singh's three-day visit to the Soviet Union in July 1990, it became clear that the thrust of the relationship was shifting from political-security to economic-commercial concerns.

The accumulating difficulties notwithstanding, close relations between India and the Soviet Union were maintained until the demise of the latter. For example, on 8 August 1991 the two countries decided to renew the 1971 Friendship Treaty for another twenty years, saying that it met the fundamental interests of both countries and provided a reliable basis for the steady development of their multifaceted ties.[6]

Just eleven days later came the coup in Moscow and the subsequent breakup of the Soviet Union. The attempted coup, its collapse within four days, the triumph of the reformers led by Boris Yeltsin and the subsequent erosion of Soviet central authority found and left Indian foreign policy directionless. When Mikhail Gorbachev was a prisoner of party hardliners, Narasimha Rao delivered lectures in India's parliament about the instructive example of over-enthusiastic reformers. The restoration of constitutional authority in Moscow was hailed in the Indian parliament on 23 August by unanimous euphoria. One member attacked the official response as "blinkered timidity and ineptitude"; another said that "our heads hang in shame before the people of the Soviet Union" as a result.[7]

---

4. BBC, *SWB*, SU/W0213A/3, 17 January 1992.
5. C. Raja Mohan, "Indo-Soviet Relations—The Return of Common Sense," *Hindu Weekly*, 18 August 1990, p. 9.
6. *Hindu Weekly*, 17 August 1991, p. 16.
7. *Hindu Weekly*, 31 August 1991, p. 6.

This mattered because the Yeltsin government of the successor-state Russia remembered who had stood up to be counted and who had stayed on the sidelines. Russia's Foreign Minister noted in a speech in Bonn on 6 September 1991 that during the coup only the alleged enemies of the old Soviet Union had proven to be true friends.[8] In failing to back the resistance to the coup, India failed to side with the winners, endorse principles of democracy and human rights and endear itself to Western governments who matter even more in the new unipolar world. That is, India's stand was neither just nor wise—a point made in the editorial and correspondence columns of the major Indian newspapers.

When the Baltic republics declared their independence, India said it would not recognise them. New Delhi took three weeks to reverse its untenable position. The decision was announced by Prime Minister P. V. Narasimha Rao on 7 September from Bonn, following Moscow's acceptance of the separation of the Baltic states.[9] Worse still, policy drift and incoherence saw India trying to maintain relations with the Soviet Union even as the latter dissolved before the eyes of the world. It was as though New Delhi was viewing events through a freeze-frame. The prime minister tried to repair the damage after the collapse of the coup. He sent exceptionally warm messages of congratulations both to Gorbachev and Yeltsin on 22 August expressing relief and happiness at the outcome and drawing attention to the abiding nature of Indo-Soviet friendship.[10]

Foreign Secretary J. N. Dixit led a delegation to Russia in 1992 and finalised a new political treaty and signed memoranda of understanding on trade and supplies of defence and power generation equipment. The Press Trust of India reported on 15 January 1992 that the new treaty contained elements of the 1971 Friendship Treaty, while the memoranda had been structured to permit flexibility for meeting the two countries' changing economic requirements.

Military

The Soviet Union acquired a dominant position among India's major arms suppliers in the 1960s and maintained it until its demise in 1991 (Figure 8.1). In the second half of the 1980s, India was the major Third World and Asian purchaser of weapons in the international arms bazaar. For the 1987–91 quinquennium, 79 percent of India's US $17.6 bn worth of arms purchases were sourced from the USSR. The close military

---

8. BBC, *SWB*, SU/1173 A1/3, 10 September 1991.

9. *Hindu Weekly*, 14 September 1991, p. 3.

10. The text of the two letters was released to the press.

cooperation between Moscow and New Delhi was maintained until the very end of the Soviet Union. For example, the INS *Vibhuti,* first in a series of missile boats being constructed in India, was commissioned in mid-1991. The small but fast warship was built indigenously under technical collaboration from the Soviet Union.[11]

India is a leading second-rank power; its power was built with significant Soviet military assistance; the Soviet Union has disintegrated: what will be the impact on India's defence posture? Problems were inevitable, for five sets of reasons. First, leaders in Moscow had concluded that a major contributor to their economic impoverishment was the alarming rate of military buildup. Second, nothing had so alarmed the West as Soviet military links with a number of Third World countries. Defence was therefore to be reined in as an instrument of foreign policy. Third, defence production in the FSU had been organised on a one-market basis. There was no comparative specialisation along particular production lines among the various constituent republics. The breakup of the union therefore disrupted defence production and deliveries to foreign customers. For example, Indian officials spent some time trying to identify the estimated 3,500 suppliers scattered around the new republics who manufactured the military equipment that India needed.[12]

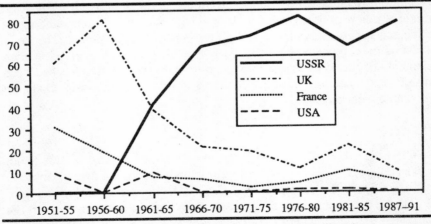

FIGURE 8.1: India's Arms Suppliers, 1951–91

SOURCES: M. Brzoska and T. Ohlson, *Arms Transfers to the Third World, 1971–85* (Oxford: Oxford University Press for SIPRI, 1987) and *SIPRI Yearbook 1992* (Oxford: Oxford University Press for SIPRI, 1992).

---

11. *Asian Defence Journal,* August 1991, p. 99.
12. S. Coll, "An Arms Rush in South Asia," *International Herald Tribune,* 6 January 1992.

Fourth, moves by the FSU towards an open economy and currency convertibility meant that the method of payment had to be renegotiated with those countries, such as India, that had conducted barter trade with the FSU. And fifth, negotiations had to be conducted to work out to mutual satisfaction how India's previous defence debt to the old Soviet Union was to be apportioned among the new republics and how the value of the rouble debt would be recalculated with the rouble in a free-fall. While India was understandably jolted by all this, there was also empathy with a country undergoing the throes of partition. For example, the division of an integrated defence force among successor-states was a familiar experience to Indians.

Economic

India was the FSU's largest developing-country trading partner. The economic relationship between India and the Soviet Union was dynamic and multifaceted. Figure 8.2 shows the steady growth in Indo-Soviet trade since 1963. It also shows that the trade balance has generally been in India's favour and that the export-import gap widened in the last five years or so. The USSR was one of India's most important single-country trading partners right until the last year of its existence. At the same time, as India's economy entered a new phase, the Soviet-East European market had begun to decline in importance for Indian exports in comparison to the industrial countries and the newly industrialising countries in Asia (Figure 8.3).

FIGURE 8.2: India's Trade with the USSR, 1963–91 (US $m)

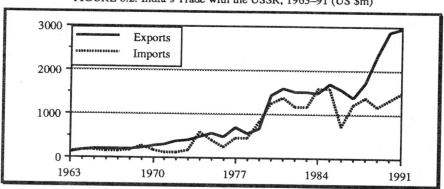

SOURCE: IMF, *Direction of Trade Statistics Yearbook,* annual volumes.

FIGURE 8.3: India's Major Export Markets by Region, 1970–91 (percentages)

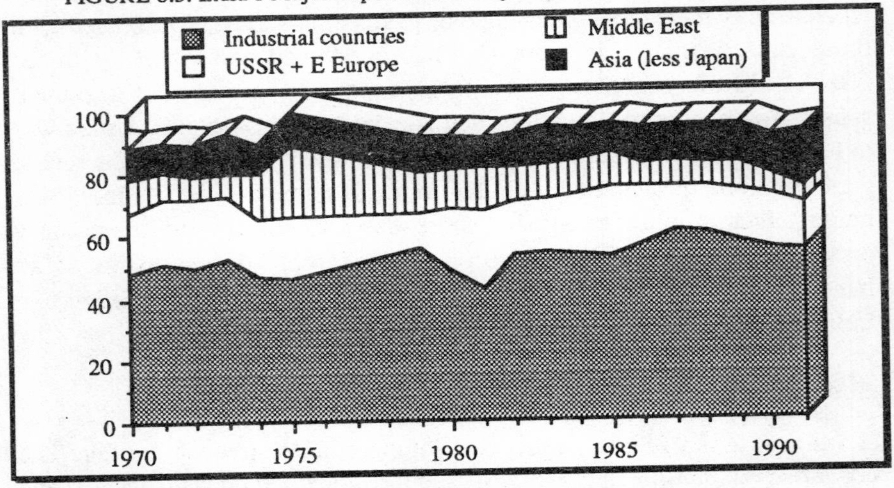

SOURCE: IMF, *Direction of Trade Statistics Yearbook,* annual volumes.

The annual report of India's Petroleum Ministry for 1991–92 noted that the ending of traditional supplies of crude oil from the FSU on a rouble-rupee barter basis had added to the hard-currency bill. Foreign Secretary Dixit had failed to obtain assurances that Russia and the other members of the CIS would resume supplies.[13] The problems affecting oil deliveries had been exacerbated by the fact that the most convenient port for shipping Russian oil to India was Odessa, which now lies in Ukraine. While continuing to import Indian goods priced in rupees, many Soviet enterprises let India run short of non-ferrous metals, newsprint and other items for which India had become reliant on Soviet suppliers.

Trade between Russia and India had more or less stopped by January 1992, with Moscow owing Rs. 32 bn in technical credits.[14] India closed trading accounts with the Soviet Union on 28 December 1991 and new accounts were opened in the name of the new CIS republics. A commentator noted on Russian TV on 3 May 1992 that Moscow was not only leaving friends in the lurch but also creating an image as an unreliable trade partner. By contrast, India had managed to find $500m worth of humanitarian aid for the FSU.[15]

---

13. *Australian,* 3 February 1992.
14. *Financial Times* (London), 7 February 1992.
15. BBC, *SWB,* SU/1372 A3/2, 5 May 1992.

Realignment of Interests

Indo-Soviet relations, in an upward trajectory since 1955, seemed to be headed downwards in the 1990s. The intimacy of the Indo-Soviet relationship had been based on conjunctions of political, military and economic interests; the future of India-CIS relations will depend on how recent events have affected the interplay of interests. The bilateral connection was important to India for modernisation and indigenisation of Indian defence forces and equipment in keeping with India's assessment of its needs, for protection of vital interests against international censure at the United Nations, for counter-balancing possible American and Chinese pressures on India and for economic assistance in the public sector.

The connection to New Delhi was useful to the Soviet Union in pursuing goals of eroding Western and containing Chinese influence in Asia, establishing its own presence in order to lend credence to claims of being an Asian and a global power, demonstrating the reality of close relations between the leading socialist state and a leading Third World state to mutual advantage, and securing an entrée to the Third World and the nonaligned movement. Indian and Soviet rhetoric on international issues often turned out to be mutually reinforcing.

Fading Conjunctions. Third-party relations used to be an important determinant of Indo-Soviet relations. The old Soviet Union had an interest in a strong and stable India while the United States was often viewed by Indians as hostile to their regional ambitions. Now events in the FSU could be the catalyst to fresh instabilities in South Asia. There is fear of the demonstration effect of the breakup of the Soviet Union on ethnic and nationalist movements all over the world, including the many fissiparous tendencies in India.[16]

Soviet global and regional interests in checking U.S. alliances and containing Chinese influence had dovetailed with the Indian foreign policy of nonalignment. Each is now also largely irrelevant. The Cold War provided the point of definition for the nonaligned movement. The end of the Cold War therefore empties the concept of nonalignment of any substantial meaning. The disappearance of one of the two poles also leaves nonalignment without its major role as a channel of contact in a rigidly bipolar world. India has lost a major ideological value as an exemplar of good relations between the leading socialist regime and a leading Third World country. Indeed questions began to be raised about some of the costs of such ties. As formerly secret files were opened by the Yeltsin

16. See, for example, Sunanda K. Datta-Ray, "State of Disunity," *Statesman Weekly*, 14 September 1991, p. 11.

administration, allegations surfaced that the CPSU Central Committee used to set aside sums of money for covert operations in India.[17]

One of the major advantages to New Delhi of its links to Moscow used to be the defence of Indian interests at the United Nations by a veto-wielding power. In the 1990–91 Gulf crisis, Moscow fell in with Washington's campaign to isolate the hitherto client regime of Saddam Hussein. President George Bush was remarkably successful in building an international coalition that held together for the duration of the war. This held two sobering policy lessons for India: Moscow's support could no longer be taken for granted in the Security Council and the United States can mobilise impressive diplomatic resources as well as being an unchallengeable economic and military power in the foreseeable future.

In the past, Indian and Soviet pronouncements in the UN and elsewhere had usually converged on major international arms control and disarmament initiatives aimed at putting the international spotlight on the U.S. nuclear arsenal. With Russia and the CIS committed to maintaining the momentum of nuclear disarmament begun by the USA and the USSR (see Figure 1.1 above), Moscow and New Delhi no longer need to camouflage their respective arms buildups in the moral high ground of rhetorical flourishes towards grand statements of international arms control.

In turn this elevates the importance of nonproliferation objectives in Moscow's goal of nuclear arms control. The disincentives to public disagreement with India on the NPT and a South Asian nuclear-weapon-free zone (NWFZ) are removed. In November 1991, Russia caused shock and consternation in India by supporting a joint Pakistani-Bangladeshi NWFZ resolution in the Disarmament Committee of the General Assembly.

Short of the nuclear threshold, the basis of the military relationship between India and Russia has also been affected. In the Gulf War the Soviet Union for the first time stood on the sidelines while a major defence client was crushingly defeated. The war was a blow to Soviet doctrines as well as weapons. There were thus three lessons for Indian defence policy: the previous history of uninterrupted delivery of Soviet arms during a war is no assurance anymore of continued deliveries in future conflicts, Soviet war-fighting doctrines have critical flaws and the technological gap between Soviet and U.S. weapon systems is widening to dangerous dimensions for Indian security.

The collapse of the Soviet Union into a collection of impoverished states necessitated a major reorientation of Indian foreign policy. Four factors transformed the basis of the relationship between India and the United States and brought forth the promise of greater harmony: the end of the Cold War,

---

17. *Hindu Weekly,* 20 June 1992, p. 7.

the start of a new cooperative relationship between Moscow and Washington, the fading of the war in Afghanistan from international consciousness and the resulting downgrading of Pakistan's strategic-cum-political importance to the United States.

India's defence forces turned their attention to Washington at the same time as global and regional strategic realignments intensified irritants between Pakistan and the U.S. while removing many old ones from the Indo-U.S. relationship. The revised U.S. perception of India's role in South Asia has been helped by policies of economic liberalisation pursued by New Delhi and by a reassessment of India as a force for stability in a troubled subcontinent. In the meantime, Moscow has greatly improved relations with Beijing. The normalisation of relations between China and the Soviet Union produced initial apprehension in India and acted as a spur to New Delhi seeking to restore cordiality to its own relations with Beijing. Visits were exchanged in 1991–92 by the Chinese premier and the President and Defence Minister of India. Tensions have been greatly reduced and border trade resumed after a lapse of some thirty years.

In February 1992 Defence Minister Sharad Pawar said that India and the U.S. were moving towards opening their defence forces and activities to each other and collaborating in some defence projects.[18] A flurry of high-level defence visits in both directions culminated in joint naval exercises on 28–29 May 1992. Ironically, one of the Indian Navy ships taking part in the exercises was the Soviet-built destroyer *INS Ranjit*. The joint exercises were small, of short duration and limited in scope. Their larger significance was not military but political: India was ending 28 years of self-imposed isolation to hold joint exercises with a foreign navy. A report on Russian TV on 8 May 1992 noted that if Moscow stopped supplying India with military items, the U.S. and its NATO allies would quickly fill the vacuum. The discussions on joint Indo-U.S. naval exercises were "a threat to Russia's geopolitical interests in South Asia, the more so as we have seriously weakened our positions in other regions."[19]

On the nuclear issue too Washington seemed to reverse its old stance and became less tolerant of Pakistan's position while less openly hostile to India. In 1992 U.S. interest shifted to capping the nuclear status quo in the subcontinent. A nuclear restraint regime was believed to be more achievable and not particularly dangerous. Disagreements between New Delhi and Washington extend beyond India's missile and nuclear programs to trade issues, especially intellectual property rights. But the differences are no longer permitted to override other common interests.

---

18. *Asian Defence Journal*, March 1992, p. 92.
19. BBC, *SWB*, SU/W0230 A/10, 15 May 1992.

The ban imposed on India and Russia in the aftermath of the sale of Russian rocket technology (discussed below) showed the connections between military and economic dimensions. From an Indian perspective, the Soviet economic link opened up direct trade contacts with the USSR, secured goods and industrial raw materials against rupee payments, enabled imports to be used as a means of increasing the range of exports, stabilised prices of traditional exports and facilitated the expansion of non-traditional exports. Externally, it helped achieve the goals of export diversification both in goods and in markets while conserving scarce foreign exchange reserves.

From the Soviet perspective, economic links with India were important because the latter was a source of significant amounts of certain raw and processed commodities, some machinery and some consumer products. India was also regarded as a reliable partner in economic cooperation, never having defaulted on credit repayments and rarely seeking even their deferral.[20] Indo-Soviet cooperation permitted reliable Soviet acquisition, on soft terms, of familiar machinery and equipment needed for the development of the Soviet economy. India provided the Soviet Union a back door to acquiring hard-currency products. Finally, and perhaps most importantly, Soviet purchases from India gave the latter the wherewithal to buy Soviet weaponry: India's military debt-servicing to the Soviet Union was costed at more than one billion dollars a year.[21]

Mutual benefits notwithstanding, Soviet trade with India had reached a plateau by the 1980s. An infrastructure of basic industries having been created with Soviet assistance, the objective base of Indo-Soviet economic cooperation had been eroded as India's needs entered a new phase of searching for Western technology. That is, the Indo-Soviet trading imbalance was structural rather than transient. Indian repayment to the Soviet Union began to exceed the value of Soviet deliveries and financial credits extended by the Soviet Union remained severely underutilised. Sectors of the Indian economy also suffered painful dislocation because of export variability caused by Soviet import volatilities. The trade gap between India and the USSR widened even further with the collapse of the international oil prices in the mid-1980s (see Figure 8.2 above)—India's 1990–91 trade surplus with the USSR was US $1.48 bn.[22]

---

20. S. Skachkov "Soviet-Indian Economic and Technical Co-operation," *Foreign Trade* (USSR), 3/1975, p. 13. Figures released by the Soviet Finance Ministry in 1990 showed that 61 countries were in debt to the USSR to the tune of 85.8 bn roubles. The three most indebted countries were Cuba (15.5 bn roubles), Vietnam (9.1 bn) and India (8.9 bn); *Current Digest of the Soviet Press* 42(9), 1990, p. 9.

21. *Economist*, 20 October 1990, p. 27.

22. *Direction of Trade Statistics Yearbook 1992* (Washington DC: IMF, 1992), p. 223.

A more fundamental problem was that in seeking Soviet aid for the development of the public sector, in the long term India ended up importing all the inefficiencies of the Soviet system. The Soviet daily *Izvestiia* blamed the economic crisis afflicting India in 1991 on an economic system based on socialism, autarky and protectionism.[23] In the long run, economic links with the USSR produced a doubly inefficient Indian economy. Trade-distorting factors led to a misallocation of resources, and the guaranteed Soviet market meant that Indian exporters did not have the competitive discipline of the international marketplace imposed on them.

Public sector enterprises built up with Soviet assistance were characterised by overmanning, poor management, recurring idle capacity, poor product quality, high unit costs and poor returns on capital. Allegations of "switch trade" by the Soviet Union (importing Indian products on soft terms and re-exporting them to hard-currency markets) were not substantiated. But India was losing hard currency in net terms by importing intermediate components from world markets to make products that were saleable only in the Soviet market for nonconvertible currency. In the Special Export Zone at Kandla (Gujarat), the net outflow from 1981–88 was estimated to have reached Rs. 6 bn.[24]

There was also the problem of currency values. The rouble-rupee arrangement enabled India to purchase Soviet arms without expending hard currency. It was also on balance trade-creating rather than trade-diverting. But Soviet authorities tended to apply double standards in establishing dollar values for rouble-local currency transactions. The dollar value of the rouble was set according to its relative purchasing power, but the same logic was not used in fixing the dollar value of Third World currencies.

Soviet analysts in turn expressed dissatisfaction with non-reciprocal Soviet generosity in the economic relationship with India. The relationship had been insulated from more general Soviet efforts to move away from soft-currency bilateral clearing arrangements. Nor were Soviet buyers always happy with the quality of Indian products. By the start of the 1990s, market and price-driven reorientations of the Soviet economy ushered in a fundamental restructuring of Soviet trading relationships.

The first implication of the drive to free-market economies in the FSU for India's trade was that it too would be guided by market calculations rather than political-cum-strategic considerations. In November 1991, the Indian Deputy Commerce Minister said that rupee settlements in India's trade with the CIS would terminate in 1994–95. After that date, India intends to build its economic relations with the sovereign republics on principles of a market

---

23. As reported in *Hindu Weekly*, 20 July 1991, p. 4.
24. James Clad, "Friends in Need," *FEER*, 9 August 1990, p. 45.

economy.[25] Second, Moscow's search for widened international trading relationships would pit India in direct competition with any number of other Third World countries for the same products. Third, Moscow's new-found recognition of quality control would test the Indian tendency to getting away with selling shoddy products on the domestic and foreign markets. Soviet Ambassador V. F. Isakov warned Indian suppliers that the Soviet market was going to become more demanding, selective and competitive.[26]

By the time of the coup in Moscow in August 1991, the problems in Indo-Soviet trade had mounted to such an extent that India's Ministry of Commerce took some radical measures to control exports to the Soviet Union. Export-promotion councils were asked to give preference to general-currency areas over the Soviet Union; exports to the USSR, especially those with an import-content in excess of 30 percent, were to be subjected to monthly scrutiny to restrict foreign exchange leakage by buying intermediate components in hard currency for making goods which were then exported to the USSR against rupee payments; incentive schemes for exports to rupee-payment areas were curtailed; and exports to the USSR were restricted by value to the annual protocol amount.[27]

Dissipating Disjunctions. If previously convergent interests have begun to diverge, then the reverse is also true. The Indo-Soviet relationship was an ideological misfit from the start, with one being the founding and most powerful communist state and the other the world's most populous democracy. The abandonment of communism in favour of democratic government makes it possible to place ties between Moscow and New Delhi on a more compatible ideological basis.

Indo-Soviet economic relations were subject from the start to continuous adaptations and adjustments caused by structural asymmetries. Even the initial establishment of a trading relationship between a socialist economy and a mixed economy was problematical. This was further complicated by India being a developing country and the USSR an advanced industrial economy. Now the need to confront similar problems might provide a ballast to chart the Indo-Russian relationship through unaccustomed turbulence. Both countries are going to be struggling to achieve economic success by means of a mixed but market-oriented liberalising economy functioning within a multiethnic, multiparty competitive federal democracy.

The Soviet invasion of Afghanistan in 1979 presented India with a challenge by exacerbating sensitive communal relations domestically,

---

25. BBC, *SWB*, SU/1234 A3/3, 20 November 1991.
26. Quoted in Clad, "Friends in Need," p. 46.
27. See Neeraj Kaushal, "For a Few Dollars More," *India Today*, 31 July 1991, pp. 78–79.

degrading the regional security environment, complicating relations with the Islamic and nonaligned countries and embarrassing India in international forums. Some commentators expressed apprehension that the Soviet retreat following the Geneva Accords of April 1988 would leave behind a chaotic situation in India's strategic area of interest.[28] In 1989 India communicated private but official concern that the Soviet Union was withdrawing its troops too soon.[29] India and the Soviet Union thus shared an interest in moderating the resurgent fundamentalism of Islam which could threaten the secular identity and territorial integrity of both states.[30]

Enduring and Emerging Complementarities. It seemed even before the breakup of the Soviet Union that India's economic ties with it would be the catalyst to opening up the Indian economy to international market forces. The Soviet self-destruction gave immediate urgency to the process. Yet there are costs to too rapid a disruption. Switching to hard currency for all bilateral transactions between India and the FSU would cause trade volumes to drop by as much as 40 percent.[31] For example, India would need to spend $800m in hard currency to replace the 4.5m tonnes of oil and petroleum products supplied by the FSU each year.[32] There would be a matching outflow of hard currency from Russia and some other republics for the purchase of Indian commodities like tea. And India would not be able to purchase present volumes of military equipment from the FSU. Given the parlous condition of the coffers of India and the republics of the FSU, and the lack of alternative suppliers for the items that they import from each other, this is not an attractive option for either partner.

The first ever rupee-payment arrangements trade protocol between India and Russia, covering the established items of trade in both directions, was signed on 22 February 1992.[33] The most significant event in Russo-Indian relations since the breakup of the Soviet Union was the three-day visit to India by Russian Secretary of State Dr Gennadii Burbulis in May 1992, during the course of which he met with the Indian president, prime minister and defence and finance ministers. A commentary on the state-controlled All

---

28. GPD, "Afghanistan: After the Russians," *Economic and Political Weekly*, 23 April 1988, pp. 817–20.

29. "The Present and Future of Afghanistan," editorial in *Frontline* (Madras), 18 February–3 March 1989, p. 14.

30. A Soviet academic writing in an official Indian publication noted that religious fundamentalism in Afghanistan "undoubtedly aggravate tension" in Soviet republics and in Kashmir; G. L. Bonderevsky, "Indo-Soviet Relations," *India Perspectives* 3 (October 1990), p. 17.

31. *Economist*, 14 September 1991, p. 32.

32. Hamish McDonald, "Looking for Friends," *FEER*, 19 September 1991, p. 25.

33. *Statesman Weekly*, 29 February 1992, p. 6.

India Radio on 4 May noted that India now has to deal with a Russia that is Eurocentric, economically dependent on Western largesse, with neither the interest nor the resources to prop up Third World regimes.

On 4 May 1992 the two countries signed a five-year trade and economic cooperation agreement according the most-favoured-nation (MFN) treatment to each other. They agreed to look for mutually advantageous solutions to all outstanding problems and to make all payments in freely convertible currencies unless otherwise specified. A second agreement was signed on the establishment of an intergovernmental commission on trade, economic, scientific and technical cooperation. The two sides also decided to set up a joint working group to monitor bilateral cooperation in the power sector.

Reviewing the results of his visit, Dr Burbulis said that his talks in New Delhi had confirmed the determination of both sides to implement the program for bilateral cooperation. Russia had renewed the export of oil, newsprint and military equipment. India had opened a Rs. 2.5 bn technical credit for exporting tea, coffee, tobacco and spices. He also announced at a press conference on 5 May 1992 that President Yeltsin would pay a visit to India in the second half of 1992.[34] (Subsequently, on 2 September 1992, ITAR-TASS reported that President Yeltsin would be visiting India in January 1993.) In other words both the structure (bilateral framework agreements) and substance (the products being traded) of economic exchange between Moscow and New Delhi marked a continuity from the days of the FSU.

One of the outstanding problems was the rupee-rouble exchange rate, another was repayment of previous credits. The Russian delegation insisted that the total sum of payments could not be readjusted on the basis of the current rouble-dollar exchange rate.[35] The larger issue really was the Russian objective of moving away from any political underpinning of its external trade and placing them on a commercial basis, but without incurring any financial costs of commercialisation of its international economic relationships. As part of the old Indo-Soviet friendship, Moscow gave large rouble credits to enable India to buy Soviet arms and industrial equipment. In an agreement signed in 1978, the value of the rouble was linked to a basket of OECD (Organisation of Economic Cooperation and Development) currencies. In early 1992 it amounted to about US $1.30.

But the rouble was to be floated on 1 July 1992 and the new rate would replace the multiplicity of different rates for different categories of transactions. In Indo-Soviet trade, for example, there were three different official rouble-rupee exchange rates in 1990: 1 rouble to Rs. 29 for tourists,

---

34. BBC, *SWB*, FE/1373 A1/2-3, 6 May 1992 and FE/1375 A2/2-3, 8 May 1992.
35. BBC, *SWB*, FE/1372 A1/2, 5 May 1992.

Rs. 20 for commercial transactions and Rs. 16 for governmental transactions. Market analysts expected the rouble to trade on the currency markets at 80 roubles to the dollar. (In fact it had fallen to 250 roubles to the dollar in September and 350 in October 1992.) That is, the anticipated value of 80 roubles to the dollar if applied to old Soviet credits to India would have shrunk the total amount owed to less than one-hundredth, from about $13 bn to about $125m. Not surprisingly, Russia tried to argue against such an outcome, insisting that the 1978 agreement used the rouble not as a currency but as a unit of account. During the discussions in May 1992, Moscow offered to reduce the value of the outstanding debt by 30 percent.

Equally unsurprisingly, India saw no reason to exempt the rupee-rouble exchange rate from commercial calculations and declined the Russian offer. The rupee has depreciated steadily since 1978, effectively increasing the debt by a factor of four. For years Indian governments have argued that the terms of the 1978 agreement were being unfairly applied in penalising India for the international weakness of its currency without a matching penalty for the rouble. With the latter to be officially recognised from 1 July 1992, the balance of negotiating power shifted to India. For military hardware is one of the very areas in which Russia is internationally competitive, and India is by far the major weapons purchaser from the FSU. Yet India too needs Russian military spares and for some years at least its low-quality goods are not going to be competitive in world markets. Before leaving this subject we should note also that India believes that Moscow is still contractually bound to non-convertible barter trade in four areas: defence equipment, and aid for power projects, coal and steel. The old basis for the Moscow-New Delhi relationship has not, therefore, disappeared entirely.

If economic reforms succeed in bringing prosperity to Russia, then of course it can re-emerge as a great power. Should that be the case, then the ideological disjunctions between India and Russia will have disappeared and a new entente could be re-established. Already in 1992 non-communist nationalists in Russia were beginning to question the wisdom of having abandoned traditional friends like Iraq, Libya and India. For example Sergei Baburin, described as "one of the ablest and most eloquent of the new nationalist leaders in the Russian parliament," argues that allies adorned Russia's great-power status and power commands respect. Similarly, one of Yeltsin's own foreign policy advisers, Sergei Stankevich, has been arguing with increasing force that Russia must stop being ashamed of behaving like a great power.[36]

---

36. Mark Frankland, "Foreign Policy and Russian Pride Discord," London Observer Service, 15 July 1992, as published in the *Otago Daily Times* (Dunedin, New Zealand), 25 July 1992.

Since the breakup of the Soviet Union, the successor-republics have been interested in scaling down defence production. But conversion of defence industries into civilian production is a complex and time-consuming business.[37] In the meantime, there remains a complementarity of interests between Russia as a major arms seller and India as a major arms purchaser. The question of spares became especially acute for India's fleet of MIG-29s in early 1992. MIGs account for about three-quarters of the Indian Air Force (IAF). India was confronted with uncertainty about the CIS republics' ability and willingness to continue supplying spares to the IAF. *Izvestiia* reported on 21 January 1992 that failure to supply combat equipment and spares to India would deprive the CIS of ability to import food, medicines and consumer goods from India.[38] Four days later, it was reported that Ukraine was prepared to sell weapons to India. Kiev, which was a major weapons manufacturing centre in the FSU, used to fulfil many of the long-term defence contracts between India and the USSR and was to resume this role.[39]

Speculative reports by the Press Trust of India in March 1992 suggested that Russia was keen to continue its military ties with India. During the forthcoming visit by a high-level delegation, PTI reported, Moscow was likely to offer sales of Charlie-class nuclear-powered submarines, MIG-31 aircraft and SU-28 fighter bombers. India's interest in these lay in the wish to counter the armada of French Mirage-2000s and U.S. F-16s that Pakistan had acquired.[40] In May 1992, Russia's Economy Minister Andrei Nechaev said that India wanted Russia to continue defence supplies, and these would be implemented in the traditional form of Russian credits.[41] However, the new credits would be at double the existing interest rate and with one-tenth of the payment being made in advance.[42] He also said that Russia had agreed to a new investment credit for the construction of nuclear power stations in India.[43]

The best evidence that relations between Moscow and New Delhi were on a slow upswing again came in an interview by Russia's ambassador to India Anatolii Drukov. He informed the *Asian Defence Journal* on 6 July 1992 that Russia was prepared to shift units for producing frontline aircraft,

37. For a general comment on this, see Inga Thorsson, "In Pursuit of Disarmament," in Ramesh Thakur, ed., *International Conflict Resolution* (Boulder: Westview, 1988), pp. 148–55.
38. BBC, *SWB*, SU/W0215 A/3, 31 January 1992.
39. BBC, *SWB*, SU/1289 B/6, 28 January 1992.
40. BBC, *SWB*, FE/1325 A2/1, 10 March 1992.
41. BBC, *SWB*, SU/W0230 A/9, 15 May 1992.
42. BBC, *SWB*, FE/1372 A1/2, 5 May 1992.
43. BBC, *SWB*, SU/W0230 A/9, 15 May 1992.

tanks, armoured cars and other military equipment for use in India and also for export to third countries. "The idea has been under discussion, but I think we have now to move from an exchange of views to the concrete deal, the contract," he said.[44] The arms production joint venture would be helped by the Russo-Indian experience in joint enterprises in other fields.

The best indication of the blurred boundaries between political, economic and military dimensions of international relationships and of the enduring strength of the Indo-Russian relationship came with the contretemps over the rocket engines deal. On 11 May 1992 Washington imposed a two-year sale and technology-transfer sanctions on both Russia and India in punishment for the sale. The U.S. insisted that the rocket technology was dual-use, capable of being diverted to military uses and therefore prohibited under the Missile Technology Control Regime. Russia was equally insistent that the sale of equipment and technology for the cryogenic rockets was consistent with the MTCR and that it was prepared to have neutral experts verify this. Both India and Russia argued further that the U.S. sanctions were motivated by commercial compulsions since the U.S. firm General Dynamics had been outbid by Glavkosmos, the Russian space agency. Russian government adviser Mikhail Maley insisted that Russia, whose people had to face serious food and other scarcities, could not afford to be more moral than Western countries which were still selling their military products on world markets.[45] A report in *Izvestiia* on 6 May 1992 noted that if Moscow disregarded the U.S. warning, it risked the loss of $4 bn worth of aid. But if it went back on the deal, it would lose a profitable contract whose fulfilment would enable the acquisition of consumer goods from India. Secretary of State Burbulis said in New Delhi in May that Russia was firmly committed to the deal in conformity with its obligations and with international norms.[46] This might well be the first Russian challenge to the U.S. in the new order.

Central Asia

Developments in Central Asia and Afghanistan concerned India firstly because of the damaging after-effects of the disintegration of the Moscow-New Delhi axis, secondly because of the desire to counter Pakistan's rising influence, thirdly because of the goal of containing the spread of Islamic consciousness and fourthly because of the need to insulate Muslim-majority Kashmir from the turmoil to the north. By the end of 1991 India was

---

44. *Asian Defence Journal*, August 1992, p. 96.
45. BBC, *SWB*, SU/W0230 A/17, 15 May 1992.
46. BBC, *SWB*, FE/1372 A1/1, 5 May 1992 and FE/1373 A1/3–4, 6 May 1992.

moving swiftly to establish direct links with the Central Asian republics, opening and upgrading diplomatic missions, exchanging high-level visits and signing bilateral cooperation agreements.

The erosion of the Islamabad-Washington strategic axis reduced the international political costs to Pakistan of establishing close relations with Azerbaijan and the Central Asian republics of the FSU. By the same token, this adds yet another element to the growing convergence between New Delhi and Washington. In time it could also provide a fresh basis to India and Russia establishing a bridge across the Islamic world (with tacit if not open U.S. support) in Southwest and Central Asia which threatens their respective border regions.

During a visit to India in January 1992, Senator Larry Pressler warned of the possibility of a threat from the confederation of nine Islamic states: five republics of the FSU and Afghanistan, Iran, Pakistan and Turkey.[47] Fears of an anti-Western Islamic bloc impelled Washington to establish embassies in all the Central Asian states. In a commentary on Radio Moscow's *World Service* on 14 February, A. Kondratiev remarked that "Moscow too is worried that a contest for political influence may turn the region into a powder keg."[48]

Speaking on 26 February 1992, Sergei Filatov, first deputy chairman of the Russian parliament, expressed concern at the growing Islamic influence of southern neighbours, especially Iran and Pakistan, on the Central Asian members of the CIS.[49] The fears were expressed more bluntly by another Russian commentator on Radio Moscow's *World Service* on 9 May 1992.[50] Should there be a marked resurgence of Islamic fundamentalism in Central and Southwest Asia, then India and Russia would have a common interest in trying to contain any further spread northwards or southwards.

Indian responses to the ferment in Central Asia were shaped not simply by calculations of present geopolitical realities and fears of importing religious turbulence but also by memories of historical invasions of the subcontinent from the north. Kazakh President Nursultan Nazarbaev, who emerged as Central Asia's most forceful international spokesman, visited India and Pakistan in February 1992. In New Delhi his words were reassuring to the audience: Kazakhstan, he declared firmly, would remain a secular state. The Central Asian republics would not join a bloc of fundamentalist states even if one were created.[51] The visit ended with the

---

signing of five agreements on diplomatic relations and trade and economic cooperation. Indian businesses were invited to invest in Kazakhstan and set up joint ventures. The visit was followed by a high-level delegation from the Indian foreign ministry visiting Kazakhstan in June.

In Pakistan Nazarbaev expressed strong support for a speedy solution to the conflict in Afghanistan. Muslims represent less than 40 percent of Kazakhstan's population, and Nazarbaev wanted to insure his republic against an upsurge of Islamic fundamentalism. He made the point in Pakistan that trade links could be maintained effectively only through Afghan territory, hence the need for a settlement of the Afghan conflict.[52]

The war in Afghanistan had spilled over into Central Asia even before the breakup of the Soviet Union. Following the visit of President Nazarbaev to New Delhi, there was speculation that Kazakhstan and India could cooperate in providing aid to the Najibullah government in Afghanistan: Kazakhstan did not consider itself to be bound by the U.S.-Soviet accords on stopping military deliveries to Kabul.[53]

By geography and religion, Pakistan occupies a ringside seat overlooking the Middle East and Central Asia. But by history, culture and geography, Pakistan is South Asian. Pakistan is therefore a conduit connecting Central and South Asia. Conscious that Central Asia's leaders feared the rise of Islamic fundamentalism, in early 1992 Pakistan finally decided to try to stabilise the post-Soviet withdrawal situation in Afghanistan in order to establish a reliable political bridge with Central Asia.[54] Pakistan has a threefold interest in Central Asia: to expand its regional influence by forging new links with the newest members of the Muslim community of nations, to secure trade links and to provide landlocked Central Asia with the most convenient outlet to the sea. All three goals would be endangered if the territory in between Central Asia and Pakistan was seething with strife. Afghanistan contains substantial segments of Tajik, Turkmen and Uzbek peoples, and any intensification of the civil war in Afghanistan could easily cross political borders to engulf the Central Asian republics.

Both India and Pakistan have economic interests in the region as well. Central Asia was developed by Tsarist and Soviet Russia as a colonial dependency which traded raw or semi-processed commodities in exchange for more expensive finished goods from the Slavic dominated republics in the FSU. The successor-states to the FSU moved to recast their economies as autonomous units by diversifying markets and sources of raw material,

52. BBC, *SWB*, SU/1314 B/8, 26 February 1992.
53. BBC, *SWB*, SU/1314 B/7, 26 February 1992.
54. See Edward A. Gargan, "Fiscal and Political Forces Move Pakistan to Seek Afghan Peace," *New York Times*, 16 February 1992.

capital and technology. Countries that used to trade with the Soviet Union as a monolithic economic actor were forced to compartmentalise their trade with the new republics. But Western firms by and large have stayed away from Central Asia for fears of political and economic instability, lack of infrastructure and unfamiliarity with local conditions. Of the more than 1,500 foreign-Soviet joint ventures set up in the Soviet Union by March 1990, only 25 were in Central Asia.[55]

By contrast, firms from India and Pakistan felt quite at home with business practices in Central Asia. They took advantage of their geographic proximity and cultural and linguistic links to establish or expand footholds there. South Asian businesses began a campaign of "guerrilla investment" in Central Asia: starting small, relying on knowledge of local people and conditions, exploiting long-established personal contacts, being prepared to visit people and spend long hours in apparently idle chatter over seemingly endless cups of tea. Western firms operate under established systems of rules centred on the contract; Central Asia was returning to its Eastern roots.

Pakistan

Given the sensitivity of the emerging situation in Central and Southwest Asia, Moscow has a particular reason to restore good relations with Islamabad. Soviet relations with Pakistan from the 1960s onwards were shaped by three factors: the latter's political and military links with China and the United States, and Moscow's own relations with India. In the 1980s a fourth factor was added to this list, namely Afghanistan.

By culture, religion and geography Pakistan lies at the confluence of three regions: the Middle East, Central Asia and South Asia. Yet participation in the multinational force failed to prevent a marginalisation of Pakistan from developments in the Middle East after the Gulf War. Pakistan's attention is therefore now concentrated on the two immediate regions to its east and north. Relations with India have been hostile since simultaneous independence in 1947 as successor-states to British India. Since the bilateral relativities favoured India, Pakistan moved to establish military links with the U.S. But Washington was interested in the relationship only in the contest of its global rivalry with Moscow; the U.S.-Pakistan alliance therefore brought India and the Soviet Union together. The parallel developments of the Sino-Soviet schism, Sino-Indian conflict and Sino-Pakistan entente in the 1960s and 1970s ensured that prospects of relations between Pakistan and the USSR were subordinated to the India

---

55. James Rupert, "Central Asia's Ties that Bind," *International Herald Tribune*, 2 December 1991.

factor. In the words of a Pakistani scholar, Islamabad was told repeatedly that "the road to Moscow was via New Delhi."[56]

The Bangladesh War of 1971, following closely on the India-USSR Friendship Treaty, left Pakistan bitter at Soviet collusion in its dismemberment at the hands of its historic enemy. The Soviet invasion of Afghanistan in 1979 revived the fears of Soviet designs while also giving Pakistan an opportunity to inflict pain on the Soviet Union in coalition with the United States and the Islamic world. There was some opposition in Pakistan to the government's policy. The war in Afghanistan exported the "Kalashnikov culture" to Pakistan. There was also fear that Pakistan was incurring the enmity of one superpower as a proxy of the other superpower which had proven unreliable as a security guarantor in the past.

The Indo-Pakistani and U.S.-Soviet axes intersected again in the 1980s just as they had done in the 1950s. With the invasion of Afghanistan, Soviet commentators began an immediate campaign of impressing upon Indian minds sinister connections between Pakistan, China and the U.S., connections that would be as threatening to Indian interests as to the Soviet Union.[57]

Towards Pakistan itself Soviet policy was one of calculated ambiguity. Pakistan was home to three million Afghan refugees, the staging ground for guerrilla attacks on Afghanistan and a frontline state in the Islamic-cum-Western attempts to dislodge the Soviet Union from Afghanistan. The Soviet response was three-pronged. First, they repeatedly urged the wisdom of accommodation between the governments in power in Kabul and Islamabad and dangled the carrot of economic assistance which would flow from an accord. Second, Moscow issued several veiled warnings to Pakistan if it persisted with its policy of providing a base to the *mujahideen*. Third, the Soviet Union was nevertheless careful not to push its intimidation to the point where it would trigger a major escalation into a war with Pakistan with incalculable regional and international consequences.

After the Soviet pullout from Afghanistan, articles and editorials in the Pakistani press revealed unease and uncertainty about India's role.[58] Pakistan's three major goals were the return of refugees to Afghanistan, the installation of a friendly government in Kabul and exclusion of India from influence in Kabul. Soviet overtures to Pakistan, directed at winning Islamabad's support for an accommodation in Kabul, the release of Soviet

---

56. Rasul B. Rais, "Pakistan in the Regional and Global Power Structure," *Asian Survey* 31 (April 1991), p. 390.

57. For example Boris Chekhonin, "Looking into the Future," *New Times* 4/80 (January 1980), p. 11.

58. *Statesman Weekly*, 19 March 1988.

prisoners of war and a curtailment of Pakistan's support for the *mujahideen* failed to gain much headway in the face of Pakistan's different agenda.

The Soviet withdrawal from Afghanistan removed one pillar of the strategic bridge between Islamabad and Washington. The end of the Cold War and the collapse of Soviet communism removed a second pillar. The moderation of Iran after the death of the Ayatollah Ruhollah Khomeini eliminated the third pillar. As the strategic overlay was removed, underlying tensions and disjunctions of interests were highlighted, for example nuclear proliferation and the rise of Islamic assertiveness.

In the Afghan war, President Zia-ul-Haq had committed Pakistan to the fundamentalist leader Gulbuddin Hikmatyar. Now it is Hikmatyar who is proving most resistant to the *mujahideen* government in Kabul and continuing the bloody civil war. Beyond Afghanistan, Pakistan has moved swiftly to capitalise on the emergence of Muslim states from the ruins of the old Soviet Union.

The disintegration of the Soviet Union thus created turmoil in Indian foreign policy but presented unexpected opportunities to Pakistan. The breakdown of the strategic partnership between Islamabad and Washington increased the temptation to exploit the opportunities, while the warming of relations between Beijing and Moscow reduced the risks of antagonising an old and trusted ally by such a course. By mid-1991 Pakistan was reported to be exploring ways of obtaining military spares and missiles from Moscow for its fleet of F-7Ps (Chinese-built MIG-21F copies).[59]

Pakistan's Minister of Economic Affairs Sardar Asif Ali held talks in Moscow on 25 November 1991 with Vice-President Aleksander Rutskoi on the development of political, trade and economic links as well as on the Afghan conflict. When Rutskoi visited Islamabad in January 1992, Pakistan announced that it would support the move to have Russia take the seat of the FSU in the UN Security Council. The two countries would also explore ways of developing cooperation in various fields.[60] On 3 March Russian radio reported that Pakistan was to explore the possibility of purchasing MIG-29 and SU-27 fighters from Russia.[61] In April an international conference was held in Moscow on relations between Pakistan and the CIS. Participants explored the possibilities of opening a port for Russia on Pakistan's coast as a means of simplifying and accelerating the turnover of goods between Pakistan and the CIS states. Other proposals included joint development of oil, gas and metal deposits and Pakistan's participation in conversion of defence factories in the CIS into civilian industries.[62]

---

59. *Asian Defence Journal*, September 1991, p. 97.
60. BBC, *SWB*, SU/1241 A3/1, 28 November 1991; SU/1245 A3/2, 3 December 1991; and FE/1264 A2/8, 28 December 1991.
61. BBC, *SWB*, SU/1325 A3/2, 10 March 1992.
62. BBC, *SWB*, SU/W0227 A/2, 24 April 1992.

Of much greater significance than general explorations of relations between Pakistan and Russia are the speedy establishment of a range of ties with the Central Asian states. Pakistan planned to establish embassies in all the Central Asian republics. In December 1991 Economics Minister Asif Ali led a team of Pakistani businessmen on a trip exploring prospects for trade in Kazakhstan, Kirgizstan, Tajikistan, Turkmenistan and Uzbekistan. In February 1992, meeting in Tehran, Pakistan, Iran and Turkey invited Azerbaijan, Kirgizstan, Tajikistan, Turkmenistan and Uzbekistan to join the Economic Cooperation Organisation (ECO). Asif Ali offered long-term credits of between $10m and $30m each to the Central Asian republics. Pakistani banks and hotels looked to open branches in Central Asia, while the latter were interested in new routes to the outside world through Pakistan. There was talk of joint ventures in cement, textiles and tourism, of Pakistani help in English-language training and of transfer of surplus power from Tajikistan to power-starved northern Pakistan. The state-owned Pakistan International Airlines opened weekly flights to Tashkent in the new year. The private-sector firm Tabbani signed $200m worth of deals for exporting consumer goods and agreed to collaborate with the Uzbek government in starting a new airline Asia Air. Pakistani businessmen responded to pleas from Kazakhstan in December 1991 and raised $100m within three days to help ward off bankruptcy.[63]

The temptation to exploit multiple points of contact against the historical Indian enemy is too strong. Prime Minister Mohammad Nawaz Sharif visited Uzbekistan in June 1992 at the head of a 150-strong delegation to inaugurate the Pakistani embassy in Tashkent. A number of bilateral agreements were signed to promote cooperation on a broad range of economic, scientific and cultural fields, reinforced by further agreements signed during President Islam Karimov's return visit to Pakistan on 12–15 August. During the official banquet on 27 June, Nawaz Sharif spoke at length on the situation in "occupied Kashmir." Karimov responded by expressing support for Pakistan's stand on resolving the Kashmir problem and assured Pakistan of Uzbekistan's support on the matter at the UN.[64]

Others

In relations with the other countries of South Asia, Moscow has generally felt little need to disturb their traditional orientations. They neither posed any threat to Soviet interests nor offered much potential to advance Soviet regional or international goals. The Soviet foreign ministry's own

---

63. Ahmed Rashid, "The Crutches Are Off," *FEER*, 9 January 1992, p. 18.
64. BBC, *SWB*, SU/1420 A3/1–2, 30 June 1992.

survey of the region for the 1985–89 period noted that the USSR had yet to establish forms of cooperation with "the so-called smaller countries of southern Asia" in a manner which would accord with their levels of development and Soviet interests.[65]

Like India, **Bangladesh** entered into barter agreements with the Soviet Union and extended cooperation to scientific and cultural fields, for example an agreement to this effect signed on 25 May 1987 during the visit of Deputy Foreign Minister Egor Rogachev.[66] Moscow also agreed to offer 40 scholarships every year. Bangladesh exported traditional products like jute, textiles and leather and tea in return for Soviet oil and machinery and equipment. Moscow was also involved in constructing power plants in Bangladesh in the 1980s.

After the breakup of the Soviet Union, the government of Bangladesh encouraged its merchants to exploit religious links and move into Azerbaijan and Central Asia. In part the motivation was to insure the country against market-closing moves elsewhere, for example the EC. Bangladesh organised trade fairs in Ashkhabad and Tashkent. One difficulty for Bangladesh is that the Central Asians want barter arrangements rather than hard-currency payments. Turkmenistan, for example, wants to export cotton, cement and oil in exchange for consumer goods. But Bangladesh needs new sources of hard-currency earnings.

Given the size and location of the **Maldives**, it is hardly surprising that that the country had virtually no contact with or significance for the Soviet Union. But it is worth remembering that the reversal of the coup in the Maldives on 3 November 1988 was executed by Indian military forces equipped largely with Soviet armaments. It was the military link with Moscow that had given India the requisite rapid reaction, long-range air insertion capability.[67]

Relations between Moscow and Kathmandu were no more substantial, although it was easier to include **Nepal** in the itinerary of Soviet dignitaries visiting South Asia. Egor Rogachev went to Kathmandu in May 1987 and held discussions on such general topics as the security situation in Asia-Pacific. The first Soviet business delegation to visit Nepal went there in January 1988. Occasionally Nepal would be included as a stop for touring Soviet officials in order to cultivate its vote in the UN General Assembly, for example in August 1988 before the 43rd Assembly session began in September.

---

65. *International Affairs* (Moscow), January 1990, pp. 77–78.

66. BBC, *SWB*, FE/8578 A2/3, 27 May 1987.

67. For an account of the incident, see Shekhar Gupta, "Maldives: A Close Shave," *India Today*, 30 November 1988, pp. 28–32.

By contrast, **Sri Lanka** has been of some international significance and therefore worthy of some Soviet attention. But traditionally Moscow viewed developments in Sri Lanka through the prism of its relations with New Delhi. The most critical point of Sri Lanka's articulation with the outside world since the mid-1980s has been the continuing ethnic violence involving the Tamils. By and large Soviet pronouncements and policies on the conflict have been guided by Indian actions.[68]

In the early phases of the insurrection, Moscow joined New Delhi in denying that it was providing arms to the Tamil guerrillas.[69] India and the Soviet Union were united also in their apprehensions about a possible Western involvement in Sri Lanka in support of the government. When Indian Foreign Minister Narain Dutt Tiwari went to Moscow in early June 1987, the developing crisis in Sri Lanka was a major topic of discussion. Indeed at about the time that Tiwari was in Moscow, Soviet-supplied AN-32 transport planes of the IAF were dropping relief supplies over the Jaffna peninsula against the objections of a hapless Sri Lankan government but with the support of Soviet commentators.[70]

Sri Lanka was also a major topic of discussion during Rajiv Gandhi's trip to the Soviet Union in July. The Indo-Sri Lanka accord of 29 July 1987, which saw the introduction of a large Indian Peace-Keeping Force (IPKF) to the Jaffna Peninsula to replace government troops there and restricted Sri Lankan options in defence-foreign policy, was warmly welcomed by Moscow. Soviet media still continued to engage in periodic vitriolic commentaries on CIA and Israeli interference in Sri Lanka, for example Radio Moscow's Tamil service on 19 October and a Tass report on 26 October 1987.[71] With the unravelling of the peace accord, Moscow maintained support for the Indian military campaign against the LTTE.[72]

As the civil war showed no signs of abating, however, and sucked India into the Tamil quagmire; as Gorbachev's New Thinking began to encourage the settlement of regional conflicts by peaceful means; and as Moscow's relations with Washington improved, Soviet perceptions began to shift. By 1989 Moscow believed that India should withdraw the IPKF from Sri Lanka and their withdrawal in 1990 was welcomed by Moscow.

---

68. See Amal Jayawardane, "The Soviet Attitude Towards the Indo-Sri Lankan Problem," *Pacific Affairs* 64 (Summer 1991).

69. See, for example, the statement from the Soviet embassy in Colombo on 30 April 1987 in BBC, *SWB*, SU/8559/A3/2, 5 May 1987.

70. See, for example, Leonid Zhegalov, "A Humanitarian Act," *New Times* 24/87 (June 1987), pp. 7–8.

71. BBC, *SWB*, SU/8709/A3/6–7, 27 October 1987 and SU/8724/A3/2–3, 13 November 1987.

72. See, for example, Sergei Irodov, "Abiding by the Agreement," *New Times* 6/88 (February 1988), p. 21.

The main preoccupation of the Sri Lankan government in 1991–92 remained the war against the LTTE. Their interest in the collapse of the Soviet Union in this period was necessarily somewhat detached. But the events in Moscow did have an echo in distant Colombo. In June 1992, *Moscow News* published an article alleging that the KGB had secretly funded Mrs. Sirimavo Bandaranaike's Sri Lanka Freedom Party in the 1989 elections. She had promised to use increased parliamentary representation to challenge the government's pro-Western foreign policy. Moreover, the KGB had paid for successful parliamentary bids by a number of its confidants from the United National Party as well.[73]

There were of course other dimensions to the Sri Lanka-USSR relationship, including cultural and scientific exchange agreements. But in general Soviet-Sri Lanka ties remained thin and shallow.

Conclusion

The collapse of the Soviet Union intersected with the end of the Cold War in two ways in South Asia. First, it simultaneously eroded the Islamabad-Washington axis and lessened U.S. suspicions of India's close links with Moscow. Second, it recreated Central Asia as a geopolitical entity with marked geographical and cultural ties to parts of South Asia. The changes produced ambivalent responses from the two leading South Asian powers. Both India and Pakistan welcomed the diminution of international tension, but both also grew uneasy at the possibility that their competitive special relationships with the superpowers would wane.

By the end of the 1980s the Soviet Union had already begun to relegate South Asia to a subordinate position vis-à-vis East Asia. The 1980s proved to be a decade of major Soviet defeats. Moscow began to reassess the costs and risks of opportunities for further penetrations in the Third World. Benefits were uncertain, gains remained elusive, but the cost was substantial. Soviet statements and writings dwelt upon three sets of concerns: the escalating costs of supporting Third World clients, the dubious political and economic records of many of these clients and the damage caused by links to unsavoury regimes to other Soviet interests, in particular to U.S.-USSR relations.

The special relationship with New Delhi had made India the centrepiece of Moscow's South Asian policy. While ties with India were largely insulated from general Soviet disillusionment with the Third World, it was nonetheless clear by 1990 that the relationship was due for demystification.

---

73. *Hindu Weekly,* 20 June 1992, p. 7.

The disappearance of the Soviet Union created an economic, strategic and policy vacuum for Indian foreign policy. Part of the reason why India has had difficulty coming to terms with the fast-unfolding events was that India was not simply losing its most important international ally; it was also confronted with a challenge to its sense of Third World solidarity and its faith in socialism. Another difficulty is that Russia has as yet no conceptual underpinning to its post-USSR foreign policy. There is no coherence or overarching framework to give meaning and direction to Moscow's conduct of external relations. But, as noted above, new policy bridges are being built between Moscow and New Delhi. An elder statesman of India's foreign policy analysts notes that "The afterglow of four decades of Indo-Soviet friendship is still to be found in Russia, Kazakhstan, Ukraine and several other republics of the Commonwealth [of Independent States]."[74]

While Yeltsin's administration lacks an India orientation, there is a reservoir of affection towards India among a large number of individuals and sectors that had had contacts with the country. A Soviet scholar had argued in 1990 that to jeopardise a tried and tested friendship with India would be "stupid... fallacious... shortsighted."[75] Among many Indians too there remains a matching goodwill in its hour of need towards a country that stood by them through good times and bad. In the winter of 1990–91, India sent a million tonnes of wheat as loan and 20,000 tonnes of rice as gift to a Soviet Union facing severe food shortages: "the least that it can do for... a staunch friend and unwavering ally of long standing," said a major Indian newspaper.[76] Dr R. I. Khasbulatov, Chairman of the Supreme Soviet of Russia, leading a 15-strong parliamentary delegation to India in August 1992, noted the common desire to strengthen bilateral cooperation. India and Russia, he said, had every reason to be proud of their collective experience over four decades; nobody had the right to subject this accumulated wealth of bilateral experience to fresh scrutiny or to hinder development of the joint heritage.[77]

Interests that New Delhi, Moscow and Washington have in common include avoiding an India-Pakistan war, the promotion of pluralist democracy and market economy, opposition to fundamentalist religious and other ethnic movements, opposition to terrorism and to drug trafficking and the establishment of secure and peaceful borders. Parallel interests on land are reinforced by convergent interests at sea. All three countries have a stake

74. Bhabani Sengupta, "Former Friends: Time to Rebuild India-Russia Ties," *Statesman Weekly*, 29 February 1992, p. 12.

75. Tatiana Shaumian, "Thirty-five Years Later," *New Times* 32/90 (August 1990), p. 7.

76. Editorial in the *Hindu Weekly*, 22 December 1990, p. 8.

77. BBC, *SWB*, FE/1455 A1/2, 10 August 1992.

in ensuring freedom of the high seas, safety of the sea lanes of communication around the entire rim of the Indian Ocean from Africa to Indochina and peace and stability around the Indian Ocean littoral. The most important significance of the joint naval exercises by India and the United States in May 1992 is that they imply a mutual acceptance of each other's legitimate strategic interests in the Indian Ocean area.

The India-Pakistan rivalry was one of the main planks of the old geopolitical alliance between Moscow and New Delhi. Now the subcontinental rivalry is being extended to Central Asia. Pakistan succeeded in inserting a sentence in the joint press release issued at the end of the May 1992 Ashkhabad summit calling for a settlement of the Kashmir problem peacefully and in accordance with the principles of the UN Charter.[78] In this competitive search for influence in the region, Pakistan has the substantial advantages of geographic proximity and shared religion. But it also faces the greater danger from both in a part of the world where borders are notoriously porous to ethnic and religious turbulence.

The rest of South Asia too faces many problems comparable to the challenges confronting Russia and the CIS. Relations between these two groups of countries, never close, is likely to remain distant as all of them concentrate on internal issues.

---

78. BBC, *SWB*, SU/1378 C3/3, 12 May 1992.

9

Regional Conflicts
Afghanistan and Cambodia

William Maley

In 1979, two regimes in Asia were overthrown by external invasion: the Khmer Rouge regime in "Democratic Kampuchea" by Vietnam and the Khalq regime in the "Democratic Republic of Afghanistan" by the USSR. In 1989, both invaders withdrew their forces, substantially remitting to the United Nations the task of seeking to rebuild a degree of domestic political order in these ravaged polities. However, the political paths which Afghanistan and Cambodia subsequently took proved to be quite different, and this chapter explores some of the reasons why. It is divided into six sections. The first briefly examines the way in which changes in the Soviet leadership from 1985 prompted shifts in official Soviet ideology and policies towards "regional conflicts." The second traces the history of the Afghanistan problem and the third the history of the Cambodian problem. The fourth and fifth sections examine the politics of these conflicts since the withdrawal of the occupation forces, and the sixth concludes with a warning.

"New Thinking"

The Soviet Union in the second half of the Brezhnev era pursued a dextrous foreign policy in which détente with the West—inaugurated at the 1972 summit between Soviet General Secretary Leonid Brezhnev and U.S. President Richard Nixon, and consolidated at the 1975 Helsinki Conference—coexisted with a more vigorous Soviet exploitation of opportunities for expansion of its ties with developing countries provided by the end of the Vietnam War and the collapse of the Portuguese Empire in

Africa.[1] This policy was reinforced by an official ideology, articulated by
Brezhnev at the 1976 Party Congress, which depicted class struggle as an
enduring feature of politics in Third World countries which a policy of
peaceful coexistence did not obliterate, and the Soviet leadership as an
appropriate partner for those forces within developing countries which were
challenging the forces of imperialism.[2] As Georgii Shakhnazarov put it,
"peaceful coexistence differs from the mere notion of peace in that it is
accompanied by ideological struggle."[3] However, at a lower level in official
establishments in the USSR, vigorous debates on the merits of such a
Weltanschauung were taking place,[4] and the emergence of M. S. Gorbachev
as General Secretary in 1985, and the inauguration in 1986 of the policy of
glasnost, allowed these debates to surface with a vengeance.

Gorbachev's advent triggered a massive program of change, prompted
by the grim condition of his inheritance,[5] and in the sphere of international
politics the result was the adoption of a new ideological position, that of so-
called "new thinking" (*novoe myshlenie*), which postulated a very different

1. For discussions of this period, see Raymond L. Garthoff, *Détente and Confrontation: American-Soviet Relations from Nixon to Reagan* (Washington DC: The Brookings Institution, 1985); and Joseph G. Whelan and Michael J. Dixon, *The Soviet Union in the Third World: Threat to World Peace?* (Washington DC: Pergamon-Brassey's, 1986).

2. For detailed discussions of the evolution of Soviet views on international relations, see William Zimmerman, *Soviet Perspectives on International Relations 1956–1967* (Princeton: Princeton University Press, 1969); Vendulka Kubálková and A. A. Cruickshank, *Marxism-Leninism and Theory of International Relations* (London: Routledge & Kegan Paul, 1980); Vendulka Kubálková and A. A. Cruickshank, *Marxism and International Relations* (Oxford: Oxford University Press, 1985); Allen Lynch, *The Soviet Study of International Relations* (Cambridge: Cambridge University Press, 1987); and Margot Light, *The Soviet Theory of International Relations* (Brighton: Wheatsheaf, 1988).

3. G. Shakhnazarov, "Problema mira: analiz osnovnykh poniatii," *Voprosy filosofii* 7/1979, p. 27.

4. See Daniel S. Papp, *Soviet Perceptions of the Developing World in the 1980s: The Ideological Basis* (Lexington: D. C. Heath, 1985); and Jerry F. Hough, *The Struggle for the Third World: Soviet Debates and American Options* (Washington DC: The Brookings Institution, 1986).

5. For some discussion of Gorbachev and his inheritance, see Moshe Lewin, *The Gorbachev Phenomenon: A Historical Interpretation* (Berkeley: University of California Press, 1988); Boris Meissner, *Die Sowjetunion im Umbruch* (Stuttgart: Deutsche Verlags-Anstalt GmbH, 1988); Abraham Brumberg, ed., *Chronicle of a Revolution: A Western-Soviet Inquiry into Perestroika* (New York: Pantheon Books, 1990); Geoffrey Hosking, *The Awakening of the Soviet Union* (London: Heinemann, 1990); Jerry F. Hough, *Russia and the West: Gorbachev and the Politics of Reform* (New York: Simon and Schuster, 1990); T. H. Rigby, *The Changing Soviet System: Mono-organisational Socialism from its Origins to Gorbachev's Restructuring* (Aldershot: Edward Elgar, 1990); Richard Sakwa, *Gorbachev and His Reforms 1985–1990* (New York: Philip Allan, 1990); Stephen White, *Gorbachev and After* (Cambridge: Cambridge University Press, 1991); and Chandran Kukathas, David W. Lovell and William Maley, eds., *The Transition from Socialism: State and Civil Society in the USSR* (London: Longman, 1991).

pattern of relations between the Soviet Union and the countries of the Third World. The search for international security was depicted in positive-sum rather than zero-sum terms; military confrontation was de-emphasised; and "national reconciliation" was mooted as an appropriate strategy in those Third World countries in which the Soviet leadership had hitherto thrown its weight behind particular ruling or non-ruling forces.[6] The entanglement of the USSR and its ally Vietnam in Afghanistan and Cambodia respectively had contributed to the emergence of this new position, and both Afghanistan and Cambodia were to benefit from its adoption, although to a lesser extent than is often thought.

Afghanistan

Afghanistan's fatal involvement with the Soviet Union can be dated from the mid-1950s, when Prime Minister Mohammad Daoud, rebuffed in his efforts to secure substantial development aid from the United States, turned instead to Afghanistan's northern neighbour.[7] Soviet aid principally took the form of low interest loans for the purchase of Soviet capital equipment and training and equipment for Afghanistan's armed forces.[8] With the removal of Daoud by the Afghan monarch Zahir Shah and the initiation in 1964 of the "New Democracy" experiment, Soviet emphasis shifted towards the promotion of radical political forces whose relatively free functioning the new climate of pluralism would permit. At the beginning of 1965, the People's Democratic Party of Afghanistan (PDPA) was officially founded under the leadership of Nur Muhammad Taraki and Babrak Karmal. However, within two years it had split into two factions, the Parcham ("Banner") faction, led by Karmal and supported particularly by Persian-speaking urban dwellers, and the Khalq ("Masses") faction, led by Taraki and Hafizullah Amin and predominantly backed by detribalised Pushtuns.[9]

---

6. For details, see Anatolii Gromyko and Vladimir Lomeiko, *Novoe myshlenie v iadernyi vek* (Moscow: Mezhdunarodnye otnosheniia, 1984); Vendulka Kubálková and A. A. Cruickshank, *Thinking New About Soviet "New Thinking"* (Berkeley: Institute of International Studies, University of California, 1989); and Robert F. Miller, *Soviet Foreign Policy Today: Gorbachev and the New Political Thinking* (Sydney: Allen & Unwin, 1991).

7. See Henry S. Bradsher, *Afghanistan and the Soviet Union* (Durham: Duke University Press, 1985), pp. 17–31.

8. See M. S. Noorzoy, "Soviet Economic Interests in Afghanistan," *Problems of Communism* 36 (May–June 1987), pp. 43–54; and Muhammad R. Azmi, "Soviet Politico-Military Penetration in Afghanistan, 1955 to 1979," *Armed Forces & Society* 12 (Spring 1986), pp. 329–50.

9. For the most detailed account of the early history of the PDPA, see Anthony Arnold, *Afghanistan's Two-Party Communism: Parcham and Khalq* (Stanford: Hoover Institution Press, 1983).

In July 1973 Daoud mounted a successful coup against the King, and established a republic. In order to do so he was obliged to rely on the tacit support of the Parcham faction, which was rewarded with a number of posts in his cabinet.[10] However, the relationship was short-lived and by 1977 they had all been removed from office. Daoud's spectacular clash with Brezhnev during a visit to the Soviet Union in 1977 brought Soviet-Afghan relations to their nadir.[11] Under pressure from the Soviet leadership, the Khalq and Parcham reunited and in April 1978, they mounted a further coup which resulted in the death of Daoud and the political order over which he had presided.

The *ancien régime* in Afghanistan had survived on the basis of a degree of legitimacy provided by its association with the long-dominant Muhammadzai dynasty,[12] of which both Zahir Shah and Daoud were members, and a considerable degree of caution in taking any steps which might mortally offend the sensibilities of rural power holders. The new regime, headed by Taraki as President and Prime Minister, with Amin and Karmal as Deputy Prime Ministers, had no claim to such legitimacy and showed much less caution. As a result, when its policies—and its cadres—met with opposition, its main tool for bolstering its position proved to be coercion. This, however, proved counter-productive, as it drove the disparate elements of Afghan society into a tighter alliance against Kabul.[13] Furthermore, the opposition which the regime faced increasingly took on an organised form, as Islamic resistance groups (*mujahideen*) developed both in Afghanistan and within the growing community of Afghan exiles in Pakistan. Scattered opposition thus escalated to insurgency[14] and confronted the new regime with a challenge which it was simply not equal to meeting.

The Soviet leadership viewed these developments with considerable alarm, but its room to manoeuvre was extremely limited. Factional strife struck the new regime within a few months of Daoud's fall, and Karmal and other senior members of the Parcham faction, with whom the Soviets

---

10. See Amin Saikal and William Maley, *Regime Change in Afghanistan: Foreign Intervention and the Politics of Legitimacy* (Boulder: Westview Press, 1991), p. 25.

11. See Abdul Samad Ghaus, *The Fall of Afghanistan: An Insider's Account* (Washington DC: Pergamon-Brassey's, 1988), pp. 178–79.

12. See William Maley, "Political Legitimation in Contemporary Afghanistan," *Asian Survey* 27 (June 1987), pp. 707–11.

13. For details, see William Maley, "Social Dynamics and the Disutility of Terror: Afghanistan, 1978–1989," in P. Timothy Bushnell, Vladimir Shlapentokh, Christopher K. Vanderpool and Jeyaratnam Sundram, eds., *State Organized Terror: The Case of Violent Internal Repression* (Boulder: Westview Press, 1991), pp. 113–31.

14. On the nature of insurgency, see Raj Desai and Harry Eckstein, "Insurgency: The Transformation of Peasant Rebellion," *World Politics* 42 (July 1990), pp. 441–65.

certainly felt more affinity than they did with the hard-line Khalqis, were exiled to diplomatic postings and then expelled from the PDPA, which naturally prompted them to gravitate to Moscow. In September 1979, a clumsy attempt by the Soviets in league with Taraki to procure Amin's replacement by Karmal misfired disastrously, resulting instead in the murder of Taraki and his replacement by Amin. Seeing an imminent danger of the replacement of a pro-Soviet regime with an Islamic republic, the Soviets in December despatched an invasion force to Kabul which killed Amin and installed Karmal and his associates in office.[15]

At this point, a full-scale war developed, with significant international ramifications. The USSR was widely condemned for its invasion and the era of détente came to an immediate halt. Afghan refugees flooded into Pakistan and Iran and the relationship between the United States and Pakistan commenced an upswing, to the consternation of India. The Soviet leadership doubtless hoped that it would rapidly crush the Afghan insurgency at low cost, as it had crushed the *Basmachi* movement in Central Asia in the 1920s.[16] This proved not to be the case. Karmal—known derisorily in Kabul as "Karmalov"—proved incapable of building even a shred of legitimacy for his "rule" and was entirely dependent upon Soviet advisers.[17] Furthermore, Soviet military power, while it succeeded in causing immense sorrow for the Afghan people,[18] managed to deliver little more than control of Kabul, Kandahar, Herat, Mazar-i-Sharif and a number of other towns—which, unable to feed themselves, were heavily dependent on supplies delivered from within the Soviet Union.

The advent of Gorbachev brought a number of changes to policy on Afghanistan. The military option was not abandoned: on the contrary, in the period after Gorbachev became General Secretary, the military campaign was stepped up, and Afghan civilian casualties rose concomitantly.[19]

---

15. For details of the invasion and its background, see Thomas T. Hammond, *Red Flag Over Afghanistan: The Communist Coup, the Soviet Invasion, and the Consequences* (Boulder: Westview Press, 1984); Anthony Arnold, *Afghanistan: The Soviet Invasion in Perspective* (Stanford: Hoover Institution Press, 1985); and Joseph J. Collins, *The Soviet Invasion of Afghanistan: A Study of the Use of Force in Soviet Foreign Policy* (Lexington: D. C. Heath, 1986).

16. On these two cases, see Eden Naby, "The Concept of Jihad in Opposition to Communist Rule: Turkestan and Afghanistan," *Studies in Comparative Communism* 19 (1986), pp. 287–300.

17. See Vladimir Snegirev, "On byl zalozhnikom kremlia: Babrak Karmal' rasskazyvaet," *Trud*, 24 October 1991.

18. Jeri Laber and Barnett R. Rubin, *"A Nation is Dying": Afghanistan under the Soviets, 1978–87* (Evanston: Northwestern University Press, 1988).

19. See Marek Sliwinski, "Afghanistan: The Decimation of a People," *Orbis* 33 (1989), p. 40; and Anthony H. Cordesman and Abraham R. Wagner, *The Lessons of Modern War: The Afghan and Falklands Conflicts* (Boulder: Westview Press, 1990), pp. 53–69.

Karmal was replaced as General Secretary of the PDPA Central Committee by Dr. Najibullah, who had headed the regime's feared secret police (KHAD) from 1980 to 1985, and who immediately announced his commitment to a policy of "national reconciliation." Given Najibullah's background, his policy was scorned by the *mujahideen* and their supporters and from October 1986 U.S.-supplied Stinger anti-aircraft missiles began to find their way in large numbers to the battlefields, effectively depriving the regime and its Soviet backers of vital air cover for combat operations against the resistance.[20] At this point, the Soviet leadership moved to Afghanise the war.

This was accomplished through the auspices of the United Nations, which from June 1982 had orchestrated indirect negotiations in Geneva between Afghanistan and Pakistan. These for years had made little progress, largely because the timetable for Soviet troop withdrawal from Afghanistan proposed by Kabul had been unacceptably long. However, in February 1988 Gorbachev proposed a ten-month withdrawal period and after intense further negotiations, a set of agreements was signed in Geneva in April 1988 providing for the withdrawal of "the foreign troops" by 15 February 1989.[21]

It would be a considerable oversimplification to see the withdrawal from Afghanistan as simply an application of the principles of "new thinking": the escalation of military activity in the early period of Gorbachev's rule suggested, on the contrary, a final attempt to secure a breakthrough in the struggle against the *mujahideen*. Some analysts, such as Richard Herrmann, have suggested that the withdrawal was related more to a "reduction in the perceived threat from the West" than to "Soviet weakness and effective American pressure."[22] This argument, however, is based on confusing a decision to change course with a decision to withdraw, as well as a misunderstanding of the sequence of events.[23] Furthermore, it does not

20. Scott R. McMichael, *Stumbling Bear: Soviet Military Performance in Afghanistan* (London: Brassey's, 1991), pp. 90–91.

21. For an exhaustive account of the negotiations, see Riaz M. Khan, *Untying the Afghan Knot: Negotiating Soviet Withdrawal* (Durham: Duke University Press, 1991).

22. Richard Herrmann, "The Soviet Decision to Withdraw from Afghanistan: Changing Strategic and Regional Images," in Robert Jervis and Jack Snyder, eds., *Dominoes and Bandwagons: Strategic Beliefs and Great Power Competition in the Eurasian Rimland* (New York: Oxford University Press, 1991), p. 238.

23. In dating the turning point in Soviet policy towards Afghanistan early in Gorbachev's term, Herrmann incorrectly places the dismissal of Babrak Karmal in May *1985*, and goes on to state that it "is important to note that this took place before the major increase in American aid to the mujahideen"; "The Soviet Decision to Withdraw from Afghanistan," p. 235. Karmal, of course, was removed in May *1986*, several months *after* it had been reported that the U.S. Administration proposed to arm the resistance with Stinger missiles; Cordesman and Wagner,

explain why the USSR maintained massive and expensive supplies to the Kabul regime even as its Eastern European glacis was allowed to collapse. A more plausible explanation is one which sees both of the factors mentioned by Herrmann as important—but to different bureaucratic hierarchies in Moscow, subject to different rates of personnel turnover, and striking bargains from which each party gained at least some benefit. On this reading of the evidence, neither development mentioned by Herrmann was sufficient to prompt a troop withdrawal, but each may have been necessary.

Cambodia

Cambodia's history has been as sorrowful as Afghanistan's. From 1863 to 1945, Cambodia was subject to a French protectorate, but in March 1945, King Norodom Sihanouk, who had been placed on the throne in 1941, grasped the opportunity provided by a sudden Japanese thrust and proclaimed the protectorate at an end. The process by which substance was given to this declaration proved to be extremely drawn out, but in 1953, France finally recognised Cambodia's independence and this was affirmed at the July 1954 conference in Geneva.

The advent of independence left Cambodia afflicted with a host of political problems. It had little claim to an institutionalised governmental system: Sihanouk had abolished the parliament in 1953 and in March 1955 he abdicated the throne in order to lead a new movement, the Sangkum, into elections held pursuant to the Geneva process. After a campaign marked by widespread intimidation, his party won all the seats, as it continued to do until he was overthrown in a coup d'état by General Lon Nol in March 1970.[24] Sihanouk's father, who had assumed the throne following the abdication, died in 1960, and Sihanouk replaced him as non-monarchical Head of State.

More serious in the long run, however, was the failure of the Geneva process to produce an integrated political order in Vietnam, which remained divided along the 17th parallel. The escalation of conflict in that country, and in particular the increasing involvement of U.S. forces following the assassination of Ngo Dinh Diem in November 1963 and the Gulf of Tonkin

---

Lessons of Modern War, p. 62. For a discussion of recently declassified Soviet archival material which identifies 13 November 1986 as the date of the crucial Politburo discussion on the future course of Soviet policy towards Afghanistan, see Michael Dobbs, "With Kabul Falling, Soviet Slide Began," *International Herald Tribune*, 17 November 1992.

24. David Chandler, *The Tragedy of Cambodian History: Politics, War, and Revolution since 1945* (New Haven: Yale University Press, 1991), pp. 81–84.

resolution in August 1964,[25] created political problems in Cambodia as well. The murder of Diem prompted Sihanouk to discontinue aid from the United States, which had been plausibly implicated in Diem's overthrow. He turned instead to France and China. This was poorly received in the West, as was the increased use of Cambodian territory by North Vietnamese and NLF (National Liberation Front) forces operating against the U.S.-backed South Vietnamese Army. At the same time, both North Vietnam and China stepped up their contacts with Cambodian communists who in 1951 had formed the Khmer People's Revolutionary Party—renamed the Khmer Workers' Party in 1960 and the Communist Party of Kampuchea in 1966. In 1968, the communists, who had been denounced by Sihanouk following the Samlaut uprising from April–August 1967, decided on a course of armed struggle, and this triggered violent oscillations in Sihanouk's position, which culminated in his appointing as Prime Minister Lon Nol, who then overthrew him.[26]

The tragic story of the five years which followed, in which Cambodia was engulfed by the U.S. bombing of Vietnamese bases which had begun in March 1969 and by the expansion of the armed struggle of the Cambodian communists, has been told in detail elsewhere.[27] The most bizarre feature of this period was undoubtedly Sihanouk's alignment with the communists, whom he claimed to lead from exile in Peking. This left him poised to return to Cambodia, although with no real power, when the Lon Nol government was overrun by the Khmer Rouge in April 1975 and replaced by a regime dominated by Khieu Samphan, Ieng Sary, Son Sen and Pol Pot.

The period between 1975 and the overthrow of the Khmer Rouge in January 1979 was notable in two respects. On the one hand, the new regime established one of the most truly totalitarian systems of rule that the world has ever known and committed atrocities on a hideous scale, although with sharp regional variations, exposing Cambodian society to unparalleled traumas.[28] On the other hand, its increasing hostility to the newly-reunited

25. See Guenter Lewy, *America in Vietnam* (New York: Oxford University Press, 1978), pp. 26–28, 32–36.

26. For a discussion of Sihanouk's extreme eccentricity, see Milton Osborne, *Before Kampuchea: Preludes to Tragedy* (Sydney: George Allen & Unwin, 1979), pp. 44–58.

27. William Shawcross, *Sideshow: Kissinger, Nixon and the Destruction of Cambodia* (London: Hogarth Press, 1991).

28. The new regime attracted a number of Western admirers who anathematised with inquisitorial fervour those who initially drew attention to the regime's resort to terror. Although some have recanted, much of the early literature on this period in Cambodia's history still leaves a bad taste in one's mouth. For a discussion of this literature, see William Shawcross, "Cambodia: Some Perceptions of a Disaster," in David P. Chandler and Ben Kiernan, eds., *Revolution and its Aftermath in Kampuchea: Eight Essays* (New Haven: Yale

Vietnam drove it closer to China and consequently away from the Soviet Union, which had become Vietnam's strongest backer and was still deeply suspicious of China, which had broken with it in 1960.[29] Border skirmishes between Vietnam and Cambodia broke out in 1977 and escalated through 1978. As Vickery has pointed out, the Cambodian and Vietnamese communists adopted quite different social and economic systems, bore the legacy of interparty rivalries over many years and were separated by a border which had never been effectively delimited on the ground.[30] To pursue such conflict was nonetheless exceedingly dangerous for the leaders of the Khmer Rouge, and when Vietnamese forces finally entered Cambodia en masse on 25 December 1978, they displaced the Khmer Rouge regime within a matter of days and put in its place a new "Cambodian National United Front for National Salvation" headed by a former Khmer Rouge cadre, Heng Samrin.

At the time of the Vietnamese invasion, some observers saw the new leaders as compromised *ab initio*. "Dependent upon the force of Cambodia's historic enemy," wrote Zasloff and Brown, "their regime will suffer from a lack of legitimacy in the eyes of the Cambodian population."[31] Given the Khmer Rouge's record while in power, this was a daring claim, although to a considerable extent it was based on the denunciation of the Vietnamese invasion by Sihanouk who, released from house arrest, had flown to New York to participate in a United Nations debate on his country.

However, it was a long while before it was put to the test, largely because the Soviet leadership proved willing to make direct contributions to the Heng Samrin regime—between the establishment of the regime and the death of Brezhnev the USSR supplied US $401m of economic aid to Cambodia[32]—as well as in effect to underwrite through its aid contributions to Vietnam a substantial proportion of the costs of maintaining the

---

University Southeast Asia Studies, Monograph Series no. 25, 1983), pp. 230–58. Karl D. Jackson, ed., *Cambodia 1975–1978: Rendezvous with Death* (Princeton: Princeton University Press, 1989) is measured and useful.

29. See Joseph Camilleri, *Chinese Foreign Policy: The Maoist Era and its Aftermath* (Oxford: Martin Robertson, 1980), pp. 225–38.

30. Michael Vickery, *Kampuchea: Politics, Economics, and Society* (London: Frances Pinter, 1986), pp. 35–42.

31. Joseph J. Zasloff and MacAlister Brown, "The Passion of Kampuchea," *Problems of Communism* 28 (January–February 1979), p. 43.

32. Leszek Buszynski, *Soviet Foreign Policy and South East Asia* (London: Croom Helm, 1986), p. 198.

Vietnamese occupation force.[33] The Soviet involvement in Cambodia was far less arduous than in Afghanistan, where its own troops were in the firing line; and it was at the expense of both U.S. and Chinese influence in the region.[34] Nonetheless, the advent of Gorbachev to office again led to a reconsideration of Soviet policy, as was apparent from Gorbachev's Vladivostok speech.[35]

It would be difficult to argue that the Vietnamese withdrawal from Cambodia was a product of changes in personnel or ideology in Moscow, although the Soviets may have prodded Vietnam from time to time: in contrast to the Soviet withdrawal from Afghanistan, it was a step long foreshadowed.[36] It is true that by the late 1980s both China and the USSR had good reasons to put an end to their decades of hostility and this increased the Soviet incentive to seek a Vietnamese withdrawal.[37] However, a number of other factors seem to have been at least as important in producing Vietnamese disengagement. Cambodia had not proved to be a quagmire for Hanoi as Afghanistan had become for Moscow. The Khmer Rouge, in stark contrast to the Afghan *mujahideen*, had a very narrow support base and were heavily dependent on support from China, and indirectly from the Association of South-East Asian Nations (ASEAN) which had denounced Vietnam's invasion and ostracised the regime which it put in place. Furthermore, the regime took on an increasingly Cambodian character which muted the negative effects of its external connections. And finally, the Soviet Union, while involved in diplomacy over the Cambodia issue, stood firm in its support of the Cambodian regime, notably through arms transfers.[38] All these factors meant that once the withdrawal of Vietnamese forces was completed in 1989, the time was opportune for an attempt at a comprehensive internal settlement.

---

33. See Carlyle A. Thayer, "Civil Society and the Soviet-Vietnamese Alliance," in Chandran Kukathas, David W. Lovell and William Maley, eds., *The Transition from Socialism: State and Civil Society in the USSR* (London: Longman, 1991), p. 203.

34. See Harry Gelman, *The Brezhnev Politburo and the Decline of Detente* (Ithaca: Cornell University Press, 1989), p. 167.

35. See Carlyle A. Thayer, "Kampuchea: Soviet Initiatives and Regional Responses," in Ramesh Thakur and Carlyle A. Thayer, eds., *The Soviet Union as an Asian Pacific Power* (Boulder: Westview, 1987), pp. 171–200.

36. See Vickery, *Kampuchea: Politics, Economics, and Society* , p. 181, n33.

37. See Richard Herrmann, "Soviet Behavior in Regional Conflicts: Old Questions, New Strategies, and Important Lessons," *World Politics* 44 (April 1992), pp. 456–57.

38. See Leszek Buszynski, "The Soviet Union and Vietnamese Withdrawal from Cambodia," in Gary Klintworth, ed., *Vietnam's Withdrawal from Cambodia: Regional Issues and Realignments* (Canberra: Canberra Papers on Strategy and Defence no. 64, Strategic and Defence Studies Centre, Research School of Pacific Studies, The Australian National University, 1990), p. 47.

The Afghan Settlement

The 1988 Geneva Accords on Afghanistan in no sense provided for a comprehensive settlement of the Afghanistan problem. They simply provided a veil behind which the USSR could beat an ignominious retreat. As a result, they were denounced by the *mujahideen,* who had been completely excluded from the negotiation process. The Soviet Union had resisted a U.S. proposal for a mutual cutoff in supplies of lethal weapons and materials to the Kabul regime and the *mujahideen* respectively, and thus retained the right to flood Afghanistan with sophisticated and highly destructive weaponry. The Geneva Accords, as I argued at the time, "simply remitted the Afghan conflict to the battlefield—possibly making little difference to Afghanistan's long-term political future, but imposing immense short-run costs on the Afghan people."[39] Subsequent developments unfortunately vindicated that grim assessment.

The determination of the Soviet leadership to provide Najibullah's regime with military support and resources with which to purchase the loyalty of a range of uncommitted rural militias seemed beyond doubt. A massive airlift of military equipment was mounted during and after the Soviet troop withdrawal,[40] and Soviet-supplied Scud B missiles, which Stinger missiles could not intercept, were used against the resistance in vast quantities. One study has concluded that the number of Scud launches in Afghanistan after the signing of the Geneva Accords exceeded the total of "all ballistic missiles fired in anger since the end of the Second World War."[41] At the very time at which this was happening, U.S. support for the resistance dried up altogether.[42] This discrepancy, together with disorganisation in the ranks of the *mujahideen,* substantially accounted for the unexpected survival of the Kabul regime.

However, some factors suggested that the support for Najibullah's regime had more to do with the self-respect of various circles in Moscow than with any abiding commitment to Najibullah himself. In March 1990 his Defence Minister, the Khalqi General Shahnawaz Tanai, mounted an unsuccessful coup attempt in Kabul. It seemed implausible that he would

39. William Maley, "The Geneva Accords of April 1988," in Amin Saikal and William Maley, eds., *The Soviet Withdrawal from Afghanistan* (Cambridge: Cambridge University Press, 1989), p. 25.

40. See J. F. Burns, "In Kabul, Soviet Airlift Brings Bread and Guns," *New York Times,* 24 May 1989, p. 12; and David Isby, "Soviet Arms Deliveries and Aid to Afghanistan 1989–91," *Jane's Intelligence Review* 3 (1991), pp. 348–54.

41. Joseph S. Bermudez, "Ballistic Missiles in the Third World—Afghanistan 1979–1992," *Jane's Intelligence Review* 4 (1992), p. 51.

42. Olivier Roy, *The Lessons of the Soviet/Afghan War* (London: Adelphi Paper no. 259, International Institute for Strategic Studies, 1991), p. 37.

have made such an attempt without Soviet support and a number of acute observers speculated that the Soviets might have attempted to stage-manage Najibullah's overthrow as a quick and easy means of justifying speedy Soviet disengagement from what remained a very costly commitment.[43]

Furthermore, as Soviet politics became more pluralistic, voices were increasingly raised against support for Najibullah—most notably from Boris Yeltsin who stated that arms supplies from Russia to Afghanistan must be stopped.[44] By mid-1991, Soviet citizens could read in their press that it was Soviet economic and military assistance that was keeping Najibullah in office; that 85 percent of Afghanistan was outside the control of the Kabul regime; that Najibullah's calls for a coalition government would entail his party's retaining control of the key Ministries of State Security, Internal Affairs, Defence, and Finance; and that the Kremlin's continuing support for the Kabul regime was prompted by fear that a free Afghan government would seek war reparations running to billions of dollars on the strength of the Nuremberg indictment, a sum which the USSR in keeping with the dictates of "new thinking" would have to pay.[45]

The failure of the coup attempt in Moscow in August 1991 resulted in the prompt removal of a number of figures suspected of supporting continued Soviet backing for the Kabul regime.[46] These included the commander of Soviet Ground Forces, General Valentin Varennikov, who in 1989 had defended the continuing involvement of Soviet advisers in Afghanistan;[47] and General Boris Gromov, force commander in Afghanistan at the time of the Soviet withdrawal, whose signature had appeared along with those of Varennikov, Aleksandr Tiziakov and Vasilii Starodubtsev on a reactionary manifesto less than a month earlier calling on the armed forces to act as "reliable guarantors of security."[48] On 13 September, Soviet Foreign Minister Boris Pankin and U.S. Secretary of State Baker announced that

---

43. See Anthony Hyman, "Afghanistan's Uncertain Future," *Report on the USSR* 2 (23 March 1990), pp. 15–16; and Anthony Arnold, "Behind Afghanistan Coup Plot," *San Francisco Chronicle*, 28 March 1990, p. 7.

44. BBC, *Summary of World Broadcasts (SWB)*, SU/0819/i, 18 July 1990.

45. A. Vasilev, "Pochemu my ne ukhodim iz Afganistana," *Komsomolskaia pravda*, 29 June 1991, p. 4.

46. For a more detailed discussion of this topic, see William Maley, "Soviet-Afghan Relations After the Coup," *Report on the USSR*, 3 (20 September 1991), pp. 11–15.

47. *Moscow News*, 20 August 1989, p. 1. See also Artyom Borovik, *The Hidden War: A Russian Journalist's Account of the Soviet War in Afghanistan* (London: Faber & Faber, 1990), pp. 247–50.

48. "Slovo k narodu," *Sovetskaia Rossiia*, 23 July 1991.

from 1 January 1992, all shipments of "lethal materials and supplies" from the superpowers to the warring parties in Afghanistan would cease.[49]

This proved decisive in the subsequent course of the Afghan conflict.[50] The Kabul regime had pinned its hopes for survival on a proposal in May 1991 by the UN Secretary-General which envisaged an intra-Afghan dialogue and a "credible and impartial transition mechanism," possibly involving the former monarch Zahir Shah, to provide the Afghan people with "the necessary assurances to participate in free and fair elections, taking into account Afghan traditions, for the establishment of a broad-based government." Yet the discontinuation of Soviet aid to Kabul shifted the correlation of forces decisively in the *mujahideen's* favour: the regime lost access to the resources which it needed to buy militia loyalty; and the main resistance commanders, freed of the threat of attack from Scud B missiles and manned bombers, were left with no compelling reason to compromise with the regime. As long as Najibullah remained in office, this was precisely what in their eyes the UN plan required of them.

The cessation of Soviet assistance made Najibullah's personal position increasingly untenable and on 18 March 1992 he announced—reportedly following an ultimatum from Benon Sevan, Head of the Office of the Secretary-General in Afghanistan and Pakistan—that he had agreed to resign from the moment a transitional mechanism took over power.[51] Had this occurred six months earlier, it might have led to a quick settlement. But coming in March 1992, it was far too late to save the UN plan.

For by March, the regime was fast heading for collapse. Its long-standing problems of legitimacy had come to a head. On the day on which Najibullah announced his intention to resign, Mazar-i-Sharif fell to a coalition of *mujahideen* and Uzbek militias affronted by a clumsy attempt by Najibullah in January to replace the commander of the border town of Hairatan. Once this occurred, the prospects that the *mujahideen* would eschew the use of military force—which was advancing their objectives far more effectively than any UN diplomatic activities had ever done— disappeared almost completely. And Sevan had been too close to Najibullah for too long to enjoy the personal authority which would have been required to rescue the Secretary-General's plan from the avalanche which was

---

49. On the process by which the Bush Administration gravitated to this position, see Minton F. Goldman, "President Bush and Afghanistan: A Turning Point in American Policy," *Comparative Strategy* 11 (1992), pp. 177–93.

50. For a detailed discussion of the collapse of the communist regime, see William Maley and Fazel Haq Saikal, *Political Order in Post-Communist Afghanistan* (Boulder: Lynne Rienner, 1992).

51. Edward A. Gargan, "Afghan President Agrees to Step Down," *New York Times*, 19 March 1992.

engulfing it. On 16 April, as panic spread through Kabul, Najibullah went into hiding after a failed attempt to flee the country. The Head of KHAD committed suicide, and the communist regime collapsed.[52] The task of rebuilding the shattered country has fallen to the resistance, and it is not a task that any sane observer would envy.

"The USSR's strategy in Afghanistan," Richard Weitz recently argued,

almost succeeded. Following the withdrawal of their troops in February 1989, Soviet officials sought a negotiated settlement that would have provided their local allies with a significant chance to remain in power yet would have reduced the USSR's economic and diplomatic costs.... Only the unexpected collapse of the Soviet central government undermined Moscow's endgame in Afghanistan.[53]

However, with the benefit of hindsight, it is clear that the Soviet hope of turning the Kabul regime into an independently viable government was illusory. The Kabul regime had no more chance of surviving without Soviet support than would a brain-dead body without a life-support machine. Some observers, it is true, clung to the myth that the Afghan communists were a distinct force. On 10 April 1992, the American commentator Selig Harrison advanced the preposterous claim that "President Najibullah could block a settlement if not given a place at the bargaining table."[54] This comment, unfortunately, revealed more about Mr Harrison than about Afghanistan.

The Cambodian Settlement

The search for a political settlement in Cambodia was fundamentally dictated by the need to detach the government's opponents from their external channels of support. While the Vietnamese-backed government may have consolidated its position sufficiently for combat forces to withdraw, this did not signify that its writ ran throughout the country. The existence of opposition movements—not simply the Khmer Rouge, but also the Khmer People's National Liberation Front (KPNLF) led by the conservative Son Sann, and Sihanouk's United National Front for an Independent, Neutral, Peaceful and Cooperative Cambodia (known by its French acronym FUNCINPEC)—meant that the dangers of a resurgence of civil war were ever-present. Furthermore, in contrast to what occurred following the invasion of Afghanistan, the Heng Samrin regime was not granted the

---

52. Steve Coll, "Afghan Leader Gives Up Power: Najibullah Flees; Guerrillas on Move," *Washington Post*, 17 April 1992.

53. Richard Weitz, "Moscow's Endgame in Afghanistan," *Conflict Quarterly* 12 (Winter 1992), p. 25.

54. Selig Harrison, "A Tightrope to Peace in Afghanistan," *International Herald Tribune*, 10 April 1992.

Cambodian seat at the United Nations, and suffered a distinct shortage of international legitimacy.[55] Thus, from shortly after the Vietnamese invasion, diplomatic maneuvering began in an attempt to procure a negotiated exit from a situation of armed confrontation.

At a United Nations Conference on Cambodia held in 1981, the ASEAN states put forward a proposal for "the disarming of all the Kampuchean factions and the creation of a neutral interim administration to organise free elections."[56] This was very close to the settlement plan which ultimately took shape in Cambodia, but a decade had to pass before the interests of the various actors had shifted to the extent required to make such a model viable. And the intervening travails proved extremely tortuous. At Thai and Chinese instigation, the three opposition groups formed a Coalition Government of Democratic Kampuchea (CGDK) in 1982.[57] The internal politics of its components proved byzantine:

> The CGDK is a total misnomer: it is not a coalition (Pol Pot's Khmer Rouge is the real power); it is not a government, having neither people, territory nor other attributes of a government; it is decidedly not democratic; and it is not in Kampuchea, being located rather on the Thai side of the border.[58]

This linking of the non-communist resistance groups with the Khmer Rouge proved a source of anguish for the West and made support for the opponents of the Phnom Penh regime controversial in a way that support for the Afghan resistance never was.[59] Sihanouk, ironically given the events of 1963–65, proved to be the linchpin of Western proposals. China was prosecuting a two-pronged policy, backing both the Khmer Rouge and Sihanouk;[60] and with the Soviet leadership prepared to accept him as figurehead, a settlement agreement based on Sihanouk was possible if the detailed modalities could be negotiated.

---

55. For details, see Ramses Amer, "The United Nations' Peace Plan for Cambodia: From Confrontation to Consensus," *Interdisciplinary Peace Research*, 3 (October–November 1991), pp. 5–9.

56. Roy Allison, *The Soviet Union and the Strategy of Non-Alignment in the Third World* (Cambridge: Cambridge University Press, 1988), p. 143.

57. For details see Craig Etcheson, "The Khmer Way of Exile: Lessons from Three Indochinese Wars," in Yossi Shain, ed., *Governments-in-Exile in Contemporary World Politics* (London: Routledge, 1991), p. 106.

58. Ramesh Thakur, "The Afghan Road to Kampuchea?" *Asian Defence Journal*, August 1988, p. 58.

59. See Peter W. Rodman, "Supping with the Devil," *The National Interest* 25 (Fall 1991), pp. 44–50.

60. On China's stance, see Steven J. Hood, "Beijing's Cambodia Gamble and Prospects for Peace in Indochina: The Khmer Rouge or Sihanouk?," *Asian Survey* 30 (October 1990), pp. 977–91.

Sihanouk in December 1987 opened direct talks with the Phnom Penh regime and in 1988 moved to distance himself from the Khmer Rouge.[61] This moved him closer to the centre of events but did not in itself produce a breakthrough. In July–August 1989, a conference was convened in Paris by President François Mitterrand,[62] but its deliberations came to naught, largely because the four Cambodian factions were uninterested in sharing power. However, the growing sense among the factions that a prolongation of conflict was not in their interests meant that prospects for a breakthrough remained positive.[63] The required breakthrough came in February 1990 when Australian Foreign Minister Gareth Evans, cognisant of the UN's positive role in supervising the elections held in Namibia in November 1989, put forward a new proposal at a meeting in Jakarta.[64] The Evans plan envisaged that the UN, as well as running elections, would oversee Cambodia's administration during a transition period with the backing of a UN peacekeeping force. The virtue of this plan was that it promised to overcome the concerns of the various factions about power-sharing: if the UN were to take over the administration of Cambodia, then no one faction had any particular need to feel that another was stealing an advantage. The plan won the support of the five permanent members of the UN Security Council, including, crucially, China. It also secured the enthusiastic backing of Congressman Stephen Solarz, a strong supporter of aid to the non-communist resistance.[65]

This did not mean that a settlement was ready to fall into place. Sino-Vietnamese suspicions remained an obstacle to be surmounted. However, the collapse of Soviet communism following the August 1991 coup attempt may have led these two powers to a sense that they had more in common than they had realised, which in turn suggested that a Cambodian settlement should be pursued.[66] In any case, on 23 October 1991 an agreement was signed in Paris which gave substance to the principles of the Evans plan. It provided for a United Nations Transitional Authority in Cambodia (UNTAC) to work with the Supreme National Council (SNC)—the

61. For an attempt to discern Sihanouk's reasoning, see Gareth Porter, "Cambodia: Sihanouk's Initiative," *Foreign Affairs* 66 (Spring 1988), pp. 809–26.

62. See Amitav Acharya, Pierre Lizée and Sorpong Peou, eds., *Cambodia—The 1989 Paris Peace Conference: Background Analysis and Documents* (New York: Kraus, 1991).

63. See Gérard Hervouet, "The Cambodian Conflict: The Difficulties of Intervention and Compromise," *International Journal* 45 (Spring 1990), p. 290.

64. See *Informal Meeting on Cambodia: Issues for Negotiation in a Comprehensive Settlement: Working Papers* (Canberra: Department of Foreign Affairs and Trade, 1990).

65. Stephen J. Solarz, "Cambodia and the International Community," *Foreign Affairs* 69 (Spring 1990), pp. 99–115.

66. See Frederick Z. Brown, "Cambodia in 1991: An Uncertain Peace," *Asian Survey* 32 (January 1992), pp. 88–96.

repository of Cambodian sovereignty, chaired by Sihanouk, and containing six members from the Phnom Penh regime and five from the resistance factions. Substantial areas of governmental activity were to be brought directly under UNTAC's authority, while others were to be under its supervision. Armed forces of the various Cambodian groups were to be moved into cantonments, disarmed and 70 percent demobilised. This would pave the way for elections to choose a constituent assembly of 120 members to develop a new constitution, which would require a two-thirds majority in order to be adopted. At this point, the constituent assembly would become a legislative assembly to create a new Cambodian government.[67]

Events since the signing of the agreement have not moved especially smoothly. At a formal level, the implantation of the new institutions envisaged by the agreement has proceeded well. Sihanouk returned to Phnom Penh in November 1991 and UNTAC began its operations in early 1992—headed by Yasushi Akashi, an experienced Japanese diplomat, with Australian Major-General John Sanderson as Force Commander, a task of enormous sensitivity in any peacekeeping operation.[68] However, at a political level, tensions are all too evident. When Khieu Samphan returned to Phnom Penh, he was attacked by an enraged crowd and had to quit the country. More seriously, the Khmer Rouge declined to cooperate with the removal of their forces to cantonments as required in the plan. Serious conflict has also broken out on the question of voter eligibility, with the Khmer Rouge claiming that Vietnamese infiltrators would be permitted to vote. On the strength of such claims, the Khmer Rouge called for Akashi's resignation.[69] Akashi in turn warned on 7 September that elections might proceed without the Khmer Rouge if they refused to disarm by November.[70] Furthermore, bodies such as Asia Watch demanded that economic sanctions be imposed against the Khmer Rouge to deprive them of profits from trade with Thai entrepreneurs, a demand on which the UN Security Council eventually acted.

At this point, it appears that elections may well be held without the participation of the Khmer Rouge. In some ways this would be a satisfactory outcome: an internationally acceptable regime would be likely to emerge, and through a process uncontaminated by the participation of a party with a grisly record of genocidal behaviour in its past. The Khmer

---

67. David Roberts, "Cambodia: Problems of a UN-brokered Peace," *World Today* 48 (July 1992), p. 130.

68. See F. T. Liu, *United Nations Peacekeeping: Management and Operations* (New York: Occasional Paper on Peacekeeping, International Peace Academy, 1990), pp. 11–16.

69. BBC, *SWB*, FE/1477/B/1, 4 September 1992.

70. BBC, *SWB*, FE/1482/B/3, 10 September 1992. Sihanouk had earlier made a similar comment: *SWB*, FE/1481/B/2, 9 September 1992.

Rouge would be isolated from their Chinese support and possibly from their commercial income as well. Yet, notwithstanding the presence of peacekeepers, the Khmer Rouge could well make a serious attempt to disrupt the elections—and there are few processes as easy to disrupt as voting. Reports of Khmer Rouge cadres infiltrating urban centres are consistent with such a strategy. More fundamentally, the establishment of a new regime in Phnom Penh is not the same as its institutionalisation. Sihanouk remains as quixotic as he was four decades ago, the problems of the country are urgent and hostilities at the elite level remain intense. All these considerations suggest that to hope that Phnom Penh will turn into New Haven is hoping for too much

Conclusion

Cambodia and Afghanistan—societies that Soviet polemicists scorned as feudal—are still with us. The Soviet Union, the first socialist society, has been consigned to history. There could be few sharper ironies in what has been an ironical century. However, the futures of Cambodia and Afghanistan lie not in the hands of the Cambodians and Afghans alone. The wider world also bears a responsibility for the reconstruction of these countries. If they are starved of resources for post-war reconstruction, there is nothing more certain than that their politics will relapse into some form of barbarism. It would be the bitterest irony of all if indifference by the West were to foster the re-emergence in Cambodia and Afghanistan of the kind of collectivist monocratic rule with which the Soviet Union, so recently departed, was so long associated.

10

Indochina

Carlyle A. Thayer

For most of the past century, Indochina has been perceived as constituting an identifiable sub-region within Southeast Asia. Originally the term Indochina referred to the five mainland states of Burma, Thailand, Laos, Cambodia and Vietnam. However during the colonial period Indochina referred to the union of the French possessions of Laos, Cambodia and Vietnam. After independence Vietnam was split along Cold War lines with Laos, Cambodia and South Vietnam being placed under the protection of the South-East Asia Treaty Organisation (SEATO). North Vietnam aligned itself with China and the Soviet Union.

Indochina re-emerged as an identifiable sub-region in the mid-1970s when communist parties came to power in each state and Vietnam succeeded in imposing itself as the hegemonic power. In 1977 it negotiated a 25-year Treaty of Friendship and Cooperation with Laos.[1] The following year Vietnam invaded and occupied Cambodia. Hanoi-Phnom Penh relations were then made subject to a similar Treaty of Friendship and Cooperation. Attempts were made to coordinate economic planning on a long-term Indochina-wide basis.

Vietnam's invasion of Cambodia was preceded by the signing of a Treaty of Friendship and Cooperation with the Soviet Union. After Vietnam's occupation of Cambodia, Hanoi declared that Indochina was a "single strategic theatre" linked to the Soviet Union.[2] The imposition of communist

---

1. Carlyle A. Thayer, "Laos and Vietnam: The Anatomy of a 'Special Relationship'," in Martin Stuart-Fox, ed., *Contemporary Laos: Studies in the Politics and Society of the Lao People's Democratic Republic* (New York: St. Martin's Press, 1982), pp. 245–73.

2. General Hoang Van Thai, "Ve Quan He Hop Tac Dac Biet Giua Ba Dan Toc Dong Duong," *Tap Chi Cong San* 1 (January 1982), pp. 17–24.

power in Cambodia was declared "irreversible." Vietnam became in fact a wholly dependent ally. These events polarised Southeast Asia and became the region's dominating security issue for a decade.

The advent of Mikhail Gorbachev to power precipitated a transformation in Moscow's relations with the socialist community in general and Indochina in particular. The Indochinese states were pressed to undertake domestic reforms and to adopt "new political thinking" in foreign policy.[3] Vietnam was encouraged to seek a negotiated settlement of the Cambodian conflict and to follow the Soviet lead in normalising relations with China.[4]

In 1989 the tectonic plates on which Cold War alignments rested began to shift. Communism collapsed in Eastern Europe and weakened in the Soviet Union. Two years later the Soviet Union itself succumbed. As a consequence, external support for communist Indochina all but ended. Vietnam was forced to withdraw from Cambodia and sue for peace. In short, the period of Vietnamese hegemony over Indochina ended.

For ten years, 1979–89, the Soviet Union was the "firm cornerstone" on which Vietnam, Laos and Cambodia based their foreign and domestic policies. In 1989–90 when the cornerstone began to crumble leaders in each of the three countries were forewarned that their bilateral relationships with Moscow would be drastically altered. When the Soviet Union finally collapsed, each of the three countries was affected differently.

Relations between the former Soviet Union (FSU) and Vietnam bottomed out before when both sides made a concerted effort to salvage what was mutually beneficial. Relations between the FSU and the other two Indochinese states lacked sufficient depth for a similar recovery and were transformed into bilateral relations with the Russian Federation. Relations with Laos were reduced to their lowest common denominator, while relations with Cambodia were abruptly terminated with the formation of the Supreme National Council and by the collapse of the Soviet Union itself.

This chapter will review these developments by tracing changes in Soviet political, military and economic relations with the states of Indochina, with an emphasis on Soviet-Vietnamese relations.

---

3. Carlyle A. Thayer, "The Soviet Union and Indochina," in Roger E. Kanet, Deborah Nutter Miner and Tamara J. Resler, eds., *Soviet Foreign Policy in Transition* (Cambridge: Cambridge University Press, 1992), pp. 236–55.

4. Carlyle A. Thayer, "Kampuchea: Soviet Initiatives and Regional Responses," in Ramesh Thakur and Carlyle A. Thayer, eds., *The Soviet Union as an Asian Pacific Power: Implications of Gorbachev's 1986 Vladivostok Initiative* (Boulder: Westview Press, 1987), pp. 171–200 and Carlyle A. Thayer, "Prospects for Peace in Kampuchea: Soviet Initiatives and Indochinese Responses," *Indonesian Quarterly*, 17:2 (1989), pp. 157–72.

Vietnam

Political

Soviet-Vietnamese relations developed an "all round" character in the decade following the signing of the 1978 treaty. One major feature of this relationship was the frequency of summit meetings between party and state leaders. Until 1990 an average of two summits were held every year during the Gorbachev period.[5] In 1990 no summit was held. It was not surprising that, as Vietnam moved to convene its seventh national party congress, it pressed for a meeting at the highest level with Soviet leaders in order to take stock of their bilateral relationship.

After a postponement at Moscow's request, the summit was eventually held in Moscow in May 1991. Vietnam sent two delegations, one led by its party leader Nguyen Van Linh and the other led by the Chairman of the Council of Ministers Do Muoi. Linh held political talks with Gorbachev, while Muoi held economic talks with his Soviet counterpart. These discussions were later characterised as "difficult and complicated" by R. L. Khamidoulin, the Soviet Ambassador to Vietnam. Gorbachev volunteered to Linh that he (Gorbachev) had made the mistake of going too far with political reforms without first restructuring the economy. Gorbachev then astounded his guest by suggesting that some of the Soviet Union's reforms could be copied by Vietnam.[6]

At the same time, Do Muoi was also having a tough time in his discussions on aid and trade. He was told frankly that the Soviet economy was in such a chaotic state, with no budget having been drawn up, that it would not be possible to discuss aid. Muoi was given the further bad news that Moscow would not cancel Vietnam's Rbl. 10 bn debt, and that Vietnam was expected to begin debt service repayments of around US $350m per year at the commencement of 1991.[7] Nothing concrete resulted from the summit and it was left to future discussions to "find some creative solution" to the problems raised, as Soviet Ambassador Khamidoulin later remarked.

Linh and Muoi returned to Vietnam sobered by their discussions. This attitude was reflected in the various reports delivered to the seventh party congress. In his address to the gathering Nguyen Van Linh observed, "foreign economic relations have been affected by sudden changes, international aid reduced substantially, the source of loans from outside to

---

5. Carlyle A. Thayer, "Civil Society and the Soviet-Vietnamese Alliance," in Chandran Kukathas, David W. Lovell and William Maley, eds., *The Transition from Socialism: State and Civil Society in the USSR* (London: Longman, 1991), p. 215.

6. *Straits Times*, 22 June 1991.

7. *Far Eastern Economic Review (FEER)*, 30 May 1991, p. 8.

plug the budget deficit stopped and the import capacity of traditional markets drastically diminished."

The Central Committee's Political Report in its review of foreign affairs noted tersely that "the relations between our country and the Soviet Union are being renewed in accordance with the interests of each people." It set as the eighth of ten tasks to be undertaken in the next five years, the strengthening of "solidarity and cooperation with the Soviet Union, to renew the mode and improve the efficiency of Vietnamese-Soviet cooperation in order to meet the interests of each country."

These official reports belie what Vietnamese leaders were saying in private. Gorbachev was now described as a "traitor to the socialist cause." In August 1991 when Kremlin hardliners attempted to seize power and oust Gorbachev, Vietnam's leaders were privately elated. They drafted a congratulatory telegram to the leaders of the coup. Only the timely intervention by the Soviet ambassador prevented its dispatch and the political embarrassment that this would have caused.[8]

The Communist Party of the Soviet Union (CPSU) was only one of four foreign parties invited to the seventh national congress of the Vietnam Communist Party.[9] At the congress, Vietnam jettisoned its long-serving foreign minister Nguyen Co Thach and replaced him with a career diplomat, Nguyen Manh Cam. This proved a fortuitous decision as Cam had previously served as Vietnam's Ambassador to Moscow. He assisted in refashioning Vietnam's relations with the states of the FSU when the Soviet Union announced its dissolution on 26 December 1991.

On the very next day, Vietnam's foreign ministry announced its recognition of and readiness to establish diplomatic relations with all states of the FSU. Russia and Ukraine were singled out in separate messages sent by Foreign Minister Cam. The following month, the Council of Ministers dispatched a special envoy, Deputy Foreign Minister Nguyen Dy Nien, to Uzbekistan, Ukraine and Belarus to establish diplomatic relations. Agreements on economic, commercial, cultural and scientific and technological cooperation between Vietnam and each of these three states were signed.

Vietnam also established diplomatic relations with all other members of the Commonwealth of Independent States, the three Baltic republics and Georgia. Vietnam's "all round" relationship with the FSU enabled it to refashion relations with the newly-independent republics by building on the

8. Based on discussions with knowledgeable sources in Hanoi in November 1991. See also Kathleen Callo, Reuter, Hanoi, 14 October 1992.

9. The others were the Lao People's Revolutionary Party (LPRP), the Khmer People's Revolutionary Party (KPRP) and the Communist Party of Cuba. The permanent representative of the Japan Communist Party in Hanoi also attended.

ties forged by tens of thousands of Vietnamese and former Soviets officials who had worked in each other's country. One by one Vietnam was able either to reaffirm or renegotiate agreements signed prior to December 1991.

For example, as early as 24 December 1991 members of the USSR-Vietnam Friendship Association renamed their organisation and began to lobby for the maintenance of existing relations. In mid-year the association sent a delegation to Vietnam to work out new forms of cooperation. Russia's Indochina specialists (academics, diplomats and aid workers) formed a professional association and in April 1992 convened an international symposium on "the Countries of Indochina and International Economic Cooperation: Potentialities and Prospects" in Moscow. In August of the same year, a delegation of the Confederation of Vietnamese Workers visited Belarus and Ukraine and negotiated a memorandum of cooperation with each of its counterparts.[10]

The actions of these groups led to a re-think of Russian policy towards Vietnam. According to a Moscow-based academician, by May 1992 it was agreed that the precipitate Soviet withdrawal of economic and military assistance to Vietnam was a mistake.[11] While the USSR could not afford such aid and this decision was understandable, he said, it was taken with too much haste. Later in the year, no doubt responding to such internal pressures, the Russian foreign minister launched his country's first foreign policy initiative towards Vietnam and Southeast Asia (see below).

In mid-1992, on the eve of the most senior state visit to Vietnam by a Russian official, a spokesman in Moscow declared, "Our relations are friendly, but they have been depoliticised and de-ideologised."[12] This transformation in Soviet-Vietnam relations has not been without problems. This has been particularly evident in the political and strategic spheres where ideology no longer serves to draw Russia (or the other states of the CIS) and Vietnam together.

A number of irritants have arisen. For example, Russian attempts to take down statues of Lenin and Ho Chi Minh and to remove Lenin's body from his mausoleum in Red Square have provoked Vietnamese editorial protests. Vietnam's leaders were reportedly disturbed by the decision to return East German party boss Eric Honecker to Germany for trial for his "shoot-to-kill" orders. Honecker is considered a staunch ally of Vietnam.[13] Vietnam has been angered by seemingly off-the-cuff statements by Boris Yeltsin that

---

10. Vietnam News Agency, 23 August 1992.

11. Discussion held in Kuala Lumpur with a Senior Fellow at the Institute for Far Eastern Studies, Academy of Sciences, May 1992.

12. AFP, 14 July 1992.

13. *FEER*, 27 August 1992, pp. 6–7.

some American servicemen captured during the Vietnam War may have been taken to the Soviet Union.[14] Vietnam denies that this is the case and is concerned that such statements may harm its warming relations with the United States. Finally, the operations of a privately-run anti-Communist radio "Voice of Freedom" from Russian territory have become a major irritant. Vietnam has made several diplomatic protests and has called on Russian authorities to close it down.[15] Russian officials have replied that under the new press laws they can take no action against a private station.[16]

Irritants in the once warm bilateral relationship have led Vietnam to restrict the movements and curtail privileges of Russian personnel stationed at Cam Ranh Bay. They are now required to show Vietnamese guards written permission from the Vietnamese commander to leave the base. A Vietnamese military source stated that this was because Russia was no longer seen as a reliable military partner. "Vietnam wants the Soviets to leave," he said:

> It's nonsense for them to stay now. In the past, we were the same society, both socialist. We had a special relationship. The Soviet Union provided military equipment and technology and training. But since Gorbachev said last year that all military supplies had to be paid for in dollars, that relationship ended.[17]

Military

The disintegration of the Soviet Union during 1990–91 had a major impact on Soviet-Vietnam military relations. The Soviet Union's fall from superpower status meant the reduction of military forces stationed abroad, including Vietnam. The Soviet Union's weakening economic position resulted in the ending of its subsidised military aid program to Vietnam. Moscow now requested that all military assistance be paid for in hard currency.

In May 1991, during the course of a summit in Moscow, Soviet and Vietnamese leaders argued over the issue of hard currency payment for Soviet military aid. According to Ambassador Rashid Khamidoulin, "Military cooperation will continue, but under a form that is under discussion. We continue to reduce our presence at the Cam Ranh Bay naval and air base and we no longer maintain a strong permanent naval or air presence there."[18] Vietnam reportedly asked Moscow for US $350–400m in

14. Voice of Vietnam Network, 20 June 1992.

15. Vietnam News Agency and Reuter dispatch from Hanoi, 13 August 1992.

16. Reuter, dispatch from Hanoi and Vietnam News Agency, 27 August 1992.

17. Kathleen Callo, Reuter, Cam Ranh, *Nation* (Bangkok) and *Sunday Times* (Singapore), 23 February 1992.

18. AFP, 22 April 1991.

annual rent for Cam Ranh Bay, an amount equal to the past annual Soviet military equipment and training.[19] Moscow suggested paying US $40m instead.[20] Soviet officials have also refused to link the rental question with the issue of Hanoi's debt repayments.

During 1991, the Soviets drew down their forces at Cam Ranh Bay, regrouped those remaining into one residential area and began returning buildings to Vietnamese control.[21] At year's end Interfax news agency reported that the last major warship, the 8,000 ton destroyer *Admiral Spiridonov*, had returned to Vladivostok. The number of Soviet submarines declined from twenty to only two or three.[22] The number of personnel stationed there dropped from a high of 4,000 to 1,000 or less by mid-1992. In mid-May 1992 formal military cooperation was brought to an end with the return to Russia of the last military adviser posted to Vietnam.[23]

Sometime during April–May Russia formulated a new foreign policy for Southeast Asia and Asia-Pacific. This new policy was announced by the Foreign Minister Andrei Kozyrev at the post-ministerial conference of the Association of South-East Asian Nations (ASEAN) in Manila in July 1992. It followed a series of provocative Chinese moves in the South China Sea.

Kozyrev proposed a number of confidence-building measures for Asia-Pacific, including limitations on the scale of naval exercises and restraint in the conduct of such exercises in international straits and areas of intensive navigation and fishing; initiation of a multilateral dialogue on establishing a crisis management system in the Asian and Pacific region to avert the buildup of military tensions; and negotiations to form an international naval force to provide freedom of navigation.[24]

Within the Southeast Asian region, Kozyrev stated Russia's willingness "to develop cooperation in the military and military-technological area with the ASEAN states with the aim of maintaining their security at the level of reasonable sufficiency." He also proposed the transformation of Subic and Cam Ranh "into logistic support centres for naval activities." [25]

---

19. *Komsomolskaia pravda*, 17 October 1990.

20. Kathleen Callo, Reuter, Cam Ranh, *Nation* and *Sunday Times*, 23 February 1992.

21. Peter Wilson-Smith, Reuter, Cam Ranh, 13 August 1992; BBC, Dateline East Asia 27 August 1992 in Singapore, *Foreign Broadcast Monitor* 198/92, 27 August 1992, p. 4. The 1,000 figure was provided by Russian Ambassador Khamidoulin but he was unsure of the number as it changed often. A Vietnamese naval lieutenant estimated that the number of Russians could be as low as 400–500.

22. Reuter, Cam Ranh, *Jakarta Post*, 14 August 1992; William Branigin, *Washington Post*, 9 September 1991.

23. *FEER*, 4 June 1992, p. 9

24. AFP, Manila, 22 July 1992; and Ellen Tordesillas, *Malaya* (Manila), 23 July 1992.

25. ITAR–TASS, Moscow World Service, 22 July 1992.

Kozyrev's initiative was designed to redefine Russia's role in the Asian-Pacific region as a great power by taking advantage of regional concerns about China's future intentions. As such it posed a dilemma for Vietnam. Up until this point Vietnam had been preparing for a Russian departure from Cam Ranh. Plans were afoot to convert the facilities to commercial use. Vietnam was also unsure if a continued Russian military presence would deter China from further land-grabbing in the Spratly archipelago.

Immediately after Kozyrev launched his initiative in Manila, Vice Premier V. A. Makharadze paid the highest-level visit to Vietnam by an official of the Russian government. Makharadze discussed mainly economic and trade issues (see below), but he and members of his entourage also raised military matters.[26] These talks were preceded by discussions in Manila between Kozyrev and his Vietnamese counterpart Cam.

Both Kozyrev and Makharadze raised with the Vietnamese the question of a continued Russian naval presence, including submarines, at Cam Ranh Bay. Kozyrev reported to the press in Manila and went so far as to say that "negotiations had begun," while Makharadze confined the issue to private discussions. Kozyrev made clear that it was Russia's view that Cam Ranh should not be closed "if the Vietnamese agree and other countries in the region take it as a centre of stability." He also noted that "We are not necessarily rushing to leave.... New terms for preserving the facility will, of course, be determined."[27]

Vietnam has reacted cautiously to these developments. Foreign Minister Cam denied reports that Russia and Vietnam had begun negotiations for a renewed Russian naval presence in Vietnam.[28] Cam stated that since changes in the FSU, "we have not met to discuss a new basis for our relationship... [there is only] an agreement in principle to discuss the issue towards the end of the year (1992)."[29]

The new Russian interest in prolonging their stay in Cam Ranh Bay and turning over its facilities for commercial use raises difficult questions for Vietnam. On the strategic level, Vietnamese leaders are casting about for a strategy to deal with China. They are concerned about Chinese naval modernisation and provocative actions in the Gulf of Tonkin and Spratly Islands. Cam Ranh Bay houses one important military asset, a functioning signals intelligence (SIGINT) station. This could prove vital to Vietnam in

---

26. Based on discussions in Hanoi in July 1992.

27. AFP, Manila, 22 July 1992; and Cameron Stewart, Manila, *Australian*, 23 July 1992.

28. Nayan Chanda, "Nyet, tovarisch," *FEER*, 6 August 1992, p. 11; and *International Herald Tribune* , 23 July 1992.

29. In October 1992 a well-placed Vietnamese source, quoting a Russian Embassy official, told the author that an unannounced Russian military delegation had arrived in Hanoi that month to open negotiations.

the event of hostilities with China over the Spratly Islands.[30] The SIGINT station has the ability to monitor Chinese communications around Hainan Island, where the South Sea fleet is based.[31]

But Vietnamese leaders are reportedly not sanguine about the ability of Russia to act as a counterweight to China. Russian public statements have been far from reassuring. Kozyrev stated with respect to the Spratly issue that "it is evident that they should be solved by political means. We are encouraged by the idea to start a joint economic development of disputed territories rather than to continue territorial claims."[32] The Russian ambassador was hardly reassuring when he stated, "We have to ensure that this question [Spratly Islands] doesn't turn into a conflict... of course, Russia won't interfere in this question, but it's important that it not become an explosive issue." [33]

Vietnam is also anxious to ensure a continued supply of military equipment and spare parts for its armed forces at affordable prices. As these forces were originally equipped by the Soviet Union, Russia would be the obvious source.[34] But here the issue is complicated by Vietnamese indebtedness to Russia and the poor state of its economy. Vietnam faces the further complication of responding to a Chinese offer to sell arms.[35]

Finally there are commercial considerations. Cam Ranh is situated in Khanh Hoa province. Local authorities there have voiced the view that the Russians should leave and the facilities there be converted into civilian use to the benefit of the local economy. Foreign business interests have reportedly proposed constructing a container port.

Economic

In 1990, Moscow informed Laos, Cambodia and Vietnam that as of January 1991, aid would be drastically curtailed and all commercial relations would be conducted in hard currency at world market prices. When the Soviet cornerstone finally crumbled only Vietnam was able to pick up the pieces and refashion its relations with the states of the former Soviet Union.

---

30. Robert Karniol, "Russia Seeks to Keep SIGINT Link," *Jane's Defence Weekly*, 12 September 1992, p. 27.

31. Reuter dispatch from Hanoi, *Nation* and *Straits Times*, 28 August 1992.

32. Dispatch from Manila, *Straits Times*, 23 July 1992.

33. Reuter, Hanoi and Vietnam News Agency, 27 August 1992.

34. A knowledgeable Russian source told the author in May 1992 that the Russian foreign ministry had agreed to continue selling arms to Vietnam provided that a mutually acceptable form of payment could be worked out.

35. BBC, Dateline East Asia 31 July 1992 in Singapore, *Foreign Broadcast Monitor* 176/92, 1 August 1992, pp. 8–9.

Soviet-Vietnamese economic relations deteriorated sharply during 1990. Economic chaos in the USSR caused Moscow to fall short of its commitments to deliver vital supplies of petroleum, oil, steel, urea and cotton. This hurt Vietnamese industry which was dependent on these materials. At the same time, Soviet companies backed out of between twenty to sixty percent of signed contracts to buy Vietnamese shoes, textiles, clothes, handicrafts and light industrial products. For its part, Vietnam defaulted on at least a quarter of its commitments.

Shortfalls in the supply of fertilizer, for example, led to a decline in rice production. This caused the market price to double. Oil and steel prices nearly trebled, while unemployment and inflation both increased. At the same time, Russia demanded that Vietnam pay dollar salaries for thousands of its experts and technicians at various projects negotiated under past cooperation agreements. Vietnam lacked the cash and many were forced to return home. The number of Soviet experts stationed in Vietnam dropped from 14,000 in 1989 to 8,000 by mid-1991.

Trade stagnated due to changes in the Soviet political system, government structure and because of the lack of an effective bilateral trade mechanism.[36] In August 1991, Vietnamese officials announced that trade with all socialist countries had fallen to 15 percent of total trade. Trade with the FSU, as a percentage of total trade, dropped from over 60 percent in the 1980s, to 50 percent in 1990 and a low of 14 percent in 1991. The imbalance shifted from 4:1 in Russia's favour in the mid-1980s to 2:1 in 1990 and came close to parity in the following year.

Attempts to place transactions on a hard-currency basis failed and some bilateral payments were made in US dollars while others were made in roubles. In late 1991 the International Monetary Fund estimated the combined impact of the loss of Soviet and Eastern European aid and trade at seven percent of Vietnam's GDP.[37]

In 1991 both sides attempted to stop the downward trend and to establish relations at a lower if more business-like level. In late January, for example, Vietnam and the USSR signed two agreements, one on trade and another on aid. Under the terms of the former agreement, future trade was to be shifted from government level to local level and companies. Trade was to be calculated at international market prices with payment in hard currency. Bilateral trade was to be balanced and the two-way total cut to less than US $1 bn in 1991.

---

36. "Quan He Kinh Te-Thuong Mai Vietnam-LB Nga Net Moi va Trach Nhiem," *Nhan Dan* , 25 July 1992.

37. International Monetary Fund, *Viet Nam—Recent Economic Developments*, 5 December 1991, p. 1.

The Soviet aid program was now scaled down to US $100m in credits and US $10m in grants.[38] Moscow also sought to recalculate Vietnam's Rbl. 10 bn debt into hard currency and get Vietnam to pay interest on Rbl. 6 bn that was due between 1991 and the end of 1995. To soften the blow, the Soviet Union promised a clearing system under which Vietnamese debt at the end of 1991 would be rolled over to 1992.

In July, Vietnam and the Soviet Union negotiated an oil agreement. And in August, on the eve of the anti-Gorbachev coup, both sides signed an agreement on economic and commercial relations and a protocol on goods exchange. Despite these positive developments, domestic chaos forced Moscow to suspend all assistance, including the package agreed to in January. Plans drawn up in the expectation that some aid would be forthcoming now had to be scrapped. According to a Vietnamese economic commentator, "In economic terms 1991 was a critical time for Vietnam. If we survived that year, we can survive anything."[39]

In the aftermath of the dissolution of the Soviet Union, Vietnam moved quickly to refurbish its economic relations with the states of the FSU. Vietnamese missions were dispatched to Russia, Ukraine and Belarus in quick succession in order to determine which agreements signed in the past would be honoured and to work out new terms where necessary. In April 1992, for example, a delegation of the Vietnam Institute of Sciences paid a working visit to Russia and Ukraine to restore and develop scientific and technical cooperation. Agreements were reached in both capitals.[40] Vietnam was understandably concerned to guarantee the future of some 2,000 Vietnamese who were studying or taking graduate courses in twenty universities in different republics of the FSU.[41]

After the collapse of the USSR, the Russian Federation claimed sixty percent of the debt owed by Vietnam and left it for the other republics to determine their share. Russia also assumed responsibility for obligations entered into by the USSR. For example, in April 1992 Russia and Vietnam signed an agreement to complete the Hoa Binh hydroelectric project.[42] In March, a labour agreement was reached with Belarus which guaranteed continued employment of Vietnamese workers and training programs.[43] Russia also assumed control of many of the joint venture partnerships

38. Murray Hiebert, "Deeper in the Red," *FEER*, 21 February 1991, p. 46.
39. Barry Wain, "Vietnam Weathers Economic Transition," *Asian Wall Street Journal*, 3 August 1992.
40. Vietnam News Agency, 4 May 1992.
41. Xuan Chinh, "How do Vietnamese Workers Fare in the CIS?" *Sunday Vietnam News* 351 (19 July 1992), p. 5.
42. Dispatch from Hanoi, *Business Times* (Singapore), 2–3 May 1992.
43. Vietnam News Agency, 20 March 1992.

negotiated with Vietnam, such as Vietsovpetro which was engaged in off-shore oil exploration.

Perhaps the most important agreement was reached in May 1992 when Vietnam and the Russian Federation signed a protocol on the status of Vietnamese "guest workers." It was estimated that as many as 50,000 Vietnamese labourers lived in the USSR when it collapsed,[44] with as many as 32,000 resident in Russia. Russia agreed to safeguard the interests of these workers in conformity with an agreement on labour cooperation signed in 1981. Further, Russia guaranteed conditions for Vietnamese workers to complete their labour contracts and to provide compensation to those workers forced to return to Vietnam before the expiration of their contracts.[45]

Significant progress was also reached in rescheduling Vietnam's ten million rouble debt. Moscow now accepted that Vietnam would pay back only Rbl. 1.1 bn by 1995 instead of Rbl. 6 bn originally scheduled. Negotiations continued on what portion would be paid back in hard currency at the exchange rates in force at the time and how much would be repaid in goods.[46]

The most important development in relations between Vietnam and the FSU occurred in July 1992 when Vietnam's Vice Premier Tran Duc Luong led a delegation to Russia, Udmurtia, Belarus and Ukraine, and his Russian counterpart V. A. Makharadze paid a return visit. Major agreements were negotiated at each stop, including a protocol for 1992 on economic cooperation and barter trade with Russia. Total trade volume was targeted to reach $800m, split evenly. Both parties agreed to compile a series of documents on the principles of cooperation in the fields of investment, taxation, banking, transport, communications, science and technology, and manpower to be signed in the future. They also agreed to cooperate in such diverse sectors as fuel, energy, agriculture and food industry, consumer goods, fishery, education and training, communication and culture.

According to TASS, Vietnam agreed to continue paying off credits extended by Moscow by supplying food and export goods and by providing services to Russian companies operating in Vietnam. Vietnam also agreed to sell rice, meat and vegetables in exchange for iron, steel, fertilizer, oil and gas. Russia agreed to help Vietnam to build factories and installations,

---

44. Kawi Chongkitthawon, *The Nation*, 11 January 1992; Sophie Quinn-Judge, "Cash 'n Carry Cadres," *FEER*, 21 May 1992, pp. 32–33.

45. Vietnam News Agency, 2 October 1992.

46. AFP, Hanoi, *Business Times*, 28 May 1992. Moscow suggested an exchange rate of Rbl. 1 to US $1.4, Hanoi proposed Rbl. 1 to US $0.96.

particularly in the energy sector, in line with commitments made by the FSU.[47]

During his visit to Belarus, Vice Premier Luong signed an agreement on investment protection and cooperation between the two countries in the field of telecommunications. While in Ukraine, Luong signed agreements on cooperation in maritime navigation and post and telecommunications, and a protocol on goods exchange for 1992.[48] The Ukraine agreed to export equipment, machines and spare parts in exchange for Vietnamese rice, tea, coffee, rubber, meat, textiles, garments and shoes.

Immediately after Luong's tour, Russian Vice Premier Makharadze paid a historic visit to Vietnam where he attended the first meeting of the inter-governmental Commission for Trade, Economic, Scientific and Technological Cooperation. Several major agreements were signed: an addendum to the protocol on goods exchange signed previously in Moscow, and cooperation in such areas as science and technology, banking, labour, communications and transport, post and telecommunications, civil aviation and fishing.[49] The two sides also agreed to sign in future agreements covering investment promotion and protection, avoidance of double taxation, and navigation.

The July exchange visits completely redefined Vietnam's relations with the FSU and with the Russian Federation in particular. Speaking at a Hanoi news conference, Makharadze said relations between Russia and Vietnam "should not and cannot be built on the old basis, that is, between a big brother and a younger one."[50] Thereafter both sides moved deliberately to refashion their bilateral relations by reviving and encouraging economic links forged in an earlier period by drawing upon the knowledge and expertise of Russians with Vietnamese experience and Vietnamese with Russian experience.

The Russian-Vietnamese economic relationship will never be as lopsided or as important as it was in the decade following the 1978 Treaty of Friendship and Cooperation. Trade figures released in September 1992 clearly indicated that both sides were struggling to reach the $400m target that had been assigned to each party. According to the Russian commercial attaché in Hanoi, in the first half of 1992 Russian exports to Vietnam totalled US $58.8m, while Vietnamese imports amounted to only US $10.8m.[51] Payment was made by letters of credit as both countries were short of hard currency.[52]

47. *Economika i Zhizn*, 6 July 1992.
48. *Vietnam News*, no. 356, 24 July 1992.
49. Voice of Vietnam, 31 July 1992.
50. *Sunday Vietnam News*, 365 (2 August 1992), p. 1.
51. Vietnam News Agency, 3 September 1992.
52. *Lao Dong*, 3 September 1992.

Laos

Soviet-Lao political relations began to experience strains in 1989 when both sides engaged in mutual recriminations about the effectiveness of their bilateral economic relations. At that time the Soviet Union provided more than half of all foreign aid received by Laos. The following year, as chaos spread across the Soviet Union, the USSR was forced to curtail its activities. The size of the Soviet diplomatic and aid mission in Laos was cut nearly in half from 950 to 450.[53]

The collapse of communism in Eastern Europe sent shock waves through the ruling Lao People's Revolutionary Party (LPRP). The party's newspaper *Pasason* declared 1989 "a nightmare year for socialism" in its New Year's day editorial. The party Secretary General, Kaysone Phomvihan, labelled these developments "confusing" and called for "vigilance" on the home front.[54] The LPRP moved quickly to insulate itself from these developments by promoting democratic reform at home and by diversifying its diplomatic relations abroad, most notably towards China, Japan and Thailand.

As the political situation inside the Soviet Union deteriorated, Vientiane and Moscow continued to act in public as if everything were normal. For example, Laos continued to give pro forma support to Gorbachev's policy of *perestroika*. A delegation of the CPSU was one of four foreign parties invited to attend the fifth congress of the Lao People's Revolutionary Party held in March 1991.[55] In August, the Lao media reported on the aftermath of the coup against Gorbachev in factual terms.[56] Privately Lao leaders were reported to be disappointed at the CPSU's loss of power. In September, Laos recognised the independence of the Baltic states.[57]

In October Laos hosted a visit by the chairman of the Coordination Council of the Presidium of the Russian Council of Ministers. Discussions were held on the best way of improving Lao-Soviet commercial transactions and stepping up the exchange of goods.[58] Finally, in November, Laos sent its usual greeting to the Soviet leadership on the occasion of the anniversary of the Great October Socialist Revolution.

---

53. *Asia Yearbook 1991* (Hong Kong), pp. 151–52; Chou Norindr, "Laos in the Deadlock," *Indochina Report*, January–March 1992, p. 13.

54. Radio Vientiane, 7 February 1990.

55. In addition to the CPSU, the Lao party congress was attended by delegations from Vietnam, Cambodia and China.

56. Lao National Radio, 26 August 1991.

57. Lao National Radio, 14 September 1991.

58. Vientiane Vitthayou Hengsat Radio Network, 23 October 1991. At the same time Deputy Prime Minister Khamphoui Keoboualapha attended a World Bank conference and urged its members not to divert aid away from Laos to Eastern Europe and USSR.

At the end of the year Laos took the collapse of the Soviet Union in stride. On 27 December the Russian ambassador to Laos informed Lao Foreign Minister Phuon Sipaseut about the establishment of the CIS. The Lao foreign minister was also informed that the Russian Federation, as the successor to the Soviet Union, would abide by all obligations and international treaties entered into by the FSU.[59] On 31 December, the Lao People's Democratic Republic formally announced its recognition of all twelve republics of the FSU and its willingness to establish diplomatic relations.[60] Thereafter Lao political and diplomatic relations have been mainly confined to the Russian Federation.

Soviet military assistance to Laos peaked at US $125m in 1983 and then declined. In 1990, Laos was informed that it would no longer receive free credits and would have to pay for equipment, spare parts and training in hard currency. The USSR also stopped training Lao military personnel. Later in the year 150 Soviet military advisers were withdrawn.[61] Laos then approached China for military assistance but was told it would have to be on a commercial basis.

As for economic assistance, during the period of Laos' Second Five-Year Plan (1986–90), it received grant aid and credits worth 571.7m roubles from socialist countries, primarily the USSR, according to Lao estimates.[62] Other sources placed Soviet grant aid at Rbl. 250m during the same period.[63] At the same time, Laos ran a large trade deficit with the Soviet Union. Soviet exports of oil, cement, vehicles and medicines totalled Rbl. 350m in the period 1986–90, while Lao exports of agricultural and forestry products, tin ore and coffee accounted for less than Rbl. 60m. In 1990, Soviet sources estimated that Laos was Rbl. 758.2m in debt to the USSR.[64]

In 1989 preliminary agreement was reached on Soviet support for the next five-year plan (1991–95) with Soviet assistance directed towards the building of roads and bridges, social welfare projects, and the construction of an oil pipeline to central Vietnam. In July 1990 Laos and USSR held discussions about "switching to a new mechanism in economic and commercial cooperation" in order that Laos could reduce its trade imbalance. This marked the high point of optimism.

At the end of 1990 Soviet officials delivered the shock news that Soviet aid would be drastically cut and that from January 1991 all commercial

59. Vientiane Radio, 28 December 1991.

60. Lao National Radio, 31 December 1991.

61. Robert Karniol, "Vientiane courts Chinese aid," *Jane's Defence Weekly*, 11 January 1992, p. 45.

62. *Asia Yearbook 1992*, p. 146.

63. *Asia Yearbook 1991*, p. 152.

64. *Izvestiia*, 1 March 1990.

transactions would be on a hard-currency basis at world market prices. It was expected that Soviet-Lao trade in 1991 would fall to half the value of the previous year. Soviet officials also informed Laos that they would be able to supply only half of Laos' oil requirements. The Soviets did promise, however, to give priority to the repair of highway eight which links the centre of Laos to Vinh on the Vietnamese coast.[65]

In January 1991 a Soviet delegation visited Vientiane and signed three documents governing bilateral economic relations. One document set out the basis for the new relationship, another provided for trade in convertible currency, while the third set out the terms for the repayment of Laos' debt to the Soviet Union.[66] In brief, the Soviet Union suspended all aid and credits to Laos while promising to apply Rbl. 50m, left unspent from the previous five-year plan, towards education and health projects such as the Lao-Soviet Friendship Hospital. No figure for debt was released, but repayment was to be in the form of goods until the year 2005. Over the past fifteen years the Soviet Union granted Laos credits worth Rbl. 750m, or 75 percent of the country's total foreign debt.

In May 1991 the Soviet Union and Laos reached an agreement on cultural and scientific cooperation for 1991–93.[67] This was the last public agreement to be signed between the LPDR and the USSR. Subsequent events made its modest objectives unattainable. Scholarships for Lao students reportedly ceased in 1991.[68] In early 1992 the Lao press carried complaints about the hardships faced by Lao students stranded in the former Soviet Union.[69]

Cambodia

Over the decade of its existence, the People's Republic of Kampuchea (PRK) too became dependent on aid from the socialist bloc to the extent that eighty percent of its annual budget was derived from this source. In the late 1980s Soviet aid to Cambodia amounted to roughly US $100m a year in trade credits, technical aid and grants. This included 190,000 tonnes of oil products, 35,000 tonnes of urea fertilizer, 20,00 tonnes each of cement and construction steel, cotton and transport vehicles and medicines.

As was the case with Vietnam and Laos, the Soviet Union exported far more to Cambodia than it received in exchange. In 1989, for example, the

---

65. AFP, 30 November 1990.
66. Martin Stuart-Fox, "Laos in 1991: On the Defensive," *Southeast Asian Affairs 1992*, p. 178.
67. Lao National Radio, 21 May 1991.
68. Chou Norindr, "Laos in the Deadlock," *Indochina Report*, January–March 1992, p. 14.
69. *Vientiane Mai*, 6 and 20 February 1992.

USSR supplied Cambodia with Rbl. 103m in goods and imported only Rbl. 20m. Soviet-Cambodia trade represented eighty-five percent of Cambodia's total trade. This massive imbalance was made up by Soviet credits. By 1990, Cambodia's total debts to the USSR were estimated at between 714 and 820m roubles.[70]

In April 1990, Soviet officials informed the Phnom Penh government that as from January 1991 all technical assistance would cease and trade would be based on world market prices in hard currency.[71] The Soviets did promise "special assistance" in providing weapons, oil and fertilizer.[72] The Soviets also expected repayment of an outstanding loan of 250m roubles which fell due at that time.

During 1990, Soviet non-military aid to the Hun Sen regime dropped by some sixty percent to a total of around US $1.5m.[73] At the same time, Soviet deliveries of strategic commodities such as oil and fertilizer declined. For example, while Cambodia needed 250,000 tonnes of oil, the Soviets could only supply 5,000 tonnes.

The Cambodian economy was hurt badly. The government nearly went bankrupt and social order began to break down. There were severe shortages of goods, including food and daily necessities. Prices sky-rocketed. For example, the cost of petrol jumped from 90 riels a litre to 500.[74] The government was forced to print paper money in order to keep up with inflation. In May, the Cambodian government decided to lay off one-fourth of its civil servants and to sell its gold reserves to meet civilian and military needs.[75]

In May 1991 officials from the USSR and Cambodia met in Phnom Penh to reshape their commercial relations and to negotiate agreements on trade and economic cooperation for 1991.[76] A protocol on cultural, scientific and technical cooperation for 1991–93 was also signed.[77] Both of these agreements were overtaken by domestic events in the Soviet Union. For example, the latter agreement included provisions for extending the service of a number of specialists working in such areas as education, health,

---

70. *Izvestiia*, 1 March 1990, *Asia Yearbook 1991*, p. 95 and AFP, Phnom Penh, *Bangkok Post*, 2 December 1991.

71. Raoul M. Jennar, *Cambodia Mission Report 19th April–10th May 1990*, p. 3.

72. Jacques Bekaert, BBC, 24 Hours Programme, 14 March 1991.

73. Justus M. van der Kroef, "Cambodia in 1990: The Elusive Peace," *Asian Survey* 31 (January 1991), p. 99.

74. *Asia Yearbook 1991*, p. 94.

75. Elizabeth Becker, *International Herald Tribune*, 6 June 1990, Jennar, *Cambodia Mission Report*, p. 3. Mike Yeong, "Cambodia 1991: Lasting Peace or Decent Interval?," *Southeast Asian Affairs 1992*, pp. 104–06.

76. TASS, 21 May 1991.

77. Voice of the People of Cambodia, 22 May 1991.

information, culture and the media. In particular, Soviet specialists were to be posted to the Cambodian-Soviet Friendship Institute of Higher Technology. However, before the end of the year, the Soviets had withdrawn nearly all their technical experts. An estimated one hundred remained at the end of 1991, down from a peak of 1,500 in 1985.[78] Early in 1992 it was reported that the Institute of Higher Technology was moribund and that UNESCO and the Asian Institute of Technology would attempt to revive it.

In 1991 Soviet aid to Cambodia dried up. The following year the Russian Federation was reported to have defaulted on its contributions to the running costs of the United Nations, while Russian helicopter pilots stationed in Cambodia under UN auspices were reported to have been paid half their salary by their government.[79] In June 1992, thirty-three nations gathered in Tokyo to set up a new international agency to coordinate economic assistance to Cambodia. Over US $880m was pledged. The Russian Federation was not among the major donors.

Yet back in 1978 the Soviet Union had supported Vietnam's invasion of Cambodia. Moscow and Hanoi became the main backers of the Phnom Penh regime. Initially the PRK was recognised only by members of the socialist bloc. In 1981 India became the sole non-communist state to extend diplomatic recognition.

After Gorbachev came to power in 1985, the Soviet Union took tentative and then more affirmative steps to secure a peaceful settlement of the Cambodian conflict on the basis of "national reconciliation."[80] This process went hand-in-hand with Sino-Soviet normalisation efforts. According to one analyst, the Soviet Union "in the throes of national disintegration, had neither resources nor political inclination to continue a struggle of dubious outcome and no strategic gain." It therefore decided to remove Cambodia as a central irritant in its bilateral relations with China.[81] Soviet diplomatic pressure was applied on Hanoi and Phnom Penh to settle the conflict through negotiations

As a result of mounting internal economic difficulties after 1989, the Soviet Union's role in Cambodia diminished. The last major meeting between party leaders was in September 1990, when Moscow hosted a visit by the General Secretary of the Khmer People's Revolutionary Party

---

78. *Asia Yearbook 1992*, p. 97, and AFP dispatch from Phnom Penh, *Bangkok Post*, 2 December 1991.

79. Voice of the Great National Union Front of Cambodia, 20 July 1992.

80. Thayer, "Prospects for Peace in Kampuchea," p. 161.

81. Frederick Z. Brown, "Cambodia in 1991: An Uncertain Peace," *Asian Survey* 32 (January 1992), pp. 88–89.

(KPRP) and President of the PRK's Council of State, Heng Samrin.[82] The last party-to-party discussions were held in June 1991 when Heng Samrin met in Hanoi with O. S. Shenin, CPSU Politburo member and delegate to the seventh national congress of the Vietnam Communist Party. No CPSU representative attended the KPRP's extraordinary national congress in October 1991.[83]

During the anti-Gorbachev coup in August 1991, Cambodian officials made two statements. On 20 August a Phnom Penh diplomat interviewed in Hanoi was quoted as hoping the Soviet Union would not be weakened by unrest as it still had a key role to play in the Cambodian peace process. "We need stability in the USSR and my main concern is not to see a civil war," he stated.[84] On 24 August, after the coup had failed, Heng Samrin said he had learned "with great elation... Gorbachev has resumed his function as the president of the USSR."

After August 1991, the Soviet role in Cambodia was confined to actions undertaken in its capacity as a permanent member of the UN Security Council. The USSR and its successor the Russian Federation recognised and gave diplomatic support to the Supreme National Council after the signing of the Cambodian peace agreement. In December 1991, the Soviet Union transferred its recognition from the State of Cambodia (formerly the PRK) to the Supreme National Council.

After the dissolution of the USSR, the former Soviet Ambassador to Cambodia, Yurii Miakotnykh, became the envoy of the Russian Federation. On 27 December he met with Norodom Sihanouk and reaffirmed that normal bilateral relations would continue. That same day Sihanouk issued two statements on behalf of the Supreme National Council, one recognised the Russian Federation as a sovereign and independent state, the other recognised the Russian Federation "as the legitimate successor of the former Soviet Union... [and] permanent member of the UN Security Council."[85] Sihanouk also issued separate statements recognising Armenia, Belarus, Kazakhstan, Kirgizstan, Moldova, Tajikistan, Ukraine, and Uzbekistan.

Moscow thus shifted its political stance from supporter of the Phnom Penh regime to a more neutral ground. In June 1992, the Russian foreign ministry issued a statement declaring, "We share the viewpoint on the need to strengthen efforts by the permanent members of the UN Security Council

---

82. Shortly thereafter, on 9 November 1990, the chief of the Soviet foreign ministry's Southeast Asia department, Genrikh Kireev, met with Prince Norodom Sihanouk in Pyongyang. Sihanouk was the nominal leader of the coalition opposing the PRK; TASS, 10 November 1990.

83. Indeed, no foreign party attended the congress; AFP, 17 October 1991.

84. Jean-Claude Chapon, AFP, Hanoi, 20 August 1991.

85. SPK News Agency, Phnom Penh, 1 January 1992.

and use all means at their disposal to influence any side whose practical steps run counter to the peace agreements."[86]

On the military front, throughout the Cambodian conflict the Soviet Union was the main supplier of weapons and equipment to the PRK armed forces. Soviet military assistance averaged US $30m a year in the late 1980s.[87] According to Western diplomats "several hundred" Soviet military advisers were posted to Cambodia. Moscow has put the figure at no more than two hundred.[88] Soviet military advisers were not impressed, however, that their assistance was being put to good use. They were openly critical of the PRK army's passive performance on the battlefield despite its numerical strength.

In 1989–90, as the peace process moved to a negotiated settlement, the Soviet Union signalled its intention to stop providing military assistance to Phnom Penh.[89] In August 1990, the Soviet and Chinese foreign ministers met just prior to a round of peace talks in Jakarta and reportedly agreed that a suspension of arms shipments would encourage a cease-fire in Cambodia.[90] It would appear that limited shipments of arms continued until 1991. Immediately after the signing of the Cambodian peace agreement, the Soviet Union cut all military ties with the Phnom Penh regime and withdrew its military liaison group headed by General Vassilii G. Beliaiev.[91]

Conclusion

Events in Eastern Europe and the Soviet Union in 1989–90 prompted both Vietnam and Laos to rethink their dependent relations with the Soviet Union. Laos responded first by focusing its energies on China, Japan and Thailand. In August 1989, for example, after a series of low-level delegations had been exchanged, Laos and China restored party-to-party ties. In October, Kaysone Phomvihan, Secretary General of the LPRP, visited Beijing. He later travelled to Japan and France in his first official foray outside the socialist bloc (visits to Thailand excepted).

In 1990 Sino-Lao economic and political relations picked up considerably. Chinese investment in Laos rose to account for more than half

86. ITAR–TASS, June 10, 1992; Reuter, Phnom Penh, *Straits Times* and AFP, London, *Nation*, 12 June 1992.

87. *Asia Yearbook 1991*, p. 95.

88. AFP, Phnom Penh, *Bangkok Post*, 2 December 1991.

89. In December 1989, Soviet Deputy Foreign Minister Egor Rogachev asserted that his government had ceased military shipments to the Phnom Penh government.

90. *Asia Yearbook 1991*, p. 94.

91. AFP, Phnom Penh, *Bangkok Post*, 2 December 1991.

of all foreign investment.[92] In March, a delegation of the Chinese Communist Party's foreign relations commission visited Vientiane. A month later the chief of staff of the Lao army and party secretary of the capital city journeyed to Beijing. The most important event came in December when Laos hosted Chinese Premier Li Peng. Three economic agreements were signed at this time, including a credit arrangement valued at Rmb. 50m (US \$9.2m) to finance economic and technical cooperation over five years.

In reviewing Laos' new external orientations, one specialist concluded, "this change is not just a question of offsetting its hitherto pivotal relationship with Moscow by substituting China, but is a measure of the current political and economic disarray in the Soviet Union and Eastern Europe matched with the prospect of a drying up of developmental assistance from that source."[93]

The Soviet-Vietnamese relationship, as symbolised by the 1978 25-year Treaty of Friendship and Cooperation, was at heart an anti-China alliance. For over a decade it served as the cornerstone of Vietnam's security and foreign policy. At the seventh party congress in June 1991 Vietnam adopted what might be termed an "omni-directional" foreign policy, declaring that it wanted to make friends with all countries regardless of social systems.

After the signing of the Cambodian peace agreement, Vietnam normalised its relations with China and all six members of the Association of Southeast Asian Nations. In October 1991 Vietnamese Premier Vo Van Kiet visited Indonesia, Thailand and Singapore. Sino-Vietnamese relations were normalised in November. Early the following year Kiet travelled to Malaysia, Brunei and the Philippines. In July 1992 Vietnam (and Laos) not only attended the twenty-fifth meeting of the ASEAN foreign ministers as an officially invited observer; it also formally acceded to the 1976 Bali Treaty.

Vietnam has rounded out its "omni-directional" foreign policy by making forays into Europe, stepping up its cooperation on the issue of Americans missing-in-action (MIA) with the United States, and developing robust economic relations with Taiwan, Hong Kong and South Korea.

Relations between Vietnam and the former Soviet Union have been depoliticised and deideologised as a result of the collapse of the USSR. The downward slide in relations has been halted and is now being reconstructed by restoring traditional economic and commercial ties. These are now being forged on a more pragmatic basis. Military relations between Russia and Vietnam, including the sale of equipment and hardware and a continued Russian naval presence at Cam Ranh Bay, are the subject of ongoing

---

92. AFP, *Straits Times*, 26 November 1990.
93. Geoffrey C. Gunn, "Laos in 1990: Winds of Change," *Asian Survey* 31 (January 1991), p. 92.

discussions. The importance of Russian-Vietnamese ties will depend on the ability of Moscow to maintain political stability and hence its ability to continue its trading relationship with Vietnam.

Vietnam's protégés in Phnom Penh have taken determined steps to move in an independent direction. In 1989 the Cambodian National Assembly adopted a declaration of neutrality which rendered the 1979 treaty with Vietnam redundant. In 1991, Cambodia withdrew all its military officers from schools in Vietnam. Vietnamese leaders were reportedly not consulted in advance about the momentous changes adopted by the KPRP at its extraordinary congress in October 1991. At that congress the KPRP dropped its communist trappings and renamed itself the Cambodian People's Party. Under the terms of the 1991 Peace Agreement, Cambodian sovereignty now resides with a Supreme National Council of which the State of Cambodia (formerly the People's Republic of Kampuchea) is a member. These and other developments clearly indicate that "the special relationship" with Vietnam is a dead letter.

New patterns of regional relations are taking shape. Some analysts speak of the emergence of a "baht zone" on mainland Southeast Asia which would link the economies of Cambodia and Laos with Thailand. Others posit the development of "growth triangles" through which northern Vietnam is linked economically to southern China and Hainan Island, while southern Vietnam develops close ties with Singapore and Bangkok. A third set of evolving relationships extends beyond Indochina and Southeast Asia to take in the growing commercial links between Vietnam and South Korea, Hong Kong, Taiwan and Japan.

What is clear is that Vietnamese hegemony has been ended and the former Soviet Union no longer looms large in political, economic or military terms. The term Indochina is rapidly losing its meaning as a coherent sub-system operating within the Southeast Asian region.

11

Southeast Asia

Pushpa Thambipillai

The momentum in the improved regional and bilateral relations between the member-countries of the Association of South-East Asian Nations (ASEAN) and the Soviet Union came to a sudden standstill with the August 1991 coup in Moscow. The beginning of the end of the Union of Soviet Socialist Republics, culminating in its disintegration, has left the relationship in a quandary. Events of late 1991 have created an air of uncertainty over the nature of future ties for member-countries of ASEAN from the bilateral and regional perspectives.

This chapter will briefly review the background relationship till 1991, then discuss the nature of the current links with the newly-independent states of the Commonwealth of Independent States (CIS). Discussion is limited to the ASEAN member-countries and issues affecting the association's immediate vicinity in Southeast Asia, without too much reference to Indochina as that is adequately covered in other chapters. Myanmar (Burma) has been excluded in this study as its foreign relations have generally not impinged on or had any impact on the rest of Southeast Asia, least of all in its relations with the the former Soviet Union (FSU).

But what is the CIS? Is it not just a loose association of most of the former components of the Soviet Union? Does it aim to represent an integrated grouping? Without a common domestic or foreign policy how does one relate to it? The policy planner is faced with these questions when trying to come to grips with the present situation. This chapter can, therefore, only view Southeast Asian countries' relations with the member-units of the CIS as independent entities. Russia being the largest and the most important (and for all practical purposes the "core," having inherited most of the external dimensions of the FSU), will be the important focus of attention. However, from the Southeast Asian perspective, some of the Central Asian republics are gaining prominence and may in future be the prime focus of interest.

Background

Unlike the major players in the region (the United States, Britain, France, China and Japan), the Soviet Union had a late start in its interactions with Southeast Asia. Its main interest was in exporting ideology and in supporting local organisations and so it did not explore commercial interests. Once ideology had found a strong base in Vietnam and its neighbouring states of Laos and Cambodia in the 1950s and 1960s, the Soviet Union was content in probing the interests of the other states in the region, but without much active involvement.[1]

Only in Indonesia did the Soviet Union succeed in establishing a firm relationship at the governmental and political party levels, bolstered by the nationalist struggle for independence. In the 1950s and 1960s, Indonesia under President Achmed Sukarno provided a fertile ground for the Soviet Union to exploit the anti-West sentiments of newly-independent Third World leaders. As compared to the others in the vicinity, Indonesia was the only country with a legal communist party which had a strong Moscow link. However, the fortunes of the Communist Party of Indonesia (PKI) were reversed with the failure of an attempted coup in 1965. The involvement of communists in the abortive coup also affected Indonesia's relations with the Soviet Union. Although strained, diplomatic relations were not broken off.

The decades between 1965 and 1985 were in many respects low points in the Soviet Union's drive into non-communist Southeast Asia. Its intentions were blocked by the wariness of local leaders towards any Soviet influence, especially with the extra-legal communist parties and other potential organisations like labour unions. Soviet-Southeast Asian relations also reflected the tensions in global and regional political and ideological rivalry and the East-West divide. However, the two decades in Soviet regional relations were by no means uniform, oscillating between cordial and tense political atmospheres.

The non-communist states of Southeast Asia were caught in the midst of the Cold War rivalry, enhanced by their fear of communist influence as

---

1. For an incisive account of the early relationships see Charles B. Mclane, *Soviet Strategies in Southeast Asia: An Exploration of Eastern Policy under Lenin and Stalin* (Princeton: Princeton University Press, 1966). See also R. A. Longmire, *Soviet Relations with South-East Asia* (London: Kegan Paul, 1989) and Leszek Buszynski, *Soviet Foreign Policy and Southeast Asia* (New York: St. Martin's Press, 1986).

perpetrated by their domestic insurgencies. Four countries—Malaysia, Singapore, the Philippines and Thailand—were faced with illegal communist movements while Indonesia's new and strongly anti-communist leadership was eliminating the last vestiges of the pre-1965 communist party. Although all the countries exchanged diplomatic relations with the Soviet Union and some even proclaimed their nonaligned status, they were clearly suspicious and cautious of the Soviet giant, and sought refuge in relations with the Western powers.

Thailand was the only self-governing Southeast Asian state after the Second World War, and thus was the first in the region to formally establish diplomatic relations. Ties were instituted in 1946 but remained inactive till about 1953. Indonesia established diplomatic relations in 1954 after Joseph Stalin had formally recognised the new republic in 1950. In both the Thai and Indonesian cases, their application to join the United Nations had some influence on their exchanging ties with the Soviet Union, an important actor (in the Security Council) in supporting the admission of new members. Despite the turmoil in Indonesia in the mid-1960s, diplomatic relations with the Soviets were not severed (while those with China were suspended in 1967 and not resumed until 1990).

Malaysia was the next Southeast Asian country to set up formal ties. Initially trade relations were established in early 1967, followed by diplomatic exchanges in late 1967. The period reflected the beginnings of a nonaligned, pragmatic orientation of the Malaysian government, as well as the confidence in international relations gained through the creation of ASEAN. Singapore established official ties in mid-1968 although a trade agreement had been concluded in early 1966 and a Soviet trade mission and a TASS office had been set up in the island. The Philippines, closely associated with the United States, was the last of the Southeast Asians to open the door to the Soviets, in mid-1976. Brunei, which became fully independent in 1984, established ties with the Soviet Union in October 1991 (the first communist state among Brunei's diplomatic friends).

Despite the expanding contacts in the sixties and seventies, the Soviet Union did not enjoy a hospitable political environment. Not only did the Asian leaders not let the Soviets get too close for comfort, the Soviet Union also constantly viewed the non-communist region as an ally of its rival, the United States. Despite their insistence on the contrary, especially by Malaysia and Indonesia, the Southeast Asian states were unwittingly entangled in the Cold War strife. For instance, the formation of ASEAN incurred the displeasure of the Soviet Union, which saw it as another attempt by the West to consolidate its interests in the region. Moscow refused to recognise ASEAN as an association reflective of a genuine interest by Southeast Asians to address common problems.[2] The region was further polarised with the escalation of the Vietnam War that pitted all the ASEAN countries against the adversaries, namely China, the Soviet Union and North Vietnam. Thailand and the Philippines were physically involved in the war, while the other three gave conditional support but were not prepared to be dragged into big-power politics. Despite their varying levels of engagement in the war and in hosting foreign military forces, ASEAN collectively issued its ZOPFAN (Zone of Peace Freedom and Neutrality) declaration in 1971. The major preoccupation was with the spread of communism and therefore the leaders tended to support the attempts of the allies against the communist forces. ZOPFAN, in practice, was thus a non-starter.

The triumph of communism in Vietnam and the rest of Indochina in 1975 did not however create a permanent division in Southeast Asia; it spurred further regional activities. ASEAN was revitalised and restructured beginning with the first ever summit in 1976 and conciliatory gestures were extended towards the Indochinese states. Attempts were made to bridge the two "blocs." But the tide of events was again halted with the Vietnamese invasion of Cambodia and the Soviet action in Afghanistan—two issues that would become the centre of contention between the ASEAN countries and the Soviet Union.

Vietnam's very close post-unification ties with the Soviet Union brought the superpower physically nearer to the rest of Southeast Asia than it had ever been before. The military presence of the Soviet Union in Vietnam was a constant reminder not only of the volatility of big-power entanglements but also the threat of communism. The years of Leonid Brezhnev, Iuri Andropov and Konstantin Chernenko were periods of relatively cool and cautious relationships for the ASEAN countries. Although there were no major incidents between the Soviet Union and the countries in the region, minor irritations, for example accusations of spying by or for the Soviets, were rampant in the ASEAN countries. Despite Soviet interest in expanding relations with countries beyond Indochina, there was little diplomatic headway. Economic and other socio-cultural transactions were also limited. The Soviet Union's firm support of Vietnam, its "bankrolling" of Vietnam's invasion of Cambodia and its own invasion of Afghanistan pitted a number of ASEAN countries against the Soviet Union in the diplomatic and socio-cultural fields. Thailand and Singapore were especially critical of the Soviet-Vietnamese collusion while Indonesia and Malaysia used the Soviet-Afghan

---

2. This period is covered by Bilveer Singh, *Soviet Relations with ASEAN 1967–88* (Singapore: Singapore University Press, 1989) and K. S. Nathan, *Detente and Soviet Policy in Southeast Asia* (Kuala Lumpur: Gateway, 1984).

issue to mobilise Islamic condemnation of the Soviet Union at a number of international forums.

The Change in Tide—Mikhail Gorbachev and the Region

The Gorbachev era, beginning in March 1985, did improve the political relations between countries in Southeast Asia and the Soviet Union. In fact, it was Gorbachev's policies in both the domestic and foreign arenas that led to improved relations after 1986. In retrospect, it can be seen that Gorbachev extended the "olive branch" by downplaying ideology and emphasising functional cooperation with most of the ASEAN members. Unlike his predecessors, he tried to give the Southeast Asian region some prominence in the mapping of the Soviet Union's foreign policies. In the now-famous July 1986 Vladivostok speech, Gorbachev made several conciliatory offers for improving bilateral relations with China and the other Asian-Pacific countries. He indicated that the Soviet Union would expand ties with the ASEAN states.[3]

In keeping with that promise Foreign Minister Eduard Shevardnadze set off the pace of diplomatic exchanges by visiting Thailand and Indonesia, the first visit by a Soviet Foreign Minister to the ASEAN capitals. Several official visits were conducted, including one by Malaysian Prime Minister Mahathir Mohamad in 1987, another by Thai Prime Minister Prem Tinsulanonda in 1988, the next by Indonesian President Suharto in 1989 and finally by Singapore Prime Minister Lee Kuan Yew in September 1990. Southeast Asia had never before seen that many exchanges of visits. In that respect, 1987–89 was indeed the heyday in Soviet-Southeast Asian relations. Although Gorbachev's "Look East" pronouncements encouraged positive responses from the Southeast Asian leaders, the Soviet Union's priorities still lay with Northeast Asia. This was illustrated by Gorbachev's visits to China and Japan, but none beyond those two countries.

Soviet willingness to reconsider involvement in Afghanistan and its changing policy on supporting Vietnam's role in Cambodia were two factors that encouraged ASEAN member-countries to modify their attitudes. The Soviet Union did finally withdraw from Afghanistan; it also played a crucial

---

3. See Robyn Lim, "Implications for Southeast Asia," in Ramesh Thakur and Carlyle A. Thayer, eds., *The Soviet Union as an Asian Pacific Power: Implications of Gorbachev's Vladivostok Initiative* (Boulder: Westview, 1987), pp. 81–91; and the chapters by Robert C. Horn (Southeast Asia), J. Soedjati Djiwandono (Indonesia), Pushpa Thambipillai (Malaysia), Wilfrido V. Villacorta (Philippines), Bilveer Singh (Singapore), Chantima Ongsuragz (Thailand) and Carlyle A. Thayer (Vietnam) in Pushpa Thambipillai and Daniel C. Matuszewski, eds., *The Soviet Union and the Asia-Pacific Region: Views from the Region* (New York: Praeger, 1989).

role in cooperating with ASEAN and later with the other permanent members of the Security Council in seeking a political settlement to the Cambodian situation. ASEAN had often made it clear that the Cambodian issue was linked to improved relations with the Soviet Union. Decreasing Soviet financial support for Vietnam, influenced by a depressed domestic economy, forced Vietnam to withdraw its troops from Cambodia. Soviet support for the UN peace proposals for its "client state" encouraged a period of positive relationships. The new Soviet diplomacy gave encouragement to Soviet watchers despite the fact that sceptics saw no substantive impetus to Gorbachev's Asian-Pacific initiatives.

Gorbachev's *glasnost* and *perestroika* had also promised expanded economic relations. With the new openness, more trade delegations from the ASEAN countries explored the markets of the Soviet Union. There were also trade visits from the Soviet Union. Although ASEAN-Soviet trade had been dismal, amounting to around one percent of total ASEAN foreign trade, there were signs that investment opportunities would improve the level of bilateral transactions. As the Soviet Union continually ran trade deficits with the ASEAN members, increased exports and joint ventures were deemed essential to improve the situation. The Soviet Union suffered a "permanent" trade deficit with all the ASEAN countries. Its major imports were primary commodities like rubber, palm oil, sugar and tapioca, while it sold chemicals and machinery in return. There was little demand for Soviet products; nevertheless, Thailand and Singapore established a number of joint ventures, for example in shipping and other trading sectors.[4]

Although the economic waves of *glasnost* and *perestroika* had their major impact on Soviet relations with Western countries, some ripples were felt in Southeast Asia. Even if there was no substantial increase in trade, at least there was more communication and more interest expressed. The choice of Vladivostok for a major policy speech brought the Soviet Far East closer to the vibrant economies of Japan and East Asia, at the same time exploring the opportunities further south. The visits by ASEAN leaders were intended to take advantage of the economic opportunities offered as the official entourage often included large numbers of prominent businessmen eager to explore the new prospects. But later, most of the entrepreneurs discovered that bureaucratic hurdles and the inconvertibility of the rouble were major deterrents to effective business relationships.

Despite the slow pace of the private sector initiatives, the Soviet public sector was keen to promote inter-regional contacts. In early 1990, during a

---

4. For an analysis of economic relations during this period see Pushpa Thambipillai, "Soviet-ASEAN Economic Relations: Opportunities for Expansion," *Indonesian Quarterly* 17:2 (1989), pp. 115–25.

visit to Singapore, Prime Minister Nikolai Ryzhkov initiated the Joint Economic Commission (comprising representatives from the public and private sectors) to promote better economic relations.[5] The Philippines, realising that it would be left behind, also cautiously entered the search for economic ties. For instance, it lifted the ban on Soviet commercial ships entering Philippine shipyards, a sensitive issue considering the fact that Subic naval base was nearby. In fact the Soviets were interested in taking advantage of the improving relationship by institutionalising the cordial ties with ASEAN. In mid-1990 the visiting Deputy Foreign Minister Egor Rogachev expressed the Soviet Union's desire to be involved in regional economic and political forums in the Asian-Pacific region and to be included in ASEAN's dialogue schemes with third countries.[6] It failed in its bid to be invited for the annual ASEAN meeting in Jakarta in 1990.

However, the gradual change in mood in bilateral relations between ASEAN and the Soviet Union, strengthened by the promise of peace in Indochina, earned the Soviets an invitation to attend the most important gathering of ASEAN leaders—the annual foreign ministers' meeting. Malaysia, as the host for the July 1991 meeting, invited both the Soviet Union and China. Thus the Soviet Union was able to establish official ties with ASEAN at the institutional level and interact with the foreign ministers of ASEAN and other dialogue partners. But the Soviet Union itself was not considered for dialogue membership for the time being.[7]

The participation at the ASEAN foreign ministers' meeting earned the Soviet Union a "respectable" place within the regional grouping. Deputy Prime Minister Iuri Masliukov, who was in Kuala Lumpur, extended his official visit to Thailand and Indonesia.

Although economics was an area of increasing interest, the financial aspects were not very promising as the Soviet Union faced a severe credit crunch. Some of the countries, for instance Malaysia and Thailand, had to offer credits to the Soviet Union to facilitate exports of palm oil and rice. Barter was another method that the cash-short country had to resort to in its trade with the region. In trying to improve economic relations, a two-day trade seminar was organised in Jakarta in mid-August, taking place just before the coup. The coup slowed momentarily the pace of activities. Has the pace recovered since then?

---

5. The Singapore-Soviet Joint Economic Commission was established in February 1990. A Singapore delegation composed of public and private sector personnel visited Moscow for talks in September of that year. See the *Straits Times*, 17 February and 18 September 1990.

6. *New Straits Times*, 9 June 1990.

7. Soviet Deputy Prime Minister Iuri Masliukov (who came in place of Foreign Minister Aleksander Bessmertnykh) and Chinese Foreign Minister Qian Qichen attended the annual foreign ministerial meeting as "guests" of the Malaysian government. The two ministers also accepted the Philippine invitation to attend the following year's meeting in Manila.

Post-Coup Uncertainty

The August coup caught the Southeast Asian leaders by surprise in much the same way as it affected others elsewhere. However, they saw it as purely an internal matter. It did not have as much of an impact on Southeast Asian strategic relations as it did in the European and American arenas. Since the Soviet Union was geographically removed from the area, the immediate concern was about how it would affect international and European politics rather than local Southeast Asian affairs. Moscow had also distanced itself politically from its Vietnamese ally by the late 1980s. One of the major concerns for ASEAN was the abortive coup's impact on the promising peace process in Cambodia since the Soviet Union had been a major participant in the negotiations.

The collapse of the East European communist systems had occurred a year earlier and it was only a matter of time before it happened in the birthplace of Marxism-Leninism. In retrospect, many saw the political crisis coming for at least a year; several challenges were mounted against Gorbachev from various factions within his ruling communist party, from the so-called "hardliners" unhappy with the unfolding of *glasnost* as well as from the impatient Western-style democrats. Prime Minister Mahathir Mohamad, speaking after the coup, blamed the West for being partly responsible by concentrating on "democracy" while failing to help the Soviet Union get the benefits of a free market system.[8] The observation may have some validity. Mahathir often speaks his mind and he has had several disagreements with the "West" and is known for his forthright comments on a number of issues. Goh Keng Swee, former Deputy Prime Minister of Singapore, when asked his views on the failure of the Soviet experiment, echoed what some others have said, that *perestroika* should have preceded *glasnost,* that there should have been economic restructuring before political openness. As the economic adviser to China, he was perhaps implying that China was on the right path to preserving its system as it has adopted several vestiges of capitalism without liberalising its political system.[9]

The imminent breakup of the empire provided some ray of hope for the business sector. Southeast Asian businessmen were reportedly encouraged by the disintegration. Based on their previous experiences they reckoned that the dissolution of the Soviet Union would ease the control by the central authorities and they would then be able to deal directly with the individual republics. However, the outlook was promising for long-term opportunities

---

8. *New Straits Times,* 22 August 1991.

9. See Goh's comments to a Japanese newspaper reproduced in the *Nikkei Weekly,* 14 March 1992.

while in the short term there was uncertainty. Those who already had business contracts continued their deals while potential ones adopted a "wait and see" attitude. A year after the coup, the promise of economic opportunities was still far from satisfactory, compared to the euphoria created within business circles earlier. It appeared that it would be several years before the benefits of decentralisation or economic reform would be felt in the FSU. Besides, the financial situation had become even tighter.

The collapse of the Soviet empire also brought into scrutiny the remaining communist states, China and Vietnam. Both reemphasised their adherence to Marxist-Leninist ideology. In practice however both—but especially Vietnam, the later entrant—were in fact exploring the merits of capitalism. This meant that suddenly there were too many attractive locations for Southeast Asian private and public economic pursuits.

CIS or SIC (Single Independent Countries)?

The eventual demise of the USSR after the coup was only a matter of time and the resignation of Gorbachev, who had pioneered Soviet-Asian relations, was less traumatic than the incidents in August. The ASEAN states welcomed the independence of the twelve former Soviet republics and later the formation of the CIS by eleven members. The establishment of formal diplomatic ties with most of the republics followed later. There was great relief to the anti-communist states in Southeast Asia that the CIS was now a non-communist grouping; therefore the new situation encouraged a more "relaxed" attitude towards the once-despised superpower and its associates.

All the ASEAN states participated in a U.S.-initiated conference on the offer of humanitarian aid to the CIS in Washington in January 1992. Another conference to consider trade and technical assistance was also attended by the ASEAN members, some of which promised their share of assistance, in Lisbon in May 1992.

From the Southeast Asian perspective, the CIS as a whole was not as relevant as parts of it. The independent republics had varying levels of interests for different states in Southeast Asia. Russia, as the "inheritor" of the Soviet Union, and as the largest state, was inevitably the most important. In keeping with its global role and its position in the United Nations, Russia also retained its special position vis-à-vis the ASEAN organisation and with the six members. Of the former Soviet republics, Southeast Asia has practically ignored the Baltic republics—Estonia, Latvia and Lithuania—although there was ample media coverage during their struggles for independence preceding the disintegration of the Soviet Union. Of the other republics in the CIS, the five Central Asian republics (the "tans") have become the focus of interest: Kazakhstan, Kirgizstan, Tajikistan, Uzbekistan and Turkmenistan, as well as Azerbaijan. One feature is that they are in the Asian sector, forming a rim around China, Afghanistan and Iran (besides Russia that has the only northern Pacific coastline). The other is that they all have a sizable Muslim and Asiatic population, a factor of interest to most of the ASEAN states.

For practical, socio-economic and political reasons, Southeast Asia has not shown much concern about the other five republics: Ukraine, Belarus, Moldova, Georgia and Armenia. Like the other "tans" they had practically no contact with Southeast Asia while within the Soviet Union. Unlike some of the "tans" there appears no likelihood of their establishing active interactions with the region despite their being newly-independent. They are viewed as "European." However, despite their geographical remoteness, significant domestic events have been covered by the Southeast Asian media, for example the issue of nuclear weapons, ethnic conflicts and internal struggles for power. The coverage undoubtedly keeps the ASEAN leadership and people informed of events in these former Soviet republics.

Relations with Russia

On the diplomatic front, Russia has retained the former embassies of the USSR in all the ASEAN capitals (except in Brunei which established official relations in 1991 but had not decided on the status of an embassy or even a non-resident ambassador when the Union was dissolved). The new year of 1992 saw the Russian embassies swapping the red hammer and sickle flag for the white, blue and red flag of the Russian Federation, rather than a yet-to-be-agreed on CIS flag. As in all the countries where it is present, the Russian embassy is expected to represent the interests of all the other republics in the CIS. And as in other countries, the non-Russian republics have yet to consider setting up their separate missions in the ASEAN capitals. The small volume of interactions as well as the financial costs involved does not, at present, warrant a multitude of embassies for the CIS.

Since the breakup, the major diplomatic activity between Russia and ASEAN has been the Russian attendance at the annual foreign ministerial meeting in Manila in July 1992, on this occasion as a guest of ASEAN. It was the second time that Moscow and Beijing had attended the annual gathering of foreign ministers. ASEAN officials at the July 1992 ministerial meeting were quoted as saying that China and Russia were likely to become regular guests of the ASEAN grouping, but elevation to dialogue partner status was unlikely at the moment.[10] Speaking at the meeting, Russian Foreign Minister Andrei Kozyrev declared "Russia's intention to be

---

10. It was also reported that Taiwan had requested a dialogue relationship, a politically sensitive issue in terms of the Chinese diplomacy. See the *Straits Times*, 23 July 1992.

constructively present in the Asian and Pacific Region and it is ready to conduct a comprehensive dialogue with the ASEAN countries," asserting that the "double-headed eagle of Russia is looking both at the West and the East with equal interest." He also offered business opportunities in his country, stating that the "Russian Far East is your natural partner."[11]

For Southeast Asian regionalism, the meeting itself was an important event because for the first time it brought together Laos and Vietnam which signed the Treaty of Amity and Cooperation, an indication that both countries may develop closer links with ASEAN. The venue also provided a forum to discuss the geopolitics of the region, including the lingering Cambodian problem and the territorial claims in the South China Sea. Although the Russians referred to their ties with Vietnam and their presence in Cam Ranh Bay, it was not clear from their statements as to the nature of their current deployment there or whether they were serious about their offer to share the facilities with other interested parties.

Russia continues to be preoccupied with internal dissent and economic problems and thus it is unlikely that it will be able to devote too much interest to Southeast Asia. Perhaps the ASEAN foreign ministerial meeting might be the only formal interaction specifically between Russia and the grouping. The Soviet Union had also been a past observer at the ASEAN Inter-Parliamentary Organisation meetings.[12] Russia was invited as an observer to the last AIP meeting in Jakarta in September 1992.

There are several other avenues for collective interaction between Russia and the ASEAN states, for example at the United Nations and at the PECC (Pacific Economic Cooperation Council) where Russia has inherited its membership from the Soviet Union. Visiting Russian technocrats have also indicated their country's interest in joining APEC (Asia Pacific Economic Cooperation) as well as the yet-to-be-established EAEC (East Asian Economic Caucus) as a means to promote Russia's Pacific Basin-oriented economic and political interests. Russian participation in inter-governmental and non-governmental activities in Southeast Asia that began in the late eighties will probably increase with the removal of Russia as an ideological adversary and its decline as a military threat, at least under present circumstances.

According to a Russian scholar,

> The previous model of Soviet relations with this part of the Asian Pacific region which was based on massive economic and military assistance to Vietnam, Laos and

---

11. Address by A. V. Kozyrev at the consultative meeting with ASEAN foreign ministers, Manila, 22 July 1992.

12. The AIP is an organisation representing government and opposition party members from the five ASEAN states (except Brunei which does not have an elected legislature).

Cambodia while economic relations with the ASEAN states remained negligible is no longer valid. Russia does not want to support one group of Southeast Asian countries against the other, moreover it is interested in maintaining an atmosphere of peace and cooperation in this area which has now become very important both economically and politically.[13]

The Asian Republics

In following the practice of the majority of other countries that have embassies in Moscow, the ASEAN governments have also accredited their Moscow missions to the other CIS republics with which they have established diplomatic relations; no separate missions have yet been set up.

Of the Asian republics, perhaps only two have shown some promise of bilateral interactions with the Southeast Asian region. Kazakhstan and Uzbekistan are two of the larger republics and more outwardly-looking than the rest of their neighbouring republics. Kazakhstan is an important state in terms of its storage of nuclear weapons of the FSU. It is also a leading industrial state and a producer of oil. President Nursultan Nazarbaev came into prominence during the breakup of the Soviet Union, and his stature as an important leader was not lost later when his republic became independent.

Singapore has established special links with Kazakhstan, given the fact that Kazakhstan has needs in computers and software as well as oil industry-related imports from Singapore. Senior Minister Lee Kuan Yew led a large delegation of business and trade-related individuals to Alma Ata in September 1991, barely a month after the Moscow coup. Nazarbaev's independent stand as well as Gorbachev's unleashing of *perestroika* enabled Lee to visit Kazakhstan directly instead of having to visit Moscow first and indirectly getting the centre's approval, as would have been the case only a short time earlier. Nazarbaev was no stranger to Lee or to Singapore as he had met Lee while on a Soviet parliamentary delegation visit to the island in 1989.

But trying to advance directly to Kazakhstan also revealed the problems—there are no direct travel links between Southeast Asia and any of the Asian republics. (Lee and his party flew in on a private jet offered by the Sultan of Brunei.) The lack of communications could, perhaps, reflect the complexities ahead in establishing any meaningful ties between Kazakhstan (and the other republics as well which are all landlocked) and the Southeast Asian countries.[14]

---

13. Gennady Chufrin, "Russian Policy in Post-Cold War Pacific Asia: Strategic Aspects," *Asian Defence Journal*, August 1992, p. 33.

14. Aeroflot links some of the ASEAN capitals to Moscow, flying via India. Some flights do stop en route in Tashkent. Recently there has been an agreement between Malaysia and Uzbekistan to commence weekly flights between the two countries.

Uzbekistan with its majority Islamic Uzbeks has strengthened its links mostly with Malaysia and to a lesser extent with Indonesia. President Islam Karimov paid official visits to Malaysia and Indonesia in June 1992, the first visit by an ex-Soviet republic leader. Uzbekistan as a major producer of cotton is interested in the ASEAN market for its products, while Malaysia and Indonesia are keen to expand their overseas markets for palm oil and other commodities. While in Malaysia, Karimov's delegation signed two accords—one on economic and technical, and another on scientific and cultural cooperation. Uzbekistan was seeking Malaysia's help in its banking and oil and gas sectors. Malaysia could offer its expertise in several fields, for example, technology in palm oil production which could be applied to cotton seed oil production. As a leading gold producer, Karimov also offered Uzbekistan's gold as collateral to woo local investors who were sceptical of the viability of the republic's economy.[15] In fact, Mahathir Mohamad had already visited Uzbekistan in 1987 during his official visit to the Soviet Union. A large number of officials and businessmen had accompanied him but nothing much had resulted immediately from that visit. A more recent visit by Malaysian Foreign Minister Abdullah Badawi to Russia, Uzbekistan, Kazakhstan, Kirgizstan and Turkmenistan in May 1992 resulted in some positive bilateral links with the Asian republics, especially in the field of technical training.[16]

Uzbekistan's contacts with the region were a forerunner to its successful application for membership of the Non-Aligned Movement (NAM). After Malaysia, the Uzbek leader visited Indonesia. In an address during his meeting with President Suharto, Karimov said that "A few years ago Indonesia seemed too far away for us. We had a natural inclination towards your country, but the ruling system in the former USSR prevented us from doing this."[17] Uzbekistan was admitted as one of the few new members at NAM's last summit meeting in Jakarta in September 1992. (Brunei was another.) The only other CIS member to have any status at all in NAM was Armenia which was accorded an observer status, while Kirgizstan has applied to be an observer.

The independent republics of CIS have already swelled the membership of the United Nations. Besides NAM, some of them may also participate in other global organisations like the Islamic Conference Organisation. As new and inexperienced players in the international arena the republics have been slow in participating in foreign affairs. They have also been hampered by domestic political and economic problems. Thus leaders in Southeast Asia

---

15. *New Straits Times*, 22 June 1992.
16. *Ibid.*, 27 May and 3 June 1992.
17. See the *Jakarta Post*, 23 June 1992.

are not too optimistic about an extensive network of bilateral ties in the short term.

Soviet Demise—Is There a Silver Lining?

The end of communist ideology in Eastern Europe and the Soviet Union which had already begun before the collapse of the Soviet Union itself was a welcome outcome for the non-communist states of ASEAN. Both domestically and externally that was a "windfall." All the ASEAN member-states had faced internal communist insurgencies from the 1940s. Malaysia and Thailand had successfully seen an end to their communist movements in the 1980s. With the fall of Eurocommunism, the insurgency movement in the Philippines lost a source of psychological support, although it had never identified closely with either the Soviet or Chinese parties. The only remaining active communist party in ASEAN, it has now been legalised by the new government of President Fidel Ramos; that has therefore taken the wind out of its sails. Governments feel more confident in addressing their domestic communist movements with the fall of international communism. Although the Chinese communist party is still very much in power and both China and Vietnam have expressed strong adherence to communist ideology, the era of "exporting communism" seems to be over, especially with the onset of a strong belief in the capitalist path to development.

Internationally, the demise and the subsequent emergence of "democratic" Russia and the CIS has lessened tensions in the Southeast Asian region. The end of the Cold War and the absorption of the Soviet Union into the Western order has ensured that there is one less undesirable superpower to meddle in domestic and regional affairs. The Soviet Union had often been accused of espionage activities in the ASEAN capitals and the activities of the embassies were often regarded with suspicion. Nationals of the various ASEAN countries were also viewed with suspicion if they established any form of contact with the Soviet embassies. Soviet cultural contacts were politely refused by most of the governments except for a few performances, and scholarships for students to study in the Soviet Union were also rejected or discouraged (as in the case of Thailand) by the governments.[18] It is too early to determine how "open" the new diplomacy will be at the governmental and non-governmental levels.

From a broad political perspective, Russia is now an ally. The dissolution of the Soviet Union also contributed to the reordering of big-

---

18. For an insight into some of Thailand's interactions with the Soviet Union, see Chantima Ongsuragz, "Soviet-Thai Relations under Gorbachev," *Indonesian Quarterly* 17:2 (1989), pp. 147–56.

power presence in Southeast Asia. The chances of the region being embroiled in superpower politics as in previous decades seem less likely. The disintegration of the USSR could have added weight to the demand by the Philippines for an end to U.S. bases treaty. Thus it hastened the American military withdrawal as the Soviet threat dissipated. This was a triumph for the anti-bases groups in the Philippines. It also led to a rethinking of America's security role in the region—in decreasing the emphasis on permanent bases, while increasing the role of mobile forces.

There has also been a reorientation of Southeast Asian leaders' attitudes towards the American military presence. There is at present open expression of support for the Americans to remain as a vital regional force. They have also expressed their willingness to offer base facilities for temporary usage, be it from cautious Brunei or from a once-reluctant Indonesia. Despite the end of the Cold War that condoned the bitter rivalry between the United States and the Soviet Union, the regional countries do not seem to be taking any chances with the possibility of any new actors and changing configurations entering into Southeast Asian geopolitics.

Southeast Asia and the CIS—Active Role or Mutual Dormancy?

It is apparent that one cannot treat Russia and the rest of the republics within the confederation of the CIS as one political entity, inasmuch as ASEAN itself cannot be considered as a unified grouping. Russia is undoubtedly the dominant player domestically within the federation and internationally as the successor of the USSR. The Southeast Asian leaders often express their uncertainty over the future of Russia's Asian relations. They are even more unsure over the Asian republics' prospective links with Southeast Asia. Political, economic or cultural interests are not substantial enough to ensure that the geographical distances between Central and Southeast Asia will be bridged effectively. The "Asian factor" may not materialise after all, despite initial enthusiasm in finding a common link among the "Asians." The Asian republics constitute "new ground" for those in Southeast Asia. For the Muslim states in Southeast Asia, even the religious connection may not seem too promising. Southwest Asia appears to have an edge over Southeast Asia in that respect. Pakistan, Iran and Turkey are geographically nearer to some of the "tans" and Azerbaijan, and have had prior cultural and commercial contacts with them (see chapter 1 above).

The current Russian leadership has not lived up to Asian expectations, at least when compared to the Gorbachev leadership. The general perception is that President Boris Yeltsin is not as international a statesman as Gorbachev was in extending friendly signals to Asia. There has been no Asian-Pacific doctrine so far; no doubt Russia is the inheritor of the Vladivostok initiative, and the only Pacific country within the CIS. Although Southeast Asia has always been in the periphery as compared to Northeast Asia, Yeltsin has yet to include Southeast Asia in his order of issues, unlike Gorbachev who indicated some interest. Also, Russian Foreign Minister Andrei Kozyrev does not appear too well versed in Asian affairs as the region is new to him. In short the Yeltsin-Kozyrev team does not seem seasoned in international diplomacy and has not impressed ASEAN leaders yet. There appears to be a heavy reliance on Eurocentred technocrats or regional power brokers, as the recent issue over the Kuriles and the cancelled Yeltsin visit have indicated. Time may improve the mutual image for both Russia and the ASEAN states.

Trade appears to offer some incentives for the ASEAN countries to strengthen their ties with Russia. However, the trade and investment enthusiasm of the *glasnost* years have waned in 1992. Domestic financial uncertainty in Russia and the CIS has discouraged expansion of links. Southeast Asian businessmen are not rushing in with new ventures but are nevertheless continuing with those that had already been established. Singapore has had the lion's share in both trade and economic ventures (see Table 5.1 above). While Malaysia has lingering interests in the purchase of the Russian MIG-29 aircraft (dating back to the late 1980s) and explores its diplomacy of trade, the Philippines, which used to play the Soviet card at the height of the Cold War, is seriously considering purchasing naval ships from Russia. Despite East-West tensions Thailand had built up its trade links with the FSU and appears to be increasing its links with Russia. Indonesia has yet to increase its potential links while Brunei has no immediate plans for the CIS.

ASEAN and the CIS are still searching for a meaningful relationship. Perhaps one should not use the term CIS at all. Countries in Southeast Asia are pursuing a wait-and-see attitude while the ex-Soviet republics grope with their newly-acquired democracies and open-market economies. There is no collective ASEAN position on the CIS or on each of its components, the only exception being the inclusion of Russia at the ASEAN foreign ministers' meeting. Each ASEAN member pursues its own interests with whichever republic it chooses.

While Russia and the CIS republics fumble with domestic and foreign issues, the ASEAN member-countries have breathing space to reconsider and reformulate their collective or bilateral positions towards the former Soviet Union.

12

The South Pacific
Retreat from Vladivostok

R.A. Herr and D.J. McDougall

At a speech in Vladivostok in July 1986, Mikhail Gorbachev fired the first shot in a volley of initiatives intended to secure the Soviet Union's re-entry into the comity of nations.[1] It is likely that Gorbachev focused on Asia-Pacific because this area posed the least regional risks for his global strategy while offering considerable opportunity for economic and political gains. In arguing for greater Soviet economic and political involvement in the Asian-Pacific region, he quite naturally placed his major emphasis on the Soviet role in Northeast Asia. Although serious attention was given also to other parts of Asia-Pacific, Australia, New Zealand and the South Pacific islands were mentioned largely in the context of a Soviet willingness to expand ties with various regional states.

In the years that followed there were significant developments in both the economic and political relationship with the Southwestern Pacific extremities of Asia-Pacific. For a while, it was the South Pacific islands which occupied the centre-stage of public notoriety. Fisheries agreements, "surrogate" state activities and strategic interest all gave this remote region an international currency which it scarcely expected or deserved. Yet hardly had Gorbachev's vision of a new international order begun to take shape when, taking on a life of its own, it broke free of his grasp. Indeed, not only did Gorbachev lose control of his creation, but he himself was very quickly overtaken and politically destroyed by it. Gorbachev's fall from power and the concomitant collapse of the USSR profoundly changed the

---

1. For a comprehensive survey of the Vladivostok speech, see Ramesh Thakur and Carlyle A. Thayer, eds., *The Soviet Union as an Asian Pacific Power: Implications of Gorbachev's 1986 Vladivostok Initiative* (Boulder: Westview, 1987).

relationship between what had been the Soviet Union and the rest of the world. The former Soviet Union (FSU) moved from being an initiator of international change to being a reactive series of states responding to externally driven change.

However, just as the extraordinary global changes which were set in train by initiatives such as those proposed in Gorbachev's Vladivostok speech and which were ultimately to be responsible for ending the Cold War did not occur overnight, so too these changes did not cease with the collapse of the Berlin Wall or the fall of the Iron Curtain. Nor will they stop with the end of the Cold War. The shape of the post-Cold War pattern of international relations—commonly called "the new world (or international) order"—therefore is still emerging. As great as the changes have been to date, it can be safely predicted that there is much more yet to come. Continuities may be more difficult to identify in some areas than the changes. This is certainly the case in assessing the impact of the emerging new world order on the South Pacific islands especially in contrast with Australia and New Zealand with regard to the Vladivostok initiatives. Indeed, the changes wrought since 1986 are so momentous that they can only be interpreted as a historical watershed.

The remarkable reduction in the influence of the Soviet Union and its successor-states since July 1986 might reasonably be assumed therefore to have overtaken what were once regarded as the "ambitious" aims of the Vladivostok speech. Certainly much of the early assessments of Vladivostok cannot be regarded as relevant today. Nonetheless it is not self-evident that the obverse is true—that is, that none of the aims remains valid. The Soviet successor-states—of which Russia is the most important—may retain some of the earlier interests expressed at Vladivostok and still be acting to achieve these. On the other hand, states such as Australia, New Zealand and those of the South Pacific have had to adjust to dealing with these Soviet successor-states in terms of their continuing interests in Asia-Pacific irrespective of how these might have been defined at Vladivostok. The South Pacific islands, however, were largely peripheral to the Asian-Pacific initiatives of Vladivostok and so have far fewer continuities under the new order. Indeed, taking the broadest view of the retreat from Vladivostok by the successor-states of the FSU, it is clear that, whatever the benefits elsewhere, the new international order is unlikely to work to enhance the position of the South Pacific islands.

Australia, New Zealand, the USSR and Its Successor-States

Given their relative size, resources, economic sophistication and political ties, both Australia and New Zealand were far more important to the Soviet

Union than was the rest of the South Pacific prior to the Vladivostok speech. And unsurprisingly therefore more of these relationships have survived the ending of the Cold War than elsewhere in the Southwest Pacific. Economically, Australia and New Zealand have traditionally been important as suppliers of primary produce to the USSR. Although the generalities of this relationship did not change significantly in the years following Vladivostok, the specifics did suffer in sympathetic reaction with the fortunes of the Soviet Union.

Australian exports to the Soviet Union consisted mainly of wool and wheat while in the case of New Zealand wool, mutton and butter were important, with beef, barley and cheese also playing some role.[2] Some industrial products (such as agricultural machinery) were imported from the Soviet Union, but mostly the trade balance was strongly in favour of Australia and New Zealand (Table 12.1).

Australian wheat sales were particularly variable during the years from Vladivostok to the ending of the Cold War, declining from A $593.8m in 1985–86 to A $7.76m in 1987–88 and A $44.29m in 1988–89.[3] The increasingly obvious Soviet economic problems which *perestroika* was intended to address began to affect the general level of trade with Oceania: the 1991 export and import volumes had fallen precipitously from their 1989 peaks for both Australia and New Zealand (Table 12.1). To encourage a revival in the traditional levels of trade which were significant to Australia's own embattled rural sector, the Australian Government extended credit facilities to the Soviet Union of A $525m in November 1990.[4]

TABLE 12.1: Soviet Trade with Australia and New Zealand, 1986–91

	Exports to USSR						Imports from USSR					
	1986	1987	1988	1989	1990	1991	1986	1987	1988	1989	1990	1991
Australia	698	487	561	810	282	376	8	12	29	40	31	28
NZ	111	103	165	181	173	127	5	7	14	14	5	2

SOURCE: *Direction of Trade Statistics Yearbook 1992* (Washington DC: IMF, 1992), pp. 86, 196.

2. Dalton A. West, "New Zealand-Soviet Relations," in Pushpa Thambipillai and Daniel C. Matuszewski, eds., *The Soviet Union and the Asia-Pacific Region: Views from the Region* (New York: Praeger, 1989), p. 176.

3. Australia, Senate Standing Committee on Foreign Affairs, Defence and Trade. *Perestroika: Implications for Australia-USSR Relations* (Canberra: Australian Government Publishing Service, 1990), p. 81.

4. Gareth Evans and Bruce Grant, *Australia's Foreign Relations in the World of the 1990s* (Melbourne: Melbourne University Press, 1992), p. 297.

Despite its initial suspicion (and outright hostility in the South Pacific, an area of strategic concern) Australia did ultimately accept that there were economic benefits to be gleaned from *perestroika*. The 1989 Garnaut Report spoke of the Soviet Union as "a significant minor player in the Northeast Asian economy"[5] and Australia therefore did devote some attention and effort to developing economic links with the Soviet (subsequently Russian) Far East. In pursuit of this objective three governors from the Russian Far East visited Australia in early 1992, and John Kerin (the Australian Trade Minister) visited the region in November 1992. Australian firms such as BHP and Comalco showed an interest in becoming involved in joint ventures in the Russian Far East.[6] Mining (particularly oil, gas, gold and diamonds), food production and telecommunications appeared to be the areas attracting most Australian attention.[7]

In addition to the economic concerns which were central to Gorbachev's Vladivostok initiative, there were also promises of significant change in the Soviet political role in Asia-Pacific. The breadth of the Soviet Union's proposed involvement could not but attract the interest of Australia and New Zealand, both in terms of their bilateral relations and in regional situations where the three states (along with other states) were involved. As will be discussed in a later section, the South Pacific was quarantined as a special case but the political possibilities in other areas did elicit a more favourable, if cautious, response. This was especially the circumstance for Australia at the bilateral level.

A focus for the development of the Soviet-Australian bilateral relationship was provided by a succession of high-level visits: by Soviet Foreign Minister Eduard Shevardnadze to Australia in March 1987, by Australian Prime Minister Bob Hawke to the Soviet Union in November 1987 and by Soviet Prime Minister Nikolai Ryzhkov to Australia in February 1990. An initial caution on Australia's part was followed by a greater willingness to accept the Soviet Union as a legitimate actor in the Asian-Pacific region and to explore the possibilities for developing the relationship further for mutual

---

5. Ross Garnaut, *Australia and the Northeast Asian Ascendancy* (Canberra: Australian Government Publishing Service, 1989), p. 171. See also Peter Drysdale, ed., *The Soviets and the Pacific Challenge* (Sydney: Allen and Unwin, 1991); Gerald Segal, *The Soviet Union and the Pacific* (Boston: Unwin Hyman, in association with the Royal Institute of International Affairs, London, 1990), ch. 6.

6. Leszek Buszynski, "Australia and the Soviet Union," in F. A. Mediansky, ed., *Australia in a Changing World: New Foreign Policy Directions* (Sydney: Maxwell Macmillan, 1992), p. 241.

7. See the report of the visit to Vladivostok by Australian ambassador to the CIS and Mongolia in September 1992 in BBC, *Summary of World Broadcasts*, SU/W0250 A/4, 2 October 1992.

benefit. The Soviet Union also believed that it could gain by giving greater attention to the relationship.

In an interview with the Melbourne *Age* in January 1987, Evgenii Samoteikin, the Soviet Ambassador to Australia, drew attention to the closeness of Australian and Soviet positions on disarmament issues such as a nuclear test ban, a regional nuclear-free zone and nuclear non-proliferation.[8] Shevardnadze's visit to Australia in March 1987 was evidence of the greater emphasis being placed on Pacific diplomacy by the Soviet Union in the wake of the Vladivostok speech. At that stage he was the highest ranking Soviet official ever to have visited Australia. In his address of welcome to Shevardnadze, Foreign Minister Bill Hayden focused particularly on the need to meet the nuclear threat and drew attention to Soviet-Australian cooperation "on Antarctic affairs, on non-proliferation matters and multilateral disarmament discussions."[9] While the Soviet Union accepted the reality of Australia's close links with the U.S., it saw advantages in encouraging more "independent" Australian policies. At the end of the visit an arrangement was set in place to provide for annual political consultations between the Soviet and Australian foreign ministers or their representatives; the venue was to alternate between Moscow and Canberra.[10]

Ironically, the nuclear ships ban adopted by the Labour Government of David Lange in New Zealand after coming to power in mid-1984 (with a consequent deterioration in its relations with the U.S.) did not make the pursuit of closer Soviet-New Zealand relations easier in the wake of Vladivostok. This almost counter-intuitive circumstance arose from the triangular relationship among New Zealand, the U.S. and the Soviet Union in the final years of the Cold War. The Soviet Union sought to exploit the ban politically and so welcomed the action which it saw as consistent with its aim of encouraging greater independence by the South Pacific countries. The Soviet Ambassador to New Zealand began to assume a higher public profile and there was a visit to New Zealand by Soviet Deputy Foreign Minister Mikhail Kapitsa in August 1986.[11] Nevertheless, Shevardnadze himself did not continue across the Tasman after his visit to Australia.[12] New Zealand, on the other hand, was reluctant to accept too readily the proffered Soviet support. Indeed, by adopting a critical stance towards the

---

8. *Age* (Melbourne), 28 January 1987.

9. *Australian Foreign Affairs Record* 58 (March 1987), pp. 120–21.

10. Geoffrey Jukes, "Australia and the Soviet Union," in F. A. Mediansky and A. C. Palfreeman, eds., *In Pursuit of National Interests: Australian Foreign Policy in the 1990s* (Sydney: Pergamon, 1988), pp. 206–07.

11. West, "New Zealand-Soviet Relations," pp. 179–80.

12. He received no invitation from the New Zealand government to do so; editors.

Soviet role in the region, Lange hoped to avoid the criticism that his anti-nuclear policies aided Soviet objectives in the region.[13]

Following the Shevardnadze visit to Australia, Hawke visited the Soviet Union in December 1987. In a lecture in Singapore on his way to the Soviet Union, Hawke highlighted the emerging Australian view of the post-Vladivostok Soviet role in Asia-Pacific:

> I would welcome a constructive involvement by the USSR in political and economic developments in the Asia-Pacific. We seek mutually beneficial cooperation with the Soviet Union in a sincere and open-minded way. But we will be observing Soviet action in, for example, Indochina and Afghanistan as indicators of good faith.[14]

In Moscow, Hawke was able to make arrangements to facilitate greater political contact between the Australian and Soviet governments. Hawke was particularly concerned with human rights issues and took up the issue of the "refuseniks" in his discussions with Gorbachev. In so doing, however, Hawke also conceded Gorbachev's primary objectives at Vladivostok—recognition as an Asian-Pacific power and reintegration into the comity of nations. Paul Kelly described Hawke's approach in these terms:

> ... the Soviets are an Asia-Pacific power, and the West has an obligation to test Mr. Gorbachev's reforms at his words. Opportunities to reduce East-West tensions and integrate the Soviet Union more into the capitalist economies must be accepted, not rejected.[15]

Further evidence of the development of the Soviet-Australian bilateral relationship was provided by the visit of Soviet Prime Minister Nikolai Ryzhkov to Australia in February 1990. This visit was important in terms of giving substance to the development of the relationship, and several agreements were signed. A Soviet-Australian fisheries cooperation agreement was signed which provided for access by the Soviet fishing fleet to selected Australian ports as well as for feasibility studies into extending fishing operations within the Australian fishing zone. Other agreements covered commodities arrangements, human contacts, consular relations, the peaceful uses of nuclear energy and the protection of the environment.[16]

---

13. See David Hegarty, "The Soviet Union in the South Pacific in the 1990s," in Ross Babbage, ed., *The Soviets in the Pacific in the 1990s* (Sydney: Brassey's, 1989), p. 117.

14. *Sydney Morning Herald,* 29 November 1987, as quoted in Graeme Gill, "Australia and the Eastern Bloc," in P. J. Boyce and J. R. Angel, eds., *Diplomacy in the Marketplace: Australia in World Affairs 1981–90* (Melbourne: Longman Cheshire, 1992), p. 232.

15. Paul Kelly, "Hawkenost: What Gorbachev sees in Australia," *Australian* (Sydney), 5–6 December 1987, p. 23.

16. *Australian Foreign Affairs and Trade: The Monthly Record* 61 (February 1990), pp. 83–88.

The regular political consultations between the two countries were to continue.

Apart from a concern with the development of bilateral relations with Australia and New Zealand, the Soviet Union saw these relationships as contributing to its wider regional diplomacy. In the then still current Cold War calculus of geopolitics, the pursuit of more independent policies by Australia and New Zealand could be seen as weakening the influence of the United States in the region. At another level, both Australia and New Zealand were seen as having a certain influence in the region. Harnessing this influence to support Soviet objectives in the Asia-Pacific would add significantly to the likelihood of Soviet success. For their part, Australia and New Zealand saw Gorbachev's Soviet Union less and less in Cold War terms and therefore were able to conceive of Soviet support as useful for some of their own regional and global objectives.

There was however considerable compartmentalisation of these developing multilateral ties. The South Pacific islands were regarded by Australia and New Zealand as a special case (see below) and thus tended to be more a source of competition than cooperation. This was especially true for the fishing agreements with Kiribati and Vanuatu and, to a lesser extent, the opening of an embassy in Port Moresby.[17] In relation to Antarctic affairs, Soviet support was far less contentious and Australia welcomed Ryzhkov's endorsement of the Franco-Australian initiative to declare Antarctica a wilderness area.[18] Soviet relations with Australia and New Zealand were similarly uneven in terms of the broader Asian-Pacific region. Although there had been more than passing Australian concern about the Soviet presence at Cam Ranh Bay in Vietnam, the announcement that that presence would be wound down was welcomed and did much to foster a more benign image of the Soviet role in this region.[19] Thus, while Soviet support for Vietnam had been one of the sources of conflict in Cambodia, Australia now saw Soviet pressure on Vietnam as a useful tool in its attempts to facilitate a resolution of the conflict. Moscow used its influence in both Hanoi and Phnom Penh to help win acceptance of the Cambodian peace accord signed in Paris in October 1991.[20]

Multilateral interests were also found in aspects of Asian-Pacific economic integration. Australian support proved useful in assisting the

17. Steve Hoadley, *The South Pacific Foreign Affairs Handbook* (Sydney: Allen and Unwin, 1992), p. 49.

18. *Monthly Record* 61 (February 1990), p. 87.

19. Gill, "Australia and the Eastern Bloc," pp. 233–34.

20. Gennady Chufrin, "The USSR and Asia in 1991: Domestic Priorities Prevail," *Asian Survey* 32 (January 1992), pp. 16–17.

Soviet Union to win observer status at the Pacific Economic Cooperation Conference (PECC) and in 1991 the Soviet Union became a full member.[21] Support from Australia and New Zealand was expected to be helpful in a similar vein in the future if Russia (as the Soviet successor-state in the Asian-Pacific region) reached the stage of seeking involvement in the Asia-Pacific Economic Cooperation (APEC) process.[22] More remotely, Russian links with the Association of South-East Asian Nations (ASEAN) could be facilitated by support from Australia and New Zealand. Although the Soviet Union never achieved the status of an ASEAN dialogue partner, in 1991 a Soviet delegation led by Deputy Prime Minister Iuri Masliukov took part as "guests" in a meeting of ASEAN foreign ministers and their dialogue partners.[23]

Whatever directions Soviet relations with Australia and New Zealand might have taken in pursuit of the Vladivostok objectives, these were cut short by the increasing domestic turmoil in the Soviet Union and the collapse of that state in late 1991. At the time of the attempted coup in August 1991, Australia expressed support for the restoration of Gorbachev as President of the Soviet Union.[24] Despite a recognition that power was shifting increasingly to Yeltsin and the republics at the expense of the central government, there was nevertheless caution in Canberra about extending diplomatic recognition to the republics prematurely. This was all the more true as Australia held a certain preference for Gorbachev's objective of retaining the Soviet Union as a confederation; a policy which ran parallel to that of the U.S. On 27 August, Hawke announced that Australia would recognise the independence of the Baltic states and nonresident accreditation was to be sought for the ambassador in Copenhagen to cover Lithuania and Latvia while the ambassador in Stockholm was to cover Estonia.[25] Senator Gareth Evans, the Australian Foreign Minister, visited the Soviet Union in November 1991 at a time when the final collapse of that state was imminent.[26] Following the establishment of the Commonwealth of Independent States (CIS) on 21 December and Gorbachev's resignation as Soviet president on Christmas Day 1991, Prime Minister Paul Keating and

---

21. *Ibid.*, p. 16; Gill, "Australia and the Eastern Bloc," p. 234.

22. See Peter Drysdale, "Soviet Prospects and the Pacific Economy," in Drysdale, ed., *The Soviets and the Pacific Challenge*, p. 13.

23. See ch. 11 above by Pushpa Thambipillai.

24. See *Monthly Record* 62 (August 1991), pp. 467–73.

25. Australian Department of Foreign Affairs and Trade, *Backgrounder*, 2 (13 September 1991), p. 2.

26. The recognition of the shift of power towards the republics is evidenced, for example, in Evans' comments on the Ukraine. See *Monthly Record* 62 (November & December 1991), pp. 780–81.

Senator Evans announced on 26 December Australia's recognition of all eleven member-states of the CIS. This meant that Australia had given diplomatic recognition to all the Soviet successor-states except Georgia. Initially at least, nonresident diplomatic representation was to be provided by Australia's Moscow embassy for the ten CIS states apart from Russia.[27]

In the wake of the collapse of the USSR, Russia predictably has emerged as the successor-state of most significance to Australia and New Zealand. Not only is Russia the most powerful of the Soviet successor-states, it is also the heir to the Soviet Union in the Asian-Pacific region. As the next largest in size and the state with aspirations to retain its global fishing and trade interests, Ukraine clearly also is of interest to Australia and New Zealand. Yet even the smaller republics may provide a basis for a continuing relationship. Interestingly, Evans and Grant in their book on Australian foreign policy refer to the possibilities of developing Australian relations with Kazakhstan on the basis of its being "entrepreneurially minded, outward-looking, resource-rich and in population terms about Australia's size."[28]

The role of ethnic communities from the Soviet successor-states could intrude, however, as a complicating factor in Australia's relations with the FSU. According to the 1986 census the number of Australians giving their ancestry in terms of ethnic groups within the FSU was as follows: Estonian 7,500; Latvian 20,610; Lithuanian 11,000; Russian 46,400; Ukrainian 28,600.[29] As with the break-up of Yugoslavia, if conflicts arise involving these national groups in the area of the FSU, this could have significant repercussions for former nationals now in Australia, and this in turn could directly affect Canberra's policy towards the CIS or any of the successor-states involved.

Russian relations with Australia and New Zealand, in the post-Soviet era, will be driven primarily by Russian foreign policy priorities in general and by the placing of the Asian-Pacific region in these priorities in particular. On both counts, the Antipodes are unlikely to figure highly in the near future. In the context of emphasising the underlying realism and pragmatism of Russian foreign policy, for example, Russian Foreign Minister Andrei Kozyrev has said: "Russia's main foreign policy priority is relations with our partners in the Commonwealth of Independent States."[30] In the Asian-

---

27. *Backgrounder* 3 (31 January 1992), p. 2.
28. Evans and Grant, *Australia's Foreign Relations*, p. 297.
29. Australia, Senate Standing Committee on Foreign Affairs, *Perestroika*, p. 10.
30. Andrei Kozyrev, "Russia: A Chance for Survival," *Foreign Affairs* 71 (Spring 1992), p. 10. For an analysis of the priorities in Russian foreign policy, see ch. 3 above by Peter Shearman.

Pacific region, Russian bilateral relations with China and Japan are seen as being pivotal, as well as the achievement of "a balanced inter-relationship in the 'rectangle' comprising Russia, the United States, Japan and China, thus contributing to greater stability and cooperation in Asia and the Pacific."[31]

Australia, in acting to maintain friendly relations between itself and the CIS, has tended to favour the relationship with Russia. When the Soviet embassy advised on 19 December 1991 that it would henceforth act as the Embassy of Russia, Evans responded the following week with the assertion that Australia "now recognises the reality of Russia as an independent state." In making this statement, Australia accepted the "continuity in statehood between Russia and the former USSR," with Russia inheriting the rights and obligations of the former Soviet Union.[32] Essentially, then, the Russian embassy in Canberra has concerned itself with looking after Russian interests in relation to Australia, with the Russian (previously Soviet) embassy in Wellington doing likewise in relation to New Zealand. However these embassies do serve a broader CIS role in some limited respects. In 1992, the Canberra embassy did have one staff member looking after matters relating to Belarus, and it was prepared to communicate information on behalf of CIS members (as with the 1992 earthquake in Kirgizstan).

Apart from its economic involvement with the post-Soviet states, Australia has been prepared to provide economic and humanitarian assistance to the CIS states. Credit lines worth A $500m have been made available to support Australian commodity exports: A $100m for grains (particularly wheat), and A $400m for wool, meat and dairy products. An additional A $45m is to be provided over five years to the European Bank for Reconstruction and Development to assist inter alia in aid to the FSU. Humanitarian assistance to the Soviet successor-states was facilitated by Senator Evans' participation in the ministerial-level coordinating conference on assistance to the FSU held in Washington on 22–23 January 1992.[33] The continuation of the annual political consultations established by Shevardnadze and Hayden in 1987 on a Russian-Australian rather than a Soviet-Australian basis has also been useful in the development of the bilateral relationship. The exchange of parliamentary delegations and the establishment of a Russian-Australian parliamentary group in the Russian parliament have also contributed to the building of ties.

Clearly Australian and New Zealand relations with the post-Soviet states have given particular emphasis to Russia. Although an honorary Australian

---

31. Kozyrev, "Russia: Chance for Survival," p. 15.
32. *Backgrounder* 3 (31 January 1992), p. 2.
33. *Ibid.*

consul has been appointed in Kiev,[34] Australia has not followed the Canadian example in making Ukraine a major focus in its policies towards the FSU. The greater political significance of Canada's Ukrainian community than its counterpart in Australia is undoubtedly a factor here. The possibility that as a major agricultural state Ukraine could be a competitor for both Australia and New Zealand if its economy were to become more productive may also be a consideration, but developing fisheries connections suggest that this is not too important a factor at this stage.

In the longer term, Russia's bilateral relations with Australia and New Zealand can be expected to be relevant to the various regional and multilateral contexts in which the three states are involved. The relationship with Australia and New Zealand, as noted earlier, could prove helpful in furthering Russia's goal of participation in international economic organisations including "regional banks and economic cooperation forums in Asia and the Pacific."[35] Australia and Russia have a common interest in facilitating a settlement in Cambodia where both states have had significant, if different, levels of involvement. Although Russia is less involved in the Middle East than was the Soviet Union and Australia's role is a minor one, a common concern for developments in this region has also been a feature of recent Russian-Australian discussions.

Disarmament issues have been another area of common concern. Although the National government in New Zealand has given less prominence to these issues than the previous Labour government, the Labor government in Australia has continued to see disarmament as an area where it can contribute to progress on a global level. It has been particularly active in seeking a comprehensive Chemical Weapons Convention and this issue has been of some significance in Russian-Australian relations. More broadly there have been a number of disarmament and arms control issues relating to the future of the nuclear weapons inherited from the Soviet Union by Russia, Ukraine, Kazakhstan and Belarus.[36] Australia and New Zealand have used their diplomatic influence to encourage a situation where Russia alone retains nuclear weapons.[37]

---

34. *Monthly Record* 62 (November and December 1991), p. 781.

35. Kozyrev, "Russia: Chance for Survival," p. 9.

36. The matter has also exercised the mind of the New Zealand Minister of Disarmament and Arms Control, Doug Graham; editors. (Ramesh Thakur is a member of the Public Advisory Committee on Disarmament and Arms Control, a statutory body to aid and advise the Minister.)

37. See, for example, Senator Evans' comments on the Ukraine in *Monthly Record* 62 (November & December 1991), p. 780.

The South Pacific Islands Since Vladivostok

While change has been a key feature of post-Vladivostok relations between the FSU and the two ANZAC powers, continuities also can be discerned. In assessing the implications of the emerging world order for the CIS and their interests in the South Pacific,[38] however, the situation is characterised overwhelmingly by the absence of any significant continuities. Successor-state interests in the South Pacific have not retreated to the point of vanishing but here, even more than has been the case with Australia and New Zealand, they are in clear retreat from the heights of the Vladivostok aspirations. A second major point of distinction is the extent to which the strategic rivalries of the time influenced interpretations of the consequences of Vladivostok for this remote region.[39] Possible Soviet interest in the small states of the South Pacific focused more on their geostrategic relevance to others than on the intrinsic merits of this putative interest. For this reason, it is difficult to assess the consequences of the retreat from Vladivostok without reflecting on the implications of the emerging world order on the islands of the South Pacific. This, in the end, was the primary context within which Vladivostok was viewed by other actors.

The extent to which geopolitics were the backdrop against which the Vladivostok initiatives were played out in the South Pacific can be seen clearly in the reaction of the region's Western sponsors to the Vladivostok speech. Soviet fisheries access agreements with Kiribati (although this preceded the Vladivostok speech, being signed in 1985) and Vanuatu (1987) were seen as direct challenges to Western security interests.[40] That this response was exaggerated and unwarranted was recently acknowledged in an unflattering popular news commentary which assessed the implications of the ending of the Cold War for the South Pacific. Greg Sheridan admitted he had come to recognise that the Pacific Islands were strategically marginal and they had always been marginal to the great issues of global geopolitics. He, for one, should have recognised this earlier instead of heightening concerns over Soviet interests in the region. Sheridan recommended that Australian relations with the region should be downgraded to something more commensurate with their true international importance.[41] Similar

---

38. The terms "South Pacific" or "South Pacific islands" in this paper refer to the Pacific Islands within the ambit of the South Pacific Commission. The term "macroregion" describes larger associations or geographic entities such as the Asian-Pacific area.

39. For a review of the impact of the Vladivostok speech on the South Pacific, see R. A. Herr, "The Soviet Union in the South Pacific," in Thakur and Thayer, eds., *The Soviet Union as an Asian Pacific Power*, pp. 135–51.

40. *Ibid.*, p. 140.

41. Greg Sheridan, "Forget the Pacific Minnows, We've Got Bigger Fish to Fry," *Australian*, 15 July 1992.

assessments have been offered in more compassionate form by other media commentators who do not share Sheridan's power-based calculations of Australian national interests in the South Pacific.[42]

Strategic suspicion over the Soviets' Vladivostok ambitions, while deep and sustained, was not uniform or immutable. As noted above, the Hawke government did begin to shift its views towards the USSR in the Soviet Union's final years. Canberra even gave qualified encouragement to a South Pacific regional role for the Soviet Union by suggesting that the Soviet Union (then at the cusp of the change from USSR to CIS) be allowed to participate in the South Pacific Forum's discussions with "dialogue partners."[43] This gesture proved futile but, despite its failure, is no less revealing of the changed perceptions towards the Soviet Union. The policy of strategic denial had elevated much smaller accommodations to the level of a security threat only a few years earlier.[44] The suggestion by Evans thus amounted to a formal declaration of the end of this South Seas variation of the Western policy of containment and also then the first step towards implementing the new world order in this region.

Post-Cold War Politics in the South Pacific

The emerging international system does not reflect solely, of course, those influences at work in the dismantling of the Cold War. There were other noteworthy forces in operation even before the improvement in relations between the United States and the Soviet Union from the mid-1980s. The (now somewhat faltering) movement towards unification in the European Community; the moves towards an Asian-Pacific economic unit; and the increasing influence of environmentalism as a factor in global politics amongst other developments throughout the 1970s and 1980s were having an impact on the conduct of international relations independently of the shifts in Cold War rivalries from the advent of Mikhail Gorbachev. Thus it would be as erroneous as it is simplistic to attempt to divine the shape of the emerging new international order solely from the ashes of the Cold War. Nevertheless, it was the overwhelming effects of the collapse of the Cold War which incorporated these other influences into an international order recognisably new and fundamentally altered.

---

42. Rowan Callick, "Regional Drift Towards Pax Americana," *Financial Review*, 6 June 1991 and "The Other (South Pacific) Summit," *Sydney Morning Herald*, 31 July 1991.
43. "Evans Tells Forum to Consider Soviet Talks," *Age*, 30 July 1991.
44. For a historical review of these reactions see R. A. Herr, "Regionalism, Strategic Denial and South Pacific Security," *Journal of Pacific History* 21 (October 1986), pp. 170–182.

Perhaps the most significant consequence of the ending of the Cold War for the small states of the South Pacific is the willingness of the world's great powers (currently defined by permanent membership of the UN Security Council) to act in unison. The concert of powers in the Security Council which orchestrated the response to the invasion of Kuwait clearly was possible only because China and the then-Soviet Union were able to work pragmatically with the Western powers. Although tested regularly since the Gulf War, the post-Cold War concert of the great powers has proved sufficiently resilient to engender both hope and fear: hope that the United Nations can work more effectively to promote peace; fear that these prospects are entirely hostage to the concert amongst the permanent members of the Security Council.

The post-Cold War activism of the United Nations has sent some reassuring signals to the small powers of the world community not least through the recently revived proposal that the UN adopt a convention specifically to protect the very small.[45] However, the implied concept of a hierarchy of powers in the Security Council's newly-found concert, if pursued to its original nineteenth century conclusion, does significantly qualify the capacity of small states to participate in global affairs even in those of direct concern to them. That the outcomes of the June 1992 "Earth Summit" in Rio de Janeiro favoured large-power positions might be taken as examples of this process at work. Those adopting a Realist perspective will belittle the possible extent of the change here, secure in the belief that "it was ever thus." Nevertheless, the implications of a Security Council routinely operating with a long-term consensus among its permanent members are such that the UN Secretary General has felt obliged to propose reforms. Included within these is a change to make the permanent membership more representative. The addition of Japan would have special significance for the Pacific.

In addition to the pragmatic concert of interests amongst the UN's great powers, the collapse of the Cold War has displayed a number of other developments which may have significant implications for the South Pacific. Disarmament has been significantly advanced at the nuclear level by reductions in great power tensions although related developments have also relaxed controls on the trade in military hardware which have made for unintended increases in risks in both the nuclear and conventional arms areas. "Atlanticism" has been revived to a significant extent and this shift to an Atlantic-European focus may well prove durable at least to the middle

---

45. This discussion draws attention to the general misuse of the term "microstate." Greater consistency would have dictated usage of something like "micropower" since it is the dimension of power rather than the quality of state authority which is usually at issue.

term. Even if the 1980s dynamism of the Asian-Pacific area reasserts itself quickly, it is more likely to be in the context of a parallel regional centre rather than the catalyst for a Pacific Century which seemed so likely only a few years ago. Very much related to this speculation, the ending of the Cold War has utterly destroyed any lingering tendency towards bipolarity in the international order and so virtually predetermined some form of multipolarity. The precise number and location of the regional concentrations of power in the new order will be of general interest to the South Pacific but the near certainty that Asia-Pacific will be one of these is of direct and immediate interest. Finally, economic rationality seems destined to replace ideological rivalry as the basis of international competition although recent events suggest that nationalism should not be totally discounted.

CIS Successor State Interests

As observed previously, the logic of Gorbachev's Vladivostok speech was not necessarily destroyed either by the ending of the Cold War or the collapse of the Soviet Union. Nevertheless, its themes have lost whatever vigour they had for the South Pacific since the internal turmoil in the former Soviet Union following the August 1991 failed coup which led to the formal demise of the Soviet Union in December. The occasional signs that, despite the difficulties, Russia still seeks to retain the initiatives of 1986,[46] cannot offset the far more dramatic evidence of Russia's retreat from Vladivostok in the South Pacific, demonstrated for example in the recently announced decision to close its Port Moresby mission. The long-held Soviet objective of diplomatic acceptance in the region, which was finally achieved in 1990,[47] has now fallen victim to Russia's post-Cold War realities. The real costs of maintaining influence and priorities closer to home have told critically in the Russian reappraisal of interests in the South Pacific.

While economic necessity, domestic distractions and pragmatism in foreign policy all help to explain the retreat from the Vladivostok ambitions for the South Pacific in recent years, these do not dictate a permanent absence from the region. Russia as a great power and Ukraine as a substantial maritime state, still have interests which could, and probably will, validate elements of Vladivostok in the future. The justifications for the Soviet Union's Asian interests based in the resources of Siberia and the economic vitality of Asia-Pacific have not changed by virtue of Russia succeeding to these interests. The Soviet Union was a great distant-water fishing nation with a global scope. It appears clear that both Russia and

---

46. "Eastern Russia Eyeing Booming Pacific Trade," *Canberra Times*, 29 September 1992.
47. Hoadley, *South Pacific Handbook*, p. 49.

Ukraine wish to continue to pursue this activity on a worldwide scale if at all possible.[48] A similar expectation could also reasonably be held for Russian interests in transport and mining.[49] Both Russia and Ukraine have succeeded to elements of the old Soviet Union's Antarctic commitments and interests; a circumstance which ensures some continuing traffic through southern oceans contiguous to the Pacific and possibly through the Pacific itself. Both will require a substantial trade network if they are to achieve their domestic economic goals.

Thus the two largest members of CIS, at least, are likely to be factors to some modest degree in Asian-Pacific calculations which could involve the South Pacific. The interest and involvement of other successor-states are more problematic. Yet, even these may find some scope for continuity. The division of the assets of the FSU among the successor-states could produce unexpected consequences. For example, if the Baltic states acquire the bulk of the Soviet icebreakers, they too may be pulled back into the Pacific through the Antarctic connection. New or expanded Asian cooperative regimes or the diplomatic initiatives of Islamic states such as Malaysia may well draw the Central Asian republics into Asian-Pacific processes in the longer term. If this were to take place, it could well have a further chain reaction effect since Russia and Ukraine would have their own Asian-Pacific interests reinforced by the interests of their CIS neighbours.

Consequences of the Retreat from Vladivostok

Whatever the direction that the interests of the successor-states of the FSU take in Asia-Pacific, the South Pacific seems unlikely to loom even as modestly large in their future interests as the region did in the Vladivostok *démarche*. However, the real significance of the Vladivostok assertions lay not in the extent of Gorbachev's ambitious claim for involvement but rather in the fact that they were made at all in the face of a Western policy of strategic denial. The implications of the end of the Cold War for Russian-CIS interests in the South Pacific naturally then have tended to be referred back to the security concerns of the Western powers rather than to the Islands. The end of the Cold War has removed so thoroughly Western concerns in this regard (quite apart from whether or not these concerns were justified previously) that the basis of Western interest in the region now is

---

48. Russia has recently established a Joint Fisheries Coordinating Committee with PNG to promote common development interests. See "Russia Offers Aid to PNG Fishing Industry," *The South Sea Digest*, 3 July 1992.

49. Despite its announced withdrawal from Port Moresby, Russia has sought to protect the Aeroflot helicopter charter with PNG's mining industries.

questioned by those who believe that these were the sole or major objectives of the Western powers. Even less cynical (security-based) assessments of the South Pacific's future can reasonably hold that defence considerations did influence external relations with the region and therefore will constitute a net loss of influence for the Islands.

Marginalisation of this region (acknowledged to be peripheral) is a source of concern to thoughtful observers primarily because the area is so heavily dependent on aid. The South Pacific historically has enjoyed high levels of aid,[50] and many link this directly to the policy of strategic denial of the 1970s and 1980s. If this suspicion is justified, then the continuance of substantial assistance may be in jeopardy. Certainly local standards of living will fall if current aid levels decline. Early evidence lends credibility to these fears since real levels of aid do appear to be falling, although it is not clear that the more relaxed security environment is necessarily responsible for this apparent decline.[51] The global recession and the rebuilding of Eastern Europe undoubtedly have also played some part as well. On the other hand, it is argued by some that the full extent of the reduction in financial assistance has been disguised by increased but inappropriate aid from more recent entrants.[52]

A second consequence of the changing global order for the Islands arises from the disarmament processes associated with the ending of the Cold War. The issue of Johnston Atoll and its use as a disposal point for chemical weapons arose directly from the thaw in U.S.-Soviet relations (as well as from the legitimisation of the environment as an item on the global agenda). Agreement on reductions over a burgeoning range of weapons systems in Europe required the removal of a large stockpile of chemical weapons from Europe. Repatriation to the U.S. within the specified time proved politically awkward given the capacity of American state courts to delay the transfer of dangerous chemicals across state borders. The Johnston Atoll Chemical Agent Disposal System facility (JACADS) offered an easy solution to the political dilemma since it was already under federal control and it had an established weapons storage and disposal capability.

The U.S. was not unaware that the Islands might object to the use of JACADS despite the distance of more than 2,000 km from Johnston Atoll to the nearest South Pacific Forum country. Still, Washington hoped that the

---

50. Te'o I. J. Fairbairn *et al.*, *The Pacific Islands: Politics, Economics, and International Relations* (Honolulu: East-West Center, 1991), p. 48.

51. "Fisheries Aid: Pattern and Sources," in Richard Herr, ed., *The Forum Fisheries Agency: Achievements, Challenges and Prospects* (Suva: University of the South Pacific, 1990), p. 188.

52. Rowan Callick, "Islands Overlooked in Sloppy Phrase," *Australian Financial Review*, 9 April 1992.

protests would be moderate. Australia was perhaps caught in an even bigger quandary on this matter, since Canberra both had sponsored the early talks to reduce the world's store of chemical weapons and has taken a leading role within the region on environmental affairs. When the August 1990 meeting of the South Pacific Forum objected to the use of the Johnston Atoll facility to destroy the chemical weapons stored in West Germany, Australia (as well as New Zealand and, arguably, the Islands) had to face an uncomfortable choice between regional fears for the environment and global responsibilities to support disarmament. For its part, the U.S. took the view that its own relationship with the Soviet Union and the reconstruction of the geostrategic map of Europe were its first priorities and pressed ahead. The Forum, while maintaining its opposition to the proposal, commissioned a study by scientists from Forum countries to assess the risks. Ironically for the Forum, this report which was made public in August 1992 came out in favour of the use of the JACADS facility.[53]

The demise of the Cold War has necessarily led to the obsolescence of the doctrine of strategic denial in the South Pacific which was itself merely a local adaptation of the general Western policy of containment. European priorities tended to dominate the strategic adjustments to the end of the Cold War and so almost an inevitable inertia has occurred with regard to rethinking security changes in the South Pacific. Indeed, it is perfectly tenable to argue that the Mount Pinatubo eruption has had the major influence on this process to date. Nevertheless, elevation of what were once second-order security issues to matters of primary regional concern is a direct result of the opportunity (and perhaps the need) to devote defence resources to other missions. The willingness of Australia and New Zealand to assist the Islands with third-party enforcement of regional coastal-state fisheries regulations through the Forum Fisheries Agency and to develop and enhance local drug regulation regimes can be taken as examples of this trend.[54]

Macroregional Change

The growing coherence and integration of Asia-Pacific as a macroregion (a region built up of smaller regional blocs) can be interpreted as something of a transition issue for the South Pacific in the new world order. It links many issues which arise from the collapse of the Cold War to those themes

---

53. Craig Skehan, "Poison-gas Destruction on Atoll Approved," *Canberra Times*, 11 August 1992.

54. The Niue Treaty, signed in July 1992, provides the legal basis for possible third-party enforcement of national and regional fisheries regulations.

which have arisen independently of these global changes. Clearly the progress towards this level of economic cooperation and integration antedates the advent of Gorbachev. Indeed it was the trend towards closer economic relations that encouraged the Soviet leader, in his Vladivostok address, to seek a window on the Pacific to participate in this growth. Nevertheless, the importance of such regional relations has been modified significantly following the demise of the Cold War's bipolar tendencies. Effective regional arrangements now are seen as the basis for claims to influence (economic, political and security) in an increasingly multipolar world. Arguably, this latter rationale has come to dominate attitudes towards the concept of the Asian-Pacific macroregion over the past year.

The more coherent Asia-Pacific becomes, the more the large and middle powers will be able to project and protect their interests through Asian-Pacific processes both globally and regionally. It is expected that use of the macroregional mechanism will confer attractive economies of scale and political leverage which enable member-states to minimise the dangers of global economic restructuring while participating in any usable gains. However, these processes are being driven by the strong to safeguard their interests; a circumstance which tends to marginalise the small and the weak including the Pacific Islands.[55] Moreover, there is the further damaging prospect that the Islands' salience to larger powers will be reduced both directly and indirectly by improved Asian-Pacific cooperation. The direct erosion of the Islands' international standing derives from the small scale of their economies. In a world where economic priorities are paramount, this will tell heavily against the South Pacific. Secondly, more effective macroregional mechanisms of consultation and cooperation will allow such states to enjoy the benefits of South Pacific access without necessarily maintaining regular bilateral contact with the Islands. Effective participation in APEC and PECC may indeed prove one of the main linkages between Russia (and perhaps other CIS members) and the Islands in the future.

A more prominent place in the Asian-Pacific macroregional institutions may be the only practical method open to the Islands to minimise the risks of Asian-Pacific integration. Such a presence, however, appears likely to be available only through some form of regional representation. Papua New Guinea with its 3.5m population could hope for separate representation (although in Asian terms this number is scarcely significant), but this could endanger the prospects of the other regional states even through a regional mechanism. From the 1989 meetings of both APEC (Canberra) and PECC (Auckland), the South Pacific region has enjoyed observer status through

---

55. Rowan Callick, "Islands Overlooked in Sloppy Phrase."

the South Pacific Forum Secretariat. The Forum Fisheries Agency provides a second, partial avenue representing the region on PECC's fisheries committee.

The Islands may find some advantages in the growth of a wider Pacific regionalism but, in terms of their exercise of sovereignty, this development does pose some risks. If the wider Asian-Pacific grouping requires collective representation by the Islands for effective participation, the scope for the pursuit of individual national interest will be necessarily limited. Already PNG has indicated some displeasure at this constraint.[56] Concomitantly with the greater integration of Asia-Pacific will be a curtailing of the traditional Western outlook of the Islands. Insofar as the Pacific Islands are a part of this Asian-Pacific integrative process, they will naturally look more and more towards Asian states for support and assistance. Australia and New Zealand, however, may experience rather less erosion of their traditional relationships with the Islands than might be expected, since they too will be on the inside of the Asian-Pacific process.

Regional and National Consequences

The retreat from Vladivostok has had or will have implications for the countries of the South Pacific at the regional level. Two sets of issues, however, stand out currently as of particular importance in terms of how the South Pacific will cope with the new world order. Each could portend adversity for the region. The first of these issue-sets concerns the trend towards multipolarity at the global level which has opened the opportunity for new regional hegemons. Japan clearly intends to be a leader in Asian-Pacific affairs in pursuit of its quest for great-power status in the new world order. This quest has induced it to also seek a regional place in the sun under South Pacific skies.[57] The second set of issues has only the most tangential relation to the collapse of the Cold War. It concerns the erosion of external goodwill and support which has followed from the apparent decline in internal stability. The 1987 Fiji coup, Bougainville's ongoing attempt at secession, political instability in Vanuatu among other events have tarnished the region's image as a special area of tranquillity and peace.

Japan sought greater influence in South Pacific regionalism even before the 1987 Kuranari Doctrine offered a formal riposte to the Vladivostok

---

56. Margaret M. Taylor (PNG Ambassador to the United States), "Australia and New Zealand from a Distance," in Ramesh Thakur, ed., *The South Pacific: Problems, Issues and Prospects* (London: Macmillan, 1991), pp. 195–96.

57. See, for example, Greg Johannes, "An Isolated Debating Society: Australia in Southeast Asia and the South Pacific," Working Paper No. 244, Strategic and Defence Studies Centre, The Australian National University, Canberra, April 1992, p. 9.

speech. Nonetheless, only in recent years has there been a clear signal that it might accept formal membership in the one regional organisation where this might be a real possibility—the South Pacific Commission (SPC). De jure membership in the SPC clearly has had significant advantages for Britain, France and the U.S., three other great powers with interests in the region, and Japan has long felt that it too is entitled to similar recognition of its regional interests. Tokyo appreciates that membership in the region by right offers more avenues for influence than is available either through the Forum's dialogue mechanism (the same mechanism that Australian Foreign Minister Gareth Evans suggested should be open to the Soviet Union in 1991) or through the other informal channels of access it enjoys in other regional associations. The Islands, however, have resisted the Japanese pressure on the grounds that it would be a retrograde step to admit further external powers into its regional organisations. They believe, with more than a little justice, that their regional priorities would be skewed by the power and interests of Japan.

The second source of regional change is entirely indigenous in origin although the impact of it may well be more severe in the pragmatic politics of the new world order. This is the crisis of legitimacy which has beset the region since the military coup in Fiji on 14 May 1987.[58] The fact that previously there had been violence and instability in various parts of the South Pacific tended to be excused as aberrations from an otherwise exemplary pattern of democratic practice. The Fiji coup destroyed a sense of innocence in this regard. Fair or not, extraregional governments have reconsidered their earlier assessments of the region's capacity for stability. There appears to be a growing feeling in some quarters that the region is prone to instability because the independence constitutions of some countries are not accepted by their populations as legitimate. Should such attitudes become the dominant perspective on the South Pacific, a wide range of relationships and activities could be affected: everything from tourism and transport to investment and banking.

Conclusions

Mikhail Gorbachev's bold bid for Pacific influence in his 1986 Vladivostok speech is now a relic of a bygone age. While the successors to the Soviet Union may have reasons to recapture some of the claims Gorbachev made in the Asian-Pacific area, Australia, New Zealand and the South Pacific are not likely to figure as prominently in these calculations as

---

58. See Ramesh Thakur and G. Antony Wood, "Paradise Regained or Paradise Defiled? Fiji under Military Rule," *International Studies* 26 (January–March 1989), pp. 15–44.

the Vladivostok initiative had hinted. Complementarities across a wide range of interests—economic, political and social—will ensure, nonetheless, that the two ANZAC powers will enjoy continuing interest from, at least, the major successor-states to the USSR. Indeed, Australia and New Zealand may well find in the longer term that an economically revived CIS may be able and willing to pursue the economic aims of Vladivostok more effectively than the Soviet Union may have done. Thus, although the emerging post-Cold War order continues to redefine the relationship between the two antipodean middle powers and the former Soviet Union, the lower levels remain significant and the future still has prospects.

The consequences for the South Pacific of the retreat from Vladivostok, however, contrast markedly. The Vladivostok initiative sought to create a relationship where one scarcely existed previously. Without a political agenda or resources, there is little to attract the CIS members back except at the margins. Ironically it is not the possibility of a Russian or CIS interest in the region but rather the clear absence of a major interest and a general indifference to whatever residual interests there may be which may prove a significant factor for the Islands in the retreat from Vladivostok and the emerging new world order. The loss of strategic importance removes one principal constituent of external interest in the region during the 1970s and 1980s. And although many traditional interests in the South Pacific will be maintained in the coming decade, the priorities attached to these interests by the states concerned are likely to be adjusted in the wake of the ongoing changes to the global balance of relations. In consequence, while no one would sensibly wish for a return to the "bad old days" of the Cold War, the South Pacific states may find that they have lost more than most in the retreat from Vladivostok.

13

Regional Order in Asia-Pacific

William T. Tow

The strategic competition traditionally underwriting Asia-Pacific's postwar security environment is receding into history. U.S. concerns regarding domestic unemployment and economic recession are superseding old preoccupations with containing ideological adversaries and deterring nuclear threats. Washington's policy planners no longer regard U.S. Pacific strategy as merely one component of a unified global deterrence posture but as a more region-specific approach, directed towards achieving crisis-avoidance and conflict resolution.

This trend has intensified since the mid-1980s when Mikhail Gorbachev assumed power in the Soviet Union and American assessments of the Soviet threat began to change substantially. The new Soviet leader rejected the arguments of Soviet hardliners that the USSR should intensify global strategic competition with the United States, and instead proposed an "All-Asian" security framework, underwritten by sweeping regional confidence-building measures, as part of a larger campaign to establish "reasonable sufficiency" as his country's strategic force posture. With the Soviet Union's eventual demise in December 1991, there was growing realisation by other Asian-Pacific states that regional and global security issues in Asia-Pacific might now be shaped, at least in part, by how economic and security issues could be successfully integrated into a coherent post-Cold War Asian-Pacific security order. Even the Asians who favour continued alliance relations with the West could agree with the assessment recently forwarded by the International Institute for Strategic Studies: "the bonds of alliance were often more based on economic self-interest than on any real fear of the Soviet Union."[1]

Debate has continued, however, over precisely what type of security arrangements and structures should eventually emerge and to what extent the Soviet successor-states will play a meaningful role in shaping any such framework. As previous chapters have reviewed the second question in some depth, the major concern here will be to identity what type of new regional security order can or should emerge to replace the politics of superpower confrontation which dominated Asian-Pacific security politics during the Cold War. The chapter's underlying argument is that great-power behaviour in the immediate post-Cold War timeframe will continue to be predicated upon perceived national security interests, and that this will preclude the rapid development of a cohesive security order in Asia-Pacific. If a major conflict in the region does not occur during the remainder of the 1990s, however, collective security mechanisms emanating from one or more of the contending regional security approaches evaluated below may thereafter be sufficient to quell local disputes and to deter the belligerents and their supporters from escalating them into wider conflicts.

An Asian-Pacific Security Order?

There has been a visible and sustained tension between those supporting realist approaches for managing security politics in postwar Asia and those advocating more liberal postures of collaboration. The realists prevailed in the design and implementation of postwar Asian-Pacific security, arguing that international security cooperation could only evolve from states' fundamental determination to survive in an anarchical and conflict-prone international society. Alliances were forged to balance against threats or to create regional and international balances of power which could ensure these states' collective survival and relative gains at their adversaries' expense. At the height of the Cold War, the United States negotiated a series of mostly bilateral defence treaties with selected Asian-Pacific states to balance what it then perceived to be a monolithic Sino-Soviet bloc threatening its own access to and influence in the region.

The liberals have challenged the realists by insisting that states' collective security behaviour can be institutionalised and managed in ways which can decrease the chances of war and enhance international cooperation and stability. They reason that the key to facilitating such outcomes is to identify important issue-areas where economic and political collaboration can lead to

---

1. IISS, *Strategic Survey 1991–1992* (London: Brassey's, 1992), p. 211.

the identification of shared norms and values that can, over time, reinforce the incentives of states to cooperate.[2]

Liberal Postures of Collaboration

The nonaligned legacy, combined with subsequent events in Indochina, led a number of Southeast Asian states to explore the advantages of institutional collaboration as an alternative to alliance affiliation as a preferred strategy of regional security. ASEAN enunciated its aspiration to apply the politics of nonalignment to Southeast Asia with the declaration of a Zone of Peace, Freedom and Neutrality (ZOPFAN) and to work for the long-term objective of strengthening regional institutional cooperation.

In the ensuing decades, ASEAN's diplomacy was devoted to achieving conflict resolution in Indochina and to coordinating regular and systematic consultations with external powers. Recently, ASEAN members and other Asian-Pacific states have attempted to define and shape a broader, pan-Asian mechanism for economic and security cooperation. The Asia-Pacific Economic Cooperation (APEC) forum, created in 1989, appears to be the strongest candidate yet for becoming the all-Pacific organisation which supporters of the liberal security approach have long envisioned.

APEC's prospects for moving towards summit diplomacy, ASEAN's increased willingness to undertake consultations and policy coordination on security matters, and the removal of the Soviet Union as a preeminent security threat are all conducive to applying a security regimes approach to Asia-Pacific. If the conditions for security regime formation postulated by Robert Jervis are valid, then increasingly explicit constraints on competition and conflict will need to be: (1) supported by the region's great powers; (2) codified into rules and norms that clearly inhibit expansionist behaviour by any one of them; and (3) reinforced by a widely shared perception that engagement in regional conflict is too costly for any state associated with the regime relative to the gains accrued.[3]

Containment and Alliance Strategies

In Asia-Pacific, each of the security regime's criteria is challenged by "realist-oriented" premises and policies. All regional military powers have intermittently expressed their willingness to explore the applicability of

---

2. Among the best known proponents of this argument are R. O. Keohane and J. Nye, *Power and Interdependence: World Politics in Transition* (Boston: Little Brown, 1978); R. Axelrod, *The Evolution of Cooperation* (New York: Basic Books, 1984); and K. Oye, "Explaining Cooperation Under Anarchy: Hypothesis and Strategies," *World Politics* 38 (October 1985).

3. "Security Regimes," *International Organization* 36 (Spring 1982), pp. 360–62.

multilateral institutions to regional security management and conflict resolution.

There is a continuing tendency for key actors in Asia-Pacific to pursue security through adopting realist postures even as superpower competition winds down. Accordingly, prospects for regional power vacuums and hegemonic competition have increased. The second criterion for regime formation thus appears difficult to meet: preventing incentives for hegemonic expansion through the establishment of rules and norms which all regional security actors can accept.

Security regime politics' applicability for the establishment of a more stable and enduring post-Cold War security order in the region ultimately will rest on the third condition: making war too costly an option for attaining relative security gains. This criterion is applicable to Asia-Pacific, with two major no-gain conflicts having been fought in Korea and Vietnam.

The liberal view is that containment and deterrence strategies which have traditionally driven realist strategy for war-avoidance in Asia-Pacific actually make conflict more probable by creating unintended "conflict spirals" or arms races emanating from potential adversaries suspecting the worst about each other's intentions behind "defensive" military preparations.[4] Realists here countered that states inherently seek relative gains and thereby will always weigh the risks of conflict with opposing powers in the context of their own relative gain as opposed to assessing how their use of force could be destabilising or unjustified, that regional stability is therefore best ensured by the maintenance of stable global and regional power balances, through the credible extension of deterrence commitments to allies by the major powers, and by tailoring arms deployment programs along clearly defensive lines.[5]

Post-Cold War Asian-Pacific Security: Contending Approaches

As the Soviet Union passed into history and U.S. levels of defence spending became increasingly accountable to hard-pressed American

---

4. R. Jervis, *Perception and Misperception in International Politics* (Princeton: Princeton University Press, 1976), pp. 62–67 and A. Mack, *Reassurance Versus Deterrence Strategies for the Asia-Pacific Region* (Canberra: Australian National University, 1991), pp. 17–18.

5. Recent representative statements of this argument include Stephen M. Walt, "The Case for Finite Containment," *International Security* 14 (Summer 1989), pp. 5–49; Terry L. Diebel, "Strategies Before Containment: Patterns for the Future," *ibid.* 16 (Spring 1992), pp. 79–108; Henry Kissinger, "Balance of Power Sustained," in Graham Allison and Gregory F. Treverton, eds., *Rethinking America's Security* (New York and London: W. W. Norton & Company, 1992), pp. 238–248; and Zbigniew Brzezinski, "Selective Global Commitment," *Foreign Affairs* 70 (Fall 1991), pp. 1–20.

taxpayers' aspirations for a "peace dividend," Washington's Asian-Pacific allies were confronted with the imperative of increasingly defining and managing their own regional security. This responsibility was not met with unbridled enthusiasm by Asian policy elites all too aware of the historical animosities, nationalist and ethnic rivalries and irredentist disputes which had previously been restrained by the superpowers' regional presence and global strategies. Fears by indigenous security policy managers that "ancient animosities might be reignited" in ways largely absent during the Cold War were coupled with a general conceptual paralysis in thinking about regional security problems outside the context of the American security umbrella.[6]

Gradually, however, some new ideas about how to organise future Asian security constructs are developing. Several distinct approaches can now be identified as guiding such discussion: a formal multilateral security network along the lines of the Conference on Security and Cooperation in Europe (CSCE); *à la carte* multilateralism; "soft regionalism" and its variant, "open regionalism"; sub-regional security politics; and an "honest broker" or "balancing wheel" bilateral security posture which builds on the current U.S.-sponsored alliance network in the region.

Formal Multilateralism

The most extensive regional security arrangement discussed is an Asian-Pacific counterpart to CSCE. A number of proposals have been advanced over the years, from the Soviet push for an Asian collective security blueprint in 1969 to Australian and Canadian suggestions for economic-cum-security consultations and dialogue in Asia-Pacific in the 1990s. The success and relevance of any formal Asian-Pacific multilateral security organisation will depend largely on its ability to generate high-level policy consultations and command adherence to its policy maxims. The process leading to this type of organisational legitimacy must necessarily be incremental, linking economic and political-military security. Accordingly, ASEAN, APEC or some other appropriate forum must first establish a credible track record for institutional cooperation on diplomatic consultations and economic management. As an American official observed at the fourth APEC ministerial conference in Bangkok in September 1992, that forum could be converted from "an annual high level dialogue into a living,

---

6. This point is discussed in depth by Russell Trood, "After the Cold War: Regional Security in Eastern Asia," *Current Affairs Bulletin* 69 (August 1992), p. 6.

breathing institution... (b)ut a headquarters and a budget do not an effective organisation make."[7]

Theorists of regional integration initially speculated that the "spillover" effects of successful cooperation in low-key "functional" sectors of economic and service activity would lead member-states to organise the mechanisms needed to collaborate effectively in "high politics" or military policy areas.[8] Over time, however, their arguments have proven to be too optimistic. The challenges of defining and implementing enduring regional security mechanisms have thus far proven to be too daunting even for the European Community or the CSCE as Europe moves unevenly towards economic integration.

Asian-Pacific states share a common but vague apprehension about future regional power vacuums forming from their own unwillingness to compromise on their territorial disputes or to overcome their historical animosities. They have, however, expended little real effort to define or promote a common regional security framework. No Asian agenda exists of universal issues such as human rights or the security of borders which dominated the CSCE discussions leading to Helsinki.

Consequently, sceptics argue that little would be gained by a formal pan-Pacific approach to security organisation other than "an excessive amount of atmospherics but a dearth of substance."[9] Marginal or peripheral regional security actors such as Canada, Australia or New Zealand would continue to view formal multilateral discussions opportunistically, using them to enhance their limited stature and influence in the region. They further postulate that China, Japan, Russia, and the United States, with their different security priorities, are far more likely to pursue national security interests in Asia through bilateral or, at best, very qualified multilateral dialogues, intent on minimising their own involvement in the disputes of smaller regional actors.[10]

À La Carte Security

Although little progress has been made in implementing comprehensive formal mechanisms for regional security, attempts to establish informal

---

7. Remarks of Robert Fauver, U.S. Acting Under-Secretary of State for Economic and Agricultural Affairs, in an address to the Fourth APEC Ministerial Conference, Bangkok, 10 September 1992 as reprinted in United States Information Agency, *Wireless File* EPF407, 10 September 1992, pp. 17–20.

8. The "spillover" concept was developed by Ernst Haas, *Beyond the National-State: Functionalism and International Organization* (Stanford: Stanford University Press, 1964).

9. Donald Hellman as cited in Patrick M. Cronin, "Perspectives on Policy and Strategy: Multilateral Security Approaches toward Asia," *Strategic Review* 20 (Spring 1992), p. 63.

10. Trood, "After the Cold War," p. 11.

security dialogues have received greater support. Australian Prime Minister Paul Keating's efforts to organise a biennial heads-of-government summit loosely associated with APEC to discuss political-security issues informally has reportedly won U.S. and Japanese support.[11] After initially resisting it, ASEAN gradually accepted and implemented Japanese Foreign Minister Tarô Nakayama's July 1991 proposal to incorporate regular security discussions into the ASEAN-Post Ministerial Conference (ASEAN-PMC) meetings with ASEAN's external "dialogue partners": the U.S., EC, Japan, China, South Korea, India, Australia and New Zealand. A Malaysian initiative to host an informal security dialogue attended by Asian-Pacific military leaders to discuss their respective countries' national security postures has also been well received.[12]

The creation of informal or ad hoc security networks to engage in dialogue about the most obvious and pressing security issues and crisis in the region has been labelled *à la carte security* by Gerald Segal, the most prominent advocate of this approach.[13] Instead of taking years to negotiate a comprehensive agenda of confidence-building, disarmament and peacekeeping measures acceptable to all interested regional parties, issue-areas would be prioritised on the basis of their urgency or ease of resolution. Inherent in this method is the underlying assumption that the frequency and intensity of consultations would generate an irresistible momentum leading to crisis or conflict resolution. The precedent of incessant ASEAN consultations and coordination on the Cambodian conflict, which led to successive resolutions in the UN General Assembly supporting ASEAN's position and which earned that organisation's consultative style the unique label of "the meat grinder," illustrates the *à la carte* concept. It incorporates "the habit of [ASEAN] ministerial consultation and cooperation... having acquired a virtual quasi-familial quality."[14]

However, there are several drawbacks to this. First, in a postwar international security environment, it has proven difficult to isolate a regional crisis and the means for resolving it from the ramifications of success or failure in other parts of the world. A second problem with the *à la carte* approach has been noted by its primary advocate: the "absence of a

11. Richard McGregor "Miyazawa Supports Keating Summit," *Australian* (Sydney), 21 September 1992; and "Keating Wins Tokyo to APEC Plan," *ibid.*, 22 September 1992.

12. Michael Vatikiotis, "Helsinki, Asian Style," *FEER*, 14 May 1992, p. 20.

13. See his "North-East Asia: Common Security or à la carte?" *International Affairs* 67 (October 1991). See also Thomas W. Robinson, "Domestic and International Trends in Asian Security: Implications for American Defense Policy," *Korean Journal of Defense Analysis* 4 (Summer 1992), p. 133.

14. Michael Leifer, "Debating Asian Security: Michael Leifer Responds to Geoffrey Wiseman," *Pacific Review* 5:2 (1992), p. 168.

multilateral security structure for East Asia comparable to NATO or the Conference on Security and Cooperation in Europe makes it necessary for the United States to confront each issue on its own. This encourages American unilateralism."[15]

Recent unsuccessful U.S. efforts to steer the Korean peninsula towards a comprehensive peace settlement reflecting its own preferences are illustrative. In 1991, Secretary of State James Baker signalled that the United States was prepared to drop its long-standing resistance to multilateral cooperation to defuse the confrontation between North and South Korea. In proposing to work with Russia, China, and Japan to resolve the Korean crisis, Baker made it clear that his initiative was not to be interpreted as a wholesale shift of the U.S. policy preference for bilateral security arrangements in the region.[16]

U.S. officials represented the initiative as directed almost exclusively towards neutralising North Korea's efforts to develop indigenous nuclear weapons—a classical application of *à la carte*. South Korea, China, and even Japan dissented from the American stated intention, instead expressing concern that Baker's "two-plus four" initiative was nothing less than a unilateral effort by Washington to decide the political fate of the two Koreas. The U.S. was forced to retreat from its original multilateral design, instead conceding the initiative to North and South Korean negotiators for reaching agreement on a peninsula-wide nuclear-weapon-free zone and a non-aggression treaty. In this instance, Asian nationalism prevailed over an American unilateralist approach to peace in Korea.

Ad hoc or *à la carte* security is a high-risk approach to security politics because it tends to downplay the imperative of preparing an adequate conceptual framework prior to advancing policy initiatives and often ignores the interconnections between domestic politics and foreign policies. Policy misinterpretations and miscalculations are better avoided by working within some type of recognisable security framework which allows for systematic consultations between allies and adversaries, and within which collaborative processes for conflict-avoidance can be identified and put into effect.

"Soft" or "Open Regionalism"

A third outlook, which most directly acknowledges the growing primacy of economics in regional and international security, can be labelled "soft" or

---

15. Segal, "A Unified East Asia Would Be Heard," *International Herald Tribune*, 29–30 November 1991, p. 6.

16. James A. Baker III, "America in Asia: Emerging Architecture for a Pacific Community," *Foreign Affairs* 70 (Winter 1991/92), pp. 5–6.

"open regionalism." Robert Scalapino has described soft regionalism as the flow of economic interaction across Asia's ideological and political boundaries in ways which intensify their stake in each others' survival and stability. Such interaction is underwritten by "Asianisation": a complex expansion of communications and interactions in multiple sectors which is fostering greater regional interdependence and is rendering obsolete the old patterns of alliance politics and Cold War confrontation.[17]

Allen Choate has described a similar process of "open regionalism" which emphasises the "structural displacement" of the United States and Soviet Union with middle-level and entrepreneurial intra-regional centres of power—China and Japan in Northeast Asia and ASEAN in Southeast Asia—and with APEC overlapping both sub-regions as a potential successor-guarantor for regional order in lieu of a declining U.S.-sponsored collective defence network. Australia, New Zealand and the South Pacific Forum have to varying degrees disassociated themselves from the old American-sponsored "strategic denial" posture in favour of establishing closer links with ASEAN via APEC. "Open regionalism" is defined as a strong private sector leading state institutions into arrangements for ongoing economic development; encouragement of regional trade liberalisation and investment flows as integral characteristics of a regional economic order; and an aversion to trade blocs. It assumes attenuation over time of the authoritarian-pluralist rule now characterising the governance of many Asian states, with a gradual reconciliation of diverse cultures and nationalities into more harmonious and democratic forms of socio-economic organisation.[18]

Those arguing that soft/open regionalism most accurately describes the security environment now unfolding in Asia-Pacific are well aware that Asian nationalism and xenophobia can overwhelm prospects for further liberalisation of Asian nations that must take place if they are to meet the challenges facing them in both the economic and political-security fields. In this sense, the regionalism they envision is a high-risk strategy.

A practical factor capable of undercutting the "regionalist" vision is that, after high levels of energy have been expended to create new regional institutions, the returns anticipated from such efforts will not be forthcoming. The rise of regional trade blocs could shut off Asian access to established markets, erosion of the global trading and financial systems can

---

17. Robert Scalapino, "Northeast Asia—Prospects for Cooperation," *Pacific Review* 5:2 (1992), p. 102 and Robert Scalapino, "The United States and Asia: Future Prospects," *Foreign Affairs* 70 (Winter 1991/92), pp. 20–21, 26.

18. See the summary of Choate's address to the Northeast Asia-United States Forum on International Policy, Institute for International Studies, Stanford University by Richard A. Deck, Project Coordinator on Asian Regionalisation, Autumn 1991 (copy in author's hands).

occur, and the "Pacific Century" can be rendered obsolete before even commencing. Political barriers still inhibit middle class development in the region and the Asian states' generally poor track record in generating the type of basic research needed to be technologically competitive with North America and Europe makes it doubtful that Asia-Pacific will match or surpass the other two regions any time soon.[19]

Common Security

Some proponents for multilateralism for Asia-Pacific argue that while the growth of informal consultative processes within ASEAN, APEC and other regional bodies is encouraging, further intra-regional consensus leading to a security regime is best attained neither through *à la carte* responses to specific crisis and problems nor through reliance upon intensified, albeit informal, economic networks. Instead they believe that enduring multilateral security arrangements and institutions can result only from regional security actors embracing a "gradualist collective security" approach. This would embody the assimilation of the remnants of Cold War Western collective defence arrangements into "building block" sub-regional security for intelligence collection, airspace and sea lane coverage, and the coordination of negotiating strategies regarding territorial and environmental questions. Eventually, a more comprehensive and enduring "common security network" would supplant the building blocks. The key to making gradualist collective security viable is that sufficient U.S. strategic power remains deployed in the area to ensure that "breathing space" is available for confidence-building measures to be implemented and to withstand initial tests before transition to a full-fledged multilateral security regime.[20]

If there is a drawback to the "building block" common security approach, it is the possible assumption that strategic collaboration is an end rather than a means to integrating national security objectives with regional security cooperation. States may not always be willing to entrust their interests to the process of organisational incrementalism implied by the gradualist collective security approach. Nor may they share common values with those states they do choose to associate with on a particular security issue. Moreover,

19. George Hicks, "So Much for the Pacific Century—It Will Be America, As Usual," *International Herald Tribune*, 29 July 1992, p. 4.

20. The best conceptual explanation of "gradualist collective security" is by Geoffrey Wiseman, "Common Security in the Asia-Pacific Region," *Pacific Review* 5:1 (1992), especially p. 44. See also Desmond Ball, *Building Blocks for Regional Security: An Australian Perspective on Confidence and Security Building Measures (CSBMs) in the Asia/Pacific Region* (Canberra: Australian National University, Canberra Papers on Strategy and Defence No. 83, 1991); and Mack, *Reassurance Versus Deterrence*, pp. 19–24.

while three separate "security complexes" exist in Asia-Pacific—Northeast Asia, Southeast Asia and the South Pacific[21]—it remains debatable to what extent the security dynamics of each complex or subregion are subject to disruption by either outside powers active in more than one subregion or by the other subregions themselves. In contrast to Southeast Asia and the South Pacific where ASEAN and the South Pacific Forum have succeeded to some extent in integrating political and economic agendas, Northeast Asia remains relatively unorganised with Japan, China and the United States regarding one anothers' policy intentions warily. All three powers may well be too strategically and economically powerful to achieve even limited success in implementing the gradualist collective security demonstrated in Southeast Asia and the South Pacific.

Bilateralism

The United States continues to pursue the same security posture in Asia-Pacific that it adopted at the outset of the Cold War. It believes that existing bilateral collective defence arrangements with Japan, South Korea, Australia and the Philippines allow it the flexibility needed to apply a classical balance-of-power strategy in the region in lieu of its old Cold War strategy of containment.

Throughout 1990–91, the Bush administration argued that only the United States could play the role of an "acceptable regional balancer" as Asian-Pacific nations come to terms with the transition from superpower global confrontation to a post-Cold War world. The bilateral alliances are symbolic of American resolve to help effect a smooth transition by impressing upon allies its version of "strategic reassurance": an over-the-horizon but nonetheless still very active U.S. force presence capable of rapidly projecting substantial military power to all parts of Asia-Pacific. Labelled "cooperative vigilance" by U.S. Defense Department officials, this emphasis on strengthening existing bilateral alliances through selective commitment, power balancing and increased burden-sharing was reflected in the Bush administration's "East Asia Strategy Initiative." Envisioning modest and conditional force reductions, EASI nonetheless attempted to justify the perpetuation of U.S. bilateral security treaties in the Pacific as the best way to avoid regional power vacuums "that other major players would be tempted or compelled to fill." It proposed to "provide a rationale for

---

21. For background on security complexes in a subregional context, see Barry Buzan, "The Southeast Asian Security Complex," *Contemporary Southeast Asia* 10 (June 1988), pp. 1–16; and Eric Herring, "'Buzantine' Security Complexes in the Pacific," *Pacific Review* 4:3 (1991), pp. 280–82.

increased cost sharing contributions to regional security by our friends/allies" via the United States exercising the diplomatic leverage needed to "localise" and "minimise" regional hostilities.[22]

Most Asian-Pacific governments have accepted the bilateral approach to the extent that the creation of more elaborate, multilateral security frameworks is not viewed as an urgent or compelling regional security priority. "Asian governments have never fully shared, or understood, the Western enthusiasm for attempting to accommodate security arrangements within multilateral frameworks... [and] have shown a marked preference for proceeding slowly, emphasising bilateral processes of dialogue and the steady development of consensus."[23] ASEAN states were upset when the United States and the Philippines were unable to reach agreement for a continued American force presence at Subic Bay and Clark Air Base and moved quickly to offer the U.S. navy access (although not permanent basing) to their own port facilities. ASEAN fears of China's ultimate intentions regarding the Spratly Islands dispute have reinforced the appeal of an American force presence. Japan and South Korea continue to regard the American strategic presence in Northeast Asia as a critical element of stability, not only against the prospects of a resurgent Russian or intensified Chinese military threats but as a strategic buffer against each other's historical animosities as Korea moves towards reunification.

Several arguments against sustaining bilateralism have surfaced in the regional security debate. One is that the politics of collective defence perpetuates the old containment and deterrence strategies of the Cold War. Regional conflict spirals thus exacerbate while incentives for regional cooperation are stymied.[24]

A second criticism logically evolves from the above point. Bilateral security relationships are often based on an expedient and temporary convergence of national security interests between allies. Such ties are not designed to endure or to reassure all regional security actors. If properly structured and sufficiently comprehensive, collective security arrangements provide a mandate for their participants to implement measures tailored to preclude and overcome threats to regional stability or to effect peaceful and positive regional change. Losses in national security autonomy are, in such arrangements, more than compensated by modifications of threat environments and by absolute gains in security.[25]

---

22. U.S. Department of Defense, *A Strategic Framework For the Asian Pacific Rim: Looking Toward the 21st Century* (Washington, DC: USDOD, April 1990).

23. Trood, "After the Cold War," p. 12.

24. Mack, *Reassurance vs. Deterrence*, pp. 14–15.

25. This point is developed by Oye, "Explaining Cooperation Under Anarchy," pp. 12–18.

A third criticism of bilateralism is that by preserving Cold War alliances other regional tensions in Asia remain suppressed which, if allowed to surface, might be resolved more rapidly and definitively. The "resurfacing of endemic regional tensions in Asia may be inevitable and ultimately healthy.... The argument that the U.S. must remain as a stabilizing force to prevent excessively powerful Asian states from disrupting the equilibrium is a relic of the Cold War.... Asian-Pacific dynamics should be unleashed to be dealt with by regional actors."[26] However, allowing latent hostilities to be unleashed on the questionable assumption that such conflicts would ultimately resolve long-simmering enmities appears, at best, to be an unacceptably high-risk strategy for attaining regional stability. Either deterrence or reassurance seem preferable to calculated bloodletting.

Regional Security and Great-Power Behaviour

If this chapter's fundamental argument that formal and effective multilateral security organisations will not emerge as predominant in Asia-Pacific over the short term is correct, then the strategic interests and policies of the major regional powers are more likely to determine the region's security order over at least the remainder of this century. In this context, several behavioural patterns are developing that will direct the shaping of that order and influence the degree to which conflicts may be experienced or avoided in the process. These include American strategic retrenchment, China's strategic resurgence, Japan's response to both these developments and Russia's possible role as a "wild card" in the short-term regional balance of power.

The United States: A Regional Policeman?

U.S. preoccupation with the Soviet global threat which fashioned its Asian-Pacific strategy during the Cold War seems to have been replaced by an apprehension over future regional hegemons. Regional security alliances and coalitions are still viewed by Washington as the primary instruments for implementing its regional security policy in Asia. But two of its most important security collaborators during the height of Soviet-American competition in the region—China and Japan—are now projected by U.S. defence planners as candidates for filling any power vacuum created by further reductions of American military power in the Pacific. This theme was underscored by a controversial (although later modified) and classified

---

26. Edward A. Olsen, "A New American Strategy in Asia?" *Asian Survey* 31 (December 1991), p. 1153.

U.S. Defense Department study, the *Defense Planning Guidance Statement* (leaked to the *New York Times* in March 1992), and later reiterated in a new version of the East Asia Strategy Initiative (quickly labelled "EASI II") submitted to Congress in July 1992. U.S. defence planners argued that the maintenance of bilateral security treaties with traditional Asian allies, a forward deployed U.S. military presence through low-key access arrangements to allied and friendly territory and complementary defence cooperation would best "ensure a rapid and flexible crisis response capability; contribute to regional stability; discourage the emergence of a regional hegemon... [and] demonstrate to friends, allies and potential enemies alike a tangible, visible U.S. interest in the security of the entire region."[27]

Left unclear in these documents was how the United States planned to reconcile growing strains in Sino-American relations resulting from human rights differences, pending jet aircraft sales to Taiwan and tariff policies with the limited but still hopeful signs that security collaboration between China and the U.S. is possible in areas of nuclear non-proliferation, conventional arms sales to troubled regions and diplomatic efforts to constrain belligerent factions in Indochina and elsewhere. Also unaddressed was how worsening U.S.-Japanese trade ties could be reconciled with a cooperative vigilance strategy clearly dependent on Japanese burden-sharing. In this context, the old bilateral frameworks and instrumentalities for managing security relations with both Asian powers appear increasingly inadequate. Both could thus emerge, by default, as threats to U.S. national security interests if more innovative American security postures are not forthcoming.

Recent American efforts to block Russia's sale of cryogenic rocket engines to India are a further example of Washington failing to establish clear security priorities in a bilateral defence context. The advantages perceived by the Americans of entering into an upgraded security relationship with the Indians after the Cold War appeared to be outweighed by a number of "conditions" which Washington subsequently attached to dealing with New Delhi. These included Indian compliance with the guidelines of the Missile Technology Control Regime (MTCR) and its willingness to sign the Nuclear Non Proliferation Treaty. To the Indians, these demands violated their sovereign prerogatives.[28]

---

27. U.S. Department of Defense, *A Strategic Framework for the Asian Pacific Rim: Report to Congress* (Washington, DC: USDOD, July 1992), p. 20.

28. For background, consult Sunanda K. Datta-Ray, "India and America: Back to Grumble-as-Usual," *International Herald Tribune*, 27 May 1992, p. 4. See also Ramesh Thakur, "India

If the United States insists that its bilateral security relations must be predicated increasingly on the friend's or ally's readiness to contribute a substantial portion of the defence burden necessary to fulfil the objectives of the alliance, it should be equally prepared to enter into compromises necessary to establish and maintain alliance goodwill. If this policy is unacceptable, then greater American acceptance of a "gradualist collective security" approach where decision-making is shared may be inevitable.

China: Towards Regional Integration or Hegemonic Strategy?

At the annual ASEAN foreign minister's meeting held in Manila in July 1992, Chinese Foreign Minister Qian Qichen suggested that China and the ASEAN states could develop "extensive and close" cooperation in moving towards establishing a more peaceful region by creating "multilevel and multichannel" dialogue mechanisms for consultations on security matters.[29]

His Malaysian counterpart, Abdullah Badawi, countered that "the beautiful [Chinese] statement on policy doesn't reconcile with what's happening on the ground."[30] ASEAN's concern over Chinese moves to award oil concessions in the Spratly Islands to American drilling companies over strong Vietnamese objections, and its passage of national legislation defining the Spratlys as part of China, overshadowed its interest in signing mutual trade agreements with or entering into security dialogues with China. Instead, ASEAN officials displayed fears about long-term Chinese strategic intentions which are widely shared by other Asian-Pacific states: that Beijing entertains pretensions to fill a regional power vacuum if U.S. forces leave or are substantially reduced in the region, and that the Chinese are embarking upon a major military buildup to enforce their strategic interests throughout East and Southeast Asia.

Following the end of communism in Eastern Europe and the FSU, and the spectacular display of U.S. military high-technology in the Gulf War, China has pursued a "dual strategy" of cooperating with the West on global security issues while staking out its own agenda in Asia-Pacific.[31] The Chinese have opted to disregard the Bush administration's rhetoric about a "new world order." They have focused upon improving ties with regional

after Nonalignment," *Foreign Affairs* 71 (Spring 1992), pp. 165–182; and Dilip Mukerjee, "Marriage of Convenience," *FEER*, 6 August 1992, p. 13.

29. Raphael Pura, "ASEAN, Wary of Chinese Moves, Offers Guidelines to Solve Territorial Disputes," *Asian Wall Street Journal Weekly*, 27 July 1992, p. 2.

30. Rodney Tasker, "Facing Up To Security," *FEER*, 6 August 1992, p. 9.

31. This theme is developed by Harry Harding, "China's American Dilemma," *Annals of the American Academy of Political Science* 519 (January 1992), pp. 18–22.

neighbours and extending selective cooperation with the West on matters of international concern such as nuclear proliferation on the Korean peninsula, peacekeeping in Cambodia and restraining arms transfers to the Middle East. In the meantime, the Chinese leadership invited Japan's emperor to visit their country and welcomed the reintroduction of Japanese investment and capital. China reestablished diplomatic relations with Indonesia after a 25-year hiatus and subsequently normalised ties with Singapore and South Korea, a development unthinkable only a few years ago. It also orchestrated a rapprochement with Vietnam, as one of the few other communist powers left in Asia-Pacific, even as it distanced itself from a North Korean regime which had become almost totally dependent upon Beijing for its economic and strategic survival.

While offering olive branches to potential adversaries, however, Beijing simultaneously issued caveats. It warned Japan against remilitarising independently of U.S. control, contested Japanese claims over the Senkaku (Diaoyutai) islands and, along with most Southeast Asian states, continued to criticise the Japanese for not fully atoning for the wrongs they inflicted on the region leading up to and during the Second World War. It made clear its uncompromising position regarding China's sovereign control over the East China Sea's contested territories, the future democratisation of Hong Kong and President George Bush's decision to sell F-16 fighters to Taiwan.

Yet it is doubtful whether China is prepared to reverse its fundamental policy of projecting the image of a "responsible" international security actor. It remains desperate for access to Western markets to sustain the rapid economic growth in its southeastern sector and to fund future military modernisation. In a telling gesture, Qian Qichen visited Israel less than a month after the F-16 sale was announced and promised his hosts that China would refrain from selling weapons systems to Middle Eastern states. China also continued to pressure the Khmer Rouge into compliance with UN peacekeeping efforts in Cambodia. The Chinese appear unwilling to risk giving Japan any impetus for embarking on a substantial arms buildup of its own or to alienate ASEAN or South Korea at a time when they desperately want to strengthen economic relations with both. Most importantly, they do not wish to precipitate an intensified American military presence in East Asia, preferring a regional security order driven by a "soft regionalism" that will allow their political system to coexist with a market economy.

Japan: Reconciling Bilateralism with Regional Leadership

While China's current military buildup is worrisome enough, the prospect of Japan using its considerable economic capacity and technological acumen to become a regional military power generates fear throughout Asia-Pacific. No amount of reassurances offered by successive Japanese leaders that their nation will never again develop force-projection capabilities appears sufficient to reassure other Asian states that Japan would not become an overwhelming security threat. Japan's recent dispatch of minesweepers to the Persian Gulf and its current deployment of a modest peacekeeping contingent to Cambodia have thus been received with mixed emotions, with ASEAN generally more supportive of Japan assuming an international security role commensurate with its economic status while China and the Koreas remain highly critical of any Japanese initiative to expand its Self Defence Force.[32]

Two factors will be paramount in determining Japan's future policies towards regional security. First, can its territorial disputes with Russia and China be resolved through negotiated settlements? If not, Japanese nationalism could intensify, eventually causing Tokyo to reassess the value of the American security relationship relative to its own national security interests. This relates to a second issue: will the U.S.-Japan Mutual Security Treaty be viewed by Japan's neighbours increasingly as less of a legitimate part of a collective defence network than a U.S. instrument to check Japanese power from dominating Asia-Pacific?

Asian-Pacific analysts increasingly argue that de facto Japanese economic hegemony in their region should be managed through multilateral groupings which could work to open Japan's domestic markets to imports and to cultivate greater levels of Japanese interdependence with other regional actors. This would mean that elements of both the soft/open regionalism and gradualist collective security approaches could be implemented on the assumption that Japan's main contribution to regional security would be economic cooperation with its neighbours. Neither approach directly confronts the problem of Japanese irredentism or how Japan could overcome its feelings of isolation in the event that it gradually concludes that the U.S. is likely to abandon it during a future regional crisis or to hedge substantially on its extended deterrence commitments under the Mutual Security Treaty. This rules out Tokyo's adoption of an ad hoc or *à la carte* strategy towards Northeast Asian security contingencies. It reinforces Japan's insistence that American forces remain in the area to work with Japanese counterparts in a bilateral context as a tangible symbol of Washington's permanent commitment to its most important Asian ally.

---

32. A particularly incisive account of Chinese suspicions is by Allen Whiting, "China and Japan: Politics Versus Economics," *Annals of the American Academy of Political Science* 519 (January 1992), especially pp. 46–47. The latest South Korean Defense White Paper openly speculates about Japan becoming a future regional military threat.

In this context, Japanese Prime Minister Kiichi Miyazawa's recent announcement that he would support the Australian proposal for an APEC heads-of-government summit if other APEC members concur is significant. The Japanese assent marks a growing conviction by Tokyo that the Bush administration's election rhetoric about linking the North American and Asian-Pacific trading areas could signify that an implicit process of organising more fluid security architectures, underwritten by U.S. force mobility, to replace the predominantly bilateral treaty network, resting on a U.S. basing presence and permanently deployed American force contingents, is now under way.

Japanese policymakers are still far from adopting a gradualist collective security posture, however. This is due to their continuing sensitivity about how more extensive Japanese military commitments to any multilateral arrangement would be received by Asian neighbours. It is also due to their concerns that too great a Japanese willingness to engage in regional defence burden-sharing would provide the U.S. Congress with a rationale to further cut U.S. force deployments in the Pacific.

Russia: From Confrontation to Cooperation?

Among the Soviet successor-states, Russia is the key military power capable of affecting the Asian-Pacific security order. Two schools of thought have surfaced as to Moscow's future impact upon regional security. The first envisions Russia as a relatively benign actor, intent upon normalising relations with Japan by resolving the northern territories quagmire, facilitating economic ties with China without militarily confronting it, and gradually moving towards a "balanced interrelationship in the "rectangle" comprising Russia, the United States, Japan, and China."[33] Under this scenario, "Russian military power will simply rust."[34]

A less optimistic contingency is that Russia's economic difficulties will intensify, playing into the hands of nationalists and conservatives who view other major Asian-Pacific powers as natural strategic rivals. Kozyrev has noted that, while the current Russian government adheres to values of global economic and political interdependence, its policies are not irreversible.[35] The implications of Russia failing to implement internal reforms and falling into protracted turmoil are certainly not lost on Japanese policymakers. The consequences of any such development would be especially dire from

---

33. Andrei Kozyrev, "Russia: A Chance For Survival," *Foreign Affairs* 71 (Spring 1992), p. 15.

34. *Strategic Survey 1991–1992*, p. 213.

35. Kozyrev, "Russia: A Chance For Survival," p. 15.

Tokyo's vantage point if accompanied by ongoing Japanese-American trade tensions which led Washington to adopt a more ambiguous stance regarding its commitments under the Mutual Security Treaty. Isolated from both the Russians and the Americans, Japan could become more susceptible to confronting Russian intransigence over the northern territories with rearmament programs of its own.[36]

Mikhail Gorbachev's Asian diplomacy was directed towards integrating an economically desperate Soviet Union into East Asia's economic miracle and offsetting American offshore military power in Northeast Asia. Japan, however, was the key to success for Gorbachev's regional security diplomacy. But when he visited Tokyo in April 1991, Japanese officials showed little interest in the Soviet president's confidence-building proposals in the absence of a breakthrough in the northern territories dispute.

A number of Russian commentators see no real chance for Gorbachev's original agenda to be pursued in any coherent fashion by Russia or the Commonwealth of Independent States (CIS).[37] The last Soviet leader's overall contributions to progress in regional security can, nevertheless, be regarded as substantial and positive in terms of the policies that he pursued towards China and the Koreas. Talks between Secretary-of-State James Baker and Soviet Foreign Minister Eduard Shevardnadze in Irkutsk in August 1990 produced a joint Soviet-American declaration that neither superpower would consider the other an adversary in Asia-Pacific and that both would act in common for the resolution of outstanding regional conflicts there. By the time that the USSR ceased to exist, American military planners could cite their concern over the "residual power projection capability of Russian naval and air forces" stationed proximate to Japan and South Korea and to a still "formidable nuclear arsenal which must still be factored into [the American] strategic calculus."[38] Clearly, however, a post-Cold War Russia was regarded as more a potential security collaborator than a strategic adversary of the West.

The Yeltsin government has done little to discredit this perception. It has negotiated monumental strategic nuclear force reductions with the Bush administration; announced that it is no longer targeting American sites with nuclear forces that are retained; and expressed an interest in working with the United States to develop jointly a proposed Global Protection Against

---

36. For a cogent assessment of these factors, see Robert E. Hunter, "The United States, Japan, and the Future of Russia," *SAIS Review* 12 (Summer/Fall 1992), pp. 65–71.

37. See, for example, the commentary by Sergei Strokan in *Moskovskimye novosti* 2 (12 January 1992), p. 12 as translated and reprinted in *Current Digest of the Post Soviet Press (CDPSP)* 44 (26 February 1992), pp. 11–12.

38. *Strategic Framework for Asian Pacific Rim: Report to Congress*, July 1992, p. 10.

Limited Strikes (GPALS) defence system against limited ballistic-missile attacks launched by third parties.

A number of Soviet analysts are proposing more specific measures for Russian cooperation with the West in an Asia-Pacific context. Not surprisingly, economics has taken priority. Moscow is enthusiastically supporting the United Nations Development Program's multibillion dollar project to convert the Tumen River Delta, stretching from the western end of the Korean peninsula to the Russian-North Korean border, into a model natural economic territory (NET) from which a huge Northeast Asian trading bloc could eventually materialise, immensely enhancing future Siberian economic development.[39] While it cannot expect to become a major trading partner of the ASEAN states anytime soon, Russia envisions its future relations with Southeast Asia to be, in the words of one Russian analyst, "largely de-ideologised and commercialised."[40]

This characterisation of Russia's security posture appears to coincide with the dominant strategic perception held by Moscow's strategic thinkers about Asian-Pacific regional security order and their own country's role in that configuration. Most Russian policymakers would like their country to play an influential and constructive but low-key role in underwriting Asian stability. Some have suggested that a joint U.S.-Russian/CIS naval presence at Cam Ranh Bay could be one step in forming a credible, if symbolic, international peacekeeping force of external powers to deter or put down regional crisis in the Spratlys or elsewhere in Asia.[41] Their more sober counterparts warn that Vietnam and ASEAN could interpret any such move as yet another episode of outside forces attempting to shape the future of their own country or region.[42]

A considered vision of what role Russia could play in a revised Asian security order has been advanced by Sergei N. Goncharov of Russia's Academy of Sciences. His basic thesis is that CIS foreign policy, above all, must reflect the domestic interests of its member-states. Accordingly, Russia and the other Soviet successor-states should adopt security postures which are non-threatening to outside powers but firmly aligned with Western economic institutions. He criticises President Yeltsin's offer to join the U.S. in research on ballistic-missile defence because China, in particular, would

---

39. See the earlier chapter by Charles E. Ziegler in this volume.

40. Eduard Grebenshchikov, "Place In The Sun," *FEER*, 13 February 1992, p. 24.

41. *Ibid.* and Clare Hollingworth, "Tensions Are Mounting in the Spratlys," *International Herald Tribune*, 21 July 1992, p. 4.

42. See commentary by Pyotr Tsvetor in *Pravda*, 23 June 1992, p. 3 as translated and reprinted in *CDPSP* 45 (22 July 1992), pp. 20–21. However, Vietnamese officials have denied that they are negotiating with Moscow for a retention of any type of Russian naval presence in their country. See Nayan Chanda, "Nyet, Tovarisch," *FEER*, 6 August 1992, p. 11.

regard any such collaboration as an effort by the nuclear superpowers to preserve hegemonic control over the global strategic environment. In response, China could align itself with elements of the Islamic world to form a counter-coalition against the northern industrial powers of North America, Europe, Russia and Japan. If such a scenario were to unfold, Russia and the CIS would comprise the front line for a new global confrontation. Goncharov concludes that "under no circumstances should there be any question of Russia's entering into any rigid politico-military alliances that could be perceived as directed against the 'East' [China and East Asia] or the 'South' [the Middle East and South Asia]."[43]

Two critical tests which could ultimately determine Russia's status in Asia-Pacific remain the ability of relatively pro-Western moderates to sustain power in Russia and Moscow's need to settle the northern territories question with Japan as the Russian economy continues to deteriorate at an alarming pace. At the time of writing, the strength of Boris Yeltsin's political base is waning rapidly. Moreover, hardline nationalists forced the Russian president to cancel his scheduled visit to Tokyo in 1992. The Japanese had already served notice that Russia would not receive any substantial economic assistance from their country unless a reversion of the contested islands to Japan was in the offing. Japan was also alarmed by intelligence reports of increased Russian weapons exports to China.[44]

The future of the FSU remains highly uncertain. Without adequate Western and Japanese economic assistance, judiciously applied without seeking to extract diplomatic leverage or premature concessions, its chances of evolving into a stable and constructive Asian-Pacific security actor would appear to be less than promising. Goncharov's approach, which closely resembles *à la carte* security may be the best short-term approach for integrating the CIS into the post-Cold War security environment.

Conclusion

With the demise of the Cold War, pressures are increasing for Asian-Pacific states to define and shape a new and more independent security order. A growing crescendo of voices within and outside the region argue that its stability, traditionally preserved by U.S. deterrence commitments, treaty alliances and offshore military forces, can now best be sustained by more indigenous arrangements which will facilitate peace, confidence-

---

43. Sergei N. Goncharov, "Russia's Special Interests—What They Are," *Izvestiia* 25 February 1992, as translated and reprinted in *CDPSP* 44 (25 March 1992), pp. 9–10.
44. Jim Hoagland, "Russian Arms to China: Japan Steps In," *International Herald Tribune*, 14 July 1992, p. 4.

building and economic development in the absence of a Soviet military presence or any other threat. To write off force capabilities and deterrence as key elements of stability in the region, however, may be premature.

Arguments that the U.S. will be able to sustain its self-acclaimed role as a post-Cold War "honest broker" for preserving Asia-Pacific's power equilibrium are tenuous, at best, if current deployment trends are objectively assessed. The Bush administration's rejection of the logic advanced by the Defense Planning Guidance Statement's initial version, and its continued adherence to the East Asia Strategy Initiative, have clearly signalled Washington's long-term intentions. An abrupt U.S. strategic retrenchment from Asia-Pacific is to be avoided but downward adjustments in U.S. security commitments to and forces deployed within the region are inevitable. Reinforcing this policy, the U.S. Congress has demanded—and received—assurances from both the Bush administration and from U.S. regional allies such as Japan and South Korea that future defence tasks in a more multipolar world will be shared more equitably as U.S. fiscal assets come under ever greater strain.

Even if most Asian-Pacific states continue to support the preservation of a less comprehensive but still operational American-sponsored bilateral security network in their region, they will increasingly be inclined to search for new alternatives in building a post-Cold War regional security order. Which approach they will ultimately pursue is not yet clear. Those favouring the formal multilateral approach argue that if Asian-Pacific states are unsuccessful in moving quickly and effectively towards a new set of tangible security arrangements, then an unrestrained regional arms race cannot be far behind. Accordingly, they support the immediate implementation of regional initiatives for peacekeeping, disarmament and confidence-building. Proponents of gradualist collective security advocate the pursuit of regional peace and stability through the sustaining of frequent but informal security dialogues between ASEAN, APEC and various other regional economic associations. They believe that these dialogues can ultimately produce a region-wide formal multilateral organisation which will effectively ensure regional peace and stability. States like China, Vietnam and even Indonesia are inclined towards the soft/open regional approach, aspiring as they do to develop Western-style economies but still wishing to avoid residual effects of overly rapid democratisation. À *la carte* adherents such as Russia believe a security policy which emphasises a "case-by-case" response to security problems and crisis will safeguard their strategic neutrality and allow them to avoid commitments that would automatically alienate other important regional actors.

Of all these security models, only the formal multilateral approach compels its participants to identify and pursue policy priorities designed to attain a specific regional security framework. Critics of the institutional approach correctly point out that post-Cold War Asia is not post-Cold War Europe—that there is a multiplicity of threats to Asian conflict-resolution which defies either bilateral or multilateral security architects to seek easy answers. Asian geography is far more vast, disparate and complex than Europe's and the recent decolonisation of many Asian states contrasts with their European counterparts' long established sovereignty and national self-confidence. The major problem of European security during the Cold War—a divided Germany underwritten by Soviet military strength—is now resolved by that country's reunification. By contrast, a reunified Korean peninsula, Taiwan's peaceful incorporation into the Chinese mainland and Japan's reacquisition of the disputed northern territories from Russia still remain elusive goals.

Prospects are increasing that as superpower competition winds down in Asia-Pacific, there will be no shortage of contending regional powers ready to vie for dominance or of regional authoritarian regimes willing to precipitate crises. In the former category, China appears to be the most serious long-term threat. Yet India fields the world's fourth largest standing army, a blue water navy and a highly trained contingent of scientists and engineers capable of quickly expanding that country's nuclear-weapons arsenal. While Japanese leaders continue to disavow remilitarisation, Japan's global economic interests are dependent upon a U.S. offshore power-projection capability to safeguard critical sea lanes of communication. If projected U.S. cutbacks take place over the remainder of this decade and translate into lower levels of commitment to the U.S.-Japan Mutual Security Treaty, or if ongoing economic tensions between Washington and Tokyo escalate into a serious political division, then Japan could reevaluate its current determination to forgo the building of offensive military forces.

More serious over the near term are potential regional flashpoints of instability. North Korea's nuclear weapons program is reportedly on hold, but its ability to pose a conventional military threat offsets recent progress in negotiations between the two Koreas. Threats to regime legitimacy in Burma, Vietnam, Laos and even in some ASEAN states could resurrect old civil wars or introduce new ones. Underlying all of this is the "Russian enigma," in which a former empire, having relinquished political control of a number of independent and restive republics, still possesses a large nuclear arsenal which could fall under the control of radical nationalists or other political extremists.

It may be that Asian policymakers will identify and implement creative solutions appropriate to these or other contingencies; they should be given every encouragement to do so. Greater thought must, however, be directed towards how, in the short-term, regional conflict-escalation could be checked until a consensus is reached over which security approach to pursue and more enduring mechanisms for regional stability are put into place.

In this context, the gradualist collective security approach is the best policy option. Moreover, Australian Prime Minister Keating's proposal that a biennial heads-of-government summit be convened under APEC auspices to incorporate region-wide security discussions appears to be the most promising initial step for a smooth transition from bilateralism to multilateralism. The summit agenda should be directed towards confronting and resolving outstanding territorial disputes, implementing phased reductions in arms expenditures and addressing ways to prevent regional nuclear proliferation. Existing bilateral security treaties between the United States and its Northeast Asian allies should be reaffirmed but in the context of acknowledging the reality of a more limited U.S. role. The current relevancy and implications of ASEAN's decision to incorporate formal discussions of security issues into its ministerial consultations, and the recent upgrading of U.S. defence relations with other ASEAN states in the aftermath of the American basing pullout from the Philippines, should be critically reviewed. Appropriate, if initially modest, additional security measures by those regional powers willing to collaborate should be considered. These might include intelligence exchanges which could increase early-warning capabilities of impending conflicts, selected joint naval or air exercises designed to emulate peacekeeping operations and the formation of a crisis prevention centre within any future APEC secretariat.

Creative strategic planning can provide a better chance that a more stable Asian-Pacific security environment can eventually be realised. The "gradualist collective security" approach may offer the region its best chance of transformation from a postwar geopolitical environment dominated by containment and confrontation to a post-Cold War milieu shaped by common security objectives and approaches. Finding mutual interests and forging common political values in an area as large and diverse as Asia will be more challenging and initially more elusive than was the shaping of a postwar European community. But achieving a common Asian-Pacific destiny would be well worth the quest.

Index